100
Years of
Psychoanalysis

André Haynal
Ernst Falzeder (eds)

100
Years of
Psychoanalysis

Contributions to the History
of Psychoanalysis

Special issue of the «Cahiers Psychiatriques Genevois»
published by the Institutions Universitaires de Psychiatrie de Genève
distributed by H. Karnac (Books) Ltd., – London
and, for Switzerland, by Médecine et Hygiène, Geneva

The texts contained in this volume were presented
at the Symposium «100 Years of Psychoanalysis»
which took place in Geneva on September 17 and 18, 1993.

Acknowledgments

Many Thanks to Mr. Mark Paterson, Director,
Sigmund Freud Copyrights Ltd.,
for his kind permission to reproduce quotations from the letters
of Sigmund Freud.

British Library Cataloguing in Publication Data
A catalogue record fot this book is available from the British Library.

© Cahiers Psychiatriques Genevois et Institutions Universitaires
de Psychiatrie de Genève, Geneva, Switzerland, 1994
Except for the contribution of Peter Loewenberg: © Loewenberg, 1993

ISBN 1-85575-090-2

In Memoriam
Raymond de Saussure
(1894-1971)

OTHER TITLES BY ANDRÉ HAYNAL

Depression and Creativity. International University Press, New York, 1985.

The Technique at Issue. Controversies in Psychoanalysis from Freud and Ferenczi to Michael Balint. GB: Karnac. London. 1988. US: *Controversies in Psychoanalytic Method. From Freud and Ferenczi to Michael Balint.* New York University Press, New York, 1989.

Psychoanalysis and the Sciences. Epistemology – History. GB: Karnac, London, 1993. US: University of California Press, Berkeley, 1993.

The Correspondence of Sigmund Freud and Sándor Ferenczi. Volume 1, 1908-1914. Introduction and scientific supervision of the editorial work by André Haynal. The Belknap Press/Harvard University Press, Cambridge, Mass., 1994.

Cahiers Psychiatriques Genevois, Special Issue, 1994, pp. 7-8

CONTENTS

Part II – Freud and his intimate Sándor Ferenczi

Commentary - Closure

Cahiers Psychiatriques Genevois, Special Issue, 1994, pp. 9-12

EDITORS AND CONTRIBUTORS

Editors and Contributors

André Haynal, M.D., psychoanalyst and psychiatrist, professor and chairman of the Department of Psychiatry at the University of Geneva, former president of the Swiss Psychoanalytic Society, twice visiting professor at Stanford University; his books include *Depression and Creativity* (New York, Int. Univ. Press); *The Technique at Issue: Controversies in Psychoanalysis from Freud and Ferenczi to Michael Balint* (London, Karnac, and NY, NewYork Univ. Press,); *Psychoanalysis and the Sciences. Epistemology & History* (London, Karnac, and Berkeley, CA, California Univ. Press), among others. He is the academic supervisor of the editing of the Freud/Ferenczi Correspondence (Cambridge, Mass., Harvard University Press).

Ernst Falzeder, Ph.D., author of a doctoral thesis on Sándor Ferenczi and Michael Balint, and of publications on history of psychoanalysis, lecturer at the University of Salzburg, coeditor of the *Freud/Ferenczi Correspondence*, former research fellow at the Balint Archives (Geneva, Switzerland), beneficiary of a grant of the Louis Jeantet Foundation.

Contributors

Carlo Bonomi, Ph.D., psychoanalyst in Florence, Italy. He is author of a forthcoming book: *You are requested to close the eyes. A history of the origins of psychoanalysis.*

Judith Dupont, M.D., psychoanalyst in Paris, editor of «Le Coq-Héron». She translated into French and edited Ferenczi's *Oeuvres complètes* (Paris,

Payot, 1963, 1974, 1984), the *Clinical Diary of Sándor Ferenczi* (1988; French, 1985; German, 1988), and contributed to the French translation of the *Freud / Ferenczi Correspondence* (Paris, Calmann-Lévy, 1992).

Olivier Flournoy, M.D., psychoanalyst in Geneva, author of several books on psychoanalysis and its history: *L'acte de passage. D'une manière de terminer sa psychanalyse* (Neuchâtel, La Baconnière, 1985); *Le temps d'une psychanalyse* (Paris, Belfond, 1979); *Théodore et Léopold. De Théodore Flournoy à la psychanalyse* (Neuchâtel, La Baconnière, 1986; *Psychanalyse 1985* (Neuchâtel, La Baconnière, 1985), and the forthcoming: *Défense de toucher ou la jouissance du dit* (Paris, Calmann-Lévy, 1994).

John Forrester, Ph.D., University Lecturer in the History and Philosophy of Science at the University of Cambridge, author of *Language and the Origins of Psychoanalysis* (London: Macmillan, 1980; French, Paris: Gallimard, 1984), *The Seductions of Psychoanalysis. Freud, Lacan and Derrida* (Cambridge: Cambridge Univ. Press, 1990) and (with Lisa Appignanesi) of *Freud's Women* (London: Weidenfeld & Nicolson, 1992). He also co-translated into English Jacques Lacan, *The Seminar. Books I & II* (1988) and is co-founder of the *Psychoanalytic Forum*, the *Cambridge Group for the History of Psychiatry, Psychoanalysis and Allied Sciences* and the *Cambridge group, Unofficial Knowledge*.

Christopher Fortune, Doctoral Fellow of the Social Sciences and Humanities Research Council of Canada in Applied Psychology at the University of Toronto (Ontario Institute for Studies in Education), currently researching and writing on Elizabeth Severn's role in the history of psychoanalysis.

Albrecht Hirschmüller, M.D., psychiatrist, neurologist and psychotherapist, doctoral thesis about Josef Breuer, scientific collaborator at the Institute of the History of Medicine at the University of Tübingen. Habilitation for history of medicine (*Freud's Encounter with Psychiatry*, Tübingen, 1991). Publications on history of psychiatry and psychoanalysis.

Axel Hoffer, M.D., psychoanalyst, assistant clinical professor at Harvard Medical School, chairman of the Psychoanalytic Institute of New England Eastin Needham, Mass., USA; together with his brother Peter, who is currently translating the correspondence between Freud and Ferenczi into English, he translated Freud's *Phylogenetic Phantasy*. Publications on technique, theory and history of psychoanalysis

Peter Loewenberg, Ph.D., psychoanalyst, professor of History and Political Psychology at the University of California in Los Angeles. He has made many important contributions to psychoanalytic theory, history of psychoanalysis and psychohistory. His major publication is *Decoding the Past* (Berkeley, California University Press, 1980).

Patrick J. Mahony, Ph.D., psychoanalyst, professor of English Literature at the University of Montreal, Canada, author of numerous books, especially on *Freud as a Writer* (New York, Int. Univ. Press, 1982; French, Paris, Les Belles Lettres, 1990), and on Freud's cases: *Cries of the Wolf Man* (New York, Int. Univ. Press, 1984), *Freud and the Rat Man* (New Haven/London, Yale Univ. Press, 1986; French, Paris, P.U.F., 1991), among many others.

R. Andrew Paskauskas, Ph.D., M.A. professor at the American College of Switzerland (Leysin, Switzerland), former professor at the Basic University Education Center of the University of the United Arab Emirates, editor of the *Freud/Jones Correspondence* (Harvard Univ. Press, 1993).

Arnold Wm. Rachman, Ph.D., psychoanalyst in New York City, professor of Clinical Psychology and associate professor of Psychiatry at the New York Medical Center, founding member and training analyst of the Sándor Ferenczi Institute in New York.

Peter L. Rudnytsky, Ph.D., professor at the Institute of Psychological Study of Arts of the University of Florida, Gainesville, USA, and author of several books: *The Persistence of Myth: Psychoanalytic and Structuralist Perspective* (New York/London, Guilford Press, 1988); *The Psychoanalytic Vocation. Rank, Winnicott, and the Legacy of Freud* (New Haven/London, Yale Univ. Press, 1991).

Jean Starobinski, M.D. and Ph.D., honorary professor of the Geneva University, president of the «Rencontres internationales de Genève», Chevalier de la Légion d'Honneur (France), author of a considerable number of books, among which: *Trois fureurs* (Paris, Gallimard, 1974), *Le remède dans le mal. Critique et légitimation de l'artifice à l'âge des Lumières* (Paris, Gallimard, 1989), etc. Recipient of the 1993 Goethe Prize awarded for his work on the history of medicine, the history of European thought and French literature.

Judith E. Vida, M.D., psychoanalyst in Los Angeles, author of numerous articles on psychoanalytic issues, among others, Ferenczi's views on female sexuality.

Freud, his Mother and Sisters, in Mourning at his Father's Grave, 1897.

The father's death was, in Freud's view, the most important event, the most poignant loss of an man's life, and he attributed his self-analysis and his writing *The Interpretation of Dreams* to this experience.

Cahiers Psychiatriques Genevois, Special Issue, 1994, pp. 13-14

INTRODUCTION

André Haynal

To cast light on the process which gave rise to psychoanalysis: the early Freud, his cultural background, his encounters with patients – women in particular – and with colleagues, philosophers or biologists, the influences that marked him, the problems that preoccupied him whilst constructing the *paradigm* of psychoanalysis, is the scope of this volume.

Psychoanalysis has deeply penetrated human sciences, literature, history, psychology, philosophy and even theology of the 20th century: our culture, from Virginia Woolf and James Joyce including the surrealists up until recent films and paintings, cannot be understood without that particular sensibility which nurtured psychoanalysis, and which in its turn enriched subsequent scientific and cultural movements. It penetrated the atmosphere of our daily lives, our nurseries and bedrooms... Moreover, it has been predominant in psychiatry in the ramifications of the diagnostic apparatus and in treatments whether psychoanalytical or thus inspired, among others...

It goes without saying that the search for a theory of affectivity, human relations and sexuality does not come about without *arousing* much emotion, inhibition, disagreement and even passion. We thought that these dissonances in the history should be shown, in order to allow admirers and critics to put forward their points of view in relation to the historical facts. The impact of psychoanalysis has been so vast that a critical appraisal of its history in an *academic* setting seems fully justified... Research on Freud should be conducted with the same academic rigour as for others, e.g. Darwin, Kant or Spinoza, that is without prejudice or institutional conservatism. The history of philosophy and of the religions

---

Translated from French by Dr. Annabel McQuillan, Geneva.

shows us that such an undertaking is possible, – a *history of ideas* can be done.

This book has two main foci: the *early* Freud on the one hand, and his *relationship* with his closest colleague Sándor Ferenczi on the other. We feel that closer examination of these two topics lately made easier by a wider access to his *correspondence*, would shed light on a group of people who, as just mentioned, changed our perception of the world in which we live.

At this point, I would like to pay tribute to our Genevan colleague Raymond de Saussure. It is to his memory that this volume is dedicated. An extraordinarily cultured man, a researcher of insatiable curiosity and exceptional courage, he was also an analysand of Freud (and of others). After his return to Geneva, he became associate professor («chargé de cours») at the University as well as a charismatic member of the European psychonalytical movement, having been one of the founders of the Paris Psychoanalytical Society in 1926. He also wrote a history of the fore-runners to psychoanalysis, notably the magnetists Mesmer and Puységur, and what he was to call «the birth of psychoanalysis».

It is impossible to make a complete list of all the thanks that are due to those who contributed to and made the publication of this volume possible, notably the Institutions Universitaires de Psychiatrie de Genève, the Institute Louis-Jeantet for the History of Medicine and the Department of Psychiatry of the University of Geneva; Colette Degive and Véronique Haynal, as well as members of the Editorial Committee: Marie-Christine Beck-Hamidi, Agnès Reffet, Helga Rieben, Maud Struchen and the principal editor Annabel McQuillan, M.D., who all worked very hard for this publication.

Part I

The Early Freud:
1893 and Afterwards

Cahiers Psychiatriques Genevois, Special Issue, 1994, pp. 17-30

THE GENESIS OF THE *PRELIMINARY COMMUNICATION* OF BREUER AND FREUD

Albrecht Hirschmüller

«A hundred years of psychoanalysis», the title of this volume alludes to the *Preliminary Communication* «On the psychical mechanism of hysterical phenomena» which saw the light of the scientific world at the beginning of 1893. The term itself «psychoanalysis», as we know, appeared for the first time three years later in Freud's work[1]. It is not the right place to explain in detail the known basic thoughts of Breuer and Freud, that is to say the idea of psychic contents that are unconscious or inadmissible to consciousness, their effect in the formation of symptoms and the therapeutic procedures which would, in attaching these contents again to conscious life, achieve a cure by setting free the strangulated affects (*eingeklemmte Affekte*) which was called the *cathartic method*. All this has been explained recently in a concise way in the editorial introduction to the corresponding passages in the supplementary volume of the *Gesammelte Werke*. Instead of this I shall deal with the actual genesis of the *Preliminary Communication*, and then in a second part of my present work examine the later differences of the two protagonists.

At the point when Josef Breuer and Sigmund Freud published their collaborative work, they were bound by fifteen years of friendship and a scientific co-operation which had lasted ten years. When in 1883 Freud first heard of Breuer's epoch-making observation on Anna O., a decisive spark sprang to life within him. But a kind of repression took place under the influence of Charcot's theory, and then of the fascinating temptation arising from the possibilities of hypnotic suggestion therapy, and it was only the disappointments that Freud suffered with this procedure that

---

Translated from German by Dr. Christine Trollope, London.

caused his interest in Breuer's method to come to life again, and led him to make his own first attempt whith the cathartic method in 1889.

Increasing theoretical breakthrough and a (very limited) experience of his own then provided the opportunity for Freud to induce Breuer, fourteen years older than himself, to collaborate with him on a publication. The decision was made in June 1892. The work appeared on 1st and 15th January 1893. How can we now imagine in detail the genesis of this text written in common by two autors?

Freud soon offered Breuer a first piece of manuscript and wrote to him somewhat later in a letter:

> The satisfaction with which I innocently handed you over those few pages of mine has given way to the uneasiness which is so apt to go along with the unremitting pains of thinking. (...) The main question, no doubt, is whether we should describe it historically and lead off with all (or two of the best) case histories, or whether, on the other hand we should start by dogmatically stating the theories we have devised as an explanation.[2]

Freud thus originally wanted to use case-material also as a support for the new theories. However, this plan was probably set aside first of all at Breuer's instigation. Interesting observations of patients had only just begun, and there was not yet complete agreement on their significance. So they limited themselves to a provisional, predominantly theoretical text.

On 12th July 1892 Freud wrote to Fliess:

> My hysteria has, in Breuer's hands, become transformed, broadened, restricted, and in the process has partially evaporated. We are writing the thing jointly, each on his own working on several sections which he will sign, but still in complete agreement. No one can yet say how it will turn out.[3]

But who wrote which parts? The *Preliminary Communication* is divided into five sections. In the first the theory is developed that hysterical patients suffer mainly from reminiscences; this is supported by three short case-histories. In the second section it is established why abreaction to the formerly repressed affects has a curative effect. The third section names *hypnoid states* as a condition of hysteria. The fourth puts forward the theory of the *hysterical attack* and considers Charcot's division into phases. The last brief passage establishes the efficacy of the cathartic method and the part it plays in the understanding *of the psychic mechanisms of hysterical phenomena*, even if not of the essence of hysteria.

Only the handwritten manuscripts could give us exact information about what has been written by one collaborator and what has been added or corrected by the other.[4] It appears however that apart from a letter from Freud of June 29th with comments[5] only two fragments have remained extant which have been printed in Vol. I of the *Standard Edition* as «Sketches for the "Preliminary Communication" of 1893»: a passage of 4 1/2 pages of print «On the theory of the hysterical attacks» dating from the end of November 1892, and a 1 1/2 page undated passage overwritten with «III».[6]

Freud often destroyed the manuscripts of his publications after they were printed. Why, then, did these particular fragments escape destruction? It has been known for a long time that a few of Breuer's pages were preserved and given back to Freud many years later.[7] But the exact circumstances of this return can been seen only in a hitherto unpublished correspondence between Freud and Breuer, found in the Freud Archives and now accessible.[8] It consists of seven letters from Breuer and one from Freud, written from 1906 to 1909. As far as we are concerned, the last of them, a letter from Breuer dated 7th October 1909, is of importance.

> Dear Professor,
> I am tidying my desk and sending back letters and pieces of writing which I believe may still be of interest to their originator.
> I have found the following pages and guess that they may interest you.
> They are obviously sketches and the draft of our Prelim. Communication of 1893. I also found mine, which contains your corrections and additions and corresponds to the printed «Communication». Only the section about attacks is missing, and I believe that you wrote this part and probably have the manuscript.
> As I find myself in possession of your work I thought it correct to put it at your disposal.
> With kindest regards
>
> > J. Breuer

On 8th October Freud confirmed their receipt:

> Very many thanks for letting me have the old drafts and sketches, which seem to me most interesting. As regard the notes on hysterical attacks, it must be as you say; but I did not keep the manuscript after it was printed.[9]

What, then, can we say about the two authors' share in the *Preliminary Communication*? We can now be sure that «Notice III» is Freud's draft for the (third) section on the hypnoid states, and that this draft was completely replaced by Breuer with a text on his own, which Freud looked through again. Also sections 1, 2 and 3 are from Breuer's pen. On the other hand Freud's text was taken as basis for Part 4, but then the passage was taken out in which the so-called principle of constancy is first mentioned.[10] The manuscript of this[11] was not left in Breuer's hands with the other parts, but appears to have been found finally somewhere among Freud's papers.

Naturally Breuer's draft for the other parts, with Freud's corrections, would have been of the greatest interest. But it is not clear where they are. In any case they were unfortunately not found among the papers which were in the possession of the Kann, Duschnitz and Ungar families and are today in the Breuer Collection in the Library of Congress.

How is the fact that Breuer gave back the papers in 1909 to be understood now? Is this a similar procedure to that of a married couple returning their love letters after separation? That usually happens at the height of the separation crisis. But that, in this case, had happened many years before. The extremely hard words about Breuer which Freud had poured out in the correspondence with Fliess had, after the turn of the century, softened to a milder tone. Was there, then, a reconciliation between Breuer and Freud? Unfortunately sources for this period are much thinner on the ground. We are therefore glad to gain from the newly-discovered letters a little additional information on the relationship between the two.

In 1906 a new edition of the *Studies on Hysteria* was considered for the first time. At first the *Preliminary Communication* was to be included in the first volume of Freud's *Sammlung kleiner Schriften zur Neurosenlehre* (collection of minor works on the theory of neuroses). Josef Breuer replied to a query in the subject on 16th May 1906:

> Dear Professor,
> I am pleased to give my consent to the reprint of our Preliminary Communication; but I add the request that a note should expressly refer to the *Studies on Hysteria* as a detailed representation of the conception sketched there.
> Your faithfully
>
> J. Breuer

A further letter followed on 19th May 1906:

> Dear Professor,
> Mr Deuticke has misunderstood me, or made a mistake in passing on my message. I have only said for my part of the book that I wish nothing to be altered in it; but I felt some doubt as to whether you would want to put this stage of development of your life's work before the public unaltered. However that has absolutely nothing to do with me, and I have absolutely no ingerence[12] in it. What I said to D. only meant that this would perhaps be an opportunity for you to commence the central parts of your work while up to now only its outworks have been presented. I am completely in agreement with the second preface and the remark dealing with you. Perhaps it would be a good idea to put the title of the treatise in «...»
> Your faithfully
>
> J. Breuer

Breuer wished to make it emphatically clear that he himself stuck firmly by viewpoints which they formerly had in common, but from which Freud had withdrawn, and it was therefore Freud's business to present and substantiate the further development of the theory. But that was exactly what Freud did not want. The affair dragged on for over a year. The next letter referring to the project is from Freud and is dated 14th October 1907:

> Dear Colleague,
> Allow me to add to my thanks for sending to me recently your treatise «On the auditory organ in birds»[13] two other communications, both of which have in common their connection with our earlier relationship.

I. Mr Deuticke, the publisher of our *Studies on Hysteria,* wants to put the second edition of the book on the market at last in 1908, and has asked me to get in touch with you on the subject. You said by that time that you would not approve anything but an unaltered impression: I am of the same opinion as far as my part is concerned. Perhaps a short «Preface to the second edition» might be desirable; as you are rightly the author first mentioned in the title, it would probably fall to you to draft it. I ask you to give me your opinion about this.

II. I have taken the liberty of having the sum of 2000 Kronen (crowns) transferred from my Post Office Savings Bank account to yours, so as to take another step towards the payment of my old debt to you after a long interval. As I have to confess to my shame that I do not know how much it is. I ask you to enlighten me with a word.

With a respect that outlasts all other changes

I am

Yours sincerely

Dr Freud

It is noteworthy that Breuer in these years sent Freud an offprint again. Perhaps this was an opportunity for Freud to take up a subject wich had strained their relationship. It is known that Freud's old financial debt to Breuer had led in 1898 to ill-feeling between them. Freud had at that time wanted to clear part of the debt, and Breuer wanted to have it settled up with an honorarium which a relative of his owed to Freud, which Freud took as overweening interference.[14] In 1907, then, Freud tried again to put an end to the matter, perhaps hoping this might be more possible in connection with the agreement on a new edition of the book on which they had once worked together.

Breuer's reply of 16th October 1907 reads as follows:

Dear Professor,

As concerns the reprint of the *Studies*, I can of course only request the un-changed reprint of my chapters (– if a reprint appears absolutely justified –) because since our work I have scarcely occupied myself intensively with the subject and the new impression would contain not only my earlier opinions, but also my present ones. Your opinion, however, have developed to such an extent that the new impres-sion has essentially the significance of a historical document. If you have not in mind to rework the theoretical and technical chapter according to your present opinions, the public must be informed why they are being presented once more with obsolete views. This preface, which can only refer to your part, can only be written by you. I suggest, then, that I explain the unchanged reprint of my chapters in three lines, and you do the same for yours.

With regard to the sum which you very kindly wish to make over to me, I must say this: I have no idea how much you ever were in debt to me; it goes without saying that these amounts were the last I would have noted; that was neither my business nor my interest. I thought, over the last few years, that the dept had already been paid in full. Only if you *know for certain* that this is *not* the case, and that the debt has reached *this amount*, I accept the payment with many thanks. If you were unable to assure me of this, I should have to take the liberty of returning the payment to your account. I therefore ask you kindly to let me know.

With the expression of my greatest respect, I am

Yours sincerely

J. Breuer

Freud's reply to Breuer's letter is not extant, but its content can be deduced from Breuer's latest reply of 19th October 1907:

> Dear Professor,
>
> If the position is as you very kindly inform me, I accept the payment of which the Post Office Savings Bank has already notified me, with many thanks, but I ask you sincerely to consider the matter now as *completely at an end*.
>
> With many thanks   J. Breuer

The reprint of *Studies on Hysteria* was delayed into 1908, and the correspondence continues with Breuer's letter of 20th June 1908:

> Dear Professor,
>
> I thank you for kindly sending me the proof sheets. I had received them directly from Deuticke, and when I got your packet I had already corrected them and sent them to Brünn at the printer's.
>
> As I have already taken the liberty of remarking, our attitude to the unchanged new impression is essentially different. I wish for it because it still corresponds in essence to my opinion. You rise it although it no longer corresponds to yours. The motivation must therefore be different, and I am not at all in a position to write the preface stating those reasons for both of us. I ask you then to write it and add the enclosed lines in second place, as they are purely personal, but the factual basis must come first.
>
> Yours faithfully   J. Breuer

Freud was now obviously expecting Breuer's preface to be moved to the top place. But this caused Breuer to change his first draft yet again, and it is to this that the next letter to Freud of 1st July 1908 refers:

> Dear Professor,
>
> I did not know what form your preface would take, and as I only wished to put in a few lines, I wrote it in such a way that it could take its place as a postscript to a longer explanation. As you too wrote the preface briefly and wished to keep the succession as it is on the title page, I had to add a few initial words. I leave out the remark that «my opinions have not changed in essence», as you are referring to this very point when stating that «I should like to give up the difference between factual and personal motivation»: it is a matter of indifference to the public whether my opinions have altered or not. Far be it from me to give any indication of our personal relationship in a publication; that goes without saying.
>
> It would be far better to let the past be past.
>
> Yours sincerely   J. Breuer

Freud probably felt this letter from Breuer as a further sign of aloofness. His reply is not extant, but Breuer for his part wrote back a card on 4th July:

> Dear Professor,
>
> Your supposition is quite correct. If I had had the remotest idea that you wished to «revive» the past, I should certainly not have declined in *this* form.
>
> Yours sincerely   J. Breuer

So the new edition of the *Studies on Hysteria* did nothing to improve decisively the personal relationship of the two co-authors. But anyway the ground was prepared on which Breuer, another year later, was able to continue the contact and give back to Freud the drafts from the time when the *Studies* took shape. However the wounds inflicted then went too deep for a reconciliation.

Freud is known to have incommoded himself by Breuer's hesitancy, his sceptical reservations in the face of apodictic formulations, and to have criticised the fact that Breuer always «knows three candidates for the position of *one* truth»[15], and decided that in reality he was not for, but against his theory. Later, after Breuer's death in 1925, he was able to correct this, and called the knowledge that all his life Breuer had taken an intensive share in the progress of psychoanalysis «balsam on a painful wound that had never healed».[16] But how was it with Breuer? Did he know of inner psychic obstacles that could oppose his collaboration with Freud? Did he know this sceptical, hesitant side of himself? We have important autobiographical documents in which Breuer expressly throws light on this side of this character, letters he exchanged with his wife in June 1877. At that time Mathilde had gone in advance, with the four children between eight years and nine months, to Gmunden im Salzkammergut, where they usually spent their summer holiday, while her husband was still occupied with his practice in Vienna. The letters are about a book they were reading together, a novel by Ivan Sergeyevich Turgenev (1818-1883) with the title «Nov'», «Virgin Soil», a book which had appeared in the same year in Russian and a little later in German translation and immediately discussed in the *Deutsche Rundschau*.[17] The letters are equally interesting for Breuer's political position and for his theoretical literary views. In the context of this paper, however, only those aspects will be shown which relate to Breuer's self-delineation. As Turgenev's novels are no longer very well known today, I must contribute to its understanding with a very brief description of contents:

Nezhdanov, one of the Russian Hamlet types often depicted by Turgenev, in outward aspect rough, realistic and a deathdefying revolutionary, a member of the «Narodniki» movement, rooted in the people, secretely cherishes idealistic, aesthetic dreams. Unlike his lover Marianna, Maschurina, who idolises him, and the gloomy revolutionary Markelov, he lacks true belief in «the Cause». His desperate efforts are doomed to failure, and he shoots himself in the end, while Marianna, following his wish, joins with Solomin, a realist from the people, who makes his mark through energy and patience. A marginal figure is Paklin, a small, limping would-be revolutionary, honest but ambivalent, awkward and clumsy, tolerated, but not taken seriously very much, and yet secretly cleverer than most of the other participants, a man who at the end through his clumsiness blurts out where the conspirators are. His aged relatives, Fomuschka and Fimuschka, are a ludicrous married couple who live like fossils from the 18th century and are alike down to the smallest detail. Such a Paklin, as Breuer writes immediately at the end of a long letter to his wife of 17th June 1877, he is himself. May God preserve him from great tasks!

Anyone who has formed a picture of Breuer's personality must above all be amazed by this comparison, this self-appraisal. And Frau Mathilde reacted with exactly this amazement, not to say indignation:

> Dearest Pepi,
> Today you made me seriously angry (...) I felt as though the blush of exasperation were rising into my cheeks as I read. So you are a Paklin. If I may not think that the monstrous heat has gone to your head, that you had to get away and already at the end of the letter were thinking of something else, then – really, I cannot say how angry I would be with you. Modesty and self-knowledge, all in honesty, and when otherwise you speak of your weakness and lack of energy, then I think it belongs to your good nature that you have such a low opinion of your virtues, yet you always look at the tiny stains on your character through a magnifying glass – but this is too much. (...).
> Do you think I would have loved you and held you as high in my enormous love as I do with other good and hard-working people, if you had been like Paklin? (...)

Breuer replied promptly, and I give a rather longer quotation from this letter:

> My sweet love,
> I am not as unfair to myself as you are to Paklin. You see him with the eyes of Nezhdanov and Maschurina. They do not look askance at him because he is worth nothing, but because he has not «the belief». He is more intelligent than any of them (...); because he feels what the circle feels and is curious, he sees the whole story from outside; but he is sceptical. He is not the stuff of which martyrs are made, nor the wood from which heroes are carved. For a martyr, he lacks the belief, for a hero the energy. But he has not at all «gone to the bad». Paklin is a very good, lovable, sensible person, whose mistake is to mix with those people at all, and to drift in a direction which is not suitable for people of his type. (...).
> Now here I come, my love! I hope you do not put me on a pedestal because I could be a hero; *that* stuff is not in me. Suppose that I had entered into such a conspiracy in the years of my youth. I would have seen how hollow the whole story is, how devoid of prospects; I would not have been able to take part in it. I might perhaps not be able to get out of it, as Solomin cannot, who judges the matter so excellently. I would stand by, try to help, if a disaster happened through acts of folly, and perhaps do it very clumsily. I would not feel the need to cry down myself and my intelligence in foolishness in order to remain «in it» like Nezhdanow, but I would feel mourning for the fallen, like Paklin.
> Where has it been written that modern man has a demon, called «but». «But» stands behind him and holds him back when he has to say his love will last for ever. Do you know what for«ever» means? he whispers, «are you sure of yourself? Are you lord and master of the unwillingness in you, of your feelings?». And the modern man we know does not say yes, he says; I believe ( ) All of us, people of the educated

middle classes, well-meaning and moderate, will not only be defeated or rather disappear in every crisis, but also play the worst part, for we have no belief. (...) How, without belief, can we fix the goals for which we long to conquer and die, even if we have the stuff of it in our character (...) What would criticism be worth if it could not even criticise itself, if it were not in a position to do its disintegrating duty against and over itself also? That is why I am on Paklin's side. Are you still angry?

It is more than clear in this letter how Breuer sees himself. He sympathises with the revolutionaries, supports them when he can, and still feels himself incapable of giving his allegiance to the «Cause» («*Sache*»), hindered by an inner tendency which he calls the «Demon But» of educated people, of sceptics without belief, of knowledgeable bourgeois, of realistically thinking politicians. This was a kind of self-estimation diametrically opposed to that of Freud. Freud was ready to fling himself into an idea, to think it through to the end with all its consequences, and for that purpose to free himself when necessary from all other ties. He expected the same from his followers. Breuer could not fulfil this expectation. So in Freud's eyes he fell into the ranks of lukewarm hangers-on, and finally was counted among the enemy, a view which Freud was not able to correct until after Breuer's death.

The *Preliminary Communication*, the first highspot of the collaboration between Breuer and Freud, already contains in itself the germ of the differences which were to become ever clearer in the following years, and which were rooted to no small extent in the different natures of the two men.

Notes

[1] *Freud* (1896a, 1896b).

[2] To Breuer, 19th June, 1892, *Standard Edition*, 1, p. 147.

[3] *Freud* (1985c, p. 32).

[4] Grubrich-Simitis, in her latest, fascinating book (1993), has effectively shown how such texts can bring to life Freud's creative way of writing.

[5] *Standard Edition*, 1, pp. 147 ff., 151-154, 149 ff.

[6] Both manuscripts are in the Freud Archives, Series B, Container 31.

[7] Freud's letter to Breuer, 8.10.1909, *Standard Edition*, 1, p. 146.

[8] I am grateful for the knowledge of this document to Gerhard Fichtner.
We gratefully acknowledge the copyright:
© 1994. A.W. Freud *et al.*, by arrangement with Mark Paterson & Associates. Extracts from Josef Breuer's letters were reproduced with the kind permission of Dr. Marie Kann, Princeton, in the name of Josef Breuer's heirs.

[9] This letter is quoted *In: Standard Edition*, 1, p. 146.

[10] This is the theory that «the nervous system endeavours to keep constant something in its functional relations that we may describe as the "sum of excitation".» (*Standard Edition*, 1, p. 153); only two years later, in the chapter on theory of the *Studies on Hysteria*, the principle of constancy is stated by Breuer, however in a specific sense deviating from Freud's original concept; cf. Hirschmüller (1989), pp. 159-164).

[11] *On the theory of hysterical attacks, Standard Edition*, 1, pp. 151-154.

[12] From the Latin *ingerere*, bring in, meddle, thus something like: influence, interference: used also as a legal term.

[13] A fairly long anatomical-physiological study by Breuer dated 1907, cf. Hirschmüller (1989, pp. 76-79).

[14] Letter to Breuer, 7.1.1898 (1961a, pp. 243-245); to Fliess, 16.1. and 22.1.1898, (1985c) pp. 294, 296.

[15] «I believe he will never forgive that in the *Studies* I dragged him along and involved him in something where he unfailingly knows three candidates for the position of *one* truth and abhors all generalizations, regarding them as presumptuous.» (1985c, p. 175).

[16] This appears from letters which he then exchanged with Breuer's son Robert; cf. Hirschmüller (1989), pp. 321-323.

[17] Deutsche Rundschau 11 (1877) (April-June) pp. 504-510. Here I use the transcription of the Russian which is usual today, but in the quotations leave the way of writing used in that time, e.g. «Turgenieff». I received the original of the two letters from Josef Breuer to Mathilde many years ago as a present from Frau Duschnitz. There exists a copy of Mathilde's reply. Copies of this correpondence can also be found in the Breuer Collection in the Library of Congress, Washington. This correspondence was not included into my dissertation in 1978 (Engl: Hirschmüller, 1989), as a publication of Breuer's letters was planned, a project which Prof. Kann could unfortunately not carry out (he died in 1981). Because of their importance the two letters will be presented here now in extracts as a preliminary to a later edition of other letters of Breuer, and will be published in their entirety elsewhere.

Appendix

Deutscher Text der erstmals veröffentlichten Briefe. Die Texte werden im allgemeinen getreu wiedergegeben. Abkürzungen wie «Mitteil[un]g» werden jedoch stillschweigend aufgelöst. Hervorhebungen erscheinen kursiv gedruckt, Auflösungen und Ergänzungen in eckigen Klammern.

Josef Breuer an Sigmund Freud, 7. Oktober 1909

Verehrter Herr Professor!
Ich räume meinen Schreibtisch auf u. sende dabei Briefe und Schriftstücke zurück, wenn ich glaube, daß sie für ihre Urheber noch Interesse haben können.
So finde ich beif[olgende] Blätter u. vermute daß sie Sie interessiren können.
Es sind offenbar Skizzen und der Entwurf zu unserer vorläuf. Mitteilung von 1893. Ich fand auch den meinigen, der Ihre Correcturen u. Zusätze enthält u. der gedruckten «Mitteilung» entspricht. Nur der Abschnitt über den Anfall fehlt da u. ich glaube, daß für diesen verfaßt haben u. wol auch das Manuskript hinterlassen m.

Da ich mich so im Besitze Ihrer Arbeit befinde, hielt ich es für richtig, sie Ihnen zur Verfügung zu stellen.

Mit besten Empfehlungen   J. Breuer

Josef Breuer an Sigmund Freud, 16. Mai 1906

Verehrter Herr Professor!

Ich gebe mit Vergnügen meine Zustimmung zum Neudrucke unserer vorl[äufigen] Mitteilung; schließe aber die Bitte an, daß eine Anmerkung ausdrücklich auf die «Studien ü[ber] H[ysterie]» verweise als auf die eingehende Darstellung der dort skizzirten Anschauung.

Hochachtungsvoll ergeben   J. Breuer

Josef Breuer an Sigmund Freud, 19. Mai 1906

Verehrter Herr Professor!

Herr Deuticke hat mich mißverstanden od. meine Äußerung irrtümlich weitergegeben. Ich habe nur für meinen Anteil an dem Buche gesagt, daß ich daran nichts geändert wünsche; meinte aber, ich zweifle, ob Sie dieß Entwicklungsstadium Ihres Lebenswerkes unverändert wieder publiciren wollten. Doch geht das mich gar nichts an, u. habe ich gar keine Ingerenz hierauf. (Ich meinte nur zu D., das wäre vielleicht eben der Anlaß für Sie, das Centrum Ihres Werkes in Angriff zu nehmen, dessen Außenwerke bisher publicirt wurden.) Ich bin mit dem zweiten Vorwort und der Sie betr. Bemerkung vollkommen einverstanden. Vielleicht empfielt [!] es sich, die Titel der Abhandlung in Anmerkung zu setzen.

Hochachtungsvoll   J. Breuer

Sigmund Freud an Josef Breuer, 14. Oktober 1907

Verehrter Herr College

Gestatten Sie mir, daß ich an den Dank für die mir letzthin übersandte Abhandlung «Über das Gehörorgan der Vögel» zwei andere Mittheilungen anknüpfe, denen beiden der Zusammenhang mit unseren früheren Beziehungen gemeinsam ist.

I. – Herr Deuticke, der Verleger unserer «Studien über Hysterie», will die zweite Auflage des Buches endlich im Jahre 1908 auf den Markt bringen und hat mich aufgefordert, darüber in Verhandlung mit Ihnen zu treten. Sie haben seinerzeit geäußert, daß Sie nichts anderes als einen unveränderten Abdruck gutheißen würden; ich bin für meinen Antheil der nämlichen Ansicht. Vielleicht wäre eine kurze «Vorrede zur zweiten Auflage» erforderlich, deren Entwurf wol Ihnen als dem auf dem Titel mit Recht voranstehenden Autor zufallen würde. Ich erbitte mir hierüber Ihre Äußerung.

II. Ich habe mir erlaubt, die Summe von Kr 2000 von meinem Postsparkassenkonto auf Ihres schreiben zu lassen, um nach langer Unterbrechung wieder einen Schritt zur Tilgung meiner alten Geldschuld an Sie zu thun. Da ich zu meiner Beschämung gestehen muß, daß ich deren Höhe nicht kenne, bitte ich Sie, mich mit einem Wort darüber zu orientiren.

Ich bin mit einer, alle sonstigen Wandlungen überdauernden, Hochachtung

Ihr ergebener   Dr. Freud

Josef Breuer an Sigmund Freud, 16. Okt. 1907

Verehrter Herr Professor!

Was den Abdruck der «Studien» anlangt, kann ich natürlich nur den unveränderten Abdruck meiner Capitel wünschen (– wenn ein Abdruck überhaupt berechtigt erscheint –), weil ich mich seit unserer Arbeit kaum intensiver mit dem Gegenstand beschäftigt habe und der Neudruck nicht bloß frühere, sondern auch meine jetzigen Anschauungen bieten würde. Ihre Anschauungen haben sich aber in solchem Maaße weiter entwickelt, daß der Neudruck wesentlich die Bedeutung eines historischen Documentes hat. Wenn Sie es nicht vorziehen, das theoretische und technische Capitel im Sinne Ihrer jetzigen Anschauungen umzuarbeiten, muß doch wol das Publikum darüber aufgeklärt werden, warum ihm überwundene Ansichten abermals vorgelegt werden. Dieses Vorwort nun, welches sich ja nur auf Ihren Anteil beziehen kann, können auch nur Sie schreiben. Ich schlage also vor, daß ich in 3 Zeilen den unveränderten Abdruck meiner Kapitel [!] motivire u. Sie es für die Ihren tun.

Was die Summe angeht, die Sie gütigst auf mich übertragen wollen, muß ich folgendes sagen. Ich habe keine Ahnung davon, wieviel Sie mir je geschuldet haben; es ist doch wol selbstverständlich, daß diese Beträge das letzte waren, was ich mir notirt hätte; das war weder meine Sache noch mein Interesse. - So war ich die letzten Jahre über der Meinung, daß die Schuld bereits vollständig beglichen sei. Nur wenn Sie *sicher wissen*, daß das *nicht* der Fall ist, und daß die Schuld *diese Höhe* erreicht, acceptire ich die Übertragung mit bestem Dank. Sollten Sie mir das nicht versichern können, muß ich mir erlauben, die Übertragung im Konto rückgängig zu machen. Ich erbitte mir deshalb eine gütige Äußerung hierüber.

Mit dem Ausdruck ausgezeichneter Hochachtung ergebenst   J. Breuer

Josef Breuer an Sigmund Freud, 19. Okt. 1907

Verehrter Herr Professor!

Wenn sich die Sache so verhält, wie Sie mir gütigst mitteilen, nehme ich die, mir bereits von der P[ost]-Sp[ar]-K[asse] angezeigte, Übertragung bestens dankend an; bitte aber herzlich, die Angelegenheit damit als *vollkommen beendet* ansehen zu wollen.

Mit bestem Danke   J. Breuer

Josef Breuer an Sigmund Freud, 20. Juni 1908

Verehrter Herr Professor!

Ich danke Ihnen für die gütige Zusendung des Correcturbogens. Ich hatte denselben von Deuticke direct erhalten u. bei Empfang Ihrer Sendung bereits corrigirt nach Brünn an die Druckerei geschickt.

Wie ich schon einmal zu bemerken mir erlaubt habe, ist unsere Stellung zu dem unveränderten Neudruck eine wesentlich verschiedene. Ich wünsche denselben, weil er im wesentlichen meiner Anschauung noch entspricht. Sie veranlassen ihn, obwol er der ihrigen nicht mehr entspricht. Die Motivirung muß also eine verschiedene sein, u. ich bin ganz außer Stande, dieß begründende Vorwort für uns beide zu schreiben. Ich bitte daher, es abzufassen und die beiliegenden Zeilen an zweiter Stelle anzufügen, da sie ja rein persönlich sind, die sachliche Begründung aber vorgehen muß.

Hochachtungsvoll   J. Breuer

Josef Breuer an Sigmund Freud, 3. Juli 1908

Verehrter Herr Professor!

Ich wußte nicht, wie Sie Ihr Vorwort gestalten würden u. da ich jedenfalls nur einige wenige Zeilen zu geben wünschte, faßte ich diese so, daß sie als Nachwort einer langen Ausführung am Platze sein konnten. Da auch Sie das Vorwort kurz fassen u. wünschen, daß die Ordnung des Titels auch hier gewahrt werde, mußte ich einige Anfangsworte beifügen. Die Bemerkung, daß sich «meine Anschauungen im wesentlichen nicht geändert haben», lasse ich weg, da sich wol nur hierauf Ihre Bemerkung beziehen kann: «ich möge auf die

Unterscheidung sachlicher u. persönlicher Motivirung verzichten«; es auch für das Publicum ganz gleichgiltig ist, ob sich meine Anschauungen geändert haben oder nicht. Irgend eine Andeutung über unser persönliches Verhältnis in eine Publication zu bringen, lagen mir absolut ferne; wie wol selbstverständlich.

Das Vergangene lassen wir wol besser u. lieber vergangen sein.

In Hochachtung ergeben   J. Breuer

Josef Breuer an Sigmund Freud, 4. Juli 1908

Verehrter Herr Professor!

Ihre Vermutung ist ganz richtig. Wenn ich auch nur im entferntesten daran gedacht hätte, daß Sie Vergangenes zu «beleben» wünschten, hätte ich gewiss nicht in *dieser* Form abgelehnt.

In Hochachtung ergebenst   J. Breuer

Mathilde an Josef Breuer, 13. Juni 1877 (Auszug)

Liebster Pepi!

Heute hast Du mich ernstlich böse gemacht [...], ich fühlte es, wie mir beim Lesen die Röthe des Unwillens ins Gesicht stieg. Also ein Paklin bist Du. Wenn ich mir nicht denken soll, daß Dir die ungeheure Hitze zu Kopfe gestiegen ist, daß Du schon fort mußtest und bei dem Ende des Briefes schon an Anderes dachtest, dann - wahrhaftig, ich kann nicht sagen, wie böse ich Dir sein müßte. Bescheidenheit und Selbsterkenntnis, alles in Ehren und wenn Du sonst von Deiner Energielosigkeit und Schwäche sprichst, dann denke ich mir wohl, wie es mit zu Deinen guten Eigenschaften gehöre, daß Du Deine Tugenden so gering achtest, die kleinen Fleckchen Deines Charakters aber stets mit dem Vergrößerungsglas betrachtest - aber das ist zu viel. [...] Glaubst Du, ich hätte Dich lieb und hielt[e] Dich nebst meiner ungeheuren Liebe noch so hoch, wie ich es tue mit anderen guten und tüchtigen Menschen, wenn Du wärst wie Paklin? [...]«

Josef an Mathilde Breuer, 14. Juni 1877 (Auszug)

Mein süßer Schatz!

Nicht ich tue mir so Unrecht, wie Du Paklin. Du siehst ihn mit den Augen der Neshdanow und Maschurina. Sie sehen nicht scheel auf ihn, weil er nichts wert wäre, sondern weil er «den Glauben» nicht hat. Er ist gescheidter als sie alle [...]; weil er dem Kreis nachempfindet und neugierig ist, hängt er als Außenglied an der ganzen Geschichte; aber er ist skeptisch. Nicht das Holz, aus dem Märtyrer gemacht werden, nicht das aus dem Helden zu schnitzen sind. Zum ersten fehlt ihm der Glaube, zum letzten die Energie. «Verkommen» aber ist er gar nicht. Paklin ist ein sehr guter, lieber, verständiger Mensch, dessen Fehler ist, überhaupt mit den Leuten zu verkehren, in einer Richtung zu treiben, die für Leute seiner Art nicht taugt. [...]

Nun komme ich, mein Schatz! Ich hoffe, Du hältst mich nicht hoch, weil ich ein Held wäre; *das* Zeug habe ich nicht. Denke dir, ich sei in jungen Jahren in so eine Conspiration gekommen. Ich müßte doch sehen, wie hohl die ganze Geschichte ist, wie aussichtslos; ich würde nicht mittun können. Ich würde vielleicht nicht zurückziehen können, wie es auch Solomin nicht tun kann, der die Sache so trefflich beurteilt. Ich würde nebenan stehen, zu helfen suchen, wenn ein Unglück durch die Tollheiten geschehen ist u. vielleicht dabei recht ungeschickt sein; das Bedürfnis, mich u. meinen Verstand in tollem Zeug zu überschreien, um *«dabei»* zu bleiben, wie Neshdanow, würde ich nicht empfinden, aber die Trauer um die Gefallenen wie Paklin.

Wo steht es doch, der moderne Mensch habe einen Dämon, der nenne sich «Aber».
«Aber» steht hinter ihm u. hält ihn zurück, wenn er sagen soll, seine Liebe werde immer
dauern. Weißt Du, was immer heißt? flüstert er, «bist du deiner selbst sicher? Bist du Herr
und Meister über das unwillkürliche in dir, deine Empfindung». Und der bekannte moderne
Mensch sagt nicht ja, er sagt: ich glaube. [...]
Wir alle, Leute der gebildeten Mittelklassen, wolmeinend und gemäßigt, werden in jeder
Krise nicht bloß unterliegen od. vielmehr verschwinden, sondern auch die schlechtere Rolle
spielen, denn wir haben keinen Glauben. [...]
Woher sollen wir glaubenslose die Ziele nehmen, für die wir sterbend siegen möchten,
auch wenn wir im Charakter das Zeug dazu hätten? [...]
Was wäre denn die Kritik wert, wenn sie nicht auch sich selbst kritisiren könnte, wenn sie
nicht im Stande wäre, auch gegen sich und über sich ihres zersetzenden Amtes zu walten.
Darum stelle ich mich zu Paklin. Bist Du noch böse? [...]

References

FREUD, S. (1896a). Heredity and the Aetiology of the Neuroses. *Standard Edition*, *3*, 143-
156.

— (1896b). Further Remarks on the Neuropsychoses of Defense. *Standard Edition*, *3*,
162-185.

— (1960). *Letters of Sigmund Freud 1873-1939*. London: Hogarth Press., 1961.

— (1985c). *The Complete Letters of Sigmund Freud to Wilhelm Fliess 1887-1904*. Cambridge,
Mass./London: Belknap.

— (1987). *Gesammelte Werke, Nachtragsband*. Frankfurt/M.: Fischer.

GRUBRICH-SIMITIS, I.(1993). *Zurück zu Freuds Texten. Stumme Dokumente sprechen
machen*. Frankfurt/M.: Fischer.

HIRSCHMÜLLER, A. (1978). *The Life and Work of Josef Breuer. Physiology and
Psychoanalysis*. New York/London: New York University Press, 1989.

— (1987). «Balsam auf eine schmerzende Wunde». Zwei bisher unbekannte Briefe Sigmund
Freuds über sein Verhältnis zu Josef Breuer. *Psyche*, *41*, 55-59.

Cahiers Psychiatriques Genevois, Special Issue, 1994, pp. 31-39

ON THE WORD
«ABREACTION»

Jean Starobinski

The word «catharsis» is generally considered to be the lexical indication used by the authors of the *Preliminary Communication* to denote the novelty of their therapeutic approach. As the word was not entirely new in medical language, the author needed to reinforce it, and added in quotation marks the word «abreaction», which was clearly a neologism.

In *An Autobiographical Study* Freud attributes these terminological innovations to Breuer:

> Breuer spoke of our method as cathartic; its therapeutic aim was explained as being to provide that the quota of affect used for maintaining the symptom, which had got on to the wrong lines and had, as it were, become strangulated there, should be directed on to the normal path along which it could obtain discharge (or *abreaction*). (Freud, 1925d [1924], S.E. 20: 22).

As far as the word «catharsis» was concerned one must stress the importance of the debate which had just taken place between philologists over the acceptance of the term in *De Poetica* by Aristotle (330, pp. 9, 58-59 and 24-28). In a very convincing manner, the philologist Jacob Bernays, uncle by marriage to Freud, proposed a meaning for this term in the same sense as it was used in Greek medicine, that is to say purgation or evacuation. In the XVIIth century, in order to define the effects of tragedy according to Aristotle, French authors spoke of «purgation des passions» and thus posed no barrier to its adoption as a medical term. It must be remembered that it was in this sense that it remained firmly anchored in the traditional medical lexicon until the XIXth century.[1] It would be useful to express in a series of metaphors, the expulsion of an affect retained enclosed (*eingeklemmt*) like a foreign body (*Fremdkörper*). Freud as

---

Translated from French by Dr. Annabel McQuillan, Geneva

cited above, made the words «*Abfuhr*», «*Katharsis*» and «*Abreaktion*» virtually synonymous: these words combining in meaning diversion, evacuation, elimination, and release with as an added plus, a hint of purification.

After he substituted the term «psycho-analysis» for «cathartic method» he no longer used the word «catharsis» except for historical references. It was also the case for the words «*Abreaktion, abreagieren*» having temporarily adopted them for the shared writing of the *Preliminary Communication* and *Studies on Hysteria* (Freud & Breuer, 1895d [1893-1895], S.E. 2). Later in *Recollecting, Repeating and Working Through* (1914) Freud was to explain what in the course of treatment had pushed abreaction into the background and brought working-through (*durcharbeiten*) to the fore.[2] The analyst has to focus his attention principally on lifting resistance. Laplanche and Pontalis (1967) on «Abreaction» write: «Emphasis placed exclusively on abreaction in determining the efficiency of psychotherapy characterized above all the period of the cathartic method. However, the notion remains in the theory of psychoanalysis for factual reasons (presence in all treatments, to various degrees according to patient type, manifestations of emotional discharge) and because fundamentally all treatment theories take into account not only *remembrance* but *repetition*. Notions like transference, working-through, acting out all imply a reference to abreaction, at the same time leading to more complex conceptualizations of treatment than simply getting rid of the traumatising affect» (p. 2). One may note, however, that Freud in the concluding chapter of *Studies on Hysteria* completes the theory of abreaction with a series of notions which were to be kept and refined in later publications: he talks not only of *analysis*, but in large measure of *repression* and *resistance* of the patient as well as the insistance of the psychotherapist.

*

The mediaeval latin word «reactio» already has the prefix *re-*, which indicates return, resistant response, secondariness. Adding the Germanic *ab-*, Freud and Breuer redoubled the prefix, and for a very specific purpose brought back a term, which, through widespread use, had lost any precise meaning. As for a word like «*mechanism*», there was a need to add a determinant complement in French in order to be specific (*réaction de ...*) or to form a composite word in German. Freud followed German usage which led to words formed by agglutination (example: *Unlustreaktion* – [reaction of unpleasure] (G.W., X, p. 260), while French forms «syntagmes» or more precisely «lexies» or «synapsies» (Dubois *et al.*, 1973). Our specialized dictionaries do not even have an entry for «reaction» alone. *The Language of Psychoanalysis* (1967) by Laplanche and Pontalis defines «defense» and not «defense reaction». The only «reaction» cited is «negative therapeutic reaction», which has a unique and very specific meaning.

In one sense, «*Abreaktion*» due to the similitude of the prefix is a doublet of «*Abfuhr*». In both words, a movement towards the exterior is indicated, which implies a starting point from where there is movement outside, that is to say «propulsion» and «disencumbrance». However, «*Abreaktion*» is not limited as «*Abfuhr*» to a material and spatial signification. The word «abreaction» benefits from an invaluable ambiguity. It may designate a mechanism, a phenomenon linked to the nervous structure and the quantity of excitation that flows therein. It may also be used to mean a transitive *action*, voluntary or involuntary. In the *Preliminary Communication* and in *Studies on Hysteria* the verb is often conjugated whether actively or passively: the subject abreacts an emotion; «an affective unit» (*Affektbetrag*) is abreacted. Abreaction is no longer something which takes place in a neutral and impersonal manner. The fact that «to abreact» can be conjugated in two ways, and the double meaning of «abreaction» alternately situates this curative phenomenon in either physiology or behaviour.

In the language of the physiologists of the XIXth century, «reaction» was the term applied to the motor branch of the reflex arc, to the point of becoming, depending on the context, virtually a synonym of «reflex». It is obvious that invoking the notion of trauma and the model of traumatic hysteria, Freud between 1892 and 1895 at least looked for an explanation of hysteria which took into consideration all the moments of a reflex arc, composing an afference from an external origin, a motor efference towards the exterior, hindered to a greater or lesser extent in its discharge. The hysteric disorder is characterized by a disturbance of the efferent motor mechanism: being either retarded or deviated it cannot take place along normal lines or within the usual time frame. In adopting a reflex model for hysterical behaviour, Freud joined the ranks of those theoreticians who had extended to include cerebral function, the model of the reflex arc – sensory excitation, motor response – shown by physiological experimentation at spinal level (Gauchet, 1992).[3] At that time, the demonstration of a reflex was a guarantee of scientific veracity. Let's however take another look at the article which Freud published in French in *Archives de Neurologie* in 1893 (Freud, 1893c, S.E. 1: 166-169). It reminds us that Charcot referred to the notion of a «*lésion dynamique*» (dynamic lesion) but that for an explanation of the hysterical neurosis he was the first to teach that «*il faut s'adresser à la psychologie*» (one has to turn to psychology). Consequently, Freud requested permission to leave neurological considerations behind and to move «*sur le terrain de la psychologie*» (into the psychological domain).

We may add that the model of the reflex arc was to reappear again and again in Freud's thinking. It is the starting point for *Instincts and their Vicissitudes* (1915c). In that essay Freud develops a theory which insists on a constant sum of excitation, precisely he had wanted to introduce into *Studies on Hysteria* (Freud & Breuer, 1895d), but with which Breuer did not agree. In order to define the fundamental concept of instinct in the 1915 study, Freud insists on the difference between simple motor action and instinctual drives. The physiological formula of reflex mobility is mentioned initially in its most classical form: «... Physiology [...] has given us the concept of a 'stimulus' and the pattern of the reflex arc, according to which a stimulus applied to living tissue (nervous substance) from the outside is discharged by action to the outside.» (Freud, 1915c, S.E. 14: 118) For the human being, Freud continued, this law is only applicable to an external stimulus; this gives rise to an evacuation in a single action. It is not the same for instinctive excitation, which arises from the interior of the organism, and is without a reciprocal motor discharge (such as flight). This distinction was already appearing in the theoretical considerations developed over the period 1892-1895.[4] Let us also note that the terms «*Abfuhr*», «*abführen*» are the same in the *Preliminary Communication*, in the *Studies* and in the study of 1915 on *Instincts and Their Vicissitudes* I have just quoted. In this later text, Freud dispenses with «abreaction» and maintains firmly «action». He thus simplifies this aspect of his terminology.

Normal psychical functioning as evoked in first texts of 1893-1895, never limits itself to an unequivocal reflex mechanism. External excitation, even *trauma*, does not have a direct effect on the motor branch of the reflex. In between the two, presentations (*Vorstellungen*) are formed, having a «quota of affect» (*Affektbetrag*) which has to be «got rid of». Normal abreaction takes place instantly along verbal or motor routes; another possibility put forward is the association of the pathological presentations to other presentations which will attenuate the traumatic effect, diffuse it and add the changes which will render the event acceptable. As soon as presentations arise they may be rendered inoffensive either by *expression* (this is abreaction proper), or by *thought*. In both cases we are dealing with the behaviour of the subject, even if initially «excitation», «presentation» and «affect» together look as if they could be taken to be physiological phenomena linked one to the other. Even in the most materialistic vision of human behaviour, the intervention of an *intention* has nothing in common with a chain reaction. The «*ab-*» of abreaction is no longer simply indicating an impersonal phenomenon, it indicates intentional exteriorisation. It has, according to Breuer and Freud an equivalent in the «*aus-*» of «*aus-drücken*».

In the case where the abreaction was not immediate, Breuer and Freud envisaged several ways in which the presentations and their associated affect could be retained, and later produce symptoms. If the event took place whilst under a hypnotic trance the presentation and the affect were supposed to go astray in a passive manner. There are in addition cases where according to the environment in which the individual finds himself, he cannot allow himself to abreact; there are also cases where the fright, offence or humiliation is actively repressed. In both cases, it leads to the formation of a foreign body like reminder situated in a «second consciousness», a so-called «subconscious»: –»groups of presentations» are separated from consciousness as the result of a «volontary act». Such were the terms used by Freud in various publications from 1892-1895 and notably in the article *The Neuro-Psychoses of Defense* [*Die Abwehr-Neuropsychosen*]. «I was repeatedly able to show that the splitting of the content of consciousness is the result of an act of will on the part of the patient; that is to say, it is initiated by an effort of will whose motive can be specified. By this I do not, of course, mean that the patient intends to bring about a splitting of his consciousness» (Freud, 1894a, S.E. 3: 46). This results in the presentation and its quota of affect being repressed and becoming manifest in symptom formation. The notions of retention, conversion and going astray into somatization are sufficiently well known that I shall not develop them here. It should suffice to emphasize the conditions which Breuer and especially Freud considered necessary for healing: the patient has to, with the doctor's help, translate back *(rückübersetzen)* into *words* (*parole*) the emotion which had been fixed in the *language* of a symptom.[5] The psychotherapeutic process of the cathartic method is to arrest «the operative force of the idea which was not abreacted in the first instance, by allowing its strangulated affect to find a way out through speech» (Breuer & Freud, 1893a [1892], S.E. 2: 17). Even if the original model drew on the pattern of a reflex arc, with its afferent and efferent branches, its excitation and response, one sees something else taking place besides the simple flow of quantities of excitation from one neurone to the other. Although Freud did his best to create a model of cerebral neurophysiology in *A Project for a Scientific Psychology* (1895, *in* 1950a), it is clear that the path he suggested from trauma to abreaction can be broken up into a number of events and behaviours that are not understood in a scientific sense: they are narrated. All the while drawing on basic neurological principles, the theory of formation and elimination of hysterical symptoms is a *story*. Instead of the schematic two movements accomplished in a reflex arc, the suppositions of Breuer and Freud stretched to cover a series of events where the unexpected may intervene at any time. The evidence is based on the patients' narrations. Within these narratives the discovery of the determination or over-determination of morbid states are *confessions* or stories told by the patients. How different they are from organic neurological illness which only allows methodological localization and isolated observation! Were organic disease to be spread out in time, it would become a set of processes, not history. One sees these organic ailments regress spontaneously or more commonly progress relentlessly. Their treatment is limited monotonously and repetitively, as Freud observed, electrotherapy, balneotherapy, rest, diet, etc. Therapeutic resources consisted of using successively all of the physical methods available. In the *Autobiographical Study* (Freud, 1925d, S.E. 20) Freud says that this is what disappointed him when he tried to apply the treatments from Erb's electrotherapy manuel, which had no greater contact with reality than a book of Egyptian dreams «such as is sold in cheap bookshops» (*ibid.*, p. 16). The cathartic method, which allowed the patient to speak through hypnosis (later it was the doctor's hand placed on the forehead, then free association), had the advantage of being able to establish, by narration, a link between the symptom and the traumatizing event retained as the principal cause, at the same time determinant and, on principle, eliminable.[6]

It was not the first time that the notion of reaction had been put forward in the XIXth century in the area of moral treatment. As soon as the distinction between the physical and moral aspects of man had become current, there was much questioning about the moral reaction to the physical, and the physical to the moral. All «energetic» measures – and some were extremely brutal – were justified in producing a «salutary reaction». Countless documents could be cited here.[7] Glancing through them, one notes in the therapeutic methods certain features in common. Most procedures consisted of making an impression upon the patient, sometimes giving him a surprise, a pleasure or a fright which was very intense. Of course, sometimes it served to bring to light an old memory. The doctor was the director of the reaction thus produced in his patient. For, according to the model inspired by the collision of bodies in physics, the psychological reaction was perceived as an isolated event which changed the course of the illness, which suddenly gave the upper hand to psychical or vital forces which opposed the sickness: a stage effect, an apparent magic stroke which results from a masterful manipulation of natural forces. False ideas, illusions, somatic complaints are suddenly dissipated: the patient speaks only to declare himself cured, back to his old self, etc. The words exchanged by doctor and patient are few. Usually one theatrical gesture sufficed: the reversal was sudden. Occasionally there was a question of relapse: which would require an intervention for each case. Therein certainly there are stories to tell. For the most part, however, the accounts took the form of short anecdotes which ran from manuels to dictionaries, from dictionaries to books of vulgarization. The theoreticians of artificial somnambulism, clairvoyance, hypnosis and suggestion often took advantage of the «reaction» in the explanations they gave. The accounts became more ample and more numerous, sometimes containing fragments of conversation with the «subjects»: these became more and more interesting provided that they were seen to be moving between different disassociated and dissimilar levels of consciousness. Thus began the era of illustrious patients, heroines through a psychiatrist or experimenter third party. «Anna O.» was one of them.

In this original case, Breuer had to increase the number of sessions of abreaction and prolong the «talking cure» in line with the increase in new symptoms. «Anna O.» did not cease to report other events (some a year away). It was not an isolated trauma but a series of traumas for which the consequences had to be stemmed. Breuer had to confront the combined series of symptoms which were presented before his eyes and their antecedents narrated by the patient. Along with the evolution of a «case», a past was constructed which had to be taken into consideration by the retelling: it is what in rhetorical terminology is called «analepsis». The initial causes of symptoms discovered one year later, formed a collection equivalent to the «*Arabian Nights*» of psychology. The major *discovery* in fact, and which Freud was going to take further than Breuer, was the efficacy of a method where the narrative voice of the patient became an effective therapeutic agent. At the same time it was necessary for the therapist to become a narrator for his part, as the person to whom the patient spoke, and in addition to inform the academic community of the new procedure. There was a lot of talking. In his fine book on Breuer, Albrecht Hirschmüller (1978) published the report written by Breuer in 1882, at the time of admission of Anna O. to the Clinique Bellevue in Kreuzlingen: the text consisted of fourteen long pages in the French edition. The account was altered and theoretical commentary added for (Freud & Breuer, 1895d) *Studies* in 1895. Quite a writing exercise for a practitioner who treated the Viennese upper classes! Why did Breuer abandon his shared research on hysteria and the neuroses? Was it only the difficulties he encountered while coping with the transference from his first patient that prevented him from continuing to treat similar patients and from following Freud in the theories of constance of energy and sexual aetiology? One could advance a much simpler hypothesis: to take on the new cathartic treatments, he would have had to spend most of his time listening to the hysterical and nervous, which would have meant giving up the rest of his medical practice. As for Freud, he did not have these problems: he had chosen when establishing his practice to become a specialist for nervous disorders. «Anyone who wants to make a living from the treatment of nervous patients must clearly be able to do something to help them. My therapeutic arsenal contained only two weapons, electrotherapy and hypnotism, for prescribing a visit to a hydropathic establishment after a single consultation was an inadequate source of income.» (Freud, 1925d, S.E. 20: 16). It cost him nothing to exclude from his practice hopeless cases of organic neurological illness. He was able to give up, without too much difficulty, a «medical» practice (with a mediocre «therapeutic arsenal») for a «psychological» practice in which he believed and which allowed regular consultations. He had great gifts as a writer to use, and he had in front of him individuals who gave the best results with the most complete narrative reconstruction of their past. He was prepared to listen to Emmy v. N. for a long time (the first patient on whom he applied Breuerian therapy in 1889), followed by all the other hysterics and neurotics. He had the talent of making people talk, of interpreting and describing. Even describing doubly: on the one hand the history of the patients and their symptoms, and on the other the instincts and their «vicissitudes». The personal biographies inseparable from a mythography («our mythology» in his own words) in which the figures are instances or psychical energies defined by their manifold scopes. Moreover, he twice had the occasion to employ again the notion of *reaction*: but when he reuses it, he gives the word another sense than the one he had attached to the primitive abreaction: it is the blocking or trapping rather than the «flowing» of excitation which Freud conceptualises in «reaction formation» (*Reaktionsbildung*). The same of course goes for «negative therapeutic reaction» (*negative therapeutische Reaktion*). The prefix of having been discarded the word «reaction» remained at the disposal of many diverse meanings.

Notes

[1] It is thus noted in the latin Lexicon medicale of Bartolomeo Castelli (Genève, de Tournes, 1746). «Catharsis» gives «purgatio»; «catharticus» gives «purgans». The article «purgatio» is particularly interesting: it distinguishes purgation occurring naturally from one produced by artificial means, drugs or enemas. In German, remedies which produced intestinal evacuation were *Abführmittel*.
In the passage which Freud has just cited it is less a «quantum of affect», more an «amount» of affect (*Affektbetrag*) (G.W. 14: 47). *Betrag* means a sum of money. *Quantum* is typical of technical translations with the intention of giving more scientific weight to Freud. A typical example is *Besetzung* which becomes *cathexis* in English. Freud himself uses *valeur affective* in French for *Affektbetrag* (G.W. 1: 54).

[2] The word *durcharbeiten* is not a Freudian neologism. It existed in German since the XVIIIth century. It appears to have been formed under the influence of Pietism, and Goethe uses it in a very specific manner in *Wahlverwandtschaften*, 1).

Gauchet shows that the extrapolation of physiological theories of medullary nervous functioning quickly led to the notion of «unconscious cerebration» (p. 30-32).

4   It should be noted that Cabanis, in his *Rapports du physique et du moral de l'homme* (1802), describes the origins of instincts in the organic sensations unconsciously experienced by embryos and foetuses.

5   I use the distinction made by Ferdinand de Saussure intentionally here, even if it is not absolutely appropriate.

6   We know that in the terminology which he borrows from Eugen Bleuler and Carl Gustav Jung, from whom he takes the notion of complex, Freud was interested in ideas (*Einfälle*) which are the reactions to excitory words, and that he paid attention to the duration of this reaction which delayed resistance etc. See S.E. 9:104-110 and S.E. 15:109-112.

7   We referred to several in «Le mot réaction: de la physique à la psychiatrie» (Starobinski, 1976, p. 3-30; the same article appeared in translation in the English edition of *Diogenes*).

References

CABANIS, P.J.G. (1802). *Rapports du physique et du moral de l'homme*. Paris.

CASTELLI, B. (1746). *Lexicon medicale*. Genève: De Tournes.

DUBOIS, J. *et al.* (1973). *Dictionnaire de linguistique*. Paris: Larousse.

FREUD, S. (1892-93). A Case of Successful Treatment by Hypnotism. *Standard Edition, 1*, 115-128.

— (1893a). On the Psychical Mechanism of Hysterical Phenomena: Preliminary Communication. *Standard Edition, 2*, 1-17.

— (1893c). Some Points for a Comparative Study of Organic and Hysterical Motor Paralyses. *Standard Edition, 1*, 155-172.

— (1894a). The Neuro-Psychoses of Defence. *Standard Edition, 3*, 41-61.

— (1895d). Studies on Hysteria. *Standard Edition, 2*.

— (1906c). Psycho-Analysis and the Establishment of the Facts in Legal Proceedings. *Standard Edition, 9*, 97-114.

— (1914g). Recollecting, Repeating and Working Through. *Standard Edition, 12*, 145-156.

— (1915c). Instincts and their Vicissitudes. *Standard Edition, 14*, 109-140.

— (1915d). Repression. *Standard Edition, 14*, 141-158.

— (1916-17). Introductory Lectures on Psycho-Analysis. *Standard Edition, 15-16*.

— (1925d). An Autobiographical Study. *Standard Edition, 20*, 1-70.

— (1950a [1887-1902]). *The Origins of Psycho-Analysis, Letters to Wilhelm Fliess, Drafts and Notes 1887-1902*. London: Imago & New York: Basic Books, 1954.

GAUCHET, M. (1992). *L'inconscient cérébral*. Paris: Seuil.

HIRSCHMÜLLER, A. (1978). *The Life and Work of Josef Breuer. Physiology and Psychoanalysis*. New York/London: New York University Press, 1989.

LAPLANCHE, J. & PONTALIS, J.B. (1967): *The Language of Psychoanalysis*. New York: Norton, 1973.

STAROBINSKI, J. (1976). Le mot réaction: de la physique à la psychiatrie. *Diogène*, n° 93, pp. 3-30.

Cahiers Psychiatriques Genevois, Special Issue, 1994, pp. 41-54

THE BALANCE OF POWER BETWEEN FREUD AND HIS EARLY WOMEN PATIENTS

John Forrester

Shortly after opening his medical practice, Freud described his «occupation» as «visiting and talking people into or out of things» (Freud, *in:* Masson, 1984, 4th February 1888, pp. 18-19). A couple of years later, in 1890, Freud located the power of the hypnotist and the psychoanalyst in the power of words, the fact of language:

> Words are the essential tool of mental treatment. A layman will no doubt find it hard to understand how pathological disorders of the body and mind can be eliminated by «mere» words. He will feel that he is being asked to believe in magic. And he will not be so very wrong, for the words which we use in our everyday speech are nothing other than watered-down magic. But we shall have to follow a roundabout path in order to explain how science sets about restoring to words a part at least of their former magical powers (Freud, 1890a, p. 283).

Talking people into and out of things; restoring to words their magical powers. This is the dimension of power that Freud initially conceived of as operating between doctor and patient.

Talking people into and out of things sounds remarkably like tricking them into doing something that they wouldn't have wanted to do otherwise. This is the voice of the young professional, cynical before his time, realizing that the exercise of his profession requires him to manipulate his clients. But Freud did not always see his metier in this cynical light. By invoking language, he brings into play a third element, something shared by both professional and client; it is this third element that gives the doctor the power to talk people into and out of things. Here is another passage from Freud's hypnotic period, in which he describes how suggestive hypnotism achieves its successes:

> Hypnotism endows the physician with an authority such as was probably never possessed by the priest or the miracle man, since it concentrates the subject's whole

interest upon the figure of the physician; it does away with the *autocratic power* of the patient's mind which, as we have seen, interferes so capriciously with the influence of the mind over the body; it automatically produces an increase of the mind's control over the body, such as is normally to be observed only as an effect of the most powerful emotions... Thus hypnotic treatment really implies a great extension of *medical power* (Freud, 1890a, p. 298; emphasis added).

What impresses the young Freud so much in hypnotism is not so much the cures one can achieve as the power it grants. Hypnotism's power stems from supplanting or dissolving the «autocratic power» of the patient's mind and transferring it to the physician.

When, in 1916, Freud reassessed the relationship between hypnotism and psychoanalysis, he used the same term, «capricious», but now, instead the word is applied to hypnotism itself, rather than the patient's mind. (Freud, 1916-1917, p. 449) This displacement is itself not entirely arbitrary or capricious; it betrays a conception of power as inherently erratic and irregular in its effects. In the early 1890s, Freud's behaviour when employing hypnotic suggestion combined with Breuer's cathartic cure showed signs of his eagerness to display the extended powers hypnotism granted him; inevitably, it seems, he chose to do so in a rather capricious and wilful manner. With Frau «Emmy von N.» (Fanny...), for instance, he blithely wiped away some of her most important memories, as if he were a behaviour therapist rather than the proto-psychoanalyst. He also could not resist playing all sorts of tricks on her to convince himself and her of the efficacy of hypnosis; the final pages of the case-history recount three such tricks, which show Freud to have been very keen to demonstrate the stupidity, the cruder hypnotic skills and the less amicable effectiveness of the other doctors who had tended to Fanny, and revealing himself to be just as crude and wilful in so doing (Freud, 1905c, pp. 98 ff.). He was using his patient to make fun of other doctors; but it was certainly at Fanny's expense, as Breuer quickly pointed out to Freud (Breuer & Freud, 1895, pp. 79-80). So central, if somewhat implicit, to Freud's later criticisms of hypnosis was the fact that the blindness of the hypnotist matched the unpredictability of its effects. There was no way of specifying the technique, of controlling the procedure. His own and other doctors' capricious use of the technique provided another reason for codifying the rules for the management of transference, the framework and so forth.

In Freud's view in 1890, what allows the doctor to exercise his function is, in one account, the power of words, and in another, a power that is equivalent to the autocratic power of the patient's mind. In order to explain the powers of hypnotism, Freud felt obliged to give an account of how the curative powers of the doctor come from elsewhere: from the patient, from language. The canonical examples come from faith-healing and fashionable cures:

> There are always fashionable treatments and fashionable physicians... These produce therapeutic results which are outside the scope of their actual power, and the same procedures effect far more in the hands of a fashionable doctor (who, for instance, may have become well-known as an attendant upon some prominent personality) than in those of another physician. Thus there are human as well as divine miracle-workers (Freud, 1890a, p. 291).

They certainly do not come from an inherent authority granted to the doctor by his knowledge:

> Outside hypnosis and in real life, credulity such as the subject has in relation to his hypnotist is shown only by a child towards his beloved parents... an attitude of similar subjection on the part of one person towards another has only one parallel, though a complete one – namely in certain love relationships where there is extreme devotion. A combination of exclusive attachment and credulous obedience is in general among the characteristics of love (Freud, 1890a, p. 296).

In 1890, then, Freud felt obliged to put forward a theory of the source of the power conferred on the physician who employs hypnotism which made the psychic dependence and pliability of patients entirely analogous to the child and the lover. All authority relations repose upon powerful affective forces – parental obedience, amorous attachment – which are also those mobilized by the hypnotist.

This is a characteristic explanatory gesture of Freud's, one which I will discuss further; before I do so, I would like to establish the starting point for my argument, which these materials have illustrated for us. Freud's use of hypnotism required him to analyse the foundations of the power and authority employed in medical practice; in effect, he presented a specific theory of hypnotism couched within the general terms of a theory of authority and power, of «powerful forces (*starken Kräfte*)» (Freud, 1890a, p. 301). In the development of Freudian theory, Power came before Sex.

But the characteristic explanatory gesture Freud employed is one to be found again as soon as sex reared its ugly head, as the puritanical English say. Freud disclaimed responsibility for the powers that hypnotism granted him, just as he was later to disclaim responsibility for eliciting transference-love. Disclaiming responsibility then required him to offer a *theory* in place of the assumption of responsibility. It is as if he said: «Neither my personal medical charisma nor the physiological helplessness of the patient are the true source of the powers that hypnotism gives to doctors; their true source is to be found not in the doctor, but in the patient – in the universal prototypes of parental authority and self-abasing love of the other.» Similarly, a few years later, when female patients expressed their sexual desires for him in the course of his therapeutic investigations, he effectively said: «Neither my personal charisma as a man nor the chronic bestiality of these women's sexual constitutions are the true source of these flagrant desires; their true source is to be found in the universal prototype of parental love.» And it should be noted that this structure of displacement of the erotic prototype into the past predates the theory of fantasy and predates the discovery of Œdipal impulses, since its structure is to be found in the final pages of *Studies on Hysteria*, written in the spring of 1895.

The hypnotic power that Freud most explicitly analysed was the benign power to heal, to cure, to remove symptoms. There was also, of course, a darker side to this power, much debated in polemics and court cases of the end of the nineteenth century: the power of the hypnotist to manipulate, to provoke immorality in the subject, to implant through suggestion in the innocent mind of the patient all manner of alien ideas and impulses (See Carroy, 1990 and Harris, 1989). Freud was not very discomforted by this figure of the evil hypnotist:

> Everything that has been said and written about the great *dangers* of hypnosis belongs to the realm of fable. If we leave on one side the misuses of hypnosis for illegitimate purposes – a possibility that exists for every other effective therapeutic method – the most we have to consider is the tendency of severely neurotic people, after repeated hypnosis, to fall into hypnosis spontaneously... People whose susceptibility goes so far that they can be hypnotised against their will, can also be protected fairly completely by a suggestion that only their physician will be able to hypnotise them (Freud, 1891, pp. 113-114).

The defence of hypnotism has two prongs: firstly, the responsibility which is incurred by its use as a therapeutic tool is shown, or implied, to be exactly the same as every other medical technique (Cf. Carvais, 1986). The onus for preventing abuse is always on the doctor. And, by implication, the fears for its abuse stem from a mistrust of other doctors' codes of medical ethics.

> It is quite interesting to find the most positive determinists suddenly defending the imperilled «personal free-will», and to hear psychiatrists who are in the habit of suffocating the «freely aspiring mental activity» of their patients with large doses of bromide, morphine and chloral, arraigning suggestive influence as something degrading to both parties (Freud, 1889, p. 94).

Freud evokes the criticisms of other doctors – the «degradation» of abusing both the doctor's and the patient's freedom, the degradation of employing a shepherd's technique and of recognising the sheep-like submissiveness of patients with respect to their doctors – only to dismiss these as fables, or as the commonplace responsibilities of medical practice. All medical practice involves the exercice of power; any medical practitioner who holds up his hands in horror at the powers made available by hypnotism is living in bad faith.

However, Freud's papers on hypnotism are not simply an analysis of the new powers granted to doctors and the possibilities of their abuse; far from it. They are just as much an account of the limitations of these powers, an account of the fact that the balance of powers never shifts entirely or predictably in favour of the doctor. And what sets the limits on those powers is the patient: «it still depends far more on the patient than on the physician with what degree of tractability a suggestion will be received – it depends once more, that is, upon the patient's choice.» (Freud, 1890a, p. 300; cf. p. 293). The patient was entirely free to remain ill, to refuse help, to undercut the authority of the doctor. And Freud eventually found it ignominious to be forced, as he inevitably was, into the hearty reassurances and trivial deceptions which any slight setback in the process required of him.

> The physician must constantly be on the look-out for a new starting-point for his suggestion, a new proof of his power, a new change in his hypnotising procedure. For him too, who has, perhaps, internal doubts about success, this presents a great and in the end exhausting strain (Freud, 1891d, p. 113).

Indeed, Freud occasionally hinted that hypnotism could never be entirely satisfactory, precisely because the authority of the physician was fraudulent, and the entire success of the operation rested on deception:

> Whereas no patient ventures to be impatient if he has still not been cured after the twentieth electrical session or an equal number of bottles of mineral water, with hypnotic treatment both physician and patient grow tired far sooner, as a result of the contrast between the deliberately rosy colouring of the suggestions and the cheerless truth. Here too, intelligent patients can make it easier for the physician as soon as they have understood that in making suggestions he is, as it were, playing a part and that the more energetically he disputes their ailment the more advantage is to be expected for them (Freud, 1891d, p. 113; cf. Forrester, 1990b, and Appignanesi & Forrester, 1992, pp. 146-167).

So, even when relying on suggestive (rather than rememorative) hypnotism in his practice, Freud's attitude was double: weary distrust of the deception it necessitated, a deception that both doctor and patient freely colluded in; and, in addition, belief that the playing of the parts assigned to them, so long as they were recognised as parts and thereby not subject to the exacting and fatiguing standards of truth, could bring success.

There is indeed the smell of failure about Freud's account of hypnotism. But it is not the failure of self-deception, nor of a world seen in the «deliberately rosy colouring of the suggestions» he found himself offering his patients. It is that more distinctively Freudian failure, arising out of the refusal to be party to deception. The truth which hypnotism brought out into the open was the fallibility of the doctor, as in the story of the Emperor's new clothes. No longer dressed up with electrical leads or the apparatus of cold baths and invigorating regimes, the doctor appeared naked in his sacred, priestly authority (Cf. Forrester, 1990a). If the patient freely places her trust in his powers, the failure of these powers is the occasion for an ever-deeper soulsearching – there is no excuse to be found, no rationalisation of the variable effects of bromides, or hydrotherapy. It is the doctor who has failed.

Other doctors were well aware of the power patients had to defeat the best – and worst – efforts of the profession. Through accepting the patient as a patient, they legitimated her symptoms, and became complicit with her resistance to her female social roles. This awareness, or suspicion, of their own complicity then accentuated their attentiveness to the moral failings and famous tricks of the hysteric: unusually intractable and self-assertive, often malingering, deceiving, capricious and irresponsible. It was the doctors who perceived the treatment as a war of wills, often degenerating into a war of attrition:

> You must expect to have your temper, your ingenuity, your nerves tested to a degree that cannot be surpassed even by the greatest surgical operations. I maintain that the man who has the nerve and the tact to conquer some of these grave cases of hysteria has the nerve and the tact that will make him equal to the great emergencies of life... (Channing, 1860, p. 22; cf. Smith-Rosenberg, 1972, pp. 208-212).

It is on this point that Freud demonstrated a new approach to the question of the recalcitrant patient; he showed how the doctor can turn failure into success.

Freud was adept at being a failure. Not only was his early career a string of failures, albeit distinguished ones – the gold-staining method, the cocaine episode, even the attempt on his return from Paris, in 1886, to make his name in Vienna by introducing the «novel» category of male hysteria, when most of his audience were already quite familiar with it (Micale, 1989, 1990a, 1990b, and Sulloway, 1979). But also, later in the development of psychoanalysis, he wrote a book about failures: slips of the tongue, misreading, mishearing, mislaying, forgetting, losing – «small failures of functioning» (Freud, 1916-1917, p. 28), «whose internal affinity with one another is expressed in the fact that they begin with the syllable «ver» (mis)» (Freud, 1916-1917, p. 26). Indeed, it is plausible to argue that the entire theory of the unconscious is couched in terms of its being a break, an interruption, a lack in some other process – something missing, a mistake (Cf. Lacan,1955-1956/1981, p. 171). Negation is, after all, the «hallmark of repression, a certificate of origin – like, let us say», «Fabriqué en France» (Freud, 1925h, p. 236).

Freud's abandoning of hypnosis was not simply giving up a method that proved unsuccessful. He decided to fight the war with his patients by other means. Instead of the ambiguously disapproving language of malingering and deception, of hysterical lying and irresponsibility, of the hysteric's childishness and ill-disciplined exaggeratedly female nature that other doctors used, Freud accentuated the vocabulary of force and power he had used to describe hypnotism, but now turned it into a language of honest hard work and skillful technique. Instead of authority and insubordination, Freud employed the quasi-physicalist language of energy, force and work. Note that the term «power» belongs in both political and physicalist semantic registers. The chapter on the psychotherapy of hysteria in *Studies on Hysteria* is couched pre-eminently in the register of technical proficiency and indefatigable energy, but the undertones of strategy, tactics, manoeuvre and negotiation are also endemic throughout.

The key term is of course «resistance»: a quasi-quantifiable measure of the work done by the analyst. Aligned with resistance are a series of other terms linking the force, the pressure, the insistence (*Drängen*) of the analyst with the intrapsychic energetics of the patient:

> It would in fact be possible for the pathogenic groups of ideas... to be brought to light by straightforward insistence (*blosses Drängen*); and since this insistence involved effort (*Anstrengung*) and so suggested the idea that I had to overcome a resistance, the situation led me at once to the theory that *by means of my psychical work I had to overcome a psychical force in the patients which was opposed to the pathogenic ideas becoming conscious (being remembered).* A new understanding seemed to open before my eyes when it occurred to me that this must no doubt be the same psychical force that had played a part in the generating of the hysterical symptom.... From all this there arose, as it were automatically *(wie von selbst)*, the thought of *defence...* a psychical force, aversion on the part of the ego, had originally driven *(gedrängt)* the pathogenic idea out of association and was now opposing its return in memory... The task of the therapist, therefore, lies in overcoming by his psychical work this resistance to association. He does this in the first place by «insisting» (*Drängen*), by making use of psychical compulsion (*Zwanges*)... (Breuer and Freud, 1895, pp. 269-270; Breuer and Freud, 1970, p. 216).

Freud's more detailed description of the therapist's task has a breathless, excited character, which reflects the mixture of metaphorical registers he is working with:

> We force our way *(Man drängt sich... ein)* into the internal strata, overcoming resistances all the time... we experiment how far we can advance with our present means and the knowledge we have acquired.... By this method we at last reach a point at which we can stop working in strata and can penetrate by a main path straight to the nucleus of the pathogenic organisation *(zum Kerne...vordringen)*. With this the struggle is won, though not yet ended... But now the patient helps us energetically. His resistance is for the most part broken (Breuer & Freud, 1895, pp. 294-529; Breuer & Freud, 1970, p. 238).

The procedure evoked here is in part forensic investigation; in part the conquistador making his way into virgin territory; in part the general conducting a military campaign; in part the ransacking and reordering of a library of documents Freud speaks of *Erinnerungsfaszikel*; in part the draw-ing-up of the balance-sheet of credits and debits; in part the quantitative assessment of the energy and work as measured by the history of the therapeutic relationship.

As I have indicated by citing the original German terms, Freud's account of the process by which the analyst discovers resistance and the mechanisms of repression and defence by which the subject protects itself are very closely linked, via the emphasis on the work that the analyst puts in. The analyst «insists», *er drängt*; because he has to work, he postulates an equivalent force on the patient's side, the resistance; and this resistance is itself an exact measure of the force that represses, *verdrängt*, the original pathogenic memory. In other words, Freud's entire theory of repression, resistance and defence, the conceptual starting-point of psychoanalysis, is based upon a phenomenological energetics of the therapeutic relationship between analyst and patient. The analyst *drängt*, the patient *verdrängt*. The verbal kinship reflects and helps sustain the underlying view of an equiva-lence of forces – a balance of powers – between patient and analyst.

When Freud reviewed this period of his development of psychoanaly-sis in *On the History of the Psycho-Analytic Movement*, he highlighted the break with hypnosis as the starting-point of psychoanalysis, since «the use of hypnosis was bound to hide this resistance» (Freud, 1914d, p. 16) from the analyst. My argument is intended, if not to correct, then to supple-ment this view. Hypnosis may have hidden this resistance, but without a prior conception of the forces at work for and against the doctor in hyp-nosis, Freud would not have been led to pay close attention to the balance of forces at play in the relationship between doctor and patient. The theory of the relationship between analyst and patient, including the essential elements of the theory of transference and resistance, emerged from the framework established by the reflections on hypnotic power, and preceded any of the more familiar theoretical elements of psychoanalysis. In 1914, Freud wrote: «Any line of investigation which recognizes these two facts (of transference and of resistance) and recognizes them as the starting-point of its work has a right to call itself psycho-analysis.» (Freud, 1914d, p. 16). Both of these concepts receive their first extensive discus-sion in the final pages of *Studies on Hysteria*, and there, in accordance with the division of labour between Breuer and Freud, they are not pri-marily theoretical terms, but rather ways in which the therapeutic rela-tionship with the patient is characterized. We should not forget that, both in the *Preliminary Communication* and the *Studies*, there is an unusual inversion of the relationship between a mentor and his apprentice: it is the younger man, Freud, who is the tried and tested practitioner, and the elder statesman, Breuer, who tries his hand at speculative theory.

Elsewhere, in my book *The Seductions of Psychoanalysis*, I described the gesture of transference as the postman's gesture: Pass it on! (Cf. Forrester, 1990c). Transference is the moment when the analyst intervenes to structure the relationship between analyst and patient around a third party, who is absent, and who is the covert recipient of the message the patient is overtly transmitting to the analyst. Resistance is then the interruption of the transmission of this message: «whatever interrupts *(stört)* the continuation of the analysis is a resistance», as Freud defined it in *The Interpretation of Dreams* (Freud, 1900a, p. 517n1). If the concept of transference casts Freud as a cross between a seducer, a matchmaker and a postman, then resistance casts him as an electrician, an accountant and a general. As we have seen, when the analyst is confronted by resistance, he insists. In this sense, the concept of resistance is a natural *continuation* of the active intervention of the hypnotist. In contrast, transference functions as a way of *exempting* the analyst from implication in the relationship with the patient: the transferential analyst is always absent. He excuses himself from responsibility. Whereas the analyst confronted by resistance takes upon himself the responsibility of continuing the analysis (where the patient has broken off) by active intervention – the pushiness, which is how I would often translate *Drang*, of interpretation.

There is another consequence that follows from considering resistance and transference as phenomenological concepts which were developed directly out of the problems of managing his relations with his patients. The dynamic and economic psychoanalytic perspectives, associated respectively with conflicts of forces and quantitative considerations of energy, have a direct relation to therapeutic practice. If one looks in reliable and intelligent guides to psychoanalytic concepts, such as Laplanche and Pontalis' magnificent *The Language of Psycho-Analysis* (1967), one finds very little reference to the practicalities of therapy in their entries about «Dynamics» and «Economics». James Strachey discusses with subtlety how *Studies on Hysteria* is «not simply the story of the overcoming of a succession of obstacles; it is the story of the *discovery* of a succession of obstacles that have to be overcome.» This elegantly expressed thought of Strachey's can be expanded as follows: psychoanalysis began with the discovery of obstacles, and its theoretical terms – such as repression and defence, the unconscious and *der Trieb* – are phenomenological correlates of the *work* the analyst does with obstacles. Yet Strachey does not theorize sufficiently the relation of these concepts to his account of the discovery of the obstacles. My argument asserts that it is necessary to do this in order to understand how the work with patients becomes the economic and dynamic points of view of the metapsychology.

I now want to turn to the more specifically sexual aspects of the relationship between Freud and his patients. I alluded to the moral contempt and distrust that many doctors expressed for their hysterics, even as they colluded with them and entered into complex therapeutic relationships in which the doctor's forcefulness, authority and character were always being tested. With Freud, and to some extent with Breuer, we find a different attitude to the patients, which is a necessary condition for establishing the right kind of balance of forces, or of social duties, for what later became the psychoanalytic relationship. The best word to characterise this relationship is «idealisation» (See Appignanesi & Forrester, 1992, pp. 63-145). I will give one lengthy quote, to remind you of the dominant tone of Freud's and Breuer's descriptions of their patients:

> Frau Emmy von N. gave us an example of how hysteria is compatible with an unblemished character and a well-governed mode of life. The woman we came to know was an admirable one. The moral seriousness with which she viewed her duties, her intelligence and energy, which were no less than a man's, and her high degree of education and love of truth impressed both of us greatly while her benevolent care for the welfare of all her dependents, her humility of mind and the refinement of her manners revealed her qualities as a true lady as well (Breuer & Freud, 1895, pp. 103-104).

Fräulein Elisabeth von R. is described in the following way:

> Her giftedness, her ambition, her moral sensibility, her excessive demand for love which, to begin with, found satisfaction in her family, and the independence of her nature which went beyond the feminine ideal and found expression in a considerable amount of obstinacy, pugnacity and reserve (Breuer and Freud, 1895, p. 161).

These paeons of praise for the hysteric are continued with later patients. Let me turn to a later example, a very important case discussed at length in a recent brilliant paper by Ernst Falzeder (Falzeder, 1994). In a letter to Pfister of 1911, Freud described a longstanding woman patient as «more than sympathetic, rather of high principles and refined». Falzeder argues that perhaps this patient is a model for Freud's confession of his experience of the «incomparable magic that emanates from a woman of high principles who confesses her passion.» (Freud, 1915a, p. 170). Whilst sharing Falzeder's intention to give historical and personal specificity to the way in which Freud builds up his account of psychoanalysis and his treatment of his patients, I am struck by the fact that so many of his women patients, from the early 1890s to the 1920s, are described in this way: as women of high principles, who have suffered from the accidents of life, and yet have struggled, in part unsuccessfully, to make what they can of their fate, their *Schicksal*.

Freud thus makes of his patient a worthy opponent. If she were not a worthy opponent, he would not be able to mobilize the therapeutic optimism or enthusiasm, he would not be able to take an interest in the patient. Having evoked the worth of the patient, the way is now open for his deployment of that familiar and extensive register of military and strategic metaphors (just to use Strachey's list, there are: *agents provocateurs*, the rate of progress of an army in the face of an enemy, the tactical struggle on a battlefield, the metaphors of behind the lines and at the front, of blocked main roads, of civil war, of frontier control, of *fueros*, the game of chess, a garrison in a conquered city, of the governors of a conquered country) (Strachey, 1974, pp. 179-183). Every analysis will necessarily be a struggle, and for this struggle to be possible, there must be sufficient forces engaged in the campaign for the armies involved to encounter resistance. A patient who surrendered immediately is firstly inconceivable – Freud's lesson as a failure at hypnosis taught him that; and the patient must also be sufficiently substantial to take the enemy seriously. For this, high moral principles are not only required; they are also visible from the outset in the contempt that such estimable patients have for their own shameful impulses and symptoms:

> His illness itself must no longer seem to him contemptible, but must become an enemy worthy of his mettle, a piece of his personality, which has solid ground for its existence and out of which things of value for his future life have to be derived... If this new attitude towards the illness intensifies the conflicts and brings to the fore symptoms which till then had been indistinct, one can easily console the patient by pointing out that these are only necessary and temporary aggravations and that one cannot overcome an enemy who is absent or not within range... The tactics to be adopted by the physician in this situation are easily justified... He is prepared for a perpetual struggle with his patient... (Freud, 1914g, pp. 152-153).

This passage, written in 1914, continues the tone of another passage, written in 1912:

> The doctor tries to compel *(nötigen)* (the patient) to fit these emotional impulses into the nexus of the treatment and of his life-history, to submit them to intellectual consideration and to understand them in the light of their psychical value. This struggle between the doctor and the patient, between intellectual and instinctual life, between understanding and seeking to act, is played out almost exclusively in the phenomena of transference. It is on that field that the victory must be won – the victory whose expression is the permanent cure of the neurosis (Freud, 1912b, p. 108).

There are two balances of forces involved here: one within the patient, theorized in terms of impulses, defences and compromise-formations. The other is its reflection, its phenomenologically prior version: the balance of forces between doctor and patient. Freud calls this second version of the balance of forces the transference-neurosis: «an intermediate region between illness and real life through which the transition from the one to the other is made» (Freud, 1914g, p. 154). We might rename this intermediate region of the transference a no-man's-land between the two warring factions. On analogy with the First World War, the moment of breakdown of the balance of power that had been constructed to keep a delicate peace in Europe from Napoleon onwards, the stalemate of the eternal no-man's-land of the transference reveals the roughly equal balance of powers that had previously been held in check by diplomacy. War – or analysis – reveals them, and the new resolution, the new balance of powers can only be found when a new intervention, a new force enters onto the battlefield. Following this metaphor, Freud the analyst is cast in the role of the United States, maybe even of Woodrow Wilson, destined to intervene in the deadlocked struggle of Europe, to force a new outcome by altering the old balance of power. What an irony this would be, if the extension of Freud's own metaphors revealed that he, one of the great Americanophobes of our time, had cast himself as the New World come to straighten out the mess of the Old!

Of course, not all patients behave like France or Germany; most behave like Switzerland. There are other paths open than the one that leads to total committment to the playground of war that is the transference. There is Dora's way: to withdraw definitively when skirmishes have only just begun. There is Baroness Marie von Ferstel's way, which we might call the Soviet way: after considerable involvement in conflict, one suffers a revolutionary transformation, extracts oneself from the struggle at any price and then badmouths the other participants in the name of other ideals. She helped Freud get his Professorship, gave him and his family ample gifts, but then «left Freud's treatment... in great anger and spread rumours most detrimental to his reputation.» (Eissler, 1979, p. 19). There is also the more traditional Russian way: passive defence, until the invading armies give up and retire to lick their wounds. Perhaps this was the story of Freud's case of female homosexuality:

> Bitterness against men is as a rule easy to gratify upon the physician; it need not evoke any violent emotional manifestations, it simply expresses itself by rendering futile all his endeavours and by clinging to the illness. I know from experience how difficult it is to make a patient understand just precisely this mute kind of symptomatic behaviour and to make him aware of this latent, and often exceedingly strong, hostility without endangering the treatment. As soon, therefore, as I recognized the girl's attitude to her father, I broke off the treatment and advised her parents that if they set store by the therapeutic procedure it should be continued by a woman doctor (Freud, 1920a, p. 164).

*

I have pursued this analogy between psychoanalytic treatment and war and diplomacy in order to make visible the fact that psychoanalysis already contains a theory of the power relations, of the balance of power, between patient and analyst: it is visible in the very terms with which

Freud describes his own activity and the inner structure of the neurosis (defence, repression, insistence) and it is incorporated into the economic and dynamic points of view. Not only that, a theory of power predates a theory of sexuality in the development of Freud's work; it is closely tied to the theory of the hypnotic rapport. With the abandoning of hypnosis, more particularly with the lessons Freud learned from his failure at hypnosis, he turned towards sexuality; but even before the sexual turn, he had never been tempted to establish a Nietzschean will to power as the fundamental principle in human relations. He would later attempt to recuperate hypnosis into psychoanalytic theory, and to explain why hypnosis and psychoanalysis are mutually exclusive: «It is obvious that anyone who makes use of hypnotism will not discover sexuality. It is used up, so to speak, in the hypnotic process.» (Freud and Jung, 1974, 118F, 11 December 1908, p. 187) And he would criticize Adler's theory of the will to power (the masculine protest) as treating the observed facts «like a spring-board that is left behind after it has been used to jump off from.» (Freud, 1914d, p. 54) My paper has a cautionary intention: we should not treat the facts of the power relations between Freud and his patients – the facts of the insistent work the analyst does, the facts of the struggle between analyst and patient in the playground of the transference – as a spring-board that is left behind after it has been used to jump off from. Psychoanalysis is not only an interminable seduction into pleasure; it is also a battle of wills and an interplay of forces and powers. Nor should we forget that power is not something left out or repressed by psychoanalysis; it is there, fully internalized and operative, in the theory of defence and resistance.

References

APPIGNANESI, L. & FORRESTER, J. (1992). *Freud's Women*. London: Weidenfeld & Nicolson/New York: Basic Books.

BREUER, J. & FREUD, S. (1895). Studies on Hysteria. *Standard Edition, 2*.

— & — (1970). *Studien über Hysterie*. Frankfurt/Main: Fischer Taschenbuch.

CARROY, J. (1990). Dédoublements. L'énigmatique récit d'un docteur inconnu. *Nouvelle Revue de Psychanalyse, 42* (Automne), 151-171.

CARVAIS, R. (1986). Le microbe et la responsabilité médicale, *In*: Salomon-Bayet C. (ed.), *Pasteur et la révolution pastorienne*. Paris: Payot, pp. 217-275.

CHANNING, W. (1860). *Bed Case: Its History and Treatment*. Boston: Ticknor & Fields.

EISSLER, K.R. (1979). A possible endangerment of psychoanalysis in the United States. *International Review of Psycho-Analysis, 6*, 15-21.

FALZEDER, E. (1993). «My grand-patient, my chief tormentor». A hitherto unnoticed case of Freud's and the consequences (forthcoming, *Psychoanalytic Quarterly*).

FORRESTER, J. (1990a). Contracting the Disease of Love: Authority and Freedom in the Origins of Psychoanalysis, *In*: Forrester, J., *The Seductions of Psychoanalysis. Freud, Lacan and Derrida*. Cambridge: Cambridge University Press, pp. 30-47.

— (1990b). Freud, Dora and the Untold Pleasures of Psychoanalysis. *In*: Forrester, J., *The Seductions of Psychoanalysis. Freud, Lacan and Derrida*, Cambridge: Cambridge University Press, pp. 48-61.

— (1990c). Who Is In Analysis With Whom? Freud, Lacan and Derrida. *In*: Forrester, J., *The Seductions of Psychoanalysis. Freud, Lacan and Derrida*, Cambridge: Cambridge University Press, pp. 221-242.

— (1889). Review of August Forel's *Hypnotism. Standard Edition, 1*, 89-102.

— (1890a). Psychical Treatment. *Standard Edition, 7*, 283-302.

— (1891d). Hypnosis. *Standard Edition, 1*, 103-114.

— (1900a). The Interpretation of Dreams. *Standard Edition, 4-5*.

— (1905c). Jokes and their Relation to the Unconscious. *Standard Edition, 8*.

— (1912b). The Dynamics of Transference. *Standard Edition, 12*, 97-108.

— (1914d). On the History of the Psycho-Analytic Movement. *Standard Edition, 14*, 1-66.

— (1914g). Remembering, Repeating and Working-Through. *Standard Edition, 12*, 145-156.

— (1915a). Observations on Transference-Love. *Standard Edition, 12*, 157-171.

— (1916-17). Introductory Lectures on Psycho-Analysis. *Standard Edition, 15-16*.

— (1920a). The Psychogenesis of a Case of Homosexuality in a Woman. *Standard Edition, 18*, 145-172.

— (1925h). Negation. *Standard Edition, 19*, 233-239.

FREUD, S. & JUNG, C.G. (1974). *The Freud/Jung Letters*. Princeton: Princeton University Press.

HARRIS, R. (1989). *Murders and Madness. Medicine, Law and Society in the Fin de Siècle*. Oxford: Clarendon Press.

LACAN, J. (1955-1956/1981). *Le Séminaire, Livre III. Les Psychoses*. Paris: Seuil.

MASSON, J.M. (1984). *The Complete Letters of Sigmund Freud to Wilhelm Fliess, 1887-1904*. Cambridge, Mass.: Harvard University Press.

MICALE, M. (1989). Hysteria and its Historiography: A Review of Past and Present Writings (1). *History of Science, 27*, 223-351.

— (1990a). Hysteria and its Historiography: The Future Perspective. *History of Psychiatry, 1*, 33-124.

— (1990b). Charcot and the Idea of Hysteria in the Male: A Study of Gender, Mental Science, and Medical Diagnostics in Late Nineteenth-Century France. *Medical History, 34*, 363-411.

SMITH-ROSENBERG, C. (1972). The Hysterical Woman: Sex Roles and Role Conflict in Nineteenth-Centura America, *In*: Smith-Rosenberg, C. (1985). *Disorderly Conduct: Visions of Gender in Victorian America*. New York/London: Oxford University Press, pp. 197-216.

STRACHEY, J. (1974). List of Analogies. *Standard Edition*, 24, 177-183.

SULLOWAY, F.J. (1979). *Freud, Biology of the Mind*. London: Burnett Books.

54

Cahiers Psychiatriques Genevois, Special Issue, 1994, pp. 55-99

WHY HAVE WE IGNORED FREUD THE «PAEDIATRICIAN»?[1]

The relevance of Freud's paediatric training for the origins of psychoanalysis

Carlo Bonomi

> «*"Dr. Herodes. Consulting hours..." "Let us hope," I remarked, "that our colleague does not happen to be a children's doctor."*»
>
> (Freud, 1900a, p. 443)

1. Why have we ignored Freud the «paediatrician»?

Since his studies in Paris and Berlin in 1885-1886, until his self-analysis in 1897, Sigmund Freud broke away from the common sense of the medical establishment and laid the essential patterns of psychoanalysis. In these crucial years, he was responsible for the department for nervous diseases at the «Public Institute for Children's Diseases» in Vienna, directed by Max Kassowitz.[2] For ten years, from 1886 to 1896, Freud worked with children three days a week, and paediatric activity effectively represented his most constant professional engagement. The importance of his work with hysterical children and his emotional involvement are amply reflected in the dream of Irma's injection in the summer of 1895 – the «specimen dream» of psychoanalysis. In this dream, Freud is helped by Otto and Leopold, his two assistants at the department for nervous children in the Kassowitz paediatric hospital (Freud, 1900a, p. 112),[3] and Otto is accused of the medical error which caused Irma's infection. Otto was the paediatrician Oskar Rie, trained by Freud himself in 1886, the year when he announced the treatment of infantile nervous diseases among the medical services offered in his private practice.[4] Leopold, who «localizes» Irma's diphtheritic infection in the dream, is described by Freud as an able diagnostician of nervous diseases in children (*ibid.*, p. 113). An important association of ideas links the «sick child to the children's hospital», and to the hospital's habit of examining children undressed, a thought which was interrupted by Freud's statement: «Frankly, I had no desire to penetrate more deeply at this point» (*ibid.*, p. 113). Finally, Irma herself turns into a young girl in the final part of the dream, which Freud had eliminated from the main text.[5]

These are only the most evident references in Irma's dream to Freud's involvement with hysterical children. Despite these clear references and the importance of the dream, Freud's paediatric activity has never been considered among his experiences relevant for the birth of psychoanalysis. There are very few studies on the beginnings of psychoanalysis which mention it, and no study which includes Freud's specific training on infantile nervous disturbances as a relevant part of his general training. This attitude is closely related to Freud's tendency to cancel the traces of his first medical involvement with hysterical children from his autobiography.[6] The most important statement in this regard is probably the one in *On the History of the Psychoanalytical Movement*, where he claimed that his discovery of infantile sexuality was «founded almost exclusively on the findings of analysis in adults, which led back into the past», since he «had no opportunity of direct observations on children».[7] This statement, however, is inconsistent with his paediatric activity at a time when the link between masturbation and children's nervous diseases was a sort of common ground in paediatric circles (Carter, 1983), and contrasts, even more, with his training under the guidance of the Berlin paediatrician Adolf Baginsky.

2. Adolf Baginsky and the sexual aetiology of infantile hysteria

After attending Charcot's lectures in Paris, Freud went to Berlin to acquire the necessary training for the position offered to him by the paediatrician Max Kassowitz in Vienna (Freud, 1925d, p. 14; Jones, 1953, I, p. 232). The choice of Berlin was Freud's, given that Kassowitz had poor relations with paediatricians in Berlin.[8] In Berlin, for about a month, Freud went daily to the policlinic where Adolf Baginsky, along with his paediatric private practice, also held courses for physicians and students.[9] In fact, Baginsky had been appointed «Privatdocent» in 1882,[10] and since then he regularly lectured during both winter and summer semesters, in addition to the so-called «vacation courses». Freud's training in 1886 has been ignored by historians of psychoanalysis. The general belief is that his training took place at the *Kaiser Friedrich Krankenhaus*, however, this hospital was not founded until 1890, four years after his training with Baginsky.[11]

Who was Adolf Baginsky, and what could Freud have learned at his policlinic (outpatient department)?

In his well-known treatise *Die Masturbation* (1899), Rohlender mentions Baginsky together with Tissot, the author of the famous *L'onanisme* (1760), and Peter Frank, the author of *System einer medizinischen Polizei* (1780), as witnesses of the spreading of the moral plague of masturbation in modern times.[12] However, whereas Tissot and Peter Frank had, a century earlier, worked on adult masturbation, Baginsky was a paediatrician and was concerned with infantile masturbation. In fact, in 1877, he published a *Handbuch der Schulhygiene* (Handbook of Scholastic Hygiene), by which he became well-known because of its moral engagement against the diffusion of masturbation among children.[13] Baginsky considered onanism as an illness of the nervous system which had its roots in unhygienic conditions and was especially dangerous because of its «infectious» character.[14] Although this idea was rather common in those days, it was developed within a specific ideological framework. Baginsky, in fact, was a modern Jew who interpreted the religious tradition on the basis of natural sciences. In particular, he believed that the ritual provisions of the Mosaic legislation were based on the physiology of the human organism, therefore representing basic hygienic-sanitary norms. He shared the diffused idea on the origins of Moses from the world of Egyptian priests; he considered antique priests as «sanitary officials», whose functions were equal to those of modern doctors, of which the most important was the prophylaxis, isolation and elimination of infections (Baginsky, 1895a). It was this approach, linking Mosaic rules and modern science of social hygiene, which was most likely to have led him to dedicate himself to paediatrics («*Kinderheilkunde*»), and which made him famous especially in the struggle against onanism and diphtheria. Moreover, Baginsky considered onanism an important cause of hysteria in children. This belief was so widespread around 1880, that Eduard Henoch – at that time the most authoritative paediatrician in Berlin – in a study on infantile hysteria, wrote that «it is more and more often heard that onanism is the main cause of these disturbances» (Henoch, 1881, p. 1008). Henoch thought that the aetiological role of masturbation was commonly exaggerated, but he still believed in it. In the next few years this thesis would become of secondary importance, for example in an 1896 study on psychic disturbances in children, Conrads wrote: «The influence of onanism has undoubtedly been overemphasized in the past years» (Conrads, 1896, p. 190).

Nevertheless, in the first book in the history of medicine dedicated to psychic disturbances in children, published in 1887, Emminghaus quotes Adolf Baginsky, together with the American paediatrician Jacobi and the Hungarian paediatrician Lindner, as supporters of the idea that masturbation was a cause of hysteria in children (Emminghaus, 1887, p. 284). Both Jacobi and Lindner had become very famous during the 1870s for their ideas on children's sexual excitement.[15] Therefore, around 1887, Baginsky was considered the German paediatrician most representative of the approach claiming the aetiological role of onanism in infantile nervous diseases. His *Lehrbuch der Kinderkrankheiten fur Aerzte und Studirende* (Handbook of Children's Diseases for Physicians and Students), among the most famous works on the subject at the end of the century, appeared in eight editions (from 1883 to 1905), and was even translated into French. In it Baginsky states that hysteria appears in similar forms in children and adults of both sexes, and masturbation is included among its main causes.[16] Baginsky recommends treatment according to aetiology, although he does not specify the treatment he applies in cases of masturbation. In fact, he considered sexuality in childhood a «reserved» question not to be openly discussed outside medical circles.[17]

Freud received his training with Baginsky precisely during this period, and given that he would for the rest of his life work on the link between infantile sexuality and neurosis, it can be assumed that his paediatric training was indeed relevant. Such an assumption, however, raises a problem, why did Freud disavow his first medical contact with infantile sexuality?[18]

3. Freud's original aversion to sexual aetiology

The above question is closely related to the «paradox» that, from 1886 to 1896, Freud did not refer to infantile onanism, despite of the fact that in the literature of the time references to onanism in children were widely diffused and emphasized.[19] In fact, it is only with his 1896 seduction theory that he started speaking of infantile sexuality.[20] Moreover, this «taboo» coincides with a crucial problem which has never been discussed, Freud's initial aversion to the genital localization of hysteria.

Since his Paris and Berlin study report, Freud opposed the genital localization of hysteria with forceful statements, connecting it to the hatred towards hysterical women and the witches persecuted in the Middle Ages.[21] Even in the presentation held at the Medical Society in Vienna on 15 October 1886, he claimed that, according to Charcot's modern views, there was no connection between the disease and genital organs (Bernfeld & Cassirer Bernfeld, 1952; Jones, 1953, I, p. 252). Several years later, as he came closer to the old sexual aetiology of neurosis,[22] he wrote that he had initially considered it an «insult».[23] Similarly, during the 1896 lecture on *The Aetiology of Hysteria*, he declared that he had initially a «personal aversion» towards the sexual aetiology.[24]

These observations show the complexity of Freud's discovery of infantile sexuality, pointing out that its starting point was a personal and enigmatic aversion towards sexual aetiology. Furthermore, the problematic character of this path is testified by the persistent distortions in his late autobiographical reconstructions. In the essay *On the History of the Psychoanalytical Movement* (1914d), he stated that he had suddenly remembered that at the time of his studies, the sexual aetiology of neurosis was suggested to him by a series of halfinsinuations by unsuspected and prominent physicians, such as Breuer, Charcot and Chrobak.[25] However, he added, these insinuations were immediately forgotten by the «innocent» young student, «ignorant» of sexual problems, as he was. This clear manipulation, which served to hide his training with Baginsky, had nevertheless enabled Freud to introduce half-truths in the reconstruction of the beginnings: in fact, he pointed out that the «scandalous idea» from which psychoanalysis had derived had not originated in himself (Freud, 1914d, p. 13-15). Later he redefined his discovery of the sexual causes as a late resurfacing of previous insinuations, «as an apparently original discovery».[26]

These autobiographical reconstructions, both revealing and concealing, essentially perpetuate the taboo of the early years. Why? The first question to be raised is: why had Freud initially experienced sexual aetiology as an «insult»?

4. The therapeutic implications of genital localization: castration of women and operations on children

We can approach this question by asking ourselves, at that time, what were the therapeutical implications of sexual aetiology? To mention one example, in 1887 Friedrich Merkel, at the University of Strasbourg, presented his dissertation in medicine entitled *Beitrag zur Casuistik der Castration bei Neurosen* (A Contribution to the Study of Castration in Neurosis), in which castration of hysterical women was defined as the most discussed problem of those times. In his rich bibliography he cited, among others, studies such as Böhmi's *Castration in Hysteroepilepsy*, Forel's *Cure of Hysteria by Castration*, Heilbrunn's *Cure of Moral Insanity by Castration*, Heydenreich's *Castration of the Woman*, Prochownich's *Contributions to the Problem of Castration*, Rudershausen's *Castration of Woman in Nervous Diseases*, Schröder's *On Castration in Neurosis*, Tissier's *On Castration of the Woman in Surgery (operation according to Hegar or to Battey)*, and Widmer's *Hysteria Cured by Castration*. These are only some of the 35 bibliographical references – many were university dissertations – cited by Merkel in his dissertation, all referring to castration of women, and all published in a very short period, from the summer of 1886 until the end of the year.[27] In these few months, the number of cases of castration quoted in the literature rose from 180 to 215 (Merkel, 1887, p. 54-55).

Although the term «castration» has a clear masculine meaning,[28] in those years it referred to the surgical treatment of nervous, psychical, and immoral (like nymphomania) disturbances of sexually mature women, consisting mainly in the extirpation of the ovaries. This type of operation was first undertaken by Hegar in 1872 (Hegar 1878),[29] and in 1896 Kroemer wrote that the women who had been operated upon had become «legions».[30]

A closely associated surgical treatment was also applied to children. In this case, however, since sexual organs were immature, it was not castration, but an «*operation*», consisting of various types of mutilation of male and female genital organs (besides male circumcision also female circumcision, the amputation or scarification of the clitoris, the cutting or cauterization *of labia minora*, infibulation, etc.), which were supposed to eliminate the local causes of continuous overstimulation of the «urogenital nerve». This practice was introduced and became widely used in 1850, particularly by the English doctor Isaac B. Brown.[31] In Germany it was illustrated by the paediatrician F.J. Behrend in 1860, assimilated in the theoretical framework of Romberg's uterus reflex neurosis theory, and was especially practiced by gynaecologists. It was considered as a «cure» of infantile onanism, representing an aetiological treatment of hysteria whenever onanism was diagnosed as its cause. Given the belief that surgical operations also had a «psychic» effect of «dissuasion» concerning bad habits, it was also recommended whenever a clear «localization» was missing. Stressing that scoldings and threats usually had a limited effect on small children, Behrend, for example, wrote:

> Dr. Johnson suggests to undertake a small operation in order to provoke such a pain with its wound that it would leave in the child a lasting psychic impression and would lead to any attempt at masturbation to hurt him. In boys the operation should be done on the prepuce, making a cut, etc. In girls it should, similarly, consist of a strong cauterization on the labia majora or inside the vagina entrance or, as doctor Gros suggests, of small excisions all around the clitoris. By means of such scarifications we have succeeded, in one case, to really eliminate the disease (Behrend, 1860, p. 328-29; my translation.)[32]

Was this the type of treatment Freud was trained in, in March 1886 in Berlin, at the policlinic of Adolf Baginsky? Judging from an article by Samuel Schäfer, based on his doctoral dissertation and published in 1884 as *Ueber Hysterie bei Kindern* (On Hysteria in Children),[33] in the paedia tric journal of which Baginsky was the main editor, this seems to be precisely the case. The dissertation was inspired by the practice and teaching of the *«Privatdocent»* Adolf Baginsky, thus representing a precious source of information. In this study it was claimed that, just as adults' sexual deprivation and overstimulation were claimed to be the main cause of hysteria, similarly also in children's hysteria, the cause was to be sought in bad sexual habits, primarily onanism (Schäfer, 1884a, p. 401). It was stressed that the diagnosis of onanism was mainly based on the examination of the genitals, the swelling and inflammation of the penis, of the *labia majora* and of the vagina (*ibid.*, p. 407). Finally, it was stated that among the main determining causes of children's hysteria,

> a role of not secondary importance is played by the illness and abnormalities of the urogenital apparatus, such as congenital phimosis, agglutination of the prepuce with the glans, inflamed and stretched clitoris. All of these conditions are able to produce special nervous states by reflex, which can also be healed by the elimination of the cause (Schäfer, 1884a, p. 407; my translation).[34]

Schäfer's study was commented on the *Wiener Medizinische Wochenschrift*, by Maximilian Herz,[35] who, together with Alois Monti, was the co-editor of Baginsky's paediatric journal in Vienna. Since Freud knew Herz, it is possible that he had influenced him in his choice of Baginsky for his paediatric training.

The causes mentioned in the above quotation are typical of the sexual aetiology which Freud opposed upon his return from Berlin, and which possibly influenced his breaking away from the medical establishment of Vienna. In fact, many years later, in his *Autobiographical Study* of 1924, he attributed the origins of his opposition to the medical establishment to the conflict, summarized in the episode of the «old surgeon», who had blamed him of being ignorant of etymology and of not knowing that hysteria came from the *«hysteron»* (i.e. the Greek word for uterus).[36] The questionable character of this late reconstruction has been emphasized by various authors, Sulloway even referred to it as the first of the «legends» which characterize the official history of psychoanalysis.[37] Although, in Freud's typical autobiographical style, it mixes up real elements with fiction, I believe that, on the contrary, this reconstruction contains an essential historical truth, which becomes evident when put in the context of the medical practice of surgical operations.

Freud was certainly not the only one to oppose mutilating operations: both Charcot and Breuer were personally against this practice and clearly expressed it. Charcot referred to it in his famous lecture of 27 February 1888 on boys' hysteria, which had a decisive influence on Freud.[38] Generally speaking, Charcot's complex work during 1884-1888 can be seen as an enlightened policy against mutilating surgical operations.[39] As for Breuer, thanks to the discovery of a part of the case history of «Nina

R.», we know that in 1894 he tried to prevent the castration of this patient of Freud's, hospitalized at the Kreuzlingen's clinic, and that he was, in principle, opposed to such operations.[40]

In reference to Freud, this question is much more complex for two reasons: firstly after having initially opposed sexual aetiology, he would again approach it to such an extent that it became the main object of his research; and secondly because it was subject to a persistent «taboo», whose core seems to be closely connected with his paediatric training in Berlin.

5. «Locus morbi» and aetiological treatment

At the time of Freud's paediatric training, a sexual aetiological diagnosis was made through a direct observation of the genital organs (and this is very probably the meaning of the association in Irma's dream of visiting children undressed). At the beginning of the 1896 lecture, *The Aetiology of Hysteria*, Freud stated that, following the pattern of the archaeologist, it was possible to make an aetiological diagnosis only by psychological means.[41] It took ten years for this revolution to take place.

The superiority of an aetiological diagnosis consisted in the possibility of a treatment focused on the causes, i.e. an aetiological treatment, like isolation or surgical operations. Yet, the mutilating character of castration also provoked many reactions, among which the main one was the loss of the traditional seat of hysteria (the uterus) and the shift from somatogenic to psychogenic ideas.[42] At the time of Freud's studies, hypnotic suggestion was emerging as the main therapeutical project alternative to castration; however, its main limitation consisted of it being a «symptomatic» treatment. Although in the following years Freud embraced the «soul-treatment», he was very sensitive to this therapeutic limitation and presumably in order to overcome this limitation, he adopted Breuer's cathartic treatment.[43] In fact, as he wrote at the end of *Studies on Hysteria* (1893-95), he considered cathartic treatments as «surgical operations».[44] We can better understand such a comparison considering that both treatments aimed at «eliminating» an extra amount of nervous excitement. «Cathartic operations» did not «add», but rather «took away», as Freud would point out many years later, when comparing analytic and suggestive methods.[45] Yet this external analogy did not represent a definite solution for Freud: in spite of everything, the cathartic treatment remained focused on the symptom.

It was through the friendship with Wilhelm Fliess that a new aetiological therapeutic solution, based on the nasal reflex neurosis theory, would appear. Many scholars have emphasised the inconsistencies of such a theory, but no one has considered it in light of the old uterus reflex neurosis theory, and of castration. If we consider it from this perspective, its major characteristic appears to be the displacement of the «*locus morbi*» from the genital organs to the so-called «genital spots» of the nose. Freud himself, while comparing the two localizations, stated that the second one opened a «broader view».[46]

The active influence of Freud on Fliess' nasal localization has also not been sufficiently considered. Discussing the question of aetiological treatment in his 1888 essay *Hysteria*, Freud not only questioned the idea that the alterations of genital organs represented a stimulus for hysterical symptoms, but when raising this doubt, he already suggested an alternative «nasal» localization.[47] Furthermore, in the Preface to the book *Neue Beitrage zur Klinik und Therapie der nasalen Reflexneurose* (New Contributions to the Theory and Therapy of Nasal Reflex Neurosis, 1893), Fliess wrote that he had been pushed in this new direction by a friend – which was Freud himself.[48]

What emerges from Freud's letters in this period is that he attributed a «messianic» value to Fliess' research, precisely because of its therapeutic implications.[49] Freud was specially enthusiastic of the possibility of the localization of peripheral disturbances, and suggested Fliess should «glorify» the advantage of localization.[50] The advantage – although Freud did not state it, since it was obvious – was the possibility of an aetiological treatment of the *status nervosus* through cauterizations or surgical operations. We should also recall that nasal surgical operations were associated with the treatment of women's masturbation.[51] In brief, we can assume that Freud attributed a «messianic value» to Fliess' research precisely because it represented a therapeutic alternative to castration, which was non-mutilating (or less mutilating). He considered the operation on the nose as «harmless» and was profoundly shaken by the dramatic outcome of the nasal operation on his patient Emma Eckstein.[52]

Emma Eckstein was operated at the beginning of 1895 by Fliess and almost died because of a medical error (Schur, 1972; Masson, 1984). Although the error was not Freud's, he nevertheless felt guilty, perhaps because he had pushed Fliess in this direction, or perhaps for deeper reasons. The problem of guilt would be reflected in the dream of Irma's injection, in which the blame for inappropriate treatment is put on the paediatrician Oscar Rie (Otto). Freud interpreted this dream as the fulfillment of the wish of not being guilty, and his associations are characterized by violent self-accusations concerning his lack of medical skill. The main point, however, is that Irma transforms herself into a young girl, and a series of details and associations indicate that the question of guilt was closely related to Freud's paediatric activity.

The influence on Freud of this dream seems to have been that of grad-ually closing the period of surgical operations and opening the one of psy-choanalysis. This took place in two phases. An immediate consequence was the early seduction theory presented in Freud's lecture *The Aetiology of Hysteria* in 1896. This theory was important since it permitted Freud to present, for the first time, a psychic model of sexual aetiological diagnosis and treatment, which finally represented a strong therapeutic project alternative to genital examinations and surgical operations. It is therefore not surprising that the term «psychoanalysis» appeared for the first time precisely in this context (Freud, 1896a p. 151; 1896b, p. 162).

It was only with his self-analysis that Freud dealt with the symbolic meaning of surgical operations. Reading *The Interpretation of Dreams* from this perspective is extremely enlightening. As pointed out by Musatti in the Preface to the Italian edition, this work is characterized by «elementary principles of justice, which function according to the law of talion: frequently in a literary sense, given that the normal punishments are death and emasculation, strangely identified.»[53] While Irma's dream opens this study, it should be stressed that it is the dream on self-dissec-tion of the pelvis in Brücke's laboratory of physiology that closes it. This dream took place in the summer of 1899, and in this «self-castration» for-mulated in the language of «physiology», Freud recognized the symbol of self-analysis. He also manifested his double tendency to reveal and conceal himself, by quoting Mephistopheles' lines from Goethe's Faust:

> *Das Beste, was du wissen kannst,*
> *Darfst du den Buben doch nicht sagen.*[54]

The dream of self-dissection is also characterized by the idea of «immortality». After self-castration, Freud wanders with aching legs until he reaches a wooden house-coffin. In the associations, the coffin was iden-tified with an Etruscan grave in which the terror of death is reversed into the fulfillment of a wish. Finally, Freud leaves the house-coffin passing over two children, lying as a bridge over the abyss.

6. **The taboo**

Freud's renouncement of surgical operations has very complex aspects. On the one hand, the preoccupation about the «future of chil-dren» is a constant topic of *The Interpretations of Dreams*, and his invol-vement in Fliess' biology and his own later contributions can be better understood as a longing for a theory on sexuality, which was alternative to the physiological models of genital overstimulation, supporting castration and surgical operations. On the other hand, in his life and work this issue is characterized by both ambivalence and taboo. The former is reflected primarily by the fact that he continued to conceive of psychic analysis as homologous to surgical operations, something which implies a precise but questionable set of judgements on sexuality and fantasies on the analytical relationship. On various occasions he used the analogy between analysis and surgery, up to the point of formulating the famous technical recommendation to operate with the coolness of a surgeon.[55] As to the taboo, it has various manifestations and it is testified by the autobiographical distortions.[56] Again, both aspects are related to the question of Freud's paediatric training.

If we reconsider Irma's dream within this framework, the insistence on paediatric practice raises the following question: why did Freud relate self-reproaches to nervous disturbances in children?

The most important crossroad of these self-reproaches is the one which relates Irma's diphtheritic infection to the death, a few years earlier, of one of his patients, Mathilde S., by treatment with Sulfonal;[57] and this death to the risk of dying of his daughter Mathilde because of diphtheria.[58] This link was expressed in the tragic sentence «this Mathilde for that Mathilde, an eye for an eye and a tooth for a tooth» (Freud, 1900a, p.112).

Hirschmüller raised the question whether Freud had not identified himself at that time with Behring, «the saviour of thousands of children» thanks to the introduction in 1894 of diphtheritic serotherapy.[59] In my opinion, this question raises a central issue which becomes sharper if brought within the frame of Freud's paediatric training with Adolf Baginsky. Baginsky was among the first to have adopted Behring's serum and already in 1895 he published a book on the results of serotherapy of diphtheria at the Berlin paediatric hospital Kaiser Friedrich. Moreover, diphtheria was his main field of interest and since the setting up of the hospital he had planned a huge «Infektions-Pavillon» (infectious building) precisely for isolating and treating children with diphtheria (and scarlet fever). He was researching the antitoxin-treatment, and Hans Aronson – who discovered that horses were the best animals for acquiring the diphtheria serum – had been his co-worker (untill 1893). In the very tense debate on the pros and cons of the serum, Baginsky was its main and most prominent supporter, even attacking the authority of Virchow, who was against its introduction. In his study of 1895 he reported that the mortality was reduced from 48.2% to 15.6% after the introduction of Aronson's antitoxin-therapy (Werner, 1990). This was the most detailed study on diphtheria, and Nothnagel asked Baginsky to include it within the series Specielle Pathologie und Therapie (Baginsky, 1898), to which Freud also contributed a study on infantile brain palsy

(Freud, 1897). Freud received the assignment from Nothnagel before Irma's dream, and it is very probable that he knew that the study on diphtheria was assigned to Baginsky. It is also to be noted that in the spring of 1895, in a letter to Fliess, he quoted the lines: «*My heart is in the coffin with Caesar*», in association both to Nothnagel's assignment and to the pains and bleeding of Emma Eckstein. These lines allude to a mourning and link Irma's dream to the dream «*non vixit*».[60]

Freud had no personal reason to identify himself with Behring; and it is more plausible that the special meaning of diphtheria reflected in Irma's dream was connected with Baginsky.[61] In fact, in the dream, the diphtheritic infection is related to «sexuality» and «localization», i.e. to those elements of sexual aetiology which are common both to Emma Eckstein's nose operation and surgical mutilations of genitals during his paediatric training. In paediatrics, moreover, quite a strong link existed between hysteria, genital illness and diphtheria.[62] For example Maximilian Herz, in his 1885 article on children hysteria, when referring to Baginsky's pupil Samuel Schäfer, wrote that an occasional cause of hysteria can be «a local or general illness, or a psychic cause, primarily a sudden and violent excitement. Among local illness, the most frequent ones are those of the urogenital parts: phimosis, agglutination of the prepuce with the glans, inflamed and stretched clitoris, etc.; among general illness, as occasional causes, typhus, diphteria, serious loss of blood and humors, are usually listed» (Herz, 1885, p.1307; my translation). Freud himself had later established a close connection between genital and nose operations. In his letter to Fliess of 24 January 1897, referring to the circumcision of one of his hysterical patients in her childhood, he had associated her mutilation on the *labium minus* to the outcome of Emma Eckstein's nose operation. And it was precisely in that same period that Mathilde suffered from diphtheria. If we reconsider, in this perspective, his self-accusations as a physician, which led him to the idea that the death of his daughter Mathilde was a punishment according to the Mosaic Law of talion, it is not difficult to imagine that what he had in mind were his own errors as a children's doctor. If this inference is correct, it would give a more precise meaning to the paediatric implications of the dream and to Irma's transformation, at the end of the dream, into a hysterical girl.

Should we deduct from what has been said that the case of Mathilde S., his patient who died from intoxication with Sulfonal, hides another case of death, or a serious accident, directly or indirectly connected to Freud's paediatric training in Berlin?

Freud associated Irma's injection to injections of morphine and cocaine. On this occasion he again alluded to a case of death, the one of his friend Ernst Fleischl. However, it should be noted that morphine was also used in the treatment of genital disturbances, and that for Freud, cocaine was closely associated to sexual aetiology and surgical operations. In his 1885 lecture on cocaine – which is mentioned in the associations of the «oto-rhino-gynaecological» dream, as Anzieu (1959-1975) defines the dream of Irma – beyond recommending cocaine as treatment of neurasthenia (Bernfeld 1953), Freud wrote that, since its discovering, cocaine had been used in the treatment of hysteria (Freud 1885, p.168). We are informed about this treatment once again through the 1885 study on hysteria in children of Maximilian Herz, the close friend of Freud who, very likely, had introduced him to Baginsky. In fact, discussing the therapy, after having stressed that onanism is often provoked by «irritative states of genitals», like the «inflamed and stretched clitoris or irritative states of the vagina» which «have to be eliminated», Hertz reported to have succeeded in healing the irritative causes of onanism in a seven years old girl only when he added a 10% solution of cocaine to the «astringents» which he put twice a day, for several weeks, in the entrance of the girl's vagina (Hertz, 1885, p. 1403)[63].

7. The Altar of Sacrifice of Pergamon Acropolis: a link between surgical operations and mythology

Freud also associated Irma's injection to Fliess' sexual aetiology and to Propylaea, the sacred entrance to the Acropolis, emphasizing that Propylaea are found not only in Athens but also in Munich (where he went to visit Fliess who was ill) (Freud, 1900a, p. 294). However, there are many elements suggesting that the German city in question was not Munich but Berlin, where its Royal Museums were, since 1875, engaged in the largest campaign of Greek and Hellenistic excavations of the end of the century (Olympia, Pergamon, Magnesia, Priene), and in which the famous Propylaea of the temple dedicated to Athena in the Acropolis of Pergamon had been rebuilt.

The association between the sexual aetiology and Propylaea, is so strange and incomprehensible, that it has never been researched, but there is an experience in Freud's life which can shed light on it and make it congruent with the paediatric implication of Irma's dream.

On 10 March 1886, during his paediatric training, Freud visited the sculptures of the Pergamon Altar of Sacrifice, which were exhibited at that time in the Royal Museum of Berlin.[64] On that day he wrote a letter to his fiancée Martha Bernays, in which he mentioned the animated scenes of struggle between gods and titans carved on the Pergamon's high-relief, he expressed emotion for hysterical children, hinted at the «secrets of children's diseases», and expressed a certain contempt for Baginsky.[65] Are there any reasons to attribute a special value to this link between the gigantomachy and Baginsky's policlinic? Furthermore, could there be a link between this visit of 10 March 1886 and the peculiar passion for archaeology which Freud would progressively develop during the following years, leading him to compulsively collect «objects found in a tomb» (according to his own definition)?[66]

Freud's so-called «archaeological metaphor» has generally been considered as having been inspired by the discovery of Troy,[67] in spite of the fact that Freud had read Schliemann's book only in 1899[68] and that the «archaeological metaphor» had come to his mind in 1892 (Breuer and Freud, 1893-1895, p. 139), and was fully developed already in the 1896 lecture on *The Aetiology of Hysteria*. Moreover, for Freud, the «archaeological metaphor» did not have only a speculative value, but primarily a symbolic and private meaning. The excavations of Pergamon are likely to have provided it.

Together with the discovery of Troy, it was the most important archaeological achievement at the end of the 19th century. The Pergamon's Acropolis – of the III and II century B.C. – is the only one to have competed in magnificence with the Acropolis of Athens, and its Altar of Sacrifice is the hugest, in dimensions and conceptions, that has been preserved from ancient times. The gigantomachy carved on the marble of the Altar dedicated to Zeus, was an allegoric work since, through the symbols of the triumph of gods over titans, of civilization over barbarity, it commemorated an historical event, the defeat of the Galatians barbarians. Moreover, it is well known that the myth of gigantomachy begins with the coupling of the mother Earth and of the father Sky, of Gea and Uranus, and the emasculation of Uranus by his son Kronos, who was pushed and armed with a sickle by his mother. It was from the bleeding of this emasculation that giants were born.

Freud referred quite often to gigantomachy.[69] This cosmogonic myth contains various essential elements of Freud's later thinking, such as primal scene, conflict and the oedipal triangle. But above all, the element which could have impressed a special and private meaning to it, is precisely the emasculation of the father by the son. This mythological emasculation could indeed have exposed the young Freud to the reversed image of surgical operations undertaken in Baginsky's policlinic, later becoming a symbol for his own interior struggle and an expression of his identification with both the triumphant god and the defeated titan. Such a hypothesis could also provide a deeper insight into the reasons which gradually led Freud to conceive myths as rejection, distortion and reversal of a definite «historical truth».

Freud was thirty when he received his training at Baginsky's policlinic and was in his fifties when he started theorizing about the complex of castration. This took place from 1908 onwards, with the case of Little Hans, and in those years he introduced the clinical problem by recalling Greek legends – i.e. gigantomachy (Freud, 1908 p. 216; 1909a, p. 8). During the following years, this private function of Greek mythology would be taken over by the so-called «phylogenetic phantasy», i.e. the idea that in prehistory the father castrated his elder sons as a punishment – a punishment which would later, depending on the level of civilization, be attenuated to simple circumcision.[70]

The uneasy path from the medical practice of castration/circumcision to the idea of castration anxiety went not only through the struggles between gods and giants, but also through repeated «historical errors» concerning who was emasculating whom, such as the quotation on Zeus emasculating Kronos (instead of Kronos emasculating Uranus),[71] and the substitution of Tarquinius Superbus with Tarquinius Priscus.[72]

The famous self-analytic study on the disturbance of memory on the Acropolis belongs to the same set of problems. In 1904, during his summer vacation, Freud unexpectedly arrived in Athens where, visiting the Acropolis, he had the strange disturbance to which thirty years later (!) he went on to refer to as «the disturbance of memory on the Acropolis». Indeed, in 1936, he described the core of this disturbance as the experience concisely summarized in the statement «*what I see here is not real*» (Freud, 1936a, p. 244). Freud explained this experience as the repetition of a previous doubt about the reality of the Acropolis: «I did not simply recollect that in my early years I had doubted whether I myself would ever see the Acropolis, but I asserted that at that time I had disbelieved in the reality of the Acropolis itself.»[73]

Commentators agree on the absurdity of this crucial statement, but if we relate it not to the Acropolis in Athens but to the one in Pergamon, partially rebuilt two thousand years later in the Center of Berlin, with its Propylaea, its Altar of Sacrifice and its animated struggles, then this statement loses its apparent absurdity. Indeed, if we consider the question within the context of Freud's paediatric training at Baginsky's policlinic, his early aversion toward sexual aetiology and later distortions and disavowals, the simple and concise sentence «what I see here is not real», once related to the issue of surgical operations, reveals an unexpected coherence. What I am suggesting is that the young Freud's emotional involvement with surgical operations seems to have shifted from the miseries and constraints of medical practice, to the terror and beauty of «archaeology» and mythological struggles, thus gaining a larger breadth, leading him to confront universal issues, while also diverting him from the grey reality.

8. Moses and the «operation»

Why had Freud returned to this disturbance after a period of thirty years had passed since his trip to Greece? During the last few years of his life, Freud became more and more sensitive to problems of rejection and disavowal. In particular, he developed the idea that myths were places where «historical truth» is not only disavowed, distorted and reversed, but also preserved – perhaps the only places where historical truth can be preserved. Furthermore, he defined his own theory of instincts as a «mythology» (Freud, 1933a, p. 95), stated that delusions and myths were similar in this regard (Freud, 1939a, p. 130 and note; 1937, p. 268), and defined psychoanalytical constructions as equivalent to delusions (Freud, 1937d, p. 268). It was in the context of this type of reflection, in *The Future of an Illusion* (1927), that he mentioned his trip to Greece in the summer of 1904: the memory of himself admiring the Aegean Sea from the top of the Acropolis had introduced, in fact, the consideration of the unreliable character – full of contradictions, changes and falsifications – of Holy Scripts (Freud, 1927d, p. 25). Freud's private reflection on the meaning of falsification seems to be connected not only to the Acropolis, but also to Moses, since in the same year he wrote a Postscript (1927) to his 1913 essay on *The Moses of Michelangelo*. These considerations would lead to the thesis that if, in spite of their absurdity, Holy Scripts were compulsively believed in, it was because of the historical truth they concealed and preserved within themselves. The study in which this thesis is developed is *Moses and Monotheism* (1939). Freud wrote the short autobiographical essay on the disturbance of memory on the Acropolis in the same period, and the relatedness of the two essays is widely acknowledged. Is it possible to find a closer connection?

The common view is that Freud's emotional and intellectual attitude towards Moses implies some kind of identification which, in the period when he was writing *Totem and Taboo*, appeared as a powerful obsession with the «titan» Moses of Michelangelo, the funeral monument of the grave of Julius II in Rome, from which the first essay on Moses originated (Freud, 1914b). The rule of drives and the mastery of rage are commonly considered as the symbolic meaning of Freud's identification with the Moses of Michelangelo.[74] In my opinion, the question is much more complex, and I suggest including also a «literal» interpretation, which regards Moses as the ruler of circumcision among Jews. Freud had a very ambivalent attitude towards circumcision, considering it as an attenuated form of emasculation, thus representing both emasculation and a great advance in the history of civilization and in the control of primeval barbarity. We can assume that for Freud, Moses reflected this ambiguity, and that his identification with the ruler of a superior degree of civilization was based on his having substituted castration with psychoanalysis.

A clue supporting this interpretation is the fact that the Moses of Michelangelo was admired by Freud for the first time during the days of his paediatric training in Berlin, when he visited the gigantomachy of Pergamon. The funeral monument of the pope Julius II was in those years exhibited in the hall of copies of famous masterpieces in the same museum,[75] and since Adolf Baginsky's approach to paediatrics was based on a «physiological» and hygienic interpretation of the Mosaic rules (including circumcision; see Baginsky, 1895, p. 474), we can assume that the statue of Moses had elicited in Freud highly contrasting feelings already in 1886. We can further speculate that this experience – in which we may again recognize the concourse of private experience, medical practice, art and mythology – had a certain role in Freud's conflictual attitude towards his Jewish identity.

The original masterpiece of the Moses of Michelangelo in Rome could have also crucially contributed to Freud's inhibition to enter Rome during the period of self-analysis. There is, in fact, an intimate connection between the Pergamon gigantomachy and the Moses of Michelangelo. Michelangelo worked on the statue in the years 1512-16 under the strong influence of the Hellenistic Laocoon-group, found in Rome in 1506, at the excavations of which Michelangelo personally assisted. Nearly four hundred years later, in 1878, the excavations of Pergamon began and, according to what we are told when the Athena-Alcinous group was dug out and liberated from the mud, the archaeologists exclaimed: «Now we also have a Laocoon!» (Kunze, 1991a, 1991b). This identification was due to the stylistic similarities between Alcinous and Laocoon, and especially to the same representation of the physical and emotional struggle against the impeding death. Moreover, these similarities later led to the identification of the Laocoon-group in Vatican as a Roman copy of an original masterpiece of Pergamon, which had been carved precisely in the period of the building of the Altar of Sacrifice.

Re-examining the interpretation of the Moses of Michelangelo, Versphol (1991) has recently stressed the plastic and topical parallel between Laocoon and Moses, with respect to the omen and feeling of the impeding death («*Todesahnung*»). While in the sculpture of the Troyan priest and prophet, the fate of death is represented by the passionate struggle of the entire body against death, Michelangelo has reproduced the same bodily tension only on the left side of the Moses, contrasting it with the calm and still posture of the right side, thus obtaining the representation of a psychological conflict elicited by the thought of impeding death. If we further compare, as it was possible for Freud, the Moses with the Pergamon struggles between gods and titans, we can recognize that on the Moses of Michelangelo, the external opposition between the still expression of the fighting gods, unaffected by the tragic events, and the tormented expression of the dying titans, corresponds to the inner dualism between the superior mission of the ruler and the human nature of the man.

Planning the grave of the pope Julius II, Michelangelo was deeply concerned not only with the main figure of the Laocoon-group, but also with the two sons of the priest, who cannot escape from the destiny of the father, and who, although innocent, must die. The emotional power raised by the issue of the sacrifice of an innocent, which is the pillar of Christianity, is reflected in Michelangelo's sculptures of the two *prigioni* (prisoners or slaves) of Louvre, which were conceived, together with the Moses, as part of the grave of Jiulius II. Like in Moses, also in the *prigioni*, death is no longer represented as a sudden outer threat, but as the counterpart of an endless inner confrontation.

The issue of sacrifice and of its basic expressions and transformations, is further connected to the question of symbols. As stressed by Verspohl (1991), Michelangelo viewed Moses, according to the Renaissance tradition, as a pendant of Saint Paul in the common search for adequate symbols. After the suppression of the false symbols (as the gold calf), the prophet dedicated his energies to the creation of symbols and forms convenient for the foundation of a community in which God was appearing through the Word (the Ten Commandments). Similarly, the apostle – who gave up the sacred symbol of the circumcision in the flesh – represented in theology the power of the Word, because of his preaching salvation thanks to the sacrifice of an innocent.

The longing for adequate symbols and forms was common to Italian Renaissance, which introduced an understanding of the sacred history mediated by the culture and art of classic Greece. Freud's late confrontation with Moses and Christianity, i.e. with the original sin, also pass through the Hellenic mythology – especially the Hellenistic Mysteries and the cults of priestly castration in Mid Asia[76] – and is focused on the question of the sacrifice and its symbols, rather than on the opposition between Judaism and Christianity.

As referred by Jones (1953), when Freud finally overcame his phobia entering Rome in 1901, he sent Martha a postcard (6.9.1901) after having visited the original Moses of Michelangelo, in which he wrote «*Plötzlich durch Mich. verstanden.*» (suddenly understood through Michelangelo). Two weeks later he wrote to Fliess that he would have bowed in front of the mutilated temple of Minerva (19.9.1901, in Freud, 1986). Minerva, the «Roman Athena», was the link between the Greek Athena and the

Catholic Maria and it was to Athena that Laocoon had been sacrified. When Carl Human began the excavations of Pergamon, he had initially attributed the marble groups to the temple of Minerva,[77] finally, when Freud entered in the *Altes Museum*, on 10 March 1886, the Athena-group was exhibited in the Rotunde, together with the Zeus-group, right in front of the Propylaea, the Hellenistic entrance of the Museum.

In brief, in the short period of Freud's stay in Berlin, we can identify a dense network of very important issues, which are able to shed light on many of the most enigmatic thoughts and phenomena of his later life. Yet, for this cross-cultural experience to have had a deep and long term influence, it had to echo some of his private experiences.

I will stress only one detail, which can link the disturbance of memory on the Acropolis, the essay on Moses and Freud's paediatric training. Freud's analysis of the revisions of the Biblical text – which, according to Freud, had been falsified, mutilated and changed into reverse in the sense of secret aims (Freud, 1939, p. 43) – focuses on the question of circumcision, or more precisely, the history of the «operation» of Moses, readily undertaken by Moses' wife Madianita in order to save his life. Freud had no hesitations in recognizing that the disavowal of the supposed assassination of the Egyptian Moses was the reason underlying the need to contradict historical truth about «operation» (ibid. p. 30; also see p. 44). Why? What private evidence did Freud have to support such an inference? Was the need to contradict historical truth about the «operation» not shared by the official history of the origins of psychoanalysis? Could this not be the meaning of the disavowal of the reality of the Acropolis? Does it make sense to apply to Freud himself what he had written about the Biblical text? For example:

> In its implications the distortion of a text resembles a murder: the difficulty is not in perpetrating the deed, but in getting rid of its traces. We might lend the word "*Entstellung*" [distortion] the double meaning to which it has a claim but of which today it makes no use. It should mean not only "to change appearance of something" but also "to put something in another place, to displace." Accordingly, in many instances of textual distortion, we may nevertheless count upon finding what had been suppressed and disavowed hidden away somewhere else, though changed and torn from its context (Freud, 1939a, p. 43).

9. **Non vixit**

The trip to Greece in 1904 and the disturbance of the memory on the Acropolis are closely connected to Freud's distressing expectation of death on a pre-fixed date.[78] Such an expectation started in the spring of

1894, corresponding to the period of the epistolary exchange between Breuer and Robert Binswanger concerning the castration of Freud's patient Nina R.. During that period Freud's nervous disturbances worsened, and he suffered a depression characterized by visions of death.[79] It was at that time that the expectation of dying at the age of 51 appeared,[80] which would later be shifted to the age of 61 and 62 and, according to Schur, was never definitely overcome. Stressing the exacerbation of Freud's emotional state in relation to the critical age of 62, Jones pointed out that the topic of death, the dread of it and the wish for it, represented a continuous preoccupation of Freud's mind, and he added, «We can even trace the beginnings of it to the sinful destruction of his little brother in his early infancy.» (Jones, 1957, p. 44).

The «little brother» was his brother Julius who died when he was 6 months old, while Sigmund Freud was 23 months old. Freud had mentioned his brother's death as the root of his feeling of guilt in the letter to Fliess of 3/4 October 1897 which, according to many scholars, represents the tragic core of self-analysis.[81] Grinstein has stressed that among Freud's reactions to Julius' death was an intense feeling of anger towards his mother; sexual assault towards women; aggression towards his father; and dread of torture, punishment, castration and death (Grinstein, 1980, p. 280). Suzanne Cassirer Bernfeld, in a famous essay on *Freud and Archeology*, compared Julius to Jesus Christ, and the associated screen memory of the «*Kasten*»[82] to a coffin, representing the Madonna with the Child, which stands on the altar of the Catholic Church (Cassirer Bernfeld, 1951).

According to Jones, Freud had referred to Julius' death also in order to explain his second fainting in front of Jung,[83] and Jones himself suggested that it could also explain the disturbance of memory on the Acropolis (Jones, 1955, p. 187). In his biography of Freud, Schur has systematically referred to the guilt originated from Julius' death, pointing to it as «the survivor's feeling of guilt», and recognizing in the dream «*non vixit*» one of the main manifestations of Freud's pathological mourning.[84] A common view among scholars is that Freud's attitude towards death,[85] his passion for archaeology and his Roman «paralysis», the split identification with Moses, and many of his symptoms, dreams and thoughts, all have a unique root closely related to the issue of Julius' death. Furthermore, through its reverberations in Freud's followers, Julius' death can be viewed as a deep source of a continuous generation of symbols.

The extraordinary power of Julius' death in generating symbols has to be imputed to its being a «screen memory». This did not escape Schur's attention, who suggested that Freud's feelings towards Julius were a displacement of the jealousy provoked by the birth of his sister Anna.[86] The point, however, is that whereas a tragic event such as a death undoubtedly contains a power of persuasion respect to Freud's pathological mourning, [87] jealousy due to the birth of a sister appears to be out of proportion to this end, lacking persuasive power. In this regard Julius' death seems to function as a myth in Freud's meaning, i.e. as something which in spite of its absurdity contains a dramatic force of persuasion, given the historical truth which it conceals and preserves at the same time.

10. A memorial to the defeated hero

It is commonly assumed that in the dream «*non vixit*» Julius is represented by Julius Caesar, while Freud identifies himself with Brutus, the murderer. This dream was inspired by the inauguration of the monument in memory of Ernst Fleischl, who was a «martyr of physiology» since he had been infected in Brücke's Laboratory of physiology – who had to suffer an infinite series of surgical mutilating operations. «I admire and love him with an intellectual passion», Freud had written before his death, «His destruction will move me as the destruction of a sacred and famous temple would have affected an ancient Greek».[88]

A similar emotion is to be found at the beginning of Freud's self-analysis, since the «Mathilde-Hella» dream of May 1897 represents the main entrance to it (McGrath, 1986, p. 200). In fact, on the 31st of May Freud wrote to Fliess that «Mathilde may have been called Hella because she has weeping so bitterly recently over the Greek defeats. She has a passion for the mythology of ancient Hellas and naturally regards all Hellenes as heroes.»[89] Since Freud's identification with defeated heroes plays a crucial role in *The Interpretation of Dreams*, it is rather important to point out that Freud's sensitivity for Mathilde's weeping is again closely related both to gigantomachy and to surgical operations.

Freud had already referred to Mathilde's passion for mythology in the previous letter of the 16th of May in association with Xenophontes' historical report on the return of Greek soldiers from Persia, i.e. the war which in classical Greece had been celebrated by utilizing the gigantomachy as an allegory of the triumph of civilization over barbarity. Two hundred years later, the king of Pergamon Eumenes II made use of the same allegory when he committed the Altar of Sacrifice, in order to celebrate the victory over the Galatian barbarians and to stress that Pergamon was to be the new Athens.

Freud had also used the same allegory quite often, and in a way which seems to commemorate the defeated heroes of surgical operations. In the letter of the 16th of May, Freud refers to a surgical operation which his son Martin had previously undergone, expressed in a distorted form in a brief «poem» concerning the throat pains of a little fawn. According to Freud, it was possible to understand precisely from the poem that Martin had undergone an operation. This was the kind of inference which he was working on at that time: in which way painful experiences were rejected, distorted and combined again in fantasies.[90] A few days later, he stated that the mechanism of creative writing was the same as that of hysterical fantasies.[91]

It is very likely that when Freud mentioned Martin's «dichterische» (i.e. «creative») distortion of his previous surgical operation, he also had in mind the circumcision of his female hysterical patient, which was associated with Emma Eckstein's nose operation. Since Freud had «dichterisch» (creatively) distorted this operation in diphtheritic pains in the dream of Irma's injection, he could have well reflected himself in the poetical attitude of his son, thus acquiring a deeper insight into the mechanism of dreams.[92]

In my opinion, it was this insight, exacerbating his split identification with the triumphant god and the defeated hero, which had provoked in Freud a «paralysis» and a writing block, forcing him to begin to face his personal involvement with surgical operations and the question of «castration» which in *The Interpretations of Dreams* is so crudely dominant in all kinds of direct, indirect, and «creatively» distorted forms.

This, however, became possible only after the «archaeological» travel in Italy of September 1897.[93] The connection between Freud's travel in Italy and his paediatric training will now be stressed, in order to draw some conclusions about the screen memory status of «Julius».

During these travels Freud visited the Etruscan tomb which would later appear associated to the dream of the dissection of the pelvis, and Luca Signorelli's *Last Judgement* in Orvieto, which would be connected to the topic «Sexuality and Death» and to the forgetfulness of «nomina propria» (Freud, 1898b). Furthermore, as it is well known, Freud had a «block» which prevented him to enter Rome, and which was later narrated through his juvenile identification with the Semitic hero Hannibal who could not conquer the Catholic Rome. I have already suggested that this block could have been related to the Moses of Michelangelo, which was first seen at the Royal Museum together with the scenes of the Pergamon gigantomachy during his paediatric training in Berlin. Freud's reference to Hannibal supports such an hypothesis, since a few years after having left Italy, Hannibal flew first to the King of Syria and later to Prusias, the King of Bythnia, taking part in the war against Eumenes II, the King of Pergamon and an ally of the Romans, and finally committed suicide (in 183 B.C.) when he was to be captured by the Roman soldiers. Freud, narrating in *The Interpretation of Dreams* the oath of young Hannibal in front of the Altar, made the slip of substituting Hamilcar

Barca with Hasdrubal – a slip later referred by Freud as having the same root as the one of Zeus emasculating Kronos (Freud, 1901b, p. 217-20). In fact, Eumenes II was the king who ordered the Pergamon gigantomachy, in order to celebrate the victories of Attalus I over the Galatians, but also his own victory over Prusias I. (Later, in 156 B.C., Prusias II would invade and destroy the Kingdom of Pergamon). Moreover, Freud associated Hannibal to Johann Joachim Winckelmann (Freud, 1900a, p. 196), the archaeologist and historian of ancient art who studied the Laocoon in the early pamphlet *Thoughts on the Imitation of Greek Works in Painting and Sculpture* (1755) and prompted Lessing to write the famous treatise *Laocoon* (1766). And, as previously stressed, the Pergamon gygantomachy, the Laocoon and the Moses of Michelangelo were strictly connected.

Also the «Catholic» qualification of Rome, as the city «neurotically» prohibited to Freud, can be traced back to the time of his paediatric training in Berlin. Although Freud would narrate his attitude towards Rome, in *The Interpretation of Dreams*, as a reaction to anti-semitism, and rooted in the «conflict between the tenacity of Jewry and the organization of the Catholic Church» (1900a, p. 197), he was well aware of the fact that his ambivalent feelings towards Rome were a question neither of faith nor of politics, but rather «deep neurotics» – as he wrote to Fliess in the letter of 3 December 1897, quoting the same Mephistopheles lines which would be also quoted when comparing the dissection of the pelvis to self-analysis. Since Freud, in the same letter, refers also to the souls burning in the hell, entering Rome could have been associated to the Jubilee, i.e. to the year in which pilgrims who enter San Pietro in Rome are given the plenary indulgence for their sins. Freud could have also contrasted, in his mind, the Catholic Jubilee to the «pagan» Jubilee which took place in Berlin in 1886. In fact, Freud's travel through Italy, in September 1897, had been dominated by the interest for «archaeology», and the Berlin 1886 Jubilee of the 100 years of the Academy of Art represented the triumph of the German imperial policy of «archaeology». A grandiose exhibition was prepared, including a copy of the Luxor obelisk which Napoleon moved to Paris, to the Place de la Concorde (the German copy included the armorial of Wilhelm I, the Prussian eagle, and imperial inscriptions), the reconstruction of the East-front of the Zeus temple of Olympia and of a part of the Pergamon Altar of Sacrifice (the relief was copied and completed in the missing parts, according to the drawings of Alexander Tondeur), and a 40-metre long «Diorama-building» in Egyptian style, which showed the imperial achievements in Africa and the visual reconstruction of the Acropolis of Pergamon. The climax of the exhibition was the «Pergamon feast», in which 1500 artists, dressed in Greek and barbarian costumes, represented the triumph of the Kings of

Pergamon over the defeated Galatians (Kunze, 1986, 1991b) – or, as had been written in the 1886 Guide to the «Pergamon- und Olympia-Panorama», the «Vernichtungskampf der Götter gegen die Giganten». Freud was already in Vienna when the exhibition was inaugurated, but he certainly knew of the Jubilee and had seen the main monuments of the exhibition.

A further clue to the connection between Freud's visit of the Royal Museum in Berlin in 1886 and the «archaeological» trip in Italy of 1897, can also be found in Freud's interest for the famous painter Luca Signorelli, whose name he had forgotten and had substituted it with the name Boltraffio when talking with a councillor of Berlin in a later «archaeological trip». In fact, during his paediatric training, it is very probable that Freud in the Royal Museum had seen one of the most famous paintings of Luca Signorelli, which is commonly considered as a paradigm of the Renaissance view of Greek mythology: Pan as god of the natural life (or «The triumph of Pan»). This painting clearly hints to the topic of "sexuality", contrasting not only with Baginsky's teaching, but also with the topic of «death» of Signorelli's fresco on the Antichrist of the Dome of Orvieto, which deeply impressed Freud in September 1897. I suggest that talking of Italian art with a person from Berlin, was crucial to Freud's forgetting the name of Luca Signorelli. Moreover, given that Boltraffio's paintings are very rare and that this painter is usually unknown outside specialist circles, it is interesting to point out that a «rare» painting of Boltraffio (as written even by Bode in the Museum guide) was exhibited with four of Signorelli's paintings in the same Museum of Berlin. A further connection between Signorelli's fresco in Orvieto and the excavations of Pergamon, is given by the fact that in the *Apocalypse* (2, 13) the throne of Satan – which is commonly viewed as an allusion to the temple of Aesculapium – is located in Pergamon.[94] Signorelli was also the author of the fresco «The testament of Moses» in the Sistina, in San Pietro, which ended the cicle of the history of Moses. Finally, Freud's first interest in the mechanism of forgetting *nomina propria* was elicited by the forgetting the name of the poet Julius Mosen,[95] the author of a poem on the sacrifice of a hero and, as stressed by several scholars, this slip seems to be related both to Julius and to Moses (McGrath, 1986, p. 291-294; Vermorel & Vermorel, 1993, p. 487; Shengold, 1993, p. 51-52).

Considering the multiple references to the Royal Museum of Berlin (the Etruscan tombs, the gigantomachy, the archaeological Jubilee, Signorelli and Boltraffio, the copy of the Moses of Michelangelo), my conclusion is that Freud, during his «archaeological» travel in Italy, was deeply concerned with Michelangelo's statue in San Pietro in Vincoli. It was upon his return to Vienna that Freud pointed out his brother Julius' death as the root of his feeling of guilt. This insight is commonly considered as foregoing the later obsession with the Moses of Michelangelo, i.e. the grave of the pope Julius II. But if we assume that this monument played a crucial role in the paralysis in front of Rome,[96] then we should reverse this chronological relation and consider the shift from the grave of Julius II to the emerging memory of Julius' death as an essential pattern of Freud's self-analytical insight.[97] Since the Moses of Michelangelo acquired its private, intense and ambivalent meaning in the context of Freud's paediatric training in Berlin and Baginsky's teaching on sexual aetiology, it can also be seen as a medium of Freud's reversal from the outer to the inner reality and from the status of a children's doctor to the one of a child. In fact, the same day when he wrote to Fliess about Julius, he had the dream in which he was bathed by his catholic nurse in water red of blood, which was associated to the «cross» (the symbol of Jesus Christ's passion), «bad treatment» and «sexual aetiology».[98] (In later years Freud would constantly refer to Jesus Christ as to the «circumcised and crucified»).

This reversal, and its echoing the legend of the birth of the titans from the bleeding of an emasculation, brings us to the conclusion of this survey on the relevance of Freud's paediatric training. As commonly assumed, this reversal was rendered possible by Freud's closing his eyes to outer reality and shifting to inner reality, symbolized by the «blindness» (of Oedipus, Faust, and other tragic heroes). Yet, blindness was constantly associated by Freud to surgical operations, and in such a way that many scholars have perceived in it a «symbol» of castration. In my opinion, we should further question the status of «symbols» in Freud's work. By reading Freud from the premises sketched in this paper, one becomes more and more convinced that Freud's style of writing is highly allegoric, thus perpetuating in various disguised forms the memory of a unique past, and unknown event – which became the secret model in Freud's understanding of the original sin.

11. Concluding remarks

In 1926, Freud had steadily defended lay analysis, and in the postscript, in which he related his early failure as «physician» to his weak sadistic inborn disposition, he stated that he continued to be suspicious towards physicians (Freud, 1926e, p. 253). He was right. The medical practice of castration, rather than having waned, was precisely then about to reach its apex. With the decline of the classical genital seat of hysteria, its medical justification was replaced by the stronger ideals of negative eugenetics. The term «eugenetic» was introduced by Francis Galton,[99] who also had an important role in Freud's self-analysis.[100] According to Galton, eugenics would breed out the vestigial barbarism of the human race, and manipulate evolution to bring the biological reality of man into consonance with its advanced moral ideals; man should have mastered the natural process, because «what Nature does blindly, slowly and ruthlessly, man may do providently, quickly, and kindly» (Kevles, 1895, p. 12). From the end of the century, castration became subordinated to the ideal of a new race without vices and imperfections, and began to be replaced by «sterilization». Laws on sterilization began to be introduced from 1907 onwards, and in thirty years (1909-1939) more than 30,000 people in the USA were officially sterilized. In Europe, after 1903, several congresses on both castration and sterilization took place. In Germany – where doctor Ploetz, the father of German eugenetics, had advanced his ideas already in 1895 in his book *The Virtue of the Race and Protection of the Weak* – requests to legalize sterilization became increasingly present only after the First World War. The law (GzVeN)[101] was adopted immediately after the coming to power of the national-socialist party in 1933. From 1934 to 1945, more than 350,000 people were legally sterilized: 60% were mentally handicapped people, of which half were children. In 1935 the law on sterilization was included in the programme of «annihilation of lives deprived of value of life» which would be applied in 1939-45, leading to the annihilation of 80,000 to 100,000 people (Bock, 1986; Finzen, 1984; Klee, 1983; Richardz, 1987; Rudnick, 1985). The days of the Holocaust were tragically confirming the «strange» equivalence between emasculation and death.

Attenuated forms of emasculation – as Freud had defined circumcision[102] – continued to be practiced as a cure for infantile onanism in western countries, primarily in the US. In 1952, René Spitz wrote a short study – supported by a bibliography with over 400 references and illustrated by atrocious examples of surgical operations on girls – in order to draw the attention of psychoanalytical circles which, according to the author, seemed to «ignore» the crude reality of the medical treatment of onanism (Spitz, 1952). This «ignoring» also raises a problem. For the first time in 1932 Freud openly spoke about surgical operation as a medical treatment of infantile masturbation, remarking that it was not at all rare in American society, and that some of his American patients had undergone it during childhood (Freud, 1933a, p. 86-87). The problem is that Freud's American patients were mainly future analysts, so, how could they have «ignored»?

This «ignoring» was the main problem with which Freud was both personally and theoretically involved. With the help of archaeology and Greek mythology, what was gradually erected in something that could be considered a stately monument in memory of the horrors of castration. In 1936, he wanted to engrave on the frontispiece of this monument the sentence «what I see is not real». Yet this memorial did not include feminine castration, in spite of its having certainly had a major role in the medical experiences of the young Freud. Finally, it is precisely this taboo which appears to be closely linked to the unaccomplished mourning which crossed both his life and his work – although, in a broader perspective, it is also possible to judge this taboo as an essential root of the unconscious dissemination of psychoanalysis in the XXth Century.

Notes

[1]   For their valuable help in the historical and bibliographical research, I would like to thank Dr. Marco Bacciagaluppi (Mailand), Cornelia Becker (Karl-Sudhoff-Institut Library, Leipzig), Anna Bellarmi (Berlin), Prof. Gerhard Fichtner (Tübingen), Dr. Albrecht Hirschmüller (Tübingen), Maren Ipsen (E.U.I. Library, Florence), Dr. Manfred Stürzbecker (Berlin), Wulf Vogel (Humboldt University Library, Berlin). My very special thanks go to Prof. Michele Ranchetti (Florence), whose general support and comments have been very precious. This paper is based on a book in preparation: *You are requested to close the eyes. A history of the origins of psychoanalysis.*

[2]   Jones, 1953, I, p. 212. As Gicklhorn & Gicklhorn (1960 p. 11-15) have stressed, this Institute ("I. öffentliches Kinder-Kranken-Ordinations-Institut, Wien, I., Steindlgasse 2; and Wien, I., Tuchlauben 8) never obtained the juridical status of «Institute» and consisted of a small number of rooms, originally property of the Kassowitz family.

[3]   In this paper the works of Freud are quoted from the Standard Edition, but confronted with the German edition whenever required.

[4]   A day after Oskar Rie's death, on 18 August 1931, Freud wrote to Marie Bonaparte that his friend had died the day before, and that 45 years earlier, when he had just married (in 1886) and had announced among his medical activities the treatment of infantile nervous diseases, Rie had attended his office, initially as a graduate student and later as his assistant, and had afterwards become the doctor of Freud's children (reported in Schur, 1972, p. 377; see also Mühlleitner, 1992, p. 271). As can be seen from the documents found by Gicklhorn & Gicklhorn (1960), the request to hold lessons at the Institute for sick Children was presented to the Council of Professors on 28 October 1886 by Dr. Richard Wittelshöfer (Lecturer in Surgery), Dr. Eduard Schiff (Lecturer in Dermatology and Syphilis), and Dr. Sigmund Freud (Lecturer in Nervous Diseases), receiving a negative answer on 3 March 1887. Nevertheless, Freud held courses on nervous illness of children during the summer semesters of 1887 and 1888 at the Institute for Children's Diseases, and in 1892 and 1893 in a place not indicated in the announcement. Oskar Rie collaborated with Freud in two studies on brain palsy in children (Freud & Rie, 1891, 1893).

[5]   This important detail is absent in the presentation of the dream, although in another chapter Freud added: «In the further course of the dream the figure of Irma acquired still other meanings, without any alteration occurring in the visual picture of her in the dream. She turned into one of the children whom we had examined in the neurological

81

department of the children hospital» (Freud, 1900a, p. 292). It is not clear whether this comment refers to the known text of Irma's dream, or if it signals a further unreported part of the dream.

6   The principal strategy in this sense, applied by Freud in his *Autobiographical Study* (1925d) and adopted also by Jones (1953), consists of presenting Freud's work on children's nervous disturbances as essentially limited to brain palsy, ignoring that it was precisely in those years that children's hysteria had not only registered a marked diffusion in clinical practice, but had moreover become, during the 1880s, the central issue in the general aetiopathogenic debate on hysteria and the main argument for the loss of the traditional «seat» of hysteria. On this issue see Kloë & Kindt (1981), who stress the central role of infantile hysteria in the transition from somatogenesis to psychogenesis by Charcot.

7   Freud, 1914, p. 18. It is to be noted that a few lines below, Freud ironically added that «the nature of the discovery was such that one should really be ashamed of having had to make it».

8   See the letter of Freud to Martha Bernays of February 10, 1886 (Freud, 1960a), according to which Kassowitz had probably advised Freud to go to Breslau. It was only after a «liberating» letter from Kassowitz that Freud decided to go to Berlin. The final decision was not taken before 10 February 1886.

9   At that time the term «Poliklinik» implied an enlarged private medical practice, in which a specialist treated his patients free of charge, while they in turn were available for didactic objectives of the specialist, who gave lessons to doctors and students in medicine. Freud used to go to the policlinic every afternoon, while he dedicated his mornings to translating Charcot's lectures from French to German. See his letter to Martha Bernays of 10 March 1886 (Freud, 1960a).

10   Adolf Baginsky was born on 22.5.1843 in Ratibor, he had studied medicine in Berlin with Virchow and Traube, and in Vienna for one year. He obtained his degree in Berlin, in 1866, and was appointed *«Privatdocent fur Kinderheilkunde»* on 7.12.1882, and *«Professor Extraordinarius»* on 3.12.1892 (*Gesamtverzeichnis des Lehrkörpers der Universität Berlin*; see also Pagel, 1901, p. 78). On the occasion of receiving the title of «Privatdocent», Baginsky held the lecture *«Das Verhältnis der Kinderheilkunde zur gesamten Medicin»*. The administrative documents of the present Humboldt University also reveal that he was nominated member of the union of professors for the vacation course (*«Feriencurse»*) – enabling him to use the title of «Professor» (in his 1886 *Report on my studies in Paris and Berlin*, Freud had in fact mentioned him as «Professor»). The register of lessons of the Friedrich-Wilhelm-Universität reveals that Adolf Baginsky – during the winter semester from 16 October 1885 to 15 March 1886 – held two courses (in his policlinic – see the next note): the first, with a change, on the pathology and therapy of infantile illness with demonstrations (Mondays, Wednesdays, Fridays, from 1-2 p.m.) and the second, free of charge, on the dangers to which students of scholastic institutions were exposed to (Saturdays, from 6-7 p.m.). These were also the lessons that Freud had presumably assisted for two weeks. In the letter to Martha Bernays of 19 March 1886, Freud wrote that he was sorry not to be able to remain for the vacation courses which were to start on 22 March (the summer semester started on April 28). The personal documents of Adolf Baginsky, found at the Humboldt University in Berlin, also reveal that his application for the nomination of *«Professor Ordinarius»* was rejected by the Ministry on 29 January 1897, on the basis of the report of the commission of the Faculty of Medicine (15.1.1897), which considered that a division of the chair in *Kinderheilkunde*, already assigned to Heubner in 1894, was useless.

[11] See *Krankenhaus-Lexikon* (Guttstadt, 1900, p. 62-63). The *Kaiser und Kaiserin Friedrich-Krankenhaus* (Reinickendorferstr. 32) was set up on the initiative of a Berlin Committee presided by Rudolf Virchow. Adolf Baginsky was appointed director and the doctor responsible for the department of internal and infective medicine, while Prof. Gluck was responsible for the surgery department. The fact that the *k. k. Friedrich-Kinderkrankenhaus* (presently the University Paediatric Clinic *Rudolf Virchow*) was founded in 1890 was well known, and is also reported in Pagel's *Biographisches Lexikon* (1901, p. 77-78; see also Werner, 1990). This erroneous indication, which has been preserved for such a long time, shows that nobody has so far dealt with this problem. In 1886, Adolf Baginsky had a private policlinic which was opened in 1872 (Pagel, 1901). According to the 1889 address book of Berlin, it was called «*Poliklinik für kranke Kinder*», was located in *Johannisstr. 3 Hochparterre*, and presumably consisted of a small number of rooms, given that half of the «Hochparterre» was occupied by a book store. Baginsky received patients on Mondays, Wednesdays, Fridays and Saturdays, from 12-1 p.m. (while from 1-2 p.m. he held lessons – see previous note).

[12] Rohlender, 1899, p. 52. Baginsky is quoted in reference to the spreading of onanism in schools, together with other authors, such as Fürbringer, Bensemann, Fournier and Moll. However, in his writings Baginsky quotes quite often Peter Frank, as he was deeply influenced by the idea of a «medical police», considering it closely linked to Mosaic hygienic rules (Baginsky, 1895).

[13] The handbook was republished in longer versions in 1883 (2^e edition) and in 1898-1900 (3^e edition, in 2 volumes).

[14] See the Chapter «Onanie» in Baginsky, 1877 (1883, 1898-1900).

[15] Jacobi, 1875-76; Lindner, 1879. Lindner would also be one of the few authors quoted as precursors by Freud in *Three Essays on the Theory of Sexuality* (1905b).

[16] Baginsky, 1889, p. 490; 1892, p. 515; 1896, p. 570. In the first edition, lacking a differentiated discussion of the various psychic disturbances, masturbation is included among minor causes. In the later editions hysteria is discussed separately. The 1887 edition has not been found, but there are good reasons to believe that it already contained such a statement.

[17] A view on the complexity of sexual aetiology and on the moral attitude of Baginsky is offered in the following passage from one of his last lectures on children's nervousness, held in 1909. At that time he avoided discussion of this question, stating «I would rather not go into the subject of youth anomalies in the sexual sphere; perhaps in no other part of the entire field [of nervous disturbances] is it so difficult to distinguish between the causes and the consequences; it is, in addition, difficult to single out, in these cases, whether it is a real pathological process, a bad habit, a conscious error, a consequence of seduction, or a bad imitation. As far as I can see, my position, contrary to the question of sexual education during youth, which today is so forcefully debated, on the one hand, is not accepted by physicians and pedagogues, and on the other hand, is judged with sympathy. Today's times, in short, are pushing towards a solution of the problem which is less reserved than the one I had recommended. We have to wait and see the consequences of free education, once it will be introduced, for the nervous system of youth. I do not expect anything good.» (Baginsky, 1909, p. 13; my translation). It has to be noted that two years before, Freud published the essay *The Sexual Enlightenment of Children* (Freud, 1907c).

[18] Some clues, which led to the belief that Freud tried from the very beginning to forget his paediatric experience in Berlin, should also be stressed. In the *Report on my Studies in*

Paris and Berlin, written immediately upon his return to Vienna, he mentions Adolf Baginsky among various other professors (Mendel, Eulenburg, Munk, Zuntz, Benno Baginsky) and doctors (Thomsen and Oppenheim) visited in Berlin, in such a way that it does not at all follow that he went to Berlin solely in order to receive his paediatric training from Adolf Baginsky. Moreover, in the letter to his friend Karl Koller of 13 October 1886 (in Freud, 1960a), he wrote that he had used his 4-week stay in Berlin exclusively for translating Charcot's new lessons (!).

[19] See: Spitz, 1952, Kern, 1973, Stengers & Van Neck, 1984. Sulloway (1979) has developed the question of the pre-Freudian discovery of infantile sexuality in the doctrinal framework of the descent theory, yet totally ignoring the crucial question of infantile hysteria. Sulloway (1979, p. 122, p. 212) has, in any case, drawn attention to the paradox of Freud's initial denial of spontaneous infantile sexuality. I believe this paradox can be explained through Freud's aversion towards the genital localization and its therapeutical implications. For a view on the link between infantile sexuality and hysteria theory among German paediatricians, see Carter, 1983.

[20] In reality, the seduction theory of 1896 (Freud, 1896a, 1896b, 1896c) is still based on a negation of infantile sexuality, given that it states that «irritations» of infantile genitals (caused by aggression and seduction) do not have any immediate effect because of the small size and the immaturity of genital organs; it is precisely this negation which permits the postulation of the posterior psychic effect of the trauma thanks to the later change brought about by maturation of genital organs. Nevertheless, it is in this context that Freud speaks, for the first time, of «active masturbation» in infancy, excluding it from the «list of the sexual noxae in early childhood which are pathogenic for hysteria», adding that the reason why masturbation is so frequently found together with hysteria is not its pathogenic action, but the fact that masturbation is frequently the consequence of an aggression or seduction (1896b, p. 165). Therefore, the pathogenic model of Freud's seduction theory represents a reversal of what he had learned in 1886 from Baginsky, although if the idea that seduction represented one of the main causes of masturbation and hysteria in children was a common ground in paediatric circles – as was stressed also by Freud in the 1896 lecture on *The Aetiology of Hysteria* – and it was shared by Baginsky too. In cases of «Verführung» (seduction) the common treatment was «isolation», according to the tradition of «moral treatment» and to the principle of «*indicatio causalis*»; nevertheless, by examining the literature of those times, one gets the idea that isolation and surgical operations (the two main «aetiological treatments») were not mutually exclusive, but could easily coexist or even be complementary (like predisposing and determining causes being complementary). Operations could be replaced by severe threats and psychic shocks, including the use of the traditional «*Ferrum candens*», which is quoted until the end of the century as a model of «psychic treatment». This background, in my opinion, makes the policy of Freud's seduction theory of 1896 more understandable.

[21] Freud, 1886. Freud wrote, among other things, that the hysterical state was «under the *odium* widespread prejudices. Among these are the supposed dependence of hysterical illness upon genital irritation...» (p. 11). Freud had borrowed from Charcot the thesis on the identity between hysteria and demoniac possession, nevertheless, he supported it with different emphasis and contents. For Charcot, it was part of the politics against genital localization, given that he stressed its «psychic» character (see primarily Charcot & Richer, 1887).

[22] This change begins at the end of 1892. In the study *A Reply to Criticism of my Paper on Anxiety Neurosis*, 1895, he wrote: «My observations had shown me that in the aetiology of the neuroses (at all events of *acquired* cases and *acquirable forms*) sexual factors play a pre-

84

dominant part and one which has been given far too little weight; so that a statement such as that 'the aetiology of the neuroses lies in sexuality', with all its unavoidable incorrectness *per excessum et defectum*, nevertheless comes nearer to the truth than do the other doctrines, which hold the field at the present time.» (p. 123). In addition: «I know very well that in putting forward my 'sexual aetiology' of the neuroses, I have brought up nothing new, and that undercurrents in medical literature taking these facts into account have never been absent. I know, too, that official academic medicine has also been aware of them, but it has acted as if it knew nothing about the matter. It has made no use of its knowledge and has drawn no inferences from it. Such behavior must have a deep-seated cause, originating perhaps in a kind of reluctance to look squarely at sexual matters, or in a reaction against older attempts at an explanation, which are regarded as obsolete.» (p. 124).

23 «...the expectation of a sexual neurosis being the basis of hysteria was fairly remote from my mind. I had come fresh from the school of Charcot, and I regarded the linking of hysteria with the topic of sexuality as a sort of insult» (Breuer & Freud, 1893-95, p. 259-60).

24 «The two investigators as whose pupil I began my studies of hysteria, Charcot and Breuer, were far from having any such presupposition; in fact they had a personal disinclination to it which I originally shared.» (Freud, 1896c, p. 199). The German expression translated into «a personal disinclination» is «*eine persönliche Abneigung entgegen*», which is not only much stronger but also has a reactive meaning, as «a personal aversion».

25 Breuer, after having been approached by the husband of one of his patients, had confided to Freud that, what was in question after all was always «privacies of the bed-chamber». Charcot, during a lively private conversation with Brouardel, had exclaimed that what was always in question was «la chose génitale, toujours... toujours... toujours». Finally, the gynecologist Chrobak had confided to him the only valid, but unprescribable, recipe: «Penis normalis – dosim – repetatur!» (1914, p. 13-15). What should be noted is the evident contradiction with his statements in 1895 and 1896, in which he recalls that he had initially opposed sexual aetiology as did his teachers Charcot and Breuer. Finally, in Kroemer's study on castration of 1896, Chrobak, who is quoted as a gynaecologist who preferred conservative cure methods (instead of castration) and recommended especially massages, is also quoted for having «operated» (castrated) 146 women – with success in more then half of the cases (Kroemer, 1896, p. 53).

26 Freud, 1925d, p. 24. It is to be noted that Freud here again tries to render credible his initial ignorance of the genital seat. For example, «What I heard from them lay dormant and inactive within me, until the chance of my cathartic experiments brought it out as an apparently original discovery. Nor was I then aware that in deriving hysteria from sexuality I was going back to the very beginnings of medicine and following up a thought of Plato's. I was not until later I learnt this from an essay by Havelock Ellis.» (*ibid.*). Here he clearly alludes to the Greek etymology of «hysteria», which takes us back to the question of genital localization.

27 The original titles quoted in Merkel's bibliographical references (1887, p. 55-56) are the following: E. Böhmi, «Castration bei Hysteroepilepsie», *Centralbl. f. Gyn.*, 22, 1886; Forel, «Heilung der Hysterie durch Castration», *Centralblatt fur Schw. Arzte*, 17, 1886; Heilbrunn, «Heilung moralischen Irreseins durch Castration», *Annales med. psycholog.* 1886; Irrenfreund, 1885, No. 11, 12, Ref.: *C. f. Gyn.* No. 40; Rudenhausen, Die Castration der Frauen bei nervösen Leiden, Diss. 1886; Schröder, «Über Castration bei Neurosen», *Naturforscherversamml.* 1886; L. Tissier, «De la castration de la femme en chirurgie» (opération d'Hegar ou de Battey), Thèse de Paris 1885, *Progrès méd.*, 8, 1886; I. Widmer, «Hysterie durch Castration geheilt», *C. f. Schweizer Ärzte*, 911, 1886, Ref.: *C. f. Gyn.* N^r. 40, 1886.

[28] In gynaecology, however, the term castration refers to both sexes.

[29] In the US, the operation was first undertaken by Battey, independently from Hegar, only three weeks later, and consequently in the American literature female castration for neuro-psychiatric reasons was called «Battey's operation» (Kroemer, 1896).

[30] Kroemer, 1896, p. 4. This study, entitled *Beitrag zur Castrationsfrage* (Contribution to the problem of castration), begins with the statement that this problem had been in the center of psychiatric controversies for over twenty years, and proceeds to examine 240 studies on castration which had appeared in the literature in those years.

[31] Spitz, 1952. On surgical operations as treatment of masturbation in children see also J. Duffy (1963), Stengers & Van Neck (1984). There are no specific historical studies on this topic, and many of the arguments advanced in the publications of those times sound rather contradictory. More details on the framework of these problems and on their evolution in paediatrics can be found in the following studies: Behrend (1860), Jacobi (1875-76), Fleischmann (1878), Schmidt (1880), Henoch (1881), Herz (1885), Jolly (1892). Although these articles also contain criticism of gynaecological practice, the one by Jolly is the first one in which it is clearly stated that «hysteria does not come from the uterus» (see note 36), and that the gynaecological treatment is, with few exceptions, inadequate. Jolly's study was influenced by Charcot's conception of infantile hysteria as illness *«par imagination»*. Jolly was in the academic commission which, in 1897, rejected Adolf Baginsky's application for «Professor Ordinarius» (see note 10).

[32] Liebermeister (1883, p. 2149), who had already adopted an enlightened and «modern» approach, after his statement that castration, extirpation of the clitoris and similar operations are to be rejected if their basis is not a local illness, says that the psychic effects that are to be obtained through such operations can also be obtained by less energetic means. As examples of «insignificant operations» which can be used for obtaining psychic effects, also in the absence of local illness, he mentions the cauterization of the clitoris, extraction of blood from the vagina, and so forth.

[33] This article is one of the main historical sources of the present study. In a footnote to the title it is written: «Der medicinischen Facultät in Leipzig als Doctor-Dissertation überreicht.» (submitted to the Leipzig Faculty of Medicine as a Doctoral thesis). Nevertheless, the thesis has not been found among dissertations either at the University of Leipzig, nor at any other German university. The study was also published as a monograph in 1884 and with the same title in Stuttgart, by the publisher Gebr. Kröner (Schäfer, 1884b), which is quoted also in the Library of Congress Catalogue.

[34] Schäfer's article contains a number of other therapeutical measures, including psychical (such as threats and moral exhortation), social (isolation from the family), pharmacological and hygienic, according to ideas common in those times. Nevertheless, in comparison with contemporary studies, he insists much more on the sexual causes, both predisposing and determinant. The quoted passage touches precisely those causes because of which the «operation» was considered an aetiological therapy.

[35] Herz, 1885. Maximilian Herz was teaching paediatrics at the University in Vienna.

[36] «But, my dear sir, how can you talk such nonsense! *Hysteron (sic)* means the uterus. So how can a man be hysterical?» (Freud, 1925d, p. 15). Bernfeld and Cassirer Bernfeld (1952, p. 147), who were the first to inquire on this episode, considered that Freud's presentation on male hysteria was not very diplomatic, as he had adopted a totally independent approach and lacked the usual modesty of the young. For similar views, see Jones (1953, I, p. 252-55). See also Ellenberger (1970) and Hirschmüller (1991). For information about what the quotation of the Greek etymology of hysteria really meant in those

86

time, see Liebermeister, 1883 (p. 2148-2149), who concludes the etymological discussion by stating that «Castration, extirpation of the clitoris and similar operations are definitely to be rejected, when they are not required by a local illness».

[37] According to Sulloway (1979, p. 39), whereas this story seems very effective, as it apparently describes Freud's first experience of hostile and irrational reception, which would characterize a life dedicated to psychoanalytical innovations, it is for its largest part a myth. Not only has it given origin to considerable misunderstandings and oversimplifications in the history of psychoanalysis, but it has also become a prototype for similar legends on Freud's life.

[38] «A Boy of Fourteen Accompanied by His Parents and His Doctor» (Charcot, 1892). Charcot's pupil, Paul Bezy, later wrote that 21 February, in the clinical study of infantile hysteria, was an historic day because, during this lesson, it was for the first time declared that it is necessary to accept this disturbance for what it represents, i.e. as a psychic disease «par excellence» (see Kloë & Kindt, 1981, p. 296). This lesson was referred to in Leçons du mardi, translated by Freud under the title Poliklinische Vorträge. Charcot, who during this lesson had stated that hysteria is for 3/4 psychic and that it is necessary to learn to treat it psychically, covertly mentions the treatment of infantile hysteria (the operation) of his teachers in terms of a «harsh punishment» (Charcot, 1892, p. 135). Freud translated the lesson and published it at the beginning of 1892, deriving from it the theory on «hysterical counter-will» (ibid, p. 156, footnote; and Freud, 1892), from which the fundamental innovations of the following few months and years derive.

[39] In Charcot's 1893 Necrology, Freud exalted «the series of uninterrupted deductions» which had led Charcot (1890) to conceive the hysterical-traumatic paralysis as psychically determined. This «series of uninterrupted deductions» dates back to 1885. Its premises are be found in lesson 6 on hysteria of young boys, and it is developed in a series of lessons dedicated to male hysteria (particularly lessons 19, 20, 21, 22), in which the concept of «traumatic suggestion» is coined. Charcot's implicit starting point was the idea, common in the medical circles of those times, that hysterical paralysis, above all those of the lower limbs, were caused physiologically by an irritated state of the «genital nerve». His argument consists of three main phases: first, the dislocation of the seat of «exquisite sensibility» from the genitals to other equivalent parts of the body (hysterogenic zones); second, the artificial reproduction by verbal suggestion in a hypnotized patient of the same paralysis which in another patient had been provoked by a physical trauma; and third, the reproduction of the same paralysis through energetic pressure on a sensitive zone. With this it was demonstrated that the effect of a «trauma» depended on a lasting «autosuggestion». The conclusion was that these paralyses were psychically determined, and therefore had to be treated psychically. Charcot was also contrary to «simulated operations». His whole endeavor acquires an extraordinary coherence precisely if viewed as a policy against castration. We can also suppose that also the famous ovary truss corresponded to the research of an alternative to mutilating operations.

[40] Hirschmüller (1987) found two extremely significant letters of Breuer to Robert Binswanger, the Kreuzlingen clinic's director, written on 12.3.94 and 23.3.94, in which he tried in a very sensitive way to avoid Nina's castration. He describes, among other things, Gersuny's negative experiences and one of his personal cases, a patient who was operated despite his contrary opinion, and was soon after seriously wasted away because of inaction, vomiting and the disappearance of all hysterical symptoms. Respect to Nina R., he considered that the neurasthenic component was dominant over the hysterical one, and this increased the reservations on the success of castration; he stressed that there were no other symptoms but leucorrhea, and that therefore a curettage or, ultimately, a

«discisio colli uteri» (dissection of the cervix) was sufficient, and that it would have been a gynecological scandal to cure a leucorrhea with the extirpation of the uterus and the ovaries. He concludes the letter to Robert Binswanger by writing «excuse me for my reactionary ideas». However, Breuer also wrote that he would leave the question to Hegar's judgement, who was precisely the doctor who had introduced, from 1872 onwards, the «operation». In reference to Nina's case, Hegar wrote to Kreuzlingen on 4.9.1894: «I am inclined to admit the patient, also when the prospect of a healing only by the treatment of the genital disturbance is not to be expected. Yet, this appears to be so important, that it will be difficult to reach the goal without its elimination or at least its partial relief through the other means.» (Unpublished document, my translation). Before going to Kreuzlingen, on 20.6.93, Nina was examined by the gynecologist of Vienna Carl Fleischmann, who made a curettage ten days later. Freud knew Carl Fleischmann well, since he assisted – or was required as a witness – the birth of his children Ernst (6.4.1892), Sophie (14.4.1893) and Anna (3.12.1895) (Israelitische Kultusgemeinde Wien, Geburtenbuch Erster Bezirk). (I thank Albrecht Hirschmüller for this information and for the unpublished documents). It is also relevant that, one year later, on July 1895 – and few weeks before Freud's dream on Irma – the younger brother of Nina R., who had a lighter hysteric neurosis, was sent by Breuer to Berlin, in order to be operated on the nose by Fliess (Hirschmüller, 1986, p. 243, p. 251).

[41] Freud, 1896c, p. 191-193. In this lecture, Freud also refers to the syphilologist model (i.e. the genitals examination), as he had already done in the study *A Reply to Criticism of my Paper on Anxiety Neurosis* (1895, p. 129), where he had emphasized the «aetiological» superiority of the method. In the new interpretation of Freud's work suggested in the present study, the various analogies with gynecologists, syphilologists and surgeons are all placed into the same matrix of the genital localization of hysteria. In addition, the functional meaning of the «archaeological metaphor», which in the last few years has constantly been criticized as a simple prejudice of the end of the last century, ought to be recognized precisely on the basis of the change concerning the direct «observation» of genitals. This approach introduces a sort of «vision» which does not use senses (touch and sight).

[42] The reactive quality of the modern ideas of the 1890s, which banished sexuality to a secondary position, was also stressed by Freud, who spoke of «a reaction against older attempts at an explanation, which are regarded as obsolete» (Freud, 1895, p. 124). Breuer would also stress this reactive character arguing that: «The unsophisticated observations of our predecessors, the residue of which is preserved in the term "hysteria", came nearer the truth than the more recent view which puts sexuality almost last, in order to save the patients from moral reproaches.» (Breuer and Freud, 1893-95, p. 247). These comments, of a «political» character, can nevertheless in some way be misleading, since the practice of «operations» (castration, dissection of the uterus, clitoridectomia, circumcision, etc.) was in fact, at that time, rapidly expanding.

[43] In the 1888 article *Hysteria* (1888b) he stated that the treatment of single hysterical symptoms did not offer a prospect of success, but that symptoms could be cured in the case of localization of the neurosis (p. 55). After having presented the hypnotic suggestion, he also described the «Breuer method» as «the method most appropriate to hysteria, because it precisely imitates the mechanism of the origin and passing of these hysterical disorders» (p. 56). This means that Freud conceived the Breuer method much closer to aetiological concerns than hypnotic suggestion.

[44] «I have often in my own mind compared cathartic psychotherapy with surgical intervention. I have described my treatments as psychotherapeutic operations...» (Breuer & Freud, 1893-95, p. 305.)

88

[45] Freud, 1905a, p. 432. This well-known comparison with the ways of creating a sculpture or a painting, defined by Leonardo *«per via di levare»* and *«per via di porre»*, may also be derived from the matrix of surgical operations.

[46] Minutes C/1 of Freud to Fliess, from the spring of 1893 (Freud, 1986). It is in this period that the possibility of surgical therapy was also included (see Michael Schröter's note 13 to the Minutes C/2).

[47] Freud, 1888, p. 56. Among the irritating somatic causes which must be removed, he included the «swelling of the turbinal». It is also relevant that, while discussing the «hysterogenic zones» at the beginning of the same essay (p. 43), he refers in an almost literary sense to a part of Charcot's lesson *On the Hysteria of Young Boys*, but omits significantly the «prepuce» – whose sensibility had been defined by Charcot as «exquisite» (Charcot, 1890, p. 88) – and adds among sensitive zones the «mucous membranes» and «sense-organs» (Freud, 1888, p. 43).

[48] See Masson, 1984, p. 74. The preface of the book is dated November 1892; in it Fliess reveals that the idea to write a book on reflex nasal neurosis was suggested to him by a «friend», who can certainly be identified as Freud (see also Freud, 1986).

[49] On the «messianic value», see Freud's letter to Fliess of 10 July 1893 (Freud, 1986). That Freud's enthusiasm for Fliess as «healer» referred also to the question of aetiological therapy, can be deducted from the therapeutical pessimism expressed by Freud in Conclusions of Minutes C/1, in which the nasal localization is contrasted with the urogenital one; and from comments of Minutes C/2 to the paper which Fliess presented under the title *«Die nasale Reflexneurosis»* at the 12th Congress of Internal Medicine, Wiesbaden, 12-15 April 1893. Fliess had accepted various of Freud's suggestions, among which the justifications for surgical therapy (see Freud, 1986, Minutes C/2, note 13 by Michael Schröter).

[50] See Minutes 0, of autumn 1894, comment to the preliminary version of Fliess' essay *«Magenschmerz und Dysmenorrhoe in neuem Zusammenhang»*, 1895; in particular, Freud's comment on p. 8 on Fliess' paper and note 8 by Michael Schröter (Freud, 1986). It is worth noting that as causal treatment of dysmenorrhea the dissection of the cervix was also recommended (Landesmann, 1890, p. 282).

[51] In the book *Über den ursachlichen Zusammenhang von Nase und Geschlechtsorgan* (On the causal link between the nose and the sexual organ), published in 1902, Fliess wrote that women who masturbated were generally dysmenorrheic and that they could definitely be cured by an operation of the nose if they really gave up this bad habit (Masson, 1984, p. 60). Masson has indicated that this passage is marked in Freud's copy of the book. See also Hirschmüller, 1986, p. 244-46.

[52] See letter to Fliess of 11 April 1895 (Freud, 1986).

[53] Freud, 1900, p. XIX of the Italian edition (Opere, vol. III, Boringhieri).

[54] Freud, 1900, p. 453. Freud would again quote these lines in his 1930 speech for the assignment of the Goethe Prize, applying them to Goethe, but also revealing even more clearly his identification with the poet, defining him as «a great self-revealer, but also... a careful concealer» (Freud, 1930b, p. 212; see also Cremerius, 1971).

[55] In Freud's texts, the analogy between surgical operations and the analytical treatment appears in: Breuer and Freud, 1893-95, p. 305; Freud, 1910a, p. 52; Freud, 1910b, p. 146.; 1912, p. 115. The analogy would again appear in Freud, 1916-17, p. 459.

[56] These two aspects of ambivalence and taboo have been further explored in Bonomi, 1993.

[57] Mathilde S., one of Freud's first patients, was hospitalized in doctor Svetlin's clinic because of a psychotic crisis with erotic contents, and was dismissed in May 1890. Freud continued to treat her with Sulfonal until the first signs of intoxication appeared, but she nevertheless died a few weeks later, on 24 September 1890, at the age of 27. Only after her death did the first signals of alarm concerning the dangers of Sulfonal begin to appear (Hirschmüller, 1989).

[58] Mathilde's diphtheria was mentioned in Freud's letter to Fliess of 7 March 1897. In the letter to Fliess of 9 November 1899, Freud wrote that his daughter had had diphtheria twice. Nevertheless, it should also be considered that Freud started writing *The Interpretation of Dreams* after having undertaken systematic self-analysis, at the beginning of 1898, and therefore it is very plausible that Mathilde's diphtheria, referred to in the associations to the dream, is precisely the one from the beginning of 1897.

[59] Hirschmüller, 1989. Until 1895, a diphtheritic septicemia almost always led to a fatal outcome, and it is only with the introduction of Behring's serotherapy that mortality had been reduced by 50%. Hirschmüller has wondered whether Freud had not wanted to become the «Behring of neurosis». This hypothesis is, however, contradicted by the fact that Freud's daughter Mathilde did not undergo serotherapy, because of the contrary opinion of both Oscar Rie and Kassowitz (see Freud's letter to Fliess of 7 March 1897).

[60] Letter to Fliess of 26 April 1895. These associations are relevant not only for Irma's dream, but also for the dream *«non vixit»*, in which Freud identified himself no longer with Antonio but with the tragic and ambivalent figure of Brutus who, although declaring his love for Julius Caesar, claims the right to having murdered the tyrant (Freud, 1900, p. 424). In my opinion this shift marks the main transformations of the self-accusations which characterize Irma's dream.

[61] A further link is given by the review of a study on diphtheria, which Freud wrote only a year after his paediatric training (Freud, 1887).

[62] Baginsky alludes to it in an early book (1874, p. 14).

[63] The gynaecological use of cocaine is especially documented in the 1887 study of William Hammond, in which a case of woman's irritation/masturbation is also reported, healed with a 20% cocaine solution, recommended also in case of male masturbation (Hammond, 1887, p.226). As well known, cocaine will later be used by Fliess and Freud in the context of nasal reflex neurosis, for cauterization of the «genital spots» of the nose. In Freud's dreams «*The Botanical Monograph*» and «*Count Thun*» (Freud, 1900), the introduction in 1884-1885 of cocaine in eye operations is presented as closely associated to sexual aetiology, treatment of hysteria and castration. The case history of an hysteric young woman reported in Kroemer's study *Beitrag zur Castrationsfrage* (1896, p. 71-74) is also worth of mention. Hospitalized at the Nietlebener Institute in 1880, the genital pains of the woman were treated with injections of morphine. She soon became addicted, and, in 1882, she was bilaterally castrated; in 1883 she was again sick and cured with morphine; in 1884-85, morphine was substituted with cocaine in order to cure the addiction.

[64] More precisely, in the «*Altes Museum*», as reported in the 1885 and 1886 guides to the Royal Museums in Berlin (Königliche Museen zu Berlin, 1885, 1886). For historical information about the excavation campaign of Pergamon, the Royal Museums and the Pergamon Museum, see Kunze, 1986, 1987, 1991; Petras, 1991.

[65] Letter of 10 March 1886 (Freud, 1960). In the letter, Freud did not explicitly refer to hysterical children. However, we can assume that he was thinking about hysterical children because: a) the reference to the «free brain» excludes idiotism; b) Freud went to Berlin to study nervous and psychic disturbances in children; c) after Charcot's teaching, he was very interested in hysteria.

66 Freud had expressed himself in this way in order to explain to the «Rat man» the archaeological metaphor, illustrating it with the collection of antique objects in his room, for which «burial had been their preservation» (Freud, 1909b, p. 176).

67 S. Cassirer Bernfeld (1951), in the first historical study dedicated to Freud's interest for archaeology, indicated that the discoveries of Heinrich Schliemann were the first to provoke his enthusiasm, and this interpretation has not been questioned since then.

68 See Freud's letter to Fliess of 28 May 1899 (Freud, 1985).

69 In the «metapsychological» chapter of *The Interpretation of Dreams* Freud compared the unconscious wishes to the defeated titans who are still trembling under the rocks (Freud, 1900, p. 553); in the crucial part of *Totem and Taboo*, he recalled the tumultuous scene of Titans together with the punishment by emasculation and the original sin (Freud, 1912-13, p. 153-54); later he compared the struggle between Eros and Death to a gigantomachy (Freud, 1930a, p. 122), and was deeply attracted by the sacrifice of the titan Prometheus, the «hero of civilization» (Freud, 1931).

70 This idea appeared in Freud's thoughts at the beginning of 1912 (letter of Freud to Ferenczi of 1 February 1912; Freud and Ferenczi, 1992); it was included in *Totem and Taboo* (1912-13), and became the core of the twelfth metapsychological essay, *Synthesis of transference neurosis* of 1915, recently found in a preliminary version by Ilse Grubrich-Simitis (Freud, 1985).

71 In *The Interpretation of Dreams* (1900) he quoted this myth twice: a first time presenting it as a source of historical information about the primeval ages of human society («The obscure information which is brought to us by mythology and legend from the primeval ages of human society gives an unpleasing picture of the father's despotic power and of the ruthlessness with which he made use of it. Kronos devoured his children, just as the wild boar devours the sow's litter; while Zeus emasculated his father and made himself ruler in his place.» (Freud, 1900, p. 256) and a second time when describing the analysis of a hysterical boy (Freud 1900, p. 619). But two years later, in chapter 10 of *The Psychopathology of Everyday Life* (1901), he pointed out that in *The Interpretation of Dreams* he committed a series of «historical errors», which had escaped his eye even when correcting the proofs, as if he «had been struck blind». He stated that rather than being casual, these errors were due to the unsuccessful concealment of certain thoughts he wanted to suppress. The quotation of Zeus emasculating Kronos was among these errors, since he had erroneously shifted this atrocity from a generation: according to Greek mythology it was, in fact, Kronos who committed it on his father Uranus (Freud, 1901, p. 218).

72 This topic was so conflictual that, a few pages before the psychological explanation of the Zeus-Kronos slip, Freud had once again made the same type of error of «generational exchange». Describing the treatment of a twelve-year-old hysterical boy – a scene representing the act of castration – he had written «Tarquinius Priscus» instead of «Tarquinius Superbus» (Freud, 1901, p. 198). Freud became aware of this new error only during a later revision of the text, and then he added a comment pointing out that substituting the name of the father for the name of the son referred to the topic of castration (cf. the note of Strachey, p. 198).

73 Ibidem. Freud's further psychological explanation of this displacement of a disbelief will not be discussed, but it should be stressed that the topic of «filial piety» connects it to the «error» of Zeus emasculating his father Kronos (Freud refers to «filial piety» in both explanations. See Freud, 1901, p. 220, and Freud, 1936, p. 244), and it should be added that this myth is also the only Greek myth which Freud refers to in those years, precisely

in the context of the problem of disavowing the evidences of the reality of emasculation (Freud, 1940) .

[74] A different view is suggested in Verspohl (1991).

[75] That is, the *Altes Museum*, whose ground level was at that time subdivided in: A. Rotunda; B. Heroes' hall; C. Etruscan Cabinet; D. Greek hall; E. Pergamon hall; F. Roman hall; G. Sculptures of Christian period; K. Ancient sculptures and copies. The copy of the Moses of Michelangelo is quoted in the guide to the Royal Museums of 1886 (Königliche Museen zu Berlin, 1886, p. 205), and in Bode, 1891, p. 154. In chapter 2 of *The Moses of Michelangelo* (1913), Freud quotes Ivan Lermolieff's (alias the Italian art critic Giovanni Morelli) use of details in order to recognize the copies from the originals. Giovanni Morelli had a quarrel with Wilhelm Bode, the famous director of the Royal Museums in Berlin, and he felt persecuted by him (Morelli, 1897). It is following these traces that I have discovered that Freud had already seen a "copy" of the Moses in the Berlin Museum in 1886. Moreover, in the same chapter of the essay on Moses, Freud quotes and criticizes a plaster copy of the statue of the Vienna Art Academy collection.

[76] For example, at the Vienna Society meeting of 7 February 1912 (within the cycle on onanism), Freud would state: «The sense of guilt has a special relationship to infantile sexuality, since it does not make its appearance with other trespasses for which children are just as severely threatened and punished (all sorts of mischievous tricks), but only with regard to sexual matters. The concept of adequate sexual satisfaction was introduced in the first article on the anxiety neurosis. Christianity did not derive solely from a reaction to Judaism; additional sources can be found in pagan religions which have preserved themselves in the Mysteries. The tendencies of Christianity derive from Mysteries; Judaism is merely a screen fantasy.» (Nunberg & Federn, 1975, p. 42; my modified translation). In *Totem and Taboo*, the original sin is discussed together with the Hellenistic cults and myths, the death by emasculation, the sacrifice of Jesus Christ, the Mysteries, the animated scenes of Titans, and the assassination of a young god (Freud, 1912-13, pp. 151-53).

[77] It was in fact the archaeologist Alexander Conze who had identified the groups as the famous gigantomachy on the basis of Lucio Ampelio's *Liber memoralis* (8, 14) (Kunze, 1991a).

[78] Freud connected the two phenomena in the letter to Jung of 19 April 1909 (Freud & Jung, 1970). In addition, a reference to this trip was included, in 1919, in the essay *The «Uncanny»* (Freud, 1919, p. 237-38), which focuses on the link between emasculation and death and is full of images of mutilations and beliefs in the returning of the dead.

[79] See Freud's letter to Fliess of 19 April 1894 (Freud, 1986).

[80] See Freud's letter to Fliess of 22 June 1894 (Freud, 1986).

[81] I will only mention two of the numerous comments. With respect to the emotional effects on the audience: «There can be no doubt of the tremendous effect of the death wish toward that first Julius which actually had coincided with his having been "got rid of"» (Shengold, 1979, p. 75). With respect to the traumatic implications for Freud: «Freud was thus not only stating an historical fact that his brother *Julius did not live* (i.e., survive as Freud had), but he also indicated a further repudiation of the entire constellation of events by implying the wish that Julius "did not live - ever," thus denying the very birth of his brother.» (Grinstein, 1980, p. 297; the author here is referring to the dream *«non vixit»*).

[82] See Freud's letter to Fliess of 15 October 1897 (in Freud, 1986)

[83] In a recent paper (Bonomi, 1993), I have argued that Freud's two episodes of fainting in front of Jung (in Bremen in 1909, and in Munich in 1912) can be related to the taboo of his paediatric training in March 1886. One of the links could be the fact that the thesis of the Egyptian origin of Jewish circumcision – which was diffusively claimed during the XIXth century and which also had a crucial role in Freud's *Moses and Monotheism* – was historically proven by professor Ebers, who had brought to Germany the penis of the mummy of the warrior Amen-em-heb, who lived under Thutmes III and Amenophy II (Amenhotep II) (from 1614 to 1555 B.C.), and professor Welker of Halle, who was able to prove, in 1878, the signs of circumcision on this mummified penis (Ploss, 1885, p. 320). Both of Freud's fainting were connected to «mummies», since the first was prompted by Jung's insistence on «moor corpses» (corpses that had been preserved thanks to a process of natural mummification); and the second, by a tense discussion on the systematic erasing of the forbidden name of the god «Amòn» by Amenhotep (II and IV), when introducing monotheism (Jones, 1953, II, p. 165-66; Jung, 1961, p. 198 onwards).

[84] Schur explained with it not only Freud's fainting in front of Jung, the superstition of dying at a pre-fixed date, his essays *The "Uncanny"*, *Beyond the Pleasure Principle* and *A Disturbance of Memory on the Acropolis*, but also the ambivalence with Fliess, the dream on Irma's injection and the dream «*non vixit*» (Schur, 1972; see primarily pp. 296299).

[85] Freud's attitude toward death is well reflected in the essay *Our Attitude toward Death* (in Freud, 1915). The first draft is dated 7.2.1915, and was later delivered as *Wir und der Tod*, at the Jewish society B'nai B'rith of Vienna. In the 8.4.1915 letter to Ferenczi, Freud defined the lecture as «a cheeky lecture, imbued with black humour». Freud closed the lecture with the following words (which had been eliminated in the published text): «At this point I have finished, and I can return from the topic of death to the other details of our life. I know what now awaits me. One of the attending brothers will be in charge of thanking me for the lecture – I dedicate to the poor fellow my brotherly sympathy, given that I did not render the task easy. He will have to dwell on the cultural rules of praise, and he has the right to say, from the heart of hearts: that the devil takes you, you have ruined my appetite.» (cit. in Grubrich-Simitis, 1993, p. 175; my translation).

[86] *Ibid*. p. 298. Freud was only 23 months old at the time of Julius'death, and Schur correctly recalls that Freud would exclude, referring to Goethe's biography (Freud, 1917), the possibility of structured feelings at such an early age. The mourning of a mother can certainly disturb the early mother-child interaction, and can also lead to a severe disorganization of the child. However, what is highly questionable in the explanation «Julius», is its narrative, i.e. a) the reasons which in Freud activated the self and object representations of «Julius» during self-analysis; b) the later use of «Julius» by Freud in justifying his fainting in front of Jung; and c) Jones' and subsequent narratives in psychoanalytic literature.

[87] On Freud's wishes of death and his pathological mourning, see Schur, 1972, p. 298, p. 216.

[88] Letter to Martha, quoted in Jones, 1953, I, p. 99, undated.

[89] Freud, 1986. The Greeks had suffered a serious defeat by the Turks, near the historically famous, blood-drenched battlefield of Pharsalos, as the Neue Freie Presse pointed out (McGrath, 1986, p. 201). The battle began the 18 April.

[90] See Minute M, enclosed to the following letter of 25 May (*ibid*.). In the same letter of 16 May, Freud stressed the «dichterische», (i.e. «creative writing») fever of his son Martin, connecting it to Fliess' biological periods (and sexual aetiology), and alluding to the taboo word «diphterisch» (see the comment of M. Schröter, the German editor of the letters, in Freud, 1986).

[91] Minute N, enclosed to the letter of the «Mathilde Hella» dream, 31 May 1897 (*ibid.*). The main root of this statement is found in Freud's analytical experience with the hysterical patient who had been brutally circumcised when she was a little girl since, in the letter of 24 January, he reported her memories of the genital mutilation as severely hysterically distorted. Few days after Mathilde risked dying because of diphtheria, and later Martin also got sick with the same diagnosis (although it was not diphtheria).

[92] It is in the same letter of 16 May that Freud announced that he had begun to work on dreams.

[93] For many months Freud was planning to visit the archaeological seat of Pompeii (which in those years was commonly called the «Hellenistic Pompeii»).

[94] In the «Gemalde-Galerie». See the guide of Royal Museums of 1886.

[95] See Freud's letter to Fliess of 26 August 1898 (Freud, 1986).

[96] A further link between Moses and the Roman phobia can be found in the second dream of the Rome Series, which contains a reference to the Mosaic topic of «the promised land seen from afar».

[97] For example, we can assume that if Freud had entered in Rome and visited the Moses of Michelangelo, he would not have recalled Julius' death.

[98] Letter of 3/4 October 1897 (Freud, 1986).

[99] The term was introduced in the book *Inquiries into the Human Faculties* (1883), but the concept was already expressed in an article which appeared in the *Macmillian's Magazine* (1865) and was developed further in *Hereditary Genius* (1869) (Kevles, 1985, p. 3).

[100] Galton's composite photographs are a key element of one of Freud's main dreams, the one of uncle Joseph. Freud had this dream in February 1897, after having received from Nothnagel the news of his application for «Professor Extraordinarius», originating therefore from the same associative matrix of Irma's dream, which has been previously pointed out. Freud again referred to Galton's composite photographs in reference to Irma's dream, and more precisely in reference to the link between Irma, his daughter Mathilde, the homonimous patient who had died, and Irma's becoming a child (Freud, 1900a, p. 292). Freud also mentioned Galton's method in *Moses and Monotheism* (1939, p. 10). Francis Galton had drawn this method in the 1870s from the photographic and anthropometric system of identifying criminals of the French policeman Alphonse Bertillon. He used this method in order to extend to man his research on heredity of *Lathyrus odoratus* (sweat pea). He presented it in the same work in which the term «eugenetics» is introduced, the *Inquiries into the Human Faculties* of 1883.

[101] Gesetz zur Verhütung erbkranken Nachwuchses.

[102] This thesis has been widely shared in psychoanalytic literature, at a clinical, anthropological and ritualistic level. Nevertheless, as Lansky and Kilborne have recently stated, «The practice of circumcision must recapture our amazement. The common consciousness is deflected from the stark reality of the attack on the penis.» (1991, p. 249).

References

ANZIEU, D. (1959-1975). *L'auto-analyse de Freud et la découverte de la psychanalyse*. 2 vol. Paris: Presses Universitaires de France.

BAGINSKI, A. (1974). *Das Leben des Weibes, Diätetische Briefe.* Berlin. Denilde's Verlag.

BAGINSKI, A. (1974). (1877, 1883, 1898-1900). *Handbuch der Schulhygiene zum Gebrauche für Ärzte, Sanitätsbeamte, Lehrer, Schulvorstände und Techniker*. Berlin: Denicke.

— (1883, 1889, 1892, 1896). *Lehrbuch der Kinderkrankheiten für Ärzte und Studierende*. Braunschweig: Verlag von Friedrich Wreden.

— (1895a). Die hygienischen Grunzüge der Mosaischen Gesetzgebung. *Deutsche Vierteljahresschrift für öffentliche Gesundheitspflege, 27*, 465-491.

— (1895b). *Die Serumtherapie der Diphterie nach den Beobachtungen im Kaiser- und Kaiserin-Friedrich-Kinderkrankhaus in Berlin*. Berlin: A. Hirschwald.

— (1898). Diphterie und diphteritischer Croup, *in*: Nothnagel H. (Hrsg.): *Specielle Pathologie und Therapie*, II Bd. Wien: A. Holder.

— (1909). Über Kindernervosität und nervöse Kinder. *Therapie der Gegenwart*, April-Mai 1909. Berlin: Julius Sittenfeld.

BEHREND, F.J. (1860). Über die Reizung der Geschlechtstheile, besonders über Onanie bei ganz kleinen Kindern, und die dagegen anzuwendenden Mittel. *Journal f. Kinderkrankheiten, 35*, 321-329.

BERNFELD, S. (1953). Freud's Studies on Cocaine, 1884-1887. *Journal of the American Psychoanalytic Association, 1*, 581-613.

—, CASSIRER BERNFELD S. (1952). Freud's First Year in Practice. *Bulletin of the Menninger Clinic, 16*, 37-49.

BOCK, G. (1986). *Zwangssterilisation im Nationalsozialismus. Studien zur Rassenpolitik und Frauenpolitik*. Opladen: Westdeutscher Verlag.

BODE, W. (1891). *Die Italianische Plastik, Handbücher der Königlichen Museen zu Berlin*. Berlin: W. Spemann.

BONOMI, C. (1993). *Freud, Jung, Ferenczi and the Vision of a Small Cut Off Penis* (Paper presented at the IV° International Conference of the Sándor Ferenczi Society, Budapest, July 18-21, 1993).

CARTER, C.K. (1983). Infantile Hysteria and Infantile Sexuality in Late Nineteenth-Century German-Language Medical Literature. *Medical History, 27*, 186-196.

CASSIRER BERNFELD, S. (1951). Freud and Archeology. *American Imago, 8*, 107-128.

CHARCOT, J.M. (1890). Leçons sur les maladies du système nerveux, *in*: *Oeuvres complètes*, tome III. Paris: Lecrosnier et Babé.

—, (1892). *Poliklinische Vorträge, I. Band, Schuljahr 1887/88*. Übersetzt von Dr. Sigm. Freud. Leipzig/Wien: Franz Deuticke.

—, RICHTER, P. (1887). *Les démoniaques dans l'art*. Paris: Delahaye et Lecrosnier.

CONRADS, H. (1896). Über Geisteskrankheiten im Kindesaltes. *Archiv für Kinderheilkunde, 19*, 175-216.

CREMERIUS, J. (1971). S. Freud – ein grosser Verhüller. *Neue Rundschau, 82*, 187-191.

DUFFY, J. (1963). Masturbation and Clitoridectomy. A Nineteenth-Century View. *Journal of the American Medical Association, 186*, 246-248.

ELLENBERGER, H.F. (1970). *The Discovery of the Unconscious: The History and Evolution of Dynamic Psychiatry*. New York: Basic Books.

EMMINGHAUS, H. (1887). *Die psychischen Störungen des Kindesalters*. Tübingen: Verlag Laupp.

FINZEN, A. (1984). *Auf dem Dienstweg: Die Verstrickung einer Anstalt in die Tötung psychisch Kranker.* Rehburg-Loccum: Psychiatrie-Verlag.

FLEISCHMANN, L. (1878). Über Onanie und Masturbation bei Säuglingen. *Wiener Medizinische Press, 19,* 8-10, 46-49.

FRANK, J.P. (1780). System einer medizinischen Polizei. Bd. 2. Mannheim.

FREUD, S. (1885b). On the General Effect of Cocaine. *In: The Cocaine Papers.* Wien/Zurich: Dunquin, 1963, pp. 45-49.

— (1887z). Rezension von: Scholz G.: Über schwere diphteritsche (*sic*) Lähmungen und deren balneotherapeutische Heilung (Berlin: Aug. Hirschwald, 1887). *Zentralblatt Kinderheilkunde, 1,* 249-250.

— (1888b). Hysteria. *Standard Edition, 1,* 41-59.

— (1892-93). A case of successful treatment by hypnotism. *Standard Edition, 1,* 115-130.

— (1893f). Charcot. *Standard Edition, 3,* 7-23.

— (1895f). A Reply to Criticism of my Paper on Anxiety Neurosis. *Standard Edition, 3,* 119-139.

— (1896a). Heredity and the Aetiology of the Neuroses. *Standard Edition, 3,* 141-156.

— (1896b). Further Remarks on the Neuro-Psychoses of Defence. *Standard Edition, 3,* 157-185.

— (1896c). The Aetiology of Hysteria. *Standard Edition, 3,* 187-221.

— (1897a). *Infantile Cerebral Paralysis.* Coral Gables, Fl.: University of Miami Press, 1968.

— (1898b). The Psychical Mechanism of Forgetfulness. *Standard Edition, 3,* 287-297.

— (1900a). The Interpretation of Dreams. *Standard Edition, 4-5.*

— (1901b). The Psychopathology of Everyday Life. *Standard Edition, 6.*

— (1905a). On Psychotherapy. *Standard Edition, 7,* 255-268.

— (1905d). Three Essays on the Theory of Sexuality. *Standard Edition, 7,* 123-243.

— (1908c). On the Sexual Theories of Children. *Standard Edition, 9,* 205-226.

— (1909b). Analysis of a Phobia in a Five-Years Old Boy. *Standard Edition, 10,* 1-147.

— (1909d). Notes Upon a Case of Obsessional Neurosis. *Standard Edition, 10,* 151-249.

— (1910a). Five Lectures on Psycho-Analysis. *Standard Edition, 11,* 1-55.

— (1910d). The Future Prospectives of Psycho-Analytic Therapy. *Standard Edition, 11,* 139-151.

— (1912e). Recommendations to Physicians Practicing Psycho-Analysis. *Standard Edition, 12,* 109-120.

— (1912-13). Totem and Taboo. *Standard Edition, 13,* 1-161.

— (1914b [1913]). The Moses of Michelangelo. *Standard Edition, 13,* 209-236.

— (1914d). On the History of the Psycho-Analytic Movement. *Standard Edition, 14,* 1-66.

— (1915b). Thoughts for the Times on War and Death. *Standard Edition, 14,* 273-300.

— (1916-17). Introductory Lectures on Psycho-Analysis. *Standard Edition, 15-16.*

— (1917b). A Child Recollection from "Dichtung und Wahrheit". *Standard Edition, 17,* 145-156.

— (1919h). The «Uncanny». *Standard Edition, 17,* 217-256.

— (1920g). Beyond the Pleasure Principle. *Standard Edition, 18,* 1-64.

FREUD, S. (1925d). An Autobiographical Study. *Standard Edition, 20,* 1-70.

— (1926e). The Question of Lay Analysis. *Standard Edition, 20,* 177-250.

— (1927c). The Future of an Illusion. *Standard Edition, 21,* 1-56.

— (1930a). Civilization and its Discontent. *Standard Edition, 21,* 57-145.

— (1930d). The Goethe Prize, Letter to Dr. Alfons Paquet. *Standard Edition, 21,* 207.

— (1932a [1931]). The Acquisition and Control of Fire. *Standard Edition, 22,* 183-193.

— (1933a [1932]). New Introductory Lectures on Psycho-Analysis. *Standard Edition, 22,* 1-182.

— (1936a). A Disturbance of Memory on the Acropolis (A Letter to Romain Rolland). *Standard Edition, 22,* 237-238.

— (1937d). Constructions in Analysis. *Standard Edition, 23,* 255-269.

— (1939a). Moses and Monotheism. *Standard Edition, 23,* 1-137.

— (1940e [1938]). Splitting of the Ego in the Process of Defence. *Standard Edition, 23,* 271-278.

— (1956a [1886]). Report on my Studies in Paris and Berlin. *Standard Edition, 1,* 5-15.

— (1960a). *Letters of Sigmund Freud 1873-1939.* New York: Basic Books, 1960; London: The Hogarth Press, 1961.

— (1985a [1915]). Übersicht der Übertragungsneurosen G.W., *Nachtragsband,* 634-651.

— (1986). *Briefe an Wilhelm Fliess 1887-1904.* Frankfurt am Main: Fischer.

—, ABRAHAM, K. (1965). *The Letters of Sigmund Freud and Karl Abraham, 1907-1926.* New York: Basic Books, 1966.

—, BREUER, J. (1893-95). Studies on Hysteria. *Standard Edition, 2.*

—, FERENCZI, S. (1992). *Correspondence, vol. 1, 1908-1914.* Cambridge, Mass.: Harvard University Press, 1994.

—, JUNG, C.G. (1974). *The Freud/Jung Letters.* Cambridge, Mass.: Harvard University Press.

—, RIE, O. (1891). Klinische Studie über die halbseitige Cerebrallähming der Kinder, *in: Beiträge zur Kinderheilkunde,* Heft 3, Hrsg. Dr. Max Kassowitz, Wien.

—, RIE, O. (1893). Zur Kenntnis der Cerebralen Diplegien des Kindesalters (im Anschuss an die Little'sche Krankheit), *in: Beiträge zur Kinderheilkunde,* Heft 3, Hrsg. Dr. Max Kassowitz, Wien.

GICKLHORN, J., GICKLHORN, R. (1960). *Sigmund Freuds Akademische Laufbahn im Lichte der Dokumente.* Wien/Innsbruck: Urban & Schwarzenberg.

GRINSTEIN, A. (1980). *Sigmund Freud's Dreams.* New York: International Universities Press.

GRUBRICH-SIMITIS, I. (1992). *Zurück zu Freud.* Frankfurt/M.: Fischer.

GUTTSTADT, A. (Hrsg.) (1900). *Krankenhaus-Lexikon für das Deutsche Reich.* Berlin: Georg Reimer.

HAMMOND, W.A. (1887) Coca. *In: Volunteer Paper.* Transactions of the *Medical Society of Virginia,* nov. 1887, pp. 212-226.

HEGAR, A. (1878). Die Castration der Frauen. *In:* Volkman, R. (Hrsg.): *Sammlung Klinischer Vorträge in Verbindung mit deutschen Klinikern,* No 136-138 (Gynäkologie No 42). Leipzig: Verlag von Breitkopf und Härtel.

HENOCH, E.H. (1881). Die hysterischen Affectionen der Kinder. *Wiener Medizinische Press,* 22/9, 916-918, 951-952, 980-982, 1006-1009.

HERZ, M. (1885). Über Hysterie bei Kindern. *Wiener Medizinische Wochenschrift, 43*, 1305-1308; *44*, 1338-1342; *45*, 1368-1371; *46*, 1401-1405.

HIRSCHMÜLLER, A. (1978). Eine bisher unbekannte Krankengeschichte Sigmund Freuds und Josef Breuers aus der Entstehungszeit der "Studien über Hysterie". *Jahrbuch der Psychoanalyse, 10*, 136-168.

— (1986). Briefe Josef Breuers an Wilhelm Fliess 1894-1898. *Jahrbuch der Psychoanalyse, 18*, 239-261.

— (1989). Freuds «Mathilde»: eine weiterer Tagesrest zum Traum. *Jahrbuch der Psychoanalyse, 24*: 128-159.

— (1991). *Freuds Begegnung mit der Psychiatrie. Von der Hirnmythologie zur Neurosenlehre.* Tübingen: Diskord.

JACOBI, A. (1875). On Masturbation and Hysteria in Young Children. *American Journal of Obstetric Diseases of Women and Children, 8*, 595-606, 1875; *9*, 218-238, 1876.

JOLLY, F. (1892). Über Hysterie bei Kindern. *Berliner Klinische Wochenschrift, 29/34*, 841-845.

JONES, E. (1953, 1955, 1957). *The Life and Work of Sigmund Freud.* 3 vol. London: The Hogarth Press.

JUNG, C.G. (1962). *Memories, Dreams, Reflections.* New York: Vintage Books, 1965.

KERN, S. (1973). Freud and the Discovery of Child Sexuality. *Hist. Child Quarterly, 1*, 117-141.

KEVLES, D.J. (1986). *In the Name of Eugenetics. Genetics and the Uses of Human Heredity.* Berkeley/Los Angeles: University of California Press.

KLEE, E. (1983). *"Euthanasie" im NS-Staat. Die "Vernichtung lebensunwerten Lebens".* Frankfurt am Main: Fischer.

KLOË, E., KINDT, H. (1981). Zur Entstehung und Entwicklung des kindlichen Hysteriebegriffes. *Gesnerus, 38*, 281-300.

Königliche Museen zu Berlin (1885), *Beschreibung der Pergamenischen Bildwerke*, 7. Aufl. Berlin: W. Spermann.

Königliche Museen zu Berlin (1886), *Führer durch die Königlischen Museen*, 6. Aufl. Berlin: W. Spermann.

KROEMER, – (1896). Beitrage zur Castrationsfrage. *Allgemeine Zeitschrift für Psychiatrie und psychisch-gerichtliche Medizin, 52*, 1-74.

KUNZE, M. (1987a). Il museo archeologico e l'Altare di Pergamo, in: *I Musei Statali a Berlino est. Storia e collezioni.* Firenze: Giunti, 1988, pp. 80-107.

— (1987b). Der Pergamonaltar - seine Wirkungen auf Kunst und Literatur, in: *"Wir haben eine ganze Kunstepoche gefunden!".* Berlin: Staatliche Museen zu Berlin, pp. 60-71.

— (1991a). *Il grande altare di marmo di Pergamo.* Staatliche Museen zu Berlin. Mainz: Philipp von Zaben.

— (1991b). *Der Altar von Pergamon.* Staatliche Museen zu Berlin.

LANDESMANN, E. (1890). *Die Therapie an den Wiener Kliniken.* Leipzig/Wien: Franz Deuticke.

LANSKY, M.R., KILBORNE, B. (1991). Circumcision and biblical narrative. *The Psychoanalytic Study of Society, 16*, 249-264.

LIEBERMEISTER, K. (1883). Über Hysterie und deren Behandlung. *Sammlung Klinischer Vorträge, 236*, 2139-2158.

LINDNER, S. (1879). Das Saugen an den Fingern, Lippen, etc., bei den Kindern (Ludeln). *Jahrbuch für Kinderheilkunde, 14*, 68-91.

MASSON, J.M.M. (1984). *The Assault on Truth: Freud's Suppression of the Seduction Theory.* New York: Farrar, Straus & Giroux.

McGRATH, W.J. (1986). *Freud's Discovery of Psychoanalysis. The Politics of Hysteria.* Ithaca/London: Cornell University Press.

MERKEL, F. (1887). *Beitrag zur Casuistik der Castration bei Neurosen.* Nürnberg: Stich.

MORELLI, G. (alias Ivan Lermolieff) (1887). *Della pittura italiana.* Milano: Fratelli Treves.

MÜHLLEITNER, E. (1992). *Biographisches Lexikon der Psychoanalyse.* Tübingen: Diskord.

NUNBERG, H., FEDERN, E. (eds) (1975). *Minutes of the Vienna Psychoanalytic Society, vol. IV: 1910-1918.* New York: International Universities Press.

PAGEL, J.L. (1901). *Biographisches Lexikon.* Leipzig.

PETRAS, R. (1987). *Die Bauten der Berliner Museumsinsel.* Berlin: Stapp.

PLOSS, H. (1885). Geschichtliches und Ethnologisches über Knabenbeschneidung. *Deutsches Archiv für Geschichte der Medizin und medizinische Geographie, 8;* repr. Hildesheim, New York: Georg Olms, 1971, pp. 312-343.

RICHARDZ, B. (1987). *Feilen, Pflegen, Töten. Zur Alltagsgeschichte einer Heil- und Pflegeanstalt bis zum Ende des Nationalsozialismus.* Göttingen: Verlag für Medizinische Psychologie.

ROHLENDER, H. (1899). *Die Masturbation. Eine Monographie für Ärzte und Pädagogen.* Berlin: Fischer's medic. Buchhandlung H. Kornfeld.

RUDNICK, M. (1985). *Behinderte im Nationalsozialismus. Von der Ausgrenzung und Zwangssterilisation zur "Euthanasie".* Weinheim/Basel: Beltz.

SCHÄFER, S. (1884a). Über Hysterie bei Kindern. *Archiv für Kinderheilkunde, 5,* 401-428.

— (1884b). *Über Hysterie bei Kindern.* Stuttgart: Kröner.

SCHUR, M. (1972). *Freud Living and Dying.* New York: International Universities Press. It. transl.: *Il caso di Freud.* Torino: Boringhieri, 1972.

SHENGOLD, L. (1979). Freud and Joseph, in: Kanzer M., Glenn J. (eds), *Freud and His Self-Analysis.* New York: Jason Aronson, pp. 67-86.

— (1993). *"The Boy will Come to Nothing!" Freud's Ego Ideal and Freud as Ego Ideal.* New Haven/London: Yale University Press.

SCHMIDT, H. (1880). Über das Vorkommen der Hysterie bei Kindern. *Jahrbuch für Kinderheilkunde und physische Erziehung,* N.F., *15,* 1-22.

SPITZ, R.A. (1952). Authority and masturbation. Some remarks on a bibliographic investigation. *Psychoanalytic Quarterly, 21,* 490-527.

STENGERS, J., VAN NECK, A. (1984). *Histoire d'une grande peur: la masturbation.* Bruxelles: Editions de l'Université de Bruxelles.

SULLOWAY, F.J. (1979). *Freud, Biologist of the. Mind.* London: Burnett Books. It. transl.: *Freud biologo della mente. Al di là della leggenda psicoanalytica.* Milano: Feltrinelli, 1982.

VERMOREL, H., VERMOREL, M. (1993). *Sigmund Freud et Romain Rolland, Correspondance 1923-1936.* Paris: Presses Universitaires de France.

VERSPOHL, F.J. (1991). Der Moses des Michelangelo. *Städel-Jahrbuch,* N.F., *13*: 155-176.

WERNER, E. (1990). Vom Kaiser- und Kaiserin-Friedrich-Kinderkrankenhaus zur Kinderklinik Universitätsklinikum Rudolf Virchow. *Kinderarzt, 9,* 1315-1322.

Cahiers Psychiatriques Genevois, Special Issue, 1994, pp. 101-119

PSYCHOANALYSIS – THE WRITING CURE

Patrick Mahony

According to a medieval maxim, anyone who claimed to have read the whole corpus of St. Augustine would most likely be a liar, since the writings of that great thinker were so voluminous. I believe that a similar maxim might hold true today for Freud, if we were to have also at our disposal the stupefying quantity of both his destroyed manuscripts and his existant but still unpublished writings. But there is another pertinent reason that I have started my presentation with Augustine. He made two incisive comments about what writing can mean to an indefatigable author, and Freud could just as well have said them about himself. The first comment, coming from Book Three of the Latin treatise *De Trinitate,* can be rendered this way: «I myself avow that in writing (this work) I have learned many things which I did not know.»[1] The second, more poignant citation comes from Letter 143, which I translate as follows: «Admittedly, therefore, I try to be among the number of those who write as they progress and who progress as they write.»[2]

We might use one more medieval reference in order to see how writing was crucial in Freud's own development. Scholastic philosophers were wont to distinguish between an *instrumentum separatum* or instrument detached from the user (such as a hammer) and an *instrumentum coniunctum* or instrument connected with the user (such as his hand). In light of this distinction, we may say that Freud's writing was carried out more or less like an extension of himself, a tracing of his inner movement. For another enlightening gloss, we may turn to Roland Barthes, perhaps the foremost Continental critic in our day on the subject of writing. Barthes distinguished between a writer, for whom writing is merely a communicative instrument, and an author, who establishes a very way of discourse and «who radically absorbs the world's *why* in a *how to write*»

(Barthes, 1964, p. 148, my translation). In this sense, Freud is clearly an author, a genuine, committed author who experienced writing as a mixture of work and pleasure. He would have sympathized with Barthes, who reflected on his own prolific activity this way:

> Writing is that *play* by which I turn around as well as I can in a narrow space: I am boxed in, I struggle between the hysteria necessary to write and the imaginative act, which oversees, guides, purifies, renders common, codifies, corrects, and imposes the aim (and vision) of a social communication... And yet: the closer I get to the work, the deeper I go into writing; I approach its unendurable depth; a desert is discovered... It is at this point of contact between writing and work that the harsh truth appears to me: *I am no longer a child.* Or rather, is it the asceticism of intense pleasure that I am discovering? (Barthes, 1975, p. 140, my translation).

The latter quotation leads us directly into the most tortuous and exalted portion of Freud's writing career called his self-analysis. Freud conducted it through, with, and in writing. Far from being a mere medium of retrospective reportage or a way of storing and retrieving information, writing was an indispensable feature with the deepest significance in Freud's self-cure. Such is my thesis, and in the course of pursuing it with you, I wish to elucidate the origins of psychoanalysis, the quality of Freud's genius, and the distinctiveness of that world masterpiece, *The Interpretation of Dreams* (Freud, 1900a).

Before moving on, we must attend to several preliminary questions. First of all, when did Freud's self-analysis take place? In our reply, we must start by dividing his self-therapy into two stages: a kind of initial, non-systematic one that began around the time that Freud was treating the patients that we can recognize in the *Studies on Hysteria* (1895d); then an intensified, systematic self-analysis that began in the summer of 1897 and, with interruptions, lasted at least up to the publication of the *Interpretation of Dreams* in November, 1899 (see Appendix). I do not want to burden you with dates but I would ask that you retain the dates more or less marking the duration of Freud's systematic self-analysis: from the summer of 1897 to November, 1899.

It is not a trivial gesture to ask what material did Freud's self-analysis focus on. Documentation amply shows that parapraxes, symptoms and screen memories were worked on in his self-analysis, yet its principal material, and not at all incidentally, revolved around dreams. Freud himself was very explicit on this matter again and again. In 1909 he told his American audience at Clark University: «If I am asked how one can become a psychoanalyst, I reply: "By studying one's own dreams"!» (Freud, 1910a, p. 33). Three years later, Freud returned to his historical pronouncement and repeated it word for word in a paper on technique

(Freud, 1912e, p. 116). Next, in his history of the psychoanalytic movement Freud reminisced this way about its earliest days:

> I soon saw the necessity of carrying out a self-analysis, and this I did with the help of a series of my own dreams which led me back through all the events of my childhood; and I am still of the opinion today that this kind of analysis may suffice for one who is a good dreamer and not too abnormal (Freud, 1914d, p. 20).

Finally, in 1926, endorsing a paper by a certain English thinker, Freud wrote that its author «carried out a systematic application of the procedure of self-analysis which I myself employed in the past for my own dreams» (Freud, 1926c, p. 280; cf. Jones, 1953, pp. 320-321 and Gay, 1988, p. 98 fn.).

The next problem confronting us, the practical modality of Freud's self-analysis, leads us further into the unique history of psychoanalysis. It is a historical irony that a frequent name for psychoanalytic treatment, the talking cure, had been coined for a very different kind of therapy and one, moreover, that preceded Freud's discovery of psychoanalysis by more than a decade.

The story is familiar: Anna O., Breuer's patient from 1880 to 1882, would jokingly refer to her cathartic treatment as «chimney-sweeping» but in a serious mood would call it a «talking cure» (Freud, 1893-1895, p. 30). A second ironical disparity of psychoanalytic history is that the other source of our clinical practice, Freud's self-analysis, was preeminently not a talking cure (nor merely a reflective, non-motoric one for that matter)[3] but a writing cure. The evidence for my thesis is extensive, both circumstantial and direct.

First, the circumstantial. It is relevant that in citing the historical precedents for free association, Freud drew attention to the fact that they had transpired in writing. For example, Freud noted that the nineteenth-century scientist Dr. Garth Wilkinson had described his own manner of writing as an enraptured laissez-faire, letting himself be guided «by an infallible instinct into the subject» and its elaboration. Another predecessor, now much more known, is the essayist Ludwig Börne, who said that to become an original writer one had only to engage in sheer scriptive improvisation for three days. We know the cryptomnesic history of this essay: the young Freud read it, but then for over half a century the reading slipped down into an unconscious transcription in Freud's own mind (Freud, 1920b, pp. 263-265). An even more telling precedent is one brought up in the *Interpretation of Dreams* itself: Schiller, let us recall, held that free association on paper is the way to overcome writer's block. Freud himself added this practical comment:

What Schiller describes as a relaxation of the watch upon the gates of Reason, the adoption of an attitude of uncritical self-observation, is by no means difficult. Most of my patients achieve it after their first instruction. I myself can do so very completely, *by the help of writing down mv ideas as they occur to me* (Freud, 1900a, p. 103, my italics).

The documentation that I have thus far adduced prompts us to conceive that Freud's self-analysis was chiefly a scriptive one dealing with dreams. But there are much more pertinent data for our conception. A generally neglected footnote in the *Studies on Hysteria* shows that as far back as the time of its composition Freud took the trouble with some of his fresh dreams «to write them down and try to solve them» (Freud, 1893-1895, p. 69 fn.). Freud's scriptive practice assumed even a greater role at the climactic point of his non-systematic self-analysis. Although it was in the course of analyzing the Irma dream that Freud discovered the secret of dreams, critics have overlooked how that dream and its immediate history are literally bathed in writing. Here's how. Being uneasy about his therapeutic treatment of Irma and wanting to lay the blame elsewhere as well as justify himself before Breuer, Freud sat down late in the day and wrote up the patient's case; the write-up was not done cursorily, for it lasted «far into the night» (Freud, 1900a, p. 108; cf. also pp. 106 and 115). According to Freud, this case history plus some alarming news about Irma's condition continued to occupy his mental activity after he fell asleep; he then had the famous dream about her. Pertinent to my thesis, the most condensed part of the dream was a chemical formula which Freud even visualized in heavy type. Immediately upon waking, in the morning of July 24, 1895, Freud noted down the dream; he then analyzed it, part by part. The dream, therefore, whose most dense section was in print, was itself bracketed by two phases of writing; in other words, day residues and associations were in scriptive form. That is not all. The same day Freud analyzed the dream he wrote to Fliess, but did not mention the writing up of his epoch-making discovery. Like his dream, Freud's letter was accusatory and – given the topic of my presentation – its opening words become even more charged: «Demon, why don't you write?... Don't you care at all any more about what I am doing» (Freud, 1985, p. 134).

The foregoing information enables us to become more to the scriptive modality of Freud's systematic self-analysis that began two years after the Irma dream. During this later period Freud hyperinvested the inscription of his dreams, associations and his analysis of them, a praxis which expanded to include his screen memories, parapraxes, transient symptoms and interactions with patients. It is quite to the point that also around this time Freud saw an uncanny resemblance between his compositional practice and that of an inspired Biblical writer; hence, while scorning the arbitrary devaluations made by his precedessors, Freud claimed that he was closely attending to dreams as if they were «Holy Writ» (Freud, 1900a, p. 514). What is more, in recording his own dreams, the practice of free association drove Freud to act like an inspired writer. Accordingly, in reporting his so-called Hollturn dream, Freud declared:

> This description is unintelligible even to myself, but I am following the fundamental rule of rendering the dream in those words which occur to me in writing it down (my translation of *G.W.* 2/3: 458 ff.; see Freud, 1900a, 455 fn.; cf. also pp. 205 and 456).

Barely several months after completing *The Interpretation of Dreams*, Freud set forth in the most direct terms his precise method of self-analysis and improvised writing. He said it this way:

> If we make use of this procedure [of free association] upon ourselves, we can best assist the investigation by *at once* writing down what are at first unintelligible associations (Freud, 1901a, p. 636, my emphasis).

Freud thereupon proceeded to jot down and analyze, in the present tense, the dream he had had the night before.[4]

The scrupulous method Freud adopted to analyze his dreams, we may say, actually involved him in more rather than less writing. As he said at one point, the «original, classical method» of analyzing one's dreams was to skip nothing: in practice, that meant to chop the dream into sequential parts and then dutifully proceed to associate «to the elements of the dream in the order in which those elements occurred» in the dream report (Freud, 1923c, p. 109). Clearly this methodical pursuit of the dream from its start to end eliminated the risk of any random procedure which would have easily conduced to overlooking some dream segments. Another scriptive strategy of Freud is more intriguing and relates subtly to his general clinical technique. You remember Freud saying this:

> If the first (dream) account given me by a patient of a dream is too hard to follow I ask him to repeat it. In doing so he rarely uses the same words. But the parts of the dream which he describes in different terms are by that fact revealed to me as the weak spot in the dream's disguise (Freud, 1900a, p. 515).

Well, we do have a few of Freud's own dreams with slightly different written versions, a discrepancy due either to a defensive reaction or to a conscious desire to disguise his dream in published form. But in other instances, such as the dreams that lend themselves to diagrammatic presentation, it seems that Freud was apt to rewrite them for the purpose of discovering more through his own associatively spatial rearrangements. For example, in presenting his well-known succinct dream about closing the eyes, Freud states: «I am accustomed (*gewöhnlich*) to write this in the following (diagrammatic) form» (Freud, 1900a, pp. 317-318; *G.W.* 2/3:

322-323), We must take the word «accustomed» for exactly what it means: not just two or three times, but many times. The implication is clear: Freud repetitively wrote the dream to find out the meanings hidden in the various ways he could graphically display it. For another example we may refer to the Villa Secerno dream, which Freud sent to Fliess with the comment: «*The way I have written it out* shows what seemed obscure and what seemed multiple» (Freud, 1985, p. 236, my italics); significantly enough, Freud wrote out this dream differently in *The Interpretation of Dreams* (1900a, p. 317).[5]

We can hardly exaggerate the importance of the fact that Freud retained his scriptive method in his self-analysis even when he dealt with material other than dreams as such. Here is Freud reporting a flash memory about his early childhood:

> I saw myself standing in front of a cupboard demanding something and screaming, while my half-brother, my senior by twenty years, held it open. Then suddenly my mother, looking beautiful and slim, walked into the room, as if she had come in from the street. These were the words in which I described (*gefasst*) the scene, of which I had a plastic picture, but I did not know what more I could make of it. Whether my brother wanted to open or shut the cupboard in my first translation (*Übersetzung*) of the picture I called it a wardrobe – why I was crying, and what the arrival of my mother had to do with it – all this was obscure to me (Freudb, 1901b, p. 50; *G.W.* 4: 59).

Note Freud's technique: much as he did with dreams, he wrote down the screen memory and closely heeded the original wording, which he called a translation.

Inscription, transcription, translation – these terms were frequently used by Freud to describe the so-called psychical systems and the vicissitudes of their traces; the triad of terms casts light on what writing both as a concept and as a practice signified for Freud. In a practical sense, the place of writing in his self-analysis was partly determined by his innate gifts as well as by external circumstances. Thus, for a considerable period during his writing cure Freud forsook giving his university lectures (Freud, 1985, pp. 332 and 347). Even more significantly, throughout his writing cure, Freud did not achieve any talking cure with his patients.[6]

Let us listen to this chronological series of Freud's epistolary laments to Fliess:

in March, 1897 – «I have not yet finished a single case» (Freud, 1985, p. 232);

later in the same month – «I am still having the same difficulties and have not finished a single case» (Freud, 1985, p. 233);

in May, 1897 – «I shall wait still longer for a treatment to be completed. It must be possible» (Freud, 1985, p. 244);

in September, 1897 – (I have) «continual disappointment in my efforts to bring a single analysis to a real conclusion» (Freud, 1985, p. 264; cf. p. 269);

in February, 1898 – «I shall not finish a single one (case) this year either» (Freud, 1985, p. 299).

Even as late as March, 1900, we hear Freud bemoaning the elusiveness of the case which he most counted on to resolve his doubts and to have confidence in his dyadic therapy (Freud, 1985, p. 403). To further gauge the bleakness of Freud's therapeutic mood, let us return to the letter 1898 in which he said that he would not finish a case either. Now in the same letter Freud announced that he had just finished composing *Sexual Aetiology of the Neuroses*, an essay that contained the following propagandistic and misleading claim: «I have in recent years almost worked out a therapeutic procedure which I propose to describe as *psychoanalytic*. I owe a great number of successes to it.» (Freud, 1898, p. 282). In brief, such contrasting contemporary private and public statements about the success of the talking cure point certainly to Freud's personal embroilment, and it is reasonable to conclude that his preeminently written cure took on that much more importance.

At this juncture one may want to object that Fliess played a capital role in Freud's analysis[7] and that although they were in contact with each other through the mail, they also did vocally communicate with each during their so-named Congresses. To that objection I would answer that we must not overestimate the extent of those dyadic encounters. We are sure that there were at least five of them during Freud's systematic self-analysis, but there may have been one or two more.[8] Yet several points must be borne in mind here. The Congresses usually lasted only one or two days. Next, there was something about these Congresses that conformed to the ordinarily accepted sense of the word, for both men were apt to deliver papers to the other or to read silently what the other wrote (see specifically Freud, 1985, pp. 287, 335, 344 and 349). Thirdly and most importantly, available evidence suggests that the Congresses were essentially intellectual exchanges.

For these and other reasons, therefore, we must not underrate the role played by writing in Freud's relationship to Fliess. From the outset of his acquaintanceship with Fliess, Freud envisaged successful writing as a shared ego ideal. In Freud's very first letter his appeal for friendship was joined with the report of compositional production: he was busy writing three essays (Freud, 1985, p. 16). In his second letter, Freud states his intention to translate a book and adds that «for recreation» he was working on two papers (Freud, 1985, p. 17).

But by 1897 Freud's disenchantment with his friend started to surface, for published research, successfully written up and published, became ever more a hypersensitive issue between the two correspondents.[9] We must realize here that Freud's disillusionment concerned not only Fliess's theoretical stance but also his lack of production as such; and in this matter, Freud did not have in mind merely a comparison of his own psychological achievements with Fliess's biological work. Indeed, it has generally gone unnoticed that between 1887 and 1900, the dates of their relatively positive friendship, even Freud's neurological publications alone far exceed in length Fliess's biological ones. To be more specific: from 1887 to 1900 Fliess published two monographs and, from what I can determine, four short articles, the whole totaling less than 400 pages. Just to mention Freud's neurological books for the same period, we have, besides the book on aphasia, a monograph written with Oscar Rie and containing some 220 pages and a bibliography of 180 titles; then a 168-page monograph dealing with central diplegias; and lastly a comprehensive treatise of some 327 pages and fourteen pages of bibliography (Jones, 1953, pp. 216-217). Let us not forget either that along with reading and summarizing the massive extant literature on dreams, between 1898 and 1900 Freud published 83 abstracts and reviews of neurological literature (in the *Jahresbericht über die Leistungen und Fortschritte auf dem Gebiete der Neurologie und Psychiatrie*). When finally we take into additional consideration for the overall period between 1887 and 1900 Freud's numerous articles on his own neurological research, the mass of his psychological publications and his translations of three books by Bernheim and Charcot, we begin to grasp the breathtaking unmatchability of Freud's creative powers and productivity.

In this whole scenario, 1897 was the watershed year for our two protagonists – Freud finished his last book on neurology (in January) and Fliess saw a book appear in print which he had completed the previous year (Freud, 1985, p. 173). But after that, from 1897 to 1900, Fliess wrote nothing except a short article. It is no surprise that reality-testing became a burning issue in the famous friendship, as Freud resorted to an impatient pressuring so that Fliess would come forth with documented evidence of successful work. Here's a chronological sampling of excerpts in Freud's correspondence that dramatically show his growing impatience with Fliess's scriptive unproductivity:

> June, 1897: (I hope) that instead of a short article you will within a year present to us a small book which solves the organic secrets (Freud, 1985, p. 254; cf. p. 304).

> February, 1899: You can write of nothing but the tremendously huge work which is all too hard for the powers of a human being (Freud, 1985, p. 344 – in this same letter Freud said that he himself had just discovered the key between dreams and neuroses).

May, 1899: A contented letter from you containing evidence of your being well and the promise that you will attempt a first presentation of your earthshaking formulas were a long-missed pleasure (Freud, 1985, p. 351) .

June, 1899: The announcement that you are engaged in research perhaps may mean, (that) instead of writing? And (thus the) postponement of the date on which I can read something of yours? (Freud, 1985, p. 356).

August, 1899: Your work apparently has changed into a pupa for me; will I be able to catch it as a butterfly, or will it fly too high for me? (Freud, 1985, pp. 365-366).

If we reflect on these passages and others, we can make the assured inference that Fliess's promise of his own great book to keep pace with the *Interpretation of Dreams* was becoming more desperate.[10]

The supreme irony was that Fliess was caught on the tenterhooks of his own theory about life's periodicity: he could not predict when he would finish that very book of his that Freud wryly called the «organically growing creation» (Freud, 1985, p. 428). As a matter of fact, the work did not see the light of day until many years after, in 1906.

The preceding discussion prepares us to examine the composition of the *Interpretation of Dreams*, which is a fascinating story in itself. We begin in 1908, when Freud prefaced the second edition of his Dreambook with the following information: «It was, I found, a portion of my own self-analysis, my own reaction to my father's death – that is to say, to the most important event, the most poignant loss, of a man's life» (Freud, 1900a, p. XXVI). Freud's retrospection needs some filling in and modification. His father died in October, 1896; in May of the following year, Freud began writing the dream book (Freud, 1985, p. 243) but quickly ran into a self-described writing block (pp. 253 and 255). Psychoanalytic scholars have overlooked that this very writing block launched Freud into the systematic self-analysis which eventually coalesced with his resumption of writing the *Interpretation of Dreams*. This compositional feature, embracing a unique mixture of scientific and therapeutic goals,[11] was such that only after completion of his masterpiece did Freud realize that the very writing of it formed part of his self-analysis.[12] Let us return for a moment to Freud's letter of May 16, 1897, where he gives a historical announcement about undertaking the Dreambook. His inaugural wording of that project is of the utmost import:

I have felt impelled to start working on the dream, where I feel so very certain (Freud, 1985, p. 243).

Notice first, Freud hyperinvested in the dream material, for it was precisely there that he felt most certain. Second, Freud's feeling of being «impelled» (*gedrängt*) is one of his recurrent references to his manner of inscriptive work at the time: again and again he spoke of having taken notes during the last «thrust» or waiting patiently for the next «thrust» (Freud, 1985, e.g., pp. 243-244, 249, 300, 301, 349). A third point about Freud's inaugurating announcement is that he uses the word «dream» to refer to his whole project. In the German text of his correspondence with Fliess, we repeatedly hear Freud talking of his scriptive project as the «dream» (*Traum*); the English translation editorially adds the word «book» in brackets, thus detracting from the force of Freud's condensation of Dreambook into «dream». The accumulated force and impact of Freud's condensation is undeniable. By the end of 1897 he was saying: «I shall force myself to write the dream in order to come out of it» (Freud, 1985, p. 278). «The dream is suddenly taking shape... the dream will be», Freud would later say (p. 353). And later again: «(I am) entirely the dream» (Freud, 1985, p. 369; German edition, p. 403, my translation).

Freud's verbal condensation was more than a figure of speech. Family members noticed that when he was composing his monumental treatise, he was in a dream-like state (Jones, 1953, p. 360 fn.). And even he himself wrote to Fliess: «The psychology is proceeding in a strange manner; it is nearly finished, composed as if in a dream» (Freud, 1985, p. 318). This process of writing the dreambook is telling, for the processive nature of Freud's understanding is inseparable from his scriptive presentation. Here is Freud again, confiding to Fliess:

> I can compose the details only in the process of writing (Freud, 1985, p. 305; cf. p. 146). It is entirely taken down [from the dictation] of the unconscious... At the start of every paragraph I did not know where I would end up (Freud, 1985, p. 319; German edition, pp. 348-349, my translation). I do not know yet how to delineate and organize (the last chapter)... but a thing like this turns out just as it will. Every attempt to make it better by itself gives it a forced quality (p. 368).

The foregoing evidence entitles us to conclude that Freud's discourse in most of his Dreambook is truly performative and ongoing. Its quintessential character is epitomized by the usage of the present tense and in that way it has the grammatical nature of the manifest dream. Accordingly, more than being just the result and account of Freud's self-analysis, the *Interpretation of Dreams* enacts and extends it.[13]

Put otherwise: dreaming and writing at the time were not so much collateral as imbricated activities for Freud, an imbrication that could even become collusive. Did not Freud write to his friend, «So far I have always known where the next dream-night would continue» (Freud, 1985, p. 268)? And when Fliess insisted that a certain important dream be dropped from the monograph, Freud yielded but went on to ask which of the dream's particular elements did Fliess object to — the reference to anxiety, to Martha, or to being without a fatherland? Whatever the objectionable elements, Freud added, he would eliminate it in one of his future dreams, for he could «have dreams like that made to order» (Freud, 1985, p. 315). It follows, then, that Freud's book about dreams was also a dream to a certain extent. The dreams and book somersaulted in a series of mutual wishes and fulfillment. The dreams were texts and pre-texts.

Were we to stop at this point, we would not fully grasp the extent to which Freud was more personally involved in writing *The Interpretation of Dreams* than any other book. Our exploration of this personal involvement leads us to see that, in Freud's mind, there was a profound link between dreams and the maternal body.

Here are excerpts from two strategic places in *The Interpretation of Dreams*, i.e., Chapters Two and Seven:

> Every dream has at least one place... a navel, as it were, by which it joins with the unknown (Freud, 1900a, p. 116 ff.; *G.W.* 2/3: 116 ff., my translation). Then this is the dream's navel, the place at which it straddles the unknown (Freud, 1900a, p. 525; *G.W.* 2/3: 530, my translation).

These two lapidary expressions anticipate another: «The finding of an object is the refinding of an object» (Freud, 1905d, p. 222). In his dream the dreamer refinds, «joins with», and even «straddles» the mother, the unknown (Strachey's desexualized rendering of *aufsitzt* or *straddles* is «reaches down into» (cf. Freud, 1900a, p. 525, and Weber, 1982, p. 75).

The suggestive power of Freud's statements is increased by the fact that the word «unknown» in German comes from a verb (*erkennen*, not *bekennen* – Anzieu, 1975, p. 215) which, like the English *know*, can be used in the biblical carnal sense. Let it be stressed. that the two appearances of the word «unknown» function as mileposts marking the exploratory distance travelled by Freud in his Dreambook. In the first citation, drawn from Chapter Two, the dream's navel is merely joined with the mother; this controlled attachment is matched by Chapter Two's main material, the Irma dream, whose deeper meanings about the maternal body were given restricted interpretation by Freud. However, towards the end of his exploration of the dream, in Chapter Seven, Freud could speak allusively about the dreamer straddling his mother. Such a libidinalization of Freud's writing is brought closer to home when we attend to the larger elements of discursive strategy in the Dreambook.

The Dreambook combines both exposition and narrative: if the focus of its exposition, the dream, is symbolic, so are the scene and movement of its narrative. In the clearest terms Freud explained the investigation in his book as a journey through nature – both its landscape, symbolic of the female genitalia, and woods, generally symbolic of the mother (Freud, 1900a, pp. 355 and 684; 1915-1917, pp. 156 and 159-160). First of all, here is what Freud privately wrote to Fliess:

> The whole thing is planned on the model of an imaginary walk. At the beginning, the dark forest of authors (who do not see the trees), hopelessly lost on wrong tracks. Then a concealed pass through which I lead the reader... and then suddenly the high ground and the view and the question: which way do you wish to go now? (Freud, 1985, p. 365).

If in this letter the dark forest designates the Dreambook's introductory historical survey of oneiric literature that was first urged by Fliess (Freud, 1985, pp. 354-355 and 362), in another letter Freud indulges in a more suggestive description: the introductory chapter is a thorny brushwood (*Dorngestrüpp*) in which most readers will get stuck and never proceed behind it to see the Sleeping Beauty (*Dornröschen*, literally, little thorny rose or hedge rose – Freud, 1985, p. 362; German edition, p. 397). As we know from the Grimms' tale that Freud is referring to, the Sleeping Beauty or embodiment of perfect feminity, struck by the curse of an evil fairy, is finally revived by the kiss of a rescuing prince. In Freud's private imagination, of course, both he and his ideal reader would be such daring co-conquistadorial princes.

Also in the *Interpretation of Dreams* Freud imagistically maps out his investigation as a journeying through a maternal landscape. The exposition in Chapter Two is symbolically identified as «passing through a narrow defile» (Freud, 1900a, p. 122); at this point Freud says that a dream fulfills a wish, but does not say infantile wish – that will come later. As the journey goes on, he takes the reader/cotraveler deeper into unconscious wishes. In Chapter Five he finally announces and explores the Œdipus complex. The preœdipal will finally come with the pitch of investigative excitement occurring in Chapter Seven, all of which was deliberately expressed in allusions (Freud, 1985, p. 362); and it is here that Freud seems to associate the deepest investigation into mental processes with a perilous descent into the archaic mother (see Mahony, 1987, pp. 119-110). Let us listen to his stark description:

> For it must be clearly understood that the easy and agreeable portion of our journey lies behind us. Hitherto, unless I am greatly mistaken, all the paths along which we have travelled have led us towards the light – towards elucidation and fuller understanding. But as soon as we endeavor to penetrate more deeply into the mental process involved in dreaming, every path will end in darkness (Freud, 1900a, p. 511).

In a word, corpus referred to both body and book, an equation later chiseled into the memorable phrase in *Moses and Monotheism:* «The distortion of a text resembles a murder» (Freud, 1939a, p. 43). And so, if the earlier part of Freud's systematic self-analysis led to the discovery of the Œdipal complex and the deceptive power of seductive fantasies, the later part of the self-analysis reshaped those fantasies, in the Dreambook, into an oedipal and preœdipal exploration of the maternal corpus.

112

Accordingly, Freud strove to have narrative strategy and epistemological investigation converge in his writing. More than a mere reaction to Fliess's writing failure, Freud's writing cure was an act of self-discovery, self recovery and growth, yes, a self-enabling and self-generative act.[14]

There's another part of our story that is so revealing. It deals with the stress[15] that led Freud to wait some six months before taking up the first draft of the *Interpretation of Dreams* and subjecting it to a second and final revision in 1899.[16] Publicly, Freud attributed the compositional delay to a lack of self-discipline (Freud, 1900a, p. 453) and to an anticipated distress over self-revelation (Freud, 1900a, p. 477). Privately to Fliess, however, Freud gave other reasons for not finishing the revision: neither could he fill in the gap owing to an important dream that had been dropped, nor could he complete the proposed connections between dreams and neuroses (cf. Freud, 1985, pp. 318, 332, 338-339, and 345). Anzieu's (1975, pp. 594, 619-620, 632, 658, 737-740) historical explanation for the publication delay partially manages to combine Freud's private and public excuses: namely the theoretical blockage that held up the revision was underpinned by unconscious fantasies about Freud's own impotence and castration; and these fantasies appeared in dreams that he could not fully verbalize[17].

In my opinion, a supplementary explanation is called for, and this will involve me in making the first major modification of my presentation's title. Freud's self-therapy was not just a writing cure, it was also a publishing cure. Much as in our own day, although in his own mode, Freud was caught in the turmoil of «publish or perish». For him, a complete œdipal victory entailed that he should follow in the steps of Shakespeare and expose his achievement in the public marketplace. Recall that in explaining the Œdipal complex in the *Interpretation of Dreams*, Freud alluded to *Hamlet* as a capital example, and added that the play was written immediately after the death of Shakespeare's father (Freud, 1900a, p. 265). Hence, if the writing of the *Interpretation of Dreams* was Freud's own filial mourning for «the most poignant loss» in his life (Freud, 1900a, p. XXVI), it was concurrently an œdipal triumph by means of a corpus that was both text and mother.

On another front, Freud was resisting the full awareness of how much the publication of the *Interpretation of Dreams* would effect an estrangement between himself and Fliess. For all its ills, their friendship had tempered a trying period so that any thought by Freud of a break-up would now be anxiogenic. Besides, in so many ways Freud's relations with Fliess proved more manageable than those with Breuer – Breuer was strictly a father figure for Freud, whereas Fliess offered the advantageous facility of being turned into a paternal and fraternal transferential object; moreover,

113

whereas Breuer was reluctant to receive communications of work in progress, Fliess could eagerly receive draft versions from Freud (Freud, 1985, p. 217). In accordance with such a dynamic Fliess figured variously in the production of *Interpretation of Dreams*. Let us note, for example, the generative significance proper to Freud's masterpiece: it began with the pregnancy of Freud's wife (the Irma dream) and ended with Freud's rushing its publication so that he could send it on time for Fliess's birthday (Freud, 1985, pp. 376 and 380). Remark too that if the co-authored *Studies on Hysteria* was Freud's first psychological book, his second was a «Dreamchild» (Freud, 1985, p. 405), which, though singly authored, nevertheless needed Fliess as «godfather» (Freud, 1985, p. 376).

On the balance, however, one must be prepared to accord a whole spectrum of meanings to the composition and publication of the *Interpretation of Dreams*. Freud felt that sending his self-proclaimed dung heap, seedling and new species (Freud, 1985, p. 353) to print would arouse «the painful feeling of parting with something which has been one's very own» (Freud, 1985, p. 376). In sum, Freud symbolically linked the book to the body of himself, his mother and Fliess, a polyvalency accompanied with anxieties of separation, castration and guilt. Yet I would suggest that the production and release of the *Interpretation of Dreams* constituted primarily an œdipal gesture, however short of complete success. I am thus led to make the second major modification of my presentation: Freud's self-analysis was a writing and publishing cure that was partial, not complete, and the subtext of *The Interpretation of Dreams* constituted a substantial amount of acting out, writing out and publishing out, whose meanings were insufficiently understood by Freud at the time.

In retrospect it is easy for us to follow the last act of the amity between Freud and his Berlin colleague, an amity that was dwindling into a memory. If Freud was desperately asking a place for dynamic influences in Fliess's dating, Fliess himself was charging that Freud's patients improved or worsened according to strict biological laws (Freud, 1985, p. 459). Freud epitomized their theoretical and personal impasse in this striking formula: «Thus we are becoming estranged from each other through what is most our own» (Freud, 1985, p. 398). Still in all, Freud was not quite ready to forsake the scriptive bond between them: bound by gratitude, Freud set about writing a kind of diary about one of his patients which he wanted to show Fliess (Freud, 1985, p.388), and Freud increased the needling of his unproductive friend (Freud, 1985, pp. 412, 421, 436, 141, and 468). By 1901 Freud found himself in an authorial imbroglio: on one hand, he withdrew the Dora case from publication because he allegedly lost his «only audience» in Fliess (Freud, 1985, pp. 450, 456, 457-458 fn.); on the other hand, Freud proposed that together they write a book on bisexuality (pp. 448 and 450. As we know, if that wish were ever fulfilled, it was only in a dream.

When correspondence was circumstantially resumed between Freud and Fliess in 1904, it dealt – not surprisingly – with none other than the subject of publication, and quickly soured into accusations about plagiarism; the very last bitter exchange between Freud and Fliess died out around the start of the summer holidays. But at the end of those holidays, as we recall, Freud visited the Acropolis; there he experienced a derealization that was brought on by guilt for surpassing his father, hence a telling residue of Freud's incomplete self-analysis and its writing out. We may now skip to 1936 when it took the celebration for another writer, Romain Rolland, in order that Freud write up his Acropolis visit as a piece of self-analysis. In the remaining part of 1936, a ghost from the past would resurrect to put Freud's self-analysis to a gruelling, nightmarish test. Precisely on December 30, Marie Bonaparte wrote to Freud that she had come upon his letters to Fliess and was ready to purchase them from the eager bookseller.

On January 3, 1937, Freud replied that these «most intimate» and «highly embarrassing» letters should not «become known to posterity» (Freud, 1985, p. 7). Thus, at both ends of his analytics Freud balked at the publication of a piece of his self-analysis – the *Interpretation of Dreams* decades earlier, and now his correspondence with Fliess. But that is not all, although the rest of our story is brief. With the news of his resurrected self-analysis fresh in his mind, Freud sat down two weeks later to write the finished copy of *Analysis Terminable and Interminable*.[18] The anguishing repercussions of the correspondence continued to remain with him, as can be measured by the fact that prior to 1936 he never talked with his daughter Anna about Fliess, and only «most sparingly» after that date (Freud, 1985, p. 4). Perhaps from our belated perspective, we can more clearly trace the continuity of the writing cure between *The Interpretation of Dreams* and *Analysis Terminable and Interminable*, and we might even risk summing them in one title: Self-analysis, dreaming, writing: terminable and interminable.

Notes

[1]   «Ego proinde fateor me ex eorum numero esse conari, qui proficiendo scribunt et scribendo proficiunt» (Augustine, *Omnia Opera*, 2: 690).

[2]   «Egoque ipse multa quae nesciebam scribendo me didicisse confitear» (Augustine, *Omnia Opera*, 8: 1218).

[3] For a while, however, it seems that Freud did analyze himself silently and without recourse to writing (Freud, 1985, pp. 284 and 294).

[4] See the German text in the *Gesammelte Werke* (2/3: 649 ff.), which renders the dream and its associations in the present tense. The resultant immediacy contrasts with the distance effect brought about by Strachey's recourse to the past tense (Freud, 1901, pp. 636 ff.).

[5] Of the four journals on drekkology or anality which Freud wrote up, at least three contained dreams (Freud, 1985, pp. 291-301). Although Freud avowed writing the journals for Fliess (p. 301), he had not sent the first one, which contained «wild dreams» that were, Freud said, «part of my self-analysis» (p. 291). Such a declaration makes clear that Fliess was not privy to all of Freud's self-analysis.

[6] The most influential of these patients was Mr. E.; we know specifically of two dreams by Freud about this patient (Freud, 1900a, pp. 435-439 and 455-459). Through dreams and memories about his nannie and his childhood libidinal attraction to «matrem nudam» (Freud, 1985, p. 268), Freud discovered his own œdipal complex and was «on the way to grasping its universal application»; thus, Freud's belief in œdipal universality was confirmed, not initiated, by one of Mr. E.'s dreams (Freud, 1901b, p. 178 – for a chronologically reverse and erroneous interpretation of this influence, see Anzieu, 1975, p. 331).

[7] Cf. Gay, 1988; Jones, 1955, pp. 6, 387 and 482; and Freud, 1985, p. 73.

[8] The dates and places of the Congresses are as follows: Berlln, September, 1897 (Freud, 1985, p. 311ff. and 355 ff.); Breslau, December, 1897 (Freud, 1985, p. 290); possibly in the Vienna surroundings, May, 1898 (Freud, 1985, pp. 314-315); possibly Aussee, July, 1898 (Freud, 1985, p. 320); Baden, December, 1898 (Freud, 1985, p. 337); Innsbruck, April, 1899 (Freud, 1985, p. 349).

[9] Martin's poetic activitv began in April, 1897 (Freud, 1985, p. 236) and, by strange historical fate (identification with his father) seemed for a while to peter out by October, 1899 (p. 377).

[10] With the onset of 1900, however, there was a two-month lull in Freud's writing (Freud, 1985, p. 404).

[11] I cannot forego making an association to the «separate» categories of the scientlfic and therapeutic: *science* and *schizo* ultimately come from the same Indo-European root, *skei* (to cut). In Greek, skhizein means to split; *science* more immediately stems from the Latin *scire*, to know, that is, to split or separate one thing from another. Thus philological examination unexpectedly sheds light on the possible restorative functions of such different entities as science and schizophrenia.

[12] Earlier during his self-analysis Freud considered writing his book to be an alternate activity (Freud, 1985, p. 299). But by the middle of 1899 he postulated an analogous relationship between the two activities – cf. the highly significant expression, «as it were» (Freud, 1900, p. 477; G.W. 2/3: 481).

[13] Compare the somewhat disparate statements in Anzieu (1975, pp. 590 and 661). This shaky conceptualization extends to Anzieu's other position that when there is a coincidence of two or three of the Dreambook's directive personages (dreamer, interpreter, narrator, theoretician), Freud becomes paralyzed. But at least the first three coincide in Freud's enactive prose.

[14] See Homans (1988, pp. 17, 26, 31-33) for later examples of self-healing in Freud's writing.

[15] See under the headings «Neurotic symptoms» (pp. 740-741) and «Hysterical symptoms» (p. 736) in the index to Volume 5 of the *Standard Edition*. Cf. Grinstein (1980, p. 20): some of the repetitiveness in the *Interpretation of Dreams* might have arisen from Freud's

«inability to deal adequately with certain unconscious material which, therefore, kept striving for expression during this period. Finally, the working through of infantile attachments, that we now take so much for granted, must have been extremely difficult for him.»

[16] In the *Interpretation of Dreams* Freud gave the impression that the work as a whole had been «finished» in 1898 and that he then waited for over a year before deciding to publish it (Freud, 1900a, p. 477; *G.W.* 2/3: 481). This is simply not true. First, Freud finished the initial draft by July, 1898, and began the second draft in May, 1899. Second, as his letters to Fliess show, the second draft underwent revisions and added the entirely new seventh chapter.

[17] Anzieu (1975, p. 313) even generalizes that a castration fantasy underlay the paralysis which Freud seemed to have experienced before making each of his great discoveries.

[18] I am relying on my photocopy of the holograph, whose first page bears the date 18.1.1937, also in Freud's handwriting.

Appendix

The dating of Freud's self-analysis is one of the quagmires of psychoanalytic scholarship, not the least due to Freud's own erroneous commentary: on November 14, 1897, he wrote that there was no sign of his self-analysis until after the summer holidays (Freud, 1985, p. 279), a statement belied, for example, by his letters of June 22 (p. 254) and July 7 (p. 255). A further difficulty is that in his correspondence to Fliess, Freud referred to his «self-analysis» as such from August 14, 1897 (p. 261) to January 3, 1899 (p. 338), although his looser allusions to this have fostered a variety of chronological interpretations. With some inconsistencies of his own, Anzieu (1975) breaks it down into three phases:

a) September-October, 1897 (pp. 582-583) – but cf. p. 311: «between June and August, 1897, Freud undertakes to make it (his self-analysis) systematic».

b) Spring, 1898, the time of Freud's writing the first version of the *Interpretation of Dreams* (pp. 582-583) – but on page 353 Anzieu assigns the first version to February-July, 1898, a dating somewhat in agreement with Kris's (Freud, 1954, p. 34) limitation of the first version to the period of the spring and summer,1898.

c) Spring-summer, 1899, the time of Freud's drafting the second version of the *Interpretation of Dreams* (pp. 582-583) – but in another place Anzieu sees the version beginning in mid-January (p. 370), an alternate quite later than autumn, 1898, which Kris proposes as the beginning of the second version (1954, p. 34). A greater dating difficulty occurs in Anzieu's irregular chronicling of the third phase of Freud's self-analysis: Freud lived «in a permanent self-analytic atmosphere» (p. 718); his self-analysis ended in 1900 (p. 733), in 1901 (pp. 724 and 729); he was in occasional self-analysis from November, 1899 to Feburary, 1901 (p. 663); his trip to Rome in September, 1901 terminated his systematic self-analysis (p. 288).

Although fully assured precision cannot be arrived at, we do have some rectifying facts at our disposal. First, Freud began his Dreambook on May, 1897 (pp. 243 and 249), i.e., before his intensified self-analysis. Second, the current term «systematic self-analysis» must be used with caution: a) Freud applied *a* «systematic» analysis to his Irma dream in 1895; b) «systematic» should neither be used freely to mean uninterupted, for Freud's systematic self-analysis was indeed one of fits and starts. Evidence will only allow Freud's self-analysis to signify one that was intensified for shorter or longer periods. Equipped with these clarifications, we may conclude the following:

a) Freud tried writing his Dreambook, quickly fell into a writing block, and then began a systematic self-analysis. Its first phase was closing toward the end of 1897; on November 5, Freud said that it was trickling (Freud, 1985, p. 277) and by November 14 he reported its continued interruption (p. 281).

b) The second phase started around the beginning of December, 1897 (pp. 284-285) and culminated in the writing of the four private «drekkological» journals, that were finished by the beginning of February, 1898 (p. 301).

c) By February 9, 1898, Freud resumed composing the first version of the Dreambook (p. 298), which he had begun before the start of his systematic self-analysis. By July 7, 1898 he finished the first version (p. 319).

d) After a period of fruitful intermittent self-analysis early in 1899 (see the letters of January 3 (p. 338) and March 2 (p. 347)), Freud started composing the second version of the Dreambook, i.e., at the end of May, 1899 (p. 353); he terminated it by September 11, 1899 and saw it published in November. The ending of this phase of the systematic self-analysis should be left an open question, for relevant traces are sporadic: on December 21, 1899 Freud (p. 392) reported an advance in self-knowledge; on March 11, 1900 he revealed that, with serious matters banished from his mind, he had not written a line for the previous two months (p. 404).

A final caveat. One must take care in interpreting Freud's claim that writing of the *Interpretation of Dreams* was part of his self-analysis. An initial writing block had induced Freud to begin a systematic self-analysis. The latter proceeded for some time before Freud got back to writing the *Interpretation of Dreams* proper.

References

ANZIEU, D. (1975). *L'auto-analyse de Freud*. 2 vols. Paris: Presses Universitaires de France.

AUGUSTINE, St. (1836). *Omnia Opera*, vols. 2 & 8. Paris: Gaume.

BARTHES, R. (1964). *Essais critiques*. Paris: Seuil.

— (1975). *Roland Barthes par Roland Barthes*. Paris: Seuil.

FREUD, S. (1893-1895). Studies on Hysteria. *Standard Edition, 2.*

— (1898a). Sexuality in the Aetiology of the Neuroses. *Standard Edition, 3,* 259-285.

— (1900a). The Interpretation of Dreams. *Standard Edition, 4-5.*

— (1901a). On Dreams. *Standard Edition, 5,* 629-686.

— (1901b). The Psychopathology of Everyday Life. *Standard Edition, 6.*

— (1905d). Three Essays on Sexuality. *Standard Edition, 7,* 123-243.

— (1910a). Five Lectures on Psycho-Analysis. *Standard Edition, 11,* 1-55.

— (1912e). Recommendations to Physicians Practising Psycho-Analysis. *Standard Edition, 12,* 109-120.

— (1914d). On the History of the Psycho-Analytic Movement. *Standard Edition, 14,* 1-66.

— (1915-1917). Introductory Lectures to Psycho-Analysis. *Standard Edition, 15-16.*

— (1920b). A Note on the Prehistory of the Technique of Analysis. *Standard Edition, 18,* 263-265.

FREUD, S. (1923c). Remarks on the Theory and Practice of Dream-Interpretation. *Standard Edition*, *19*, 107-121.

— (1926c). Prefatory Note to a Paper by E. Pickworth Farrow. *Standard Edition*, *20*, 280.

— (1937c). Analysis Terminable and Interminable. *Standard Edition*, *23*, 209-253.

— (1939a). Moses and Monotheism. *Standard Edition*, *23*, 1-137.

— (1954). *The Origins of Psychoanalysis*. London: Imago.

— (1985). *The Complete Letters of Sigmund Freud to Wilhelm Fliess*. Cambridge, Mass.: Harvard University Press.

GAY, P. (1988). *Freud: A Life for Our Time*. New York: Norton.

GRINSTEIN, A. (1980). *Sigmund Freud's Dreams*. New York: International Universities Press.

HOMANS, P. (1988). Disappointment and the Ability to Mourn: De-Idealization as a Psychological Theme in Freud's Life, Thought, and Social Circumstances., 1906-1914. *In*: Stepansky, P. (ed.): *Freud: Appraisals and Reappraisals*, vol. 2. Hillsdale, N.J.: Analytic Press, pp. 3-101.

JONES, E. (1953-1955). *The Life and Work of Sigmund Freud*, vols. 1 & 2. New York: Basic Books.

MAHONY, P. (1979). Friendship and its Discontents. *Contemporary Psychoanalysis*, *15*, 55-109.

— (1987). *Freud as a Writer*. 2nd enlarged edition. New Haven: Yale University Press.

WEBER, S. (1982). *The Legend of Freud*. Minneapolis: University of Minnesota Press.

Cahiers Psychiatriques Genevois, Special Issue, 1994, pp. 121-133

«MOTHER, HAVE YOU GOT A WIWIMAKER TOO?» FREUD'S REPRESENTATION OF FEMALE SEXUALITY IN THE CASE OF LITTLE HANS

Peter L. Rudnytsky

It is by now a commonplace to observe that Freud's case histories are themselves great works of literature that demand to be read with the sophisticated techniques of literary criticism.[1] Whatever one may think of Freud's ideas, there can be no doubt of his brilliance as a writer. Indeed, it is a testimony to Freud's genius that his works continue to be sources of instruction and inspiration for each new generation of readers however much one finds in them to dispute.

The case of Little Hans, entitled *Analysis of a Phobia in a Five-Year-Old Boy* (1909), has a special place in the annals of psychoanalysis because it is the first recorded instance of a child analysis. Part of the distinctiveness of the case, moreover, is that the child in question, whose real name was Herbert Graf, was not analyzed by Freud himself (though he did see the child for a single consultation) but by his own father, the musicologist Max Graf, who belonged to the small group of Freud's adherents that in 1908 became the Vienna Psychoanalytic Society. The complex narrative structure inherent in any case history, which must strive to capture the dynamics both of the treatment process and of the patient's life, is thus compounded by the way that Freud's text contains extensive extracts of dialogue and other material reported by the father, punctuated by Freud's editorial comments. The effect is to create a multilayered text, much like a work of modernist fiction, in which Hans plays the part of the hero, the father of the unreliable and Freud of the omniscient narrator. Underlying these formal intricacies is what would be deemed by today's standards a highly irregular transferential situation, in which the father combined the roles of parent and analyst and had in addition his own deeply invested relationship to Freud.[2] Hans's mother, moreover, had herself been a patient of Freud's, and it was thanks to her that her husband had been introduced first to Freud's work and then to the man himself in 1900 (Graf, 1942, p. 467). Rather than the therapy of an individual child, therefore, the case of Little Hans is better understood as an instance of family therapy, a precursor of Freud's own even more ill-advised experiment in commingling parental and professional roles in his prolonged analysis of his daughter Anna (Mahony, 1992).[3]

In what follows, I shall approach the case of Little Hans from a feminist standpoint. Precisely because it constitutes Freud's quintessential depiction of the crystallization of masculine sexuality and identity, I shall argue that this text likewise shows the genesis of his views on sexual difference and *female* sexuality, which are then codified in his notorious later papers. It thus calls for a critique along the lines of that provided by Luce Irigaray (1974) in her brilliant dissection of the chapter on «Femininity» in the *New Introductory Lectures on Psycho-Analysis* (1933.)[4] Accordingly, I shall examine Freud's confused and misogynistic attitudes toward female sexuality in Little Hans and show their connection to his phallocentric perspective; in a brief coda, I shall contend that the case also reveals a heterosexist bias.

The first words of Little Hans, spoken before the age of three and two years before the outbreak of his phobia, to be reported by his father and quoted by Freud in his case history, are the question: «Mother, have you got a wiwimaker *(Wiwimacher)* too?» (*G.W.*, 7:245; *S.E.*, 10:7).[5] Like the first communication by a patient entering analysis, these words acquire an ever-increasing resonance and can by the end of the process be seen to have held the key to the entire mystery. Strictly speaking, Hans's «analysis», if we deign to refer to the didactic interest taken by his father in Hans's condition by this term, has not yet commenced; but insofar as Hans's analysis now exists only in the form of Freud's written record, everything that is contained therein may be said to belong to it.

The question of whether or not women possess a penis is no less urgent for the whole of Freudian theory than it is for Little Hans's analysis. Indeed, if we regard all of Freud's writings as fragments of his interminable self-analysis, it is not difficult to surmise that the introduction of this issue as a leitmotiv is determined chiefly by Freud's own preoccupations. When, in *The Infantile Genital Organization*, Freud codifies his conviction that initially «for both sexes, only one genital, namely the male one, comes into account» by the interpolation of the phallic phase into his libido theory (Freud, 1923e, p. 142), he does so with reference to the case of Little Hans.[6] Pursuing the same line of thought, he later explains fetishism (1927e) exclusively in phallic terms as a defense against castration anxiety, triggered by the boy's glimpse of the female genitals, a substitute for the disavowed missing penis of the mother.

In probing the way that sexual difference is presented in the case of Little Hans, we find confusion perpetrated at every turn by adults – by Little Hans's parents, but above all by Freud – and the child doing his best to sort things out for himself. To Hans's repeated queries about whether she has a wiwimaker, his mother answers «of course» and «naturally» (*G.W.*, 7:245, 247; *S.E.*, 10:7, 10). Like his parents' promulgation of the fable that the stork is responsible for bringing his baby sister Hanna, this misleading account of the female genitalia deserves to be called a lie. Linked to sexual difference is the distinction between what is animate and inanimate, and here too the wiwimaker comes into play. At three and three quarters, Hans sees a locomotive from which water is being released and says it is «making wiwi». He wonders where its wiwimaker is located. He adds on reflection: «A dog and a horse have a wiwimaker; a table and a chair don't.» On this Freud comments: «So he has gained an essential characteristic for differentiating between the animate and the inanimate» (*G.W.*, 7:246-47; *S.E.*, 10:9).

The confusion into which Hans is led by those who should know better is not only anatomical but also semantic. Indeed, in the interplay between biological and linguistic frames of reference in the term «wiwimaker» we can observe the penis in the process of becoming the phallus or transcendental signifier in the full Lacanian sense of this term. For although by «wiwimaker» Hans most obviously means «penis», the word itself refers to an organ for urination, which women of course do possess. Thus, in one sense Hans's mother is correct to say that she does have a wiwimaker, though not in the disingenuous way that she implies. That Hans is concerned not simply with whether women have a penis but with how they urinate is made clear when he asks his father: «But how do girls make wiwi if they don't have a wiwimaker?» His father gives him an evasive answer: «They don't have a wiwimaker like yours. Haven't you seen when Hanna has been given a bath?» Moments earlier, however, Hans's father had told him that «girls and women don't have a wiwimaker» (*G.W.*, 7:267; *S.E.*, 10:31). These statements do not cohere. The father uses «wiwimaker» ambiguously to say both that women possess an anatomy unlike Hans's and that they do not have a penis. He thus simultaneously defines women in terms of a lack when measured against a male norm and adumbrates the possibility of regarding the two sexes as different but equal (though the word «wiwimaker» retains an androcentric bias that forever precludes this possibility from being realized).

Freud, as I have indicated, far from mitigating Little Hans's bewilderment, actually exacerbates it. His ready acceptance of the equation between the female and the inanimate is especially disturbing. (As one of my students at the University of Florida exclaimed, «I guess I'm a table!»).

In the final section of his narrative, «Epicrisis»,[7] Freud reiterates that Hans «discovers that on the basis of the readiness-to-hand *(Vorhandenseins)* or absence of the wiwimaker one can differentiate between what is living and lifeless» (*G.W.*, 7:341; *S.E.*, 10:106). By treating this hypothesis even provisionally as a «discovery» on Hans's part, instead of as a childish error, Freud remakes Hans in his own image as a phallocrat. Of course, Hans uses his own body as a basis for comparison and wonders how his mother and other females are different. But the point of his questions is precisely to clarifiy *how* they are different, not to assume that they must be identical. That is *Freud's* mistake, not Hans's. He writes of Hans's displays of affection toward boy as well as girl playmates: «Hans is homosexual, as all children may well be, completely in accordance with the not to be overlooked fact that he only *knows one kind of genital*, a genital like his own» (*G.W.*, 7:344-345; *S.E.*, 10:110; Freud's italics). By employing the collective noun «children» *(Kinder)* instead of the gender-specific «boys» *(Knaben)*, Freud elides the situation of girls, who presumably also take their own bodies as a point of reference even though, according to his own theory, they too only know one kind of genital – that belonging to males.[8] (How girls, who apparently know only genitals *unlike* their own, could ever become homosexual remains entirely mysterious in Freud's account.)

Freud's insistence on the primacy of the phallus is allied to his conviction of the centrality of the castration complex to the discovery of sexual difference. The case of Little Hans provides the prototype upon which he bases this claim; not coincidentally, the term «castration complex» is first introduced with reference to it.[9] In a pattern that Freud does not hesitate to call «typical for the sexual development of the child» (*G.W.*, 7:245; *S.E.*, 10:7), Hans is first threatened by his mother with castration as a punishment for masturbation and later catches sight of the genitalia of his baby sister, which brings home to him the reality of this threat. The structure of retrospective signification linking these two events exemplifies a distinctively psychoanalytic mode of temporality. As Freud remarks, «it would be entirely the typical procedure if the threat of castration now came to effect through *deferred action (nachträglich)*» (*G.W.*, 7:271; *S.E.*, 10:35).

In order to realize how deep an impression the case of Little Hans left on Freud's thinking, it suffices to quote the following passage from «Femininity» in the *New Introductory Lectures:*

> In [boys] the castration complex arises after they have learnt from the sight of the female genitals that the organ which they value so highly need not necessarily accompany the body. At this the boy recalls to mind the threats he brought on himself by his doings with that organ, he begins to give credence to them and falls under the influence of fear of castration, which will be the most powerful motive force in his subsequent development (1933a, p. 124-125).

Freud does not cite the analysis of Little Hans as corroboration, but it is clear that he has relied on it as a precedent. Not only is there an identical sequence of events – a verbal threat followed by a visual glimpse – but Freud's emphasis on the gaze that defines the female genitalia in terms of absence is crucial to the case. The primacy of the phallus thus has as its corollary the primacy of the gaze, and both define female sexuality simply as the negative of the male. The above-quoted passage from «Femininity» continues: «The castration complex of girls is also started by the sight of the other sex» (*S.E.*, 22:125).[10]

Hans's father's equivocal pronouncements about the female genitalia are efforts to implement the advice of Freud. In order to rid Hans of his desire to see his mother's genitals and set him on the «way to sexual enlightenment», Freud counsels, his father should inform him at a propitious moment that «his mama and all other female beings – as indeed he could know from Hanna – do not possess a wiwimaker at all» (*G.W.*, 7:264; *S.E.*, 10:28). The problem here again is that of defining women solely in terms of privation. As Jules Glenn has observed, «Hans was to be told that a girl has no penis, thus indicating that she is deficient,» and not that a girl «has a vulva (including the clitoris), vagina, and uterus» (1980, p. 125).[11] Although it might not have been necessary to enter with Little Hans into such encyclopedic detail concerning the female anatomy, it surely ought to have been possible to present the facts of life to him in a less distorted way. When Freud writes that «the enlightenment... that women truly do not have a wiwimaker can only have shattered his self-confidence and awakened his castration complex» (*G.W.*, 7:271; *S.E.*, 10:36), he is right in his assessment of the traumatic effects on Little Hans of his father's lessons, but wrong to dignify misinformation by calling it «enlightenment».

Despite Freud's recommendation that Hans be told that women do not have a wiwimaker, moreover, Hans's father persists in using this word. «You know, don't you, how Hanna's wiwimaker looks?» (*G.W.*, 7:297; *S.E.*, 10:62), he asks later in the analysis; and he doggedly insinuates (notwithstanding his son's denials) that Hans has seen his mother's genital area: «Perhaps black hair by the wiwimaker, when you were curious and looked» (*G.W.*, 7:302; *S.E.*, 10:67). Thus, just as Hans's mother leads him into confusion by her affirmative answers to his question about whether she has a wiwimaker, so his father undercuts such accurate information as he does impart about the difference between the sexes by continuing to speak of girls and women as possessing wiwimakers.

In keeping with its function as a transcendental signifier, the dilemmas facing Hans are in large measure caused by the fact that the word «wiwimaker» is used by his parents with a range of connotations – penis, urinary organ, genital organ, and genital area – and these multiple meanings are never disentangled for him. Because the primary definition of «penis» cannot be escaped even when the metonymic reference is more general, however, the word, as I have already indicated, inevitably carries a sexist overtone.[12] Freud's semantics prove even slipperier than those of Hans's parents. In a lengthy footnote near the beginning of the narrative, which expatiates on Hans's alleged inability to credit his perception that his baby sister does not have a wiwimaker, Freud adds that «behind the error a piece of correct recognition is hidden. The little girl to be sure also possesses a little wiwimaker, which we call the clitoris, even though it doesn't grow, but remains stunted» (*G.W.*, 7:249*n*1; *S.E.*, 10:12*n*3). In this version, his contention is not that women don't have penises, but that they have vestigal ones. To the other meanings of wiwimaker, therefore, we must add that of the clitoris. The best retort to Freud's demeaning view of this organ is provided by Jodi Bray, one of my students at the University of Florida, who has remarked that the clitoris «grows to the size necessary to perform its very useful functions» (1992, p. 8). Indeed, the clitoris grows larger as the child matures and undergoes tumescence during sexual activity. Little Hans seems to have grasped this truth more securely than Freud, for to his father's statement that when Hanna grows up her wiwimaker will not look like his, he replies: «I know that. It will be the way it is, only bigger» (*G.W.*, 7:297; *S.E.*, 10:62).

In view of Freud's own obfuscation of the complexities of the female genitals, it is ironic that he should remark: «The child naturally lacks an essential piece in the understanding of sexual relations as long as the female genital is undiscovered» (*G.W.*, 7:323; *S.E.*, 10:87). That children of both sexes lack a knowledge of the vagina is an integral component of Freud's phallocentric perspective. What makes this contention most outrageous in context is its complete irrelevance to the foregoing conversation between Hans and his father, which has to do not with the female body but with Hans's doubts about the father's role in procreation and how he can «belong» to the latter when it is his mother who has brought him into the world.[13]

Just as Freud imposes his theory of the ignorance of the vagina, so he refuses to believe that it is possible for boys to envy women their procreative capacity. Notwithstanding Freud's denials, however, Hans on numerous occasions voices a desire to give birth to children as his mother has done. To his father's assertion: «You would like to be the Daddy and be married to Mommy, would like to be as big as I am and have a moustache, and would like Mommy to have a child», Hans replies: «Daddy, and until I'm married I'll only have one when I want to, when I'll be married to Mommy, and if I don't want to have a child, God doesn't want it either, when I've gotten married» (*G.W.*, 7:320; *S.E.*, 10:92). The confused syntax here captures the child's primary process thinking, but what comes through unmistakably is that Hans, despite his father's Freudian promptings, desires not simply to marry but to *be* Mommy. The child's identifications are multiple, maternal as well as paternal. Most strikingly, Hans shows that he has introjected his mother's ambivalent attitude toward becoming pregnant, since his declaration, «if I don't want to have a child, God doesn't want it either», is a direct allusion to his mother's words in an earlier quarrel with his father (*G.W.*, 7:327; *S.E.*, 10:91). Ignoring all this empirical evidence, Freud insists in a footnote: «There is no necessity here to ascribe to Hans a feminine trait of longing to have children» (*G.W.*, 7:328; *S.E.*, 10:93).[14]

Further proof of Hans's awareness of the female anatomy is his mockery of the hypothesis that his sister Hanna was brought by the stork. When Hans tells his father that until the preceding year, when the newly born Hanna accompanied the family by train on their summer holiday to Gmunden, «*But always before that she travelled with us in the box*», the «box», as Freud interprets in a footnote, «is naturally the womb» of the mother (*G.W.*, 7:304; *S.E.*, 10:69-70; Freud's italics).[15] Freud continues: «What can the assertion that the preceding summer Hanna already travelled to Gmunden «in the box» mean other than his knowledge of the pregnancy of his mother?» (*G.W.*, 7:305; *S.E.*, 10:71). Just as absurdity in dreams, according to Freud, often heralds mockery in the latent dream thoughts, so Hans's seemingly nonsensical replies to his father's questions are a way of saying, in Freud's paraphrase: «*If you can expect me to believe that the stork brought Hanna in October, when I already noticed mother's big body in the summer when we travelled to Gmunden, then I can require you to believe my lies*» (*G.W.*, 7:305; *S.E.*, 10:70-71; Freud's italics). Hans likewise indicates a grasp of the concept of a fetus when he tells his father: «She was already in the world a long time, even when she wasn't there yet» (*G.W.*, 7:308; S.E., 10:73).

In addition to noticing his mother's pregnancy, Hans conveys a comprehension of sexual intercourse through two fantasies involving himself and his father. In the first, as he says, «I was with you in Schönbrunn near the sheep, and then we crawled under the cord, and we told the guard at the entrance of the garden about it, and he packed us up» (*G.W.*, 7:275; *S.E.*, 10:40). In the second, «I was travelling with you on the train, and we smashed a window, and the guard took us away» (*G.W.*, 7:276; *S.E.*, 10:41). Freud sums up Hans's conception of sexual intercourse near the conclusion of the case history:

> It must have to do with an act of violence, which one carried out on the Mama, with a smashing, a creating of an opening, a forcing into an enclosed space, the impulse to which the child could feel in himself. But although he was on the way, aided by the sensations in his penis, to postulating the existence of the vagina, he still

could not solve the riddle [*das Rätsel nicht lösen*], because to his knowledge no such thing existed as his wiwimaker needed; much rather did the conviction that his Mama possessed a wiwimaker like his own stand in the way of the solution [*Lösung*]. (G.W., 7:366; *S.E.*, 10: 134-135).

As so often, Freud is at once incontrovertibly right and alarmingly wrong – right in his interpretation of Hans's fantasies and wrong in his assertion that Hans is ignorant of the existence of the vagina. For what is the «enclosed space» into which Hans imagines forcing himself, that opening he longs to penetrate, if not his mother's vagina, the reality of which he is more than dimly aware, just as he intuits her possession of the womb in which she carries his baby sister?

What is mysterious in all this is not the mentation of Little Hans but how Freud could persist so resolutely in not seeing what lay before him in plain sight. Time after time, Freud introduces evidence that demonstrates womb envy or an accurate picture of the female sexual organs on the part of Little Hans, yet disregards it and insists on his own bizarre theories of the maternal penis and female castration.[16] Although a biographical examination of the origins of Freud's phallocentrism is beyond my scope here, suffice it to say that feminist scholars have convincingly traced many of his difficulties to his conflicted relationship with his preœdipal mother (Roith, 1987; Sprengnether, 1990). But I hope to have made it clear that a feminist perspective is no less relevant to reading the case history of the male Little Hans than that of the more celebrated heroine Dora. With the benefit of hindsight, it is salutary to contrast the obsolescence of Freud's views on gender with the percipience of Karen Horney, the first and still one of the most incisive of his feminist critics. She writes:

> On the one hand, of course, a boy will automatically conclude that everyone else is made like himself; but on the other hand his phallic impulses surely bid him instinctively to search for the appropriate opening in the female body – an opening, moreover, that he himself lacks, for the one sex always seeks in the other that which is complementary to it or of a nature different from its own (1932, p. 140).

Although not referring to Little Hans, Horney's remarks are a far more adequate interpretation of his sexual fantasies than Freud's claim that «to his knowledge no such thing existed as his wiwimaker needed». Equally pertinently, though again without appealing to Little Hans for confirmation, Horney challenges Freud's exclusive preoccupation with penis envy by observing that «in boys of the same age, we meet with parallel expressions in the form of wishes to possess breasts or to have a child» (1933, p. 151).[17] And without mentioning Freud by name, Horney intimates the personal origins of his theoretical blindness: «If the grown man continues to regard woman as the great mystery, in whom is a secret he cannot divine, this feeling of his can only relate ultimately to one thing in her: the mystery of motherhood. Everything else is merely a residue of his dread of this» (1932, p. 141).

As a coda to this discussion, it cannot be overlooked that Freud evinces an attitude toward homosexuality no less prejudiced than that toward female sexuality. Recent work in gay and lesbian studies has built on and carried further the intellectual revolution wrought by feminism, while at the same time providing a cautionary reminder that the politics of gender and sexuality need to be analyzed separately.[18] In their preoccupation with issues of *gender* difference, in other words, feminists are in danger of eliding equally important issues of *sexual* difference.

I cite three instances of Freud's heterosexist bias in Little Hans, all from the first section of the case. Right at the outset, after introducing Hans's question to his mother about whether she has a wiwimaker, Freud reports that Hans saw a cow being milked and said that milk was coming out of its wiwimaker. Then, invoking his own earlier data in the Dora case, Freud assures the reader that «one does not need to be unduly shocked if one finds in a female being the idea of sucking at the male member», since it has an innocent origin in the experience of sucking at the mother's breast, and the cow's udder provides a ready visual link between the breast and the penis (*G.W.*, 7:245; *S.E.*, 10:7). But why does Freud limit his exculpation to women, since fellatio is manifestly an act also performed by men? The answer can only be that he is thinking exclusively in heterosexual terms. Several pages later, Freud describes the four-year-old Hans's verbal and physical displays of affection toward a male cousin of five and exclaims: «Our little Hans seems to be truly a paragon of depravities!» (*G.W.*, 7:252; *S.E.*, 10:15). And again, Freud recounts how Hans did not retract his desire to sleep with the fourteen-year-old Mariedl despite a threat from his mother that he would have to leave the house: «Our little Hans conducted himself like a real man in the face of his mother's challenge, in spite of his homosexual proclivities» (*G.W.*, 7:254; *S.E.*, 10:17). Homosexuals, therefore, are not real men. These remarks are all admittedly intended to be lighthearted, but it is precisely their casual nature that allows us to catch Freud offguard, as it were, to glimpse the bourgeois prejudices that are veiled in his more circumspect theoretical pronouncements. That Freud's disparagement of homosexuality, no less than of female sexuality, is seriously disturbing cannot, I think, be doubted, and it should be censured by all those who are drawn to psychoanalysis as a means not of oppressing but of emancipating the human spirit.

Notes

[1] See Marcus (1974) for an early and exemplary demonstration of this claim with respect to the Dora case.

[2] That this relationship was a conflictual one is attested by the fact that, despite Max Graf's reverence for Freud's «creative imagination and real genius», when Freud in 1910 compelled his followers to choose between attending his group or Adler's, Graf refused «to submit to Freud's 'do' or 'don't'... and nothing was left for me but to withdraw from his circle» (1942, p. 475; see Silverman, 1980, p. 115).

[3] Apparently, the experiments in unconventional analysis continued in the Graf household. In a February 2, 1910 letter to Jung, Freud writes: «I should have thought it impossible to analyze one's own wife. Little Hans's father has proved to me that it can be done. In such analysis, however, it just seems too difficult to observe the technical rule whose importance I have lately begun to suspect: "surmount counter-transference"» (McGuire, 1974, p. 291). One wonders what Freud thought of the impediment presented by this «technical rule» when it came to his own analysis of Anna. On the case of Little Hans as family therapy, see Strean (1967).

[4] For other powerful readings of Freud in the French feminist tradition, see Cixous & Clément (1975) and Kofman (1980). None of these writers, however, deals with Little Hans.

[5] Because this paper is based on a reading of Little Hans in the original German, all passages from this case history are my own translation. For ease of reference, volume and page citations will be provided to both the *Gesammelte Werke* and the *Standard Edition*. Strachey's translation of *Wiwimacher* as «widdler» is an inspired one, but in order to preserve the verb form «to make wiwi» I prefer a more literal rendering. Other works will be cited from the *Standard Edition*.

[6] In his notes to this paper in the *Standard Edition*, James Strachey draws attention to Freud's allusions to the case of Little Hans in his twofold claim that boys look for a penis not only in all living creatures but also in inanimate objects and that they ward off threats of castration by convincing themselves that girls do possess a penis, but a small one, which will soon grow bigger (Freud, 1923e, pp. 142n1, 144n1).

[7] The German word *«Epikrise»* is defined as a «concluding critical judgment of a course of illness from the side of the doctor» (Duden). Strachey's translation in the Standard Edition of «Discussion» is lackluster.

[8] In 1923 Freud appended a footnote to this passage directing the reader to *The Infantile Genital Organization* and asserting that Hans finds himself at the period of sexual development that «is quite generally characterized through its acquaintance with only one genital – the masculine. In contrast to the later period of maturity, it consists not in genital primacy, but in the primacy of the phallus» (*G.W.*, 7:345; *S.E.*, 10:110). Hans himself commits a linguistic error comparable to Freud's when he declares: «And all men are wiwimakers» (*G.W.*, 7:269; *S.E.*, 10:34), using the generic word for people *(Menschen)* in place of the restricted word for males *(Männer)*. This universalization of the masculine perspective finds its most famous expression in Freud's epochal invocation of the Œdipus myth in *The Interpretation of Dreams:* «It is the fate of all of us, perhaps, to direct our first sexual impulse toward our mother and our first hatred and our first murderous wish against our father» (1900a, 262), where, again, the subject-position of girls is completely elided. As feminists have taught us, such solecisms can have far-reaching consequences.

⁹ Although in a note to the case of Little Hans in the *Standard Edition* Strachey identified what he believed to be the first appearance of the term (10:8n1), he later corrected himself and acknowledged that Freud had used it in print earlier in *The Sexual Theories of Children* (1908c, p. 217n1). But here, too, Freud is summarizing material from Hans's analysis, so the castration complex retains its connection with this case. Strachey's self correction is pointed out by Lindon (1992, pp. 377-378). See also the entry «Castration Complex» in Laplanche & Pontalis (1967, pp. 56-60).

¹⁰ «*The gaze is at stake from the outset.* Don't forget what "castration", or the knowledge of castration, owes to the gaze, at least for Freud» (Irigaray, 1974, p. 47). «It is the boy who looks and is horrified first, and... the little girl merely doubles and confirms by reduplication what he is supposed to have seen. Or not seen» (p. 49).

¹¹ «The pleasure gained from touching, caressing, parting the lips and vulva simply does not exist for Freud... Just as he will never refer to the pleasure associated with the sensitivity of the posterior wall of the vagina, the breasts, or the neck of the womb» (Irigaray, 1974, p. 29).

¹² Although Freud says nothing about it in this case, the male genitals consist of a scrotum and testicles as well as a penis. In *The Infantile Genital Organisation*, however, in a footnote to the passage about the penis as a criterion for distinguishing between the animate and inanimate that refers to Little Hans, Freud remarks on «what a small degree of attention the other part of the male genitals, the little sac with its contents, attracts in children. From all one hears in analyses, one would not guess that the male genitals consisted of anything more than the penis» (*S.E.*, 19:142). But given the belief of many children that the scrotal sac functions as a container for urine, and the emphasis on «making wiwi» in the case of Little Hans, it may be Freud himself, and not his young patient, who is guilty of forgetting about the testicles in this analysis (Silverman, 1980, pp. 114-15).

¹³ The German text of this dialogue indicates a slippage in Hans's mind between the awareness that «a boy gets *(kriegt)* a girl and a girl gets a boy'» and his father's reply that «A boy doesn't get *(bekommt)* children. Only women, mommies get children.» Hans is struggling with the connection – and the distinction – between having sex and having children and obtaining no help from his father. Similarly, just as the word «wiwimaker» can be used equivocally to refer either to the urinary or genital organs possessed by members of both sexes or to the exclusively masculine penis, so Hans asks how he can «belong» *(gehören)* to his father when his mother has given him birth. The concept of «belonging» is no less ambiguous than that of the wiwimaker, only here the model is female rather than male since the father both is and is not a parent like the mother. Hans's father, again, makes matters not less but more obscure by successively telling Hans: (a) that Hans «belongs» both to him and Hans's mother; (b) that Hanna «belongs» only to Mommy and not to Hans; and (c) that Hanna belongs at once to him, Mommy, and Hans. The concept of «belonging» has been expanded to encompass being not simply a parent but any family member, and Hans is left to sort out how being a sibling differs from being a mother or a father (*G.W.*, 7:322-23; *S.E.*, 10:87).

¹⁴ What is more, the theory, expounded to Hans by both his parents, that «children grow in the Mommy and then, when great pains come, are brought into the world by being pressed out like a "lumpf"», not only contributes to his anal fixation but reinforces his fantasy that pregnancy is something of which he too is capable (*G.W.*, 7:323; *S.E.*, 10:87).

¹⁵ Just before this he says in another footnote that both the box and the bathtub are for Hans «representations of the space in which babies are found» (*G.W.*, 7:304; *S.E.*, 10:69).

¹⁶ To give one more example, when Hans laughs at the sight of Hanna's wiwimaker Freud claims that this is «the first time that he acknowledges the difference between the male and female genital in this way, instead of denying it», but earlier he had quoted Hans's

131

declaration, after his mother had given birth to Hanna, «But out of my wiwimaker there comes no blood» (*G.W.*, 7:257, 248; *S.E.*, 10:21, 10). Hans pinpoints one crucial difference between the male and female genitalia, but Freud is unable to give him credit for it.

[17]   «Why not *also* analyze the "envy" for the vagina? Or the uterus? Or the vulva? Etc. The "desire" felt by each pole of sexual difference "to have something like it too?"» (Irigaray, 1974, p. 52).

[18]   For an outstanding synthesis of gay and lesbian scholarship in Shakespeare studies, see Traub (1992). Traub defines «sex» as «those anatomical, biological distinctions by which cultures differentiate between males and females»; «gender» as «the culturally prescribed roles and behaviors available to the two «sexes»; and «sexuality» as «erotic desires and practices, including but not limited to the direction and scope of erotic preference (i.e., object choice)» (p. 21).

References

BRAY, J. (1992). Young Lover or Reluctant Œdipus: The Identified Patient in the Case of Little Hans. Unpublished Manuscript.

CIXOUS, H. & CLÉMENT, C. (1975). *The Newly Born Woman.* Minneapolis: University of Minnesota Press, 1988.

FREUD, S. (1900a). The Interpretation of Dreams. *Standard Edition, 4-5.*

— (1908c). On the Sexual Theories of Children. *Standard Edition, 9*, 205-226.

— (1909b). Analysis of a Phobia in a Five-Year-Old Boy. *Standard Edition, 10*, 5-149.

— (1923e). The Infantile Genital Organization of the Libido. *Standard Edition, 19*, 139-145.

— (1927e). Fetishism. *Standard Edition, 21*, 147-157.

— (1933a). New Introductory Lectures on Psycho-Analysis. *Standard Edition, 22*, 5-182.

GLENN, J. (1980). Freud's Advice to Hans's Father. The First Supervisory Sessions. *In*: Kanzer, M. & Glenn, J. (eds), *Freud and his Patients*. New York: Aronson, 1980, pp. 121-127.

GRAF, M. (1942). Reminiscences of Professor Sigmund Freud. *Psychoanalytic Quarterly, 11*, 465-476.

HORNEY, K. (1932). The Dread of Woman: Observations on a Specific Difference in the Dread Felt by Men and by Women Respectively for the Opposite Sex. *In*: Horney, K., *Feminine Psychology*. New York: Norton, 1973, pp. 133-146.

— (1933). The Denial of the Vagina: A Contribution to the Problem of the Genital Anxieties Specific to Women. *In*: Horney, K., *Feminine Psychology*. New York: Norton, 1973, pp. 147-161.

IRIGARAY, L. (1974): *Speculum of the Other Woman*. Ithaca: Cornell University Press, 1987.

KOFMAN, S. (1980). *The Enigma of Woman: Woman in Freud's Writings*. Ithaca: Cornell University Press, 1985.

LAPLANCHE, J. & PONTALIS, J.B. (1967). *The Language of Psycho-Analysis*. New York: Norton, 1973.

LINDON, J.A. (1992). A Reassessment of Little Hans, His Parents, and His Castration Complex. *Journal of the American Academy of Psychoanalysis, 20*, 375-394.

McGUIRE, W. (ed.) (1974). *The Freud-Jung Letters: The Correspondence Between Sigmund Freud and Carl Gustav Jung*. Princeton: Princeton University Press.

MAHONY, P.(1992). Freud as Family Therapist: Reflections. *In*: Gelfand T. & Kerr J. (eds), *Freud and the History of Psychoanalysis*. Hillsdale, N.J.: Analytic Press, pp. 307-317.

MARCUS, S. (1974). Freud and Dora: Story, History, Case History. *In*: *Freud and the Culture of Psychoanalysis: Studies in the Transition from Victorian Humanism to Modernity*. Boston: Allen and Unwin, 1984, pp. 42-86.

ROITHE, E. (1987). *The Riddle of Freud: Jewish Influences on His Theory of Female Sexuality*. London: Tavistock.

SILVERMAN, M.A. (1980). A Fresh Look at the Case of Little Hans. *In*: Kanzer, M. & Glenn, J. (eds), *Freud and his Patients*. New York: Aronson, 1980, pp. 95-127.

SPRENGNETHER, M. (1990). *The Spectral Mother: Freud, Feminism, and Psychoanalysis*. Ithaca: Cornell University Press.

STREAN, H.S. (1967). A Family Therapist Looks at «Little Hans». *Family Process*, 6, 227-233.

TRAUB, V. (1992). *Desire and Anxiety: Circulations of Sexuality in Shakespearean Drama*. New York: Routledge.

Cahiers Psychiatriques Genevois, Special Issue, 1994, pp. 135-150

SIGMUND FREUD'S
PSYCHO-SOCIAL IDENTITY

Peter Loewenberg

«*Hebraism and Hellenism, between these two points of influence moves our world. At one time it feels more powerfully the attraction of one of them, at another time of the other; and it ought to be, though it never is, evenly and happily balanced between them.*»

Matthew Arnold

Whoever knows only one thing about Freud knows something wrong, which is to say, knows something which standing alone is out of balance and is therefore only a partial truth. I will place Freud in the fecund creative historical-sociological tradition of those who are marginal to mainstream western culture, they are *in* western culture but not *of* it. The excitement of their lives and discoveries is that they are initially peripheral to the larger society, they stand on its boundaries, and therefore they have a cultural vantage point of both clarity of perception and vulnerability whose discoveries are adopted by the culture to become central to its intellectual *corpus*. This in/out position of straddling boundaries is also the professional stance of psychoanalysts toward the lives of their analysands.

Today there is a substantial literature and a heated current debate about Freud's cultural and social identity. We have before us in the scholarship essentially five understandings on Freud's historico-social identifications:

I appreciate the critique of an earlier version of this essay by Jerald Simon and Peter Baldwin.

1. as a secular north German atheist;
2. as a product of Habsburg Austrian culture;
3. as a Jew who secularized Judaism in psychoanalysis;
4. as harboring a Christian, particularly Roman Catholic, consciousness;
5. as an Hellenic pagan.

To dilate briefly on each of these categories:

A) Freud was a secular atheist and positivistic scientist. This is the interpretation of Peter Gay whose researches on Freud are prodigious. He pictures Freud as a product of the Germanic cultural world and essentially the product of north German culture:

> It was not Asian wisdom that Freud offered the world but German wisdom. Now this, in the cosmopolitan scientific atmosphere of the nineteenth century, meant European wisdom[1]... In truth Freud could have developed his ideas in any city endowed with a first-rate medical school and an educated public large and affluent enough to furnish him with patients[2]... Medical Vienna [was] a German city. It was in that city, and that city alone, that Freud developed and felt most at home... The intellectual instrument that led him to his psychoanalytic theories was not Jewish or Austrian.[3]

There is only a partial truth, or a one sided distortion, in Gay's analysis. He is speaking of only one of the determinants of Freud's identity. On the issue of national cultural influences on Freud, let us say he is one-quarter correct. Of course it is an absurdity to place a quantum on fragments of an identity, which is based on psychological identifications. But operating by the points of the cultural compass, I say «one-quarter» because Vienna, prior to the First World War, stood at the social and cultural crossroads of Europe.

Freud did have an important north German political orientation in his student days.[4] He adored his Prussian teacher in neurophysiology, Ernst Brücke, whom the colleagues in Berlin called «our Ambassador to the Far East»,[5] and after whom he named his third son Ernst.[6] But there was also a strong connection to western Europe, to France where Freud had received a fellowship to study in Paris with Jean-Martin Charcot, for whom he named his first son Martin. His two half-brothers lived in England. He envied them for being able to raise their children in a land relatively free of anti-Semitism.[7] Freud named his next son Oliver, to honor the leader who re-admitted the Jews to England. As he tells us:

> My second son, to whom I had given the first name of a great historical figure (Cromwell) who had powerfully attracted me in my boyhood, especially since my visit to England. During the year before the child's birth I had made up my mind to use his name if it were a son and I greeted the new-born baby with it with a feeling of high *satisfaction*.[8]

Gay is resolute in holding that there is nothing essentially «Jewish» in Freud, his ideas, or the structure of his thought:

> It was as an atheist that Freud developed psychoanalysis... Freud became a psy-
> choanalyst in large part *because* he was an atheist... A believer, whether Jew or
> Christian, could never have founded psychoanalysis[9]... Since Freud considered reli-
> gious faith – all religious faith, including Judaism – as a subject of psychoanalytic
> study, he could approach it only from the perspective of the atheist[10]... His irreligiosi-
> ty was fundamental to his scientific stance, essential to his psychoanalytic theory.[11]

Gay takes Freud out of the social context of being born of Galician
Jewish parents in Moravia and growing up in Habsburg Austria, specifically in Vienna's Second District, the Leopoldstadt, where many of the
Eastern European Jews lived. Leopoldstadt had the largest concentration
of Jews in Vienna. They made up 9% of the population of the city, but in
1880 Jews accounted for one-third of the people of Leopoldstadt and
48.3% of all Viennese Jews lived there.[12]

For the Eastern European, particularly Jewish, influence in Freud's
life and thought, it is necessary to do no more than to cite *Jokes and their
Relation to the Unconscious* (1905), which is infused with Eastern
European, especially Galician, Jewish humor. It is often referred to
among psychoanalytic candidates as «the Jewish joke book.» The work is
filled with Jewish *Schnorrers* (beggars), travellers on trains, bath houses,
and *Schadchens* (marriage brokers). It includes Freud's analysis of the
psychology of Jewish humor, which is interpreted as an acceptable mode
of expressing hostility and as one-up-manship, as if to say, «we know our
faults and can mock them much better than you ever could.» Freud writes:

> The jokes made about Jews by foreigners are for the most part brutal comic stor-
> ies in which a joke is made unnecessary by the fact that Jews are regarded by forei-
> gners as comic figures. The Jewish jokes which originate from Jews admit this too;
> but they know their real faults as well as the connection between them and their good
> qualities, and the share which the subject has in the person found fault with creates
> the subjective determinant (usually so hard to arrive at) of the jokework.
> Incidentally, I do not know whether there are many other instances of a people
> making fun to such a degree of its own character.[13]

As to the fourth point of the cultural compass, the Helleno-Latin
world across the Alps in the Mediterranean south, we need only refer to
Freud's papers on Michelangelo, Da Vinci, the Acropolis, and what Carl
Schorske termed his «Rome neurosis»[14]. Freud travelled to Italy five times
between 1895 and 1898 while he was struggling with his self-analysis and
writing the *Interpretation of Dreams*, without being able to reach the
Eternal City. He identified with the Carthaginian general Hannibal:

> Like him, I had been fated not to see Rome... Hannibal, whom I had come to
> resemble in these respects, had been the favourite hero of my later school days... And
> when in the higher classes I began to understand for the first time what it meant to
> belong to an alien race, and antisemitic feelings among the other boys warned me
> that I must take up a definite position, the figure of the semitic general rose still
> higher in my esteem. To my youthful mind Hannibal and Rome symbolized the

conflict between the tenacity of Jewry and the organization of the Catholic church. And the increasing importance of the effects of the anti-semitic movement upon our emotional life helped to fix the thoughts and feelings of those early days. Thus the wish to go to Rome had become in my dream-life a cloak and symbol for a number of other passionate wishes.[15]

The Freudian case of psychotherapy I find most endearing for his faith in Hellas' curative powers is his prescription for Bruno Walter's hysterical paralysis of his right arm. Freud told him to go directly to Sicily, do nothing for a few weeks but drink in the beauty of the Greek antiquities, and come home and conduct the orchestra – Freud would take the responsibility for any failure.[16]

B) Freud was squarely rooted in the society and politics of Habsburg Austria and particularly the culture of *fin-de-siècle* Vienna. The case that his conscious thought and unconscious dream life were permeated by the class and national struggles of failing Austrian political liberalism was compellingly made and precisely explicated in the researches of Carl Schorske and William Mc Grath.[17]

C) Freud had a Jewish religious identification which was more pervasive than he recognized or acknowledged. There is a substantial scholarly literature on this theme.[18] This view, stressing the Jewish religious rather than cultural identification, is given its most articulate expression in the recent work of Y.H. Yerushalmi, who polemicizes against Gay and wishes to resuscitate Freud's Jewish religious identity. He locates the particular source of this identity in Freud's Galician Jewish father Jakob. He finds «in Freud a sense of otherness *vis-à-vis* non-Jews which... seems to have been primal, inherited from his family and early milieu, and it remained with him throughout his life.»[19] In a «Monologue with Freud» Yerushalmi postulates his meaning of psychoanalysis as

> itself a further, if not final, metamorphosed extension of Judaism, divested of its illusory religious forms... I think you believed that just as you are a godless Jew, psychoanalysis is a godless Judaism. But I don't think you intended us to know this.[20]

D) Freud functioned with a series of latent Christian identifications, particularly with Austro-Hungarian Roman Catholicism. Some of his childhood religious socialization was by a Czech nanny, a peasant woman who took him to church and taught him Christian notions of a heaven and damnation in hell. The powerful social pressures of Austrian anti-Semitism inhibited his professional career advancement.[21]

E) Freud had a decisive cultural identification with the classical civilization of Attic Greece. This view emphasizes the importance of Freud's humanistic gymnasium education with its languages and philosophy of antiquity. For the stratum of Austrian secular Jewish intelligentsia of the late nineteenth century to which Freud belonged the culture of reference was Hellenic-Latin.[22] Freud was a Hellenic pagan in four main dimensions of his personality:

1. most importantly in his oedipal triumph over his poor Jewish merchant father;

2. his admiration and identification with the aesthetics of what he viewed as a superior culture, and the geography of Mediterranean antiquity;

3. his enlightened plea for a tolerant non-judgmental sexual morality;

4. his personal philosophy of stoicism and in the manner in which he faced his terminal illness and death.

In sum, Freud's psycho-social identity was a dynamic interplay of the four points of the cultural compass of which Vienna was the late nineteenth century center, and of the five psycho-cultural influences which are evident: Germanic science, Austrian liberal politics, Jewish religious values, Habsburg Christian culture, and Hellenic paganism.

*

The definition of Freud's historico-social position which I wish to propose is that Freud was a larger than life exemplar of the center of a three generational late nineteenth century process by which large parts of European Jewry embraced Western enlightenment, science, modernity, religious reform, and secularism. His father Jakob was a wandering wool merchant from the Galician shtetl of Buczacz and in his life made the move, which correlated with political emancipation, from religious orthodoxy to Haskalah which saw Judaism as a religion of universal enlightenment.[23] Jakob Freud's home was religiously observant, though not strictly orthodox. Ernest Jones says Sigmund «was certainly conversant with all Jewish customs and festivals.[24]» Sigmund Freud was of the transition generation of Central European Jewry in the brief heyday of political Liberalism when the pace of assimilation was at its maximum. He stood between the observant household of his parents and the totally secularized upbringing of his own children. His wife Martha, who came from a strictly orthodox Hamburg home, was forced to give up Sabbath observance and kosher dietary laws when she married him. Freud briefly considered conversion to Protestantism at the time of their wedding in order to avoid an orthodox Jewish ceremony. His friend and patron Josef Breuer dissuaded him by murmuring, «too complicated».[25] Sigmund continued the westernizing momentum of his father to receive a secular higher education, become a free professional, a scientist, and a path breaking cultural innovator not just for the Jews, but for humankind.

History is always a tension of change and stasis, of new developments and transformations, and of conservative continuities with the past. Whereas Gay only wishes to consider the new and most forward secular position of Freud, Yerushalmi chooses to focus on the traditional themes in his *corpus* which contain where he came – from his father, Galicia, and the observant Jewish past. The position of social marginality was defined by Stonequist:

> Because of his in-between situation, the marginal man may become an acute and able critic of the dominant group and its culture. This is because he combines the knowledge and insight of the insider with the critical attitude of the outsider. His analysis is not necessarily objective – there is too much emotional tension underneath to make such an attitude easy of achievement. But he is skillful in noting the contradictions and «hypocrisies» in the dominant culture. The gap between its moral pretensions and its actual achievements jumps to his eye.[26]

Stonequist explicitly refers to Freud when he analyses the cultural creativity of Jews as a function of their marginality in society.[27]

I will draw on the understandings of this problem of Jewish cultural creativity in the modern world by three great twentieth century scholars, a sociologist, an economist, and an historian, whose work illuminates the particular case of Sigmund Freud and his Jewish heritage. These are the German Jew converted to Protestantism, Georg Simmel; the American gentile, Thorstein Veblen; and the Polish-Jewish Marxist, Isaac Deutscher. Their work is as relevant to our comprehension of the historical Freud as are his own poignant understandings of his cultural position and his relation to nationalism and Judaism.

The earliest description of socio-cultural marginality and its implications was by the sociologist Georg Simmel, a Jew who was baptized as a Protestant at birth. He was denied a professorship in Germany until he was fifty-six. When he was a candidate for a chair at the University of Heidelberg, he was successfully attacked in a letter to the Baden Minister of Culture as: «surely an Israelite through and through, in his outward appearance, in his bearing, and in his mental style *(Geistesart)*.[28]» When Simmel finally received a professorship, it was at the boundary of the German Reich, in territorially ambiguous and culturally marginal Alsace, at the University of Strasbourg. His sociological analysis reflected the jeopardy and insight, the sense of precarious insecurity and acute perception, of a person between cultures.

It is due to Simmel, who in 1908 first defined «the stranger» as a distinctive phenotype subject to analysis, that we today have the culturally marginal outsider as a category of sociological understanding. The stranger is present, but not entirely integrated in the culture. Simmel denoted European Jews as «the classical example» of «the stranger» who is not merely:

> The wanderer who comes today and goes tomorrow, but rather as the person who comes today and stays tomorrow. He is, so to speak, the *potential* wanderer: although he has not moved on, he has not quite overcome the freedom of coming and going. He is fixed within a particular spatial group, or within a group whose boundaries are similar to spatial boundaries. But his position in this group is determined, essentially, by the fact that he has not belonged to it from the beginning, that he imports qualities into it, which do not and cannot stem from the group itself.[29]

The stranger is involved in «a specific form of interaction», a special relationship to his culture of residence: he is not merely an outsider, he is also a potential critic. In what we would today term the psychoanalytical object relations idiom of optimal distance, Simmel spoke of:

> That synthesis of nearness and distance which constitutes the formal position of the stranger... He is not radically committed to the unique ingredients and peculiar tendencies of the group, and therefore approaches them with the specific attitude of «objectivity.» But objectivity does not simply involve passivity and detachment; it is a particular structure composed of distance and nearness, indifference and involvement.[30]

In 1919 Thorstein Veblen, the Wisconsin born son of Norwegian immigrant parents, and America's most original native social scientist, penned a profound essay entitled *The Intellectual Preeminence of Jews in Modern Europe*, in response to the Balfour Declaration. Veblen was a notable philosemite who obviously identified with the Jews, hailing them as «the vanguard of modern inquiry,» and drawing attention to:

> A fact which must strike any dispassionate observer – that the Jewish people have contributed much more than an even share to the intellectual life of modern Europe. So also it is plain that the civilisation of Christendom continues today to draw heavily on the Jews for men devoted to science and scholarly pursuits. It is not only that men of Jewish extraction continue to supply more than a proportionate quota to the rank and file engaged in scientific and scholarly work, but a disproportionate number of the men to whom modern science and scholarship look for guidance and leadership are of the same derivation... they count particularly among the vanguard, the pioneers, the uneasy guild of pathfinders and iconoclasts, in science, scholarship, and institutional change and growth.[31]

Veblen stresses that it is the departure from one cultural tradition, but not yet being fully assimilated or at home in another, which is the fragile position of creativity. His point, counter to Yerushalmi and others who elevate Freud's debt to the Jewish religious tradition, would be that Freud *had* to leave religious orthodoxy and its rigidity to become a creative pathbreaker.

> It appears to be only when the gifted Jew escapes from the cultural environment created and fed by the particular genius of his own people, only when he falls into the

alien lines of gentile inquiry and becomes a naturalized, though hyphenate, citizen in the gentile republic of learning, that he comes into his own as a creative leader in the world's intellectual enterprise. It is by loss of allegiance, or at the best by force of a divided allegiance to the people of his origin, that he finds himself in the vanguard of modern inquiry.[32]

According to Veblen, among the attributes of the Jewish mind which are requisites «for any work of inquiry» are «a skeptical frame of mind... a degree of exemption from hard-and-fast preconceptions, a skeptical animus, *Unbefangenheit*, release from the dead hand of conventional finality.» Veblen's identification with the Jews is nowhere clearer than when he writes of their position of restless alienation. There is a heavy price in anxiety to pay for being an innovator and challenger of received orthodoxy. Veblen invokes the myth of the wandering Jew as his metaphor for the intellectual:

> The intellectually gifted Jew is in a peculiarly fortunate position in respect of this requisite immunity from the inhibitions of intellectual quietism. But he can come in for such immunity only at the cost of losing his secure place in the scheme of conventions into which he has been born, and at the cost, also, of finding no similarly secure place in that scheme of gentile conventions into which he is thrown. For him as for other men in the like case, the skepticism that goes to make him an effectual factor in the increase and diffusion of knowledge among men involves a loss of that peace of mind that is the birthright of the safe and sane quietist. He becomes a disturber of the intellectual peace, but only at the cost of becoming an intellectual wayfaring man, a wanderer in the intellectual no man's land, seeking another place to rest, farther along the road, somewhere over the horizon.[33]

Isaac Deutscher, who authored a monumental trilogy of the life of Leon Trotsky as well as a biography of Stalin and other works on the Soviet Union and Marxism, penned an analysis in 1958 of what he termed *The non-Jewish Jew* by which he meant the «great revolutionaries of modern thought: Spinoza, Heine, Marx, Rosa Luxemburg, Trotsky, and Freud.[34]» They had in common «something of the quintessence of Jewish life and of the Jewish intellect.» These qualities include determinism, a dialectical manner of thinking, a relativity of moral standards, a commitment to knowledge being inseparable from action *(Praxis)*, and a belief in the ultimate solidarity of man. Deutscher is the only one of the major theorists of social marginality whom we consider who explicitly subsumed Freud's work in his generalizations.

> They are all, from Spinoza to Freud, determinists, they all hold that the universe is ruled by laws inherent in it and governed by *Gesetzmässigkeiten* (conformity to natural laws). They do not see reality as a jumble of accidents or history as an assemblage of caprices and whims of rulers. There is nothing fortuitous, so Freud tells us, in our dreams, follies, or even in our slips of the tongue[35]... As Jews they dwelt on the borderlines of various civilizations, religions, and national cultures. They were born and brought up on the borderlines of various epochs. Their mind matured where the most diverse cultural influences crossed and fertilized each other. They lived on the

margins or in the nooks and crannies of their respective nations. Each of them was in society and yet not in it, of it and yet not of it. It was this that enabled them to rise in thought above their times and generations, and to strike out mentally into wide new horizons and far into the future.[36]

Of Freud Deutscher said his «mind matured in Vienna in estrangement from Jewry and in opposition to the Catholic clericalism of the Habsburg capital.[37]» Although Deutscher did not avail himself of Freud's ideas in his historical research, to its detriment I think, he had an appreciative and accurate understanding of what Freud was about:

> He transcends the limitations of earlier psychological schools. The man whom he analyses is not a German, or an Englishman, a Russian, or a Jew – he is the universal man who is part of nature and part of society, the man whose desires and cravings, scruples and inhibitions, anxieties and predicaments are essentially the same no matter to what race, religion, or nation he belongs. From their viewpoint the Nazis were right when they coupled Freud's name with that of Marx and burned the books of both.[38]

I wish to correlate the theses of our socio-historical culture critics with the position Freud created – the unique vantage point of the psychoanalyst in the clinical situation. Psychoanalysts must be both empathic with and detached from their analysands. They stand with one foot in and one foot out of the emotional field or life space of the analysand in order to have an independent perspective. Psychoanalysts are intimately involved in the lives of patients and use their own responses and internal objects as tools of cognition, yet they are also outsiders who must maintain appropriate boundaries and distance, sometimes connoted as clinical «neutrality», to help analysands gain their full autonomy.

*

When considering Freud's socio-cultural identity, we are well advised to consider what he himself had to say about it. He often gave the subject of his Jewish identity candid and explicit attention, as when he describes his encounters with academic anti-Semitism in his autobiography:

> When, in 1873, I first joined the University, I experienced some appreciable disappointments. Above all, I found that I was expected to feel myself inferior and an alien because I was a Jew. I refused absolutely to do the first of these things. I have never been able to see why I should feel ashamed of my descent or, as people were beginning to say, of my «race». I put up, without much regret, with my non-acceptance into the community; for it seemed to me that in spite of this exclusion an active fellow-worker could not fail to find some nook or cranny in the framework of humanity. These first impressions at the University, however, had one consequence which was afterwards to prove important; for at an early age I was made familiar with the fate of being in the Opposition and of being put under the ban of the «compact majority» (The reference is to Henrik Ibsen's *Enemy of the People*). The foundations were thus laid for a certain degree of independence of judgement.[39]

Freud was well aware of his own social marginality as a Jew in Europe, and of the cultural marginality of psychoanalysis. This comes to the fore most clearly in his correspondence with his disciple and colleague, Karl Abraham of Berlin. The letters often involve the *Realpolitik* of their infant psychoanalytic movement. A crisis occurred with the impending defection of Carl Gustav Jung from the psychoanalytic movement in 1908. Freud plead with Abraham for forbearance:

> Please be tolerant and do not forget that it is really easier for you than it is for Jung to follow my ideas, for... you are closer to my intellectual constitution because of racial kinship, while he as a Christian and a pastor's son finds his way to me only against great inner resistances. His association with us is all the more valuable for that. I nearly said that it was only by his appearance on the scene that psycho-analysis escaped the danger of becoming a Jewish national affair.[40]

Freud acknowledged to Abraham the structural affinity between Talmudic reasoning and the logic of psychoanalytic explanation and shared his feelings of a special Jewish sensibilty for psychoanalysis as well as his resentment that being Jewish was held against him and his ideas:

> After all, our Talmudic way of thinking cannot disappear just like that. Some days ago a small paragraph in *Jokes* strangely attracted me. When I looked at it more closely, I found that, in the technique of apposition and in its whole structure, it was completely Talmudic[41]... On the whole it is easier for us Jews, as we lack the mystical element[42]... I think that we as Jews, if we wish to join in, must develop a bit of masochism, be ready to suffer some wrong. Otherwise there is no hitting it off. Rest assured that, if my name were Oberhuber, in spite of everything my innovations would have met with far less resistance.[43]

When Freud considered the forces of resistance to psychoanalysis for a French-Swiss Jewish journal, *La Revue Juive* of Geneva, he broached the subject of the decisive role of his being Jewish:

> Finally, with all reserve, the question may be raised whether the personality of the present writer as a Jew who has never sought to disguise the fact that he is a Jew may not have had a share in provoking the antipathy of his environment to psychoanalysis. An argument of this kind is not often uttered aloud. But we have unfortunately grown so suspicious that we cannot avoid thinking that this factor may not have been quite without its effect. Nor is it perhaps entirely a matter of chance that the first advocate of psycho-analysis was a Jew. To profess belief in this new theory called for a certain degree of readiness to accept a situation of solitary opposition – a situation with which no one is more familiar than a Jew.[44]

Freud's most forthright and articulate statement of his Jewish identity was in a message to the Jewish fraternal lodge B'nai Brith, which he had joined in 1895, and for many years regularly attended twice a month. This address alludes to his atheism, a conviction he was to argue at length in the ensuing year in *The Future of an Illusion*[45], but also stresses his deep and firm commitment to values of Jewish culture:

What bound me to Jewry was (I am ashamed to admit) neither faith nor national pride, for I have always been an unbeliever and was brought up without any religion though not without a respect for what are called the «ethical» standards of human civilization... But plenty of other things remained over to make the attraction of Jewry and Jews irresistible – many obscure emotional forces, which were the more powerful the less they could be expressed in words, as well as a clear consciousness of inner identity, the safe privacy of a common mental construction. And beyond this there was a perception that it was to my Jewish nature alone that I owed two characteristics that had become indispensable to me in the difficult course of my life. Because I was a Jew I found myself free from many prejudices which restricted others in the use of their intellect; and as a Jew I was prepared to join the Opposition and to do without agreement with the «compact majority»[46].

There are two great allegories for the understanding of Freud's identity and the essence of psychoanalysis, one pagan the other Judaic in origin. I think of the great pagan allegory of Aenaeas who, as he leaves the burning Troy, returns into the flaming city to rescue his aged father, carry him out on his back, leading his son by the hand, to go forth and found Rome:

But now the fire roars across the walls; the tide of flame flows nearer. «Come then, dear father, mount upon my neck; I'll bear you on my shoulders. That is not too much for me. Whatever waits for us, we both shall share one danger, one salvation»... This said, I spread a tawny lion skin across my bent neck, over my broad shoulders, and then take up Anchises; small Iülus now clutches my right hand; his steps uneven, he is following his father; and my wife moves on behind.[47]

The other allegory is the aged Freud in what must have been one of the saddest moments of his life, when psychoanalysis had been destroyed in the Germanophone world and his family and followers were forced to flee into exile. He then derived strength from Jewish history and values of intellection, recalling in *Moses and Monotheism* the sacking of Jerusalem:

The Jews retained their inclination to intellectual interests. The nation's political misfortune taught it to value at its true worth the one possession that remained to it – its literature. Immediately after the destruction of the Temple in Jerusalem by Titus, the Rabbi Jochanan ben Zakkai asked permission to open the first Torah school in Jabneh. From that time on, the Holy Writ and intellectual concern with it were what held the scattered people together.[48]

When in March 1938, Freud at last conceded that he had to escape Vienna as a refugee, he drew on this story of Jewish spiritual survival and said: «We are going to do the same. We are, after all, used to persecution by our history, tradition and some of us by personal experience.[49]»

Freud taught us that we involuntarily carry the past in us whether we will it or not. Our choice is the extent we wish to be aware of our burdens and strengths from our personal and cultural past. For those of us who have learned from Freud, as we stand at the centenary of the birth of psychoanalysis and now face its second century, we may see portions of Freud's past living in his heritage as we realize it.

Notes

[1] *Peter Gay: Freud. Jews and other Germans*, New York, Oxford University Press, 1978, p. 92.

[2] *Peter Gay: Freud: A Life for Our Time*, New York, W. W. Norton, 1988, p. 10.

[3] *Peter Gay: Reading Freud: Explorations & Entertainments*, New Haven, Yale University Press, 1990, pp. 61, 62-63.

[4] *William J. Mc Grath: Dionysian Art and Populist Politics in Austria*, New Haven, Yale University Press, 1974, pp. 247-248.

[5] *Siegfried Bernfeld:* Freud's Earliest Theories and the School of Helmholtz, *Psychoanalytic Quarterly 13* (1944), 341-361. The quotation is on p. 349.

[6] For the naming of the Freud children, see *Gay:* Six Names in Search of an Interpretation, *In: Reading Freud*, pp. 54-73.

[7] *Peter Loewenberg:* A Hidden Zionist Theme in Freud's «My Son, the Myops...» Dream, *Journal of the History of Ideas 31*, 1 (January-March, 1970), 129-132.

[8] *Freud S.: The Interpretation of Dreams* (1900), *In: Standard Edition of the Complete Psychological Works of Sigmund Freud*, translated under the general editorship of James Strachey in collaboration with Anna Freud, assisted by Alix Strachey and Alan Tyson, 24 vols, London, Hogarth Press, 1953-75, hereafter *S.E.*, 5, 447-448.

[9] *Peter Gay: A Godless Jew: Freud. Atheism. and the Making of Psychoanalysis*, New Haven, Yale University Press, 1987, pp. 37, 41, 146-147.

[10] *Gay: Freud*, p. 603.

[11] *Gay: Reading Freud*, p. 59.

[12] *Marsha L. Rosenblit: The Jews of Vienna, 1867-1914: Assimilation and Identity*, Albany, State University of New York Press, 1983, p. 76.

[13] *Freud: Jokes and their Relation to the Unconscious*, 1905, *S.E.*, 8, 111-112.

[14] *Carl E. Schorske:* Politics and Patricide in Freud's *Interpretation of Dreams, In: Fin-de-Siècle Vienna: Politics and Culture*, New York, Alfred A. Knopf, 1980, pp. 189-193.

[15] *Freud: Interpretation of Dreams, S.E.*, 4, 196-197.

[16] *Bruno Walter: Theme and Variations: An Autobiography*, trans. James A. Galston, New York, Alfred A. Knopf, 1946, pp. 164-166.

[17] *Schorske:* Fin-de-Siècle Vienna, pp. 181-207; William J. Mc Grath, *Freud's Discovery of Psychoanalysis: The Politics of Hysteria*, Ithaca, Cornell University Press, 1986.

[18] *Sander L. Gilman: The Case of Sigmund Freud: Medicine and Identity at the Fin-de-Siècle*, Baltimore: Johns Hopkins University Press, 1993; *Jerry V. Diller: Freud's Jewish Identity: A Case Study in the Impact of Ethnicity,* Cranbury, N.J.: Associated University Presses, 1991; *Lary Berkower:* The Enduring Effect of the Jewish Tradition Upon Freud, *American Journal of Psychiatry*, 125: 8 February, 1969, 1067-1073; *Martin S. Bergmann:* Moses and the Evolution of Freud's Jewish Identity, *Israel Annals of Psychiatry and Related Disciplines*, 14: 1, March, 1976, 3-26, also reprinted in *Mortimer Ostow: Judaism and Psychoanalysis*, New York, Ktav, 1982, pp. 115-142; *David Bakan: Sigmund Freud and the Jewish Mystical Tradition*, New York: Van Nostrand, 1958; *Ernst Simon:* «Sigmund Freud, the Jew,» *Leo Baeck Institute Yearbook*, II, London, East and West

Library, 1957, pp. 270-305; *Peter Loewenberg*: Sigmund Freud as a Jew: A Study in Ambivalence and Courage, *Journal of the History of the Behavioral Sciences*, 7 (4), October, 1971, 363-369; *Emanuel Rice*: *Freud and Moses: The Long Journey Home*, Albany, NY, SUNY Press, 1990; *Yosef H. Yerushalmi*: *Judaism Terminable and Interminable: an Exploration of Freud's «Moses and Monotheism»*, New Haven, Yale University Press, 1991; *Dennis B. Klein*: *Jewish Origins of the Psychoanalytic Movement* New York, Praeger, 1981; *Leonard Shengold*: «Freud and Joseph» *In: Mark Kanzer and Jules Glenn*, eds.: *Freud and His Self-Analysis*, New York, Jason Aronson, 1979, pp. 67-86; *Robert S. Wistrich*: «The Jewish Identity of Sigmund Freud», *In: The Jews of Vienna in the Age of Franz Joseph*, Oxford, Oxford University Press, 1989, pp. 537-582, also «The Jewishness of Sigmund Freud», *In: Between Redemption and Perdition: Modern Antisemitism and Jewish Identity*, London: Routledge, 1990, pp. 71-85.

[19]   *Yerushalmi*, p. 39.

[20]   *Yerushalmi*, p. 99.

[21]   *Kenneth A. Grigg:* All Roads Lead to Rome: The Role of the Nursemaid in Freud's Dreams, *Journal of the American Psychoanalytic Association*, XXI (1973), 108-126; *Paul C. Vitz*: *Sigmund Freud's Christian Unconscious*, New York, Guilford Press, 1988; *John Murray Cuddihy*: *The Ordeal of Civility: Freud, Marx, Levi-Straus,. and the Jewish Struggle with Modernity*, New York, Basic Books, 1974.

[22]   *Suzanne Cassirer Bernfeld:* Freud and Archeology, *American Imago*, 8: 2 (June, 1951), 107-128; and *Marthe Robert*: *From Oedipus to Moses: Freud's Jewish Identity*, trans. Ralph Manheim, Garden City, NY, Anchor/Doubleday, 1976; *Peter Loewenberg*: The Pagan Freud, *In: Robert S. Wistrich*, ed.: *Austrians and Jews in the Twentieth Century*, New York, St. Martin's Press, 1992, pp. 124-141.

[23]   *Bergmann, in Ostow: Judaism and Psychoanalysis*, p. 116.

[24]   *Ernest Jones: The Life and Work of Sigmund Freud*, New York: Basic Books, 1953, Vol. I, p. 19.

[25]   *Jones*, I, 167; II (1955), 17.

[26]   *Everett V. Stonequist: The Marginal Man: A Study in Personality and Culture Conflict*, New York, Charles Scribner's Sons, 1937, pp. 154-155, see also the section on *The Jews* pp. 76-82 .

[27]   *Stonequist*, p. 81.

[28]   The author of the letter was Dietrich Schaefer, a student of Treitschke. As quoted in *Gay: Freud, Jews and Other Germans*, p. 121.

[29]   *Georg Simmel:* The Stranger (1908), *In: Kurt H. Wolff*, trans. and ed.: *The Sociology of Georg Simmel*, New York, Free Press, 1950, p. 402 .

[30]   *Simmel*, p. 404.

[31]   *Thorstein Veblen:* The Intellectual Pre-Eminence of Jews in Modern Europe, *The Political Science Quarterly*, XXXIV (March 1919), reprinted in *Leon Ardzrooni*, ed.: *Essays in Our Changing Order*, New York: Viking, 1934, pp. 221-224, *passim*.

[32]   *Veblen*, 225-226.

[33]   *Veblen*, pp. 226-227.

[34]   *Isaac Deutscher: The Non-Jewish Jew and other essays*, ed. Tamara Deutscher, London, Oxford University Press, 1968, p. 26.

[35] *Deutscher*, p. 35.

[36] *Deutscher*, p. 27.

[37] *Deutscher*, p. 30.

[38] *Deutscher*, pp. 34-35.

[39] *Freud:* An Autobiographical Study, 1925, *S. E.*, 20, 9.

[40] *Freud to Abraham:* May 3, 1908, *In: A Psycho-Analytic Dialogue: The Letters of Sigmund Freud and Karl Abraham*, ed. Hilda C. Abraham and Ernst L. Freud, trans. Bernard Marsh and Hilda C. Abraham, New York, Basic Books, 1965, p. 34.

[41] *Freud to Abraham*, May 11, 1908, *Letters*, p. 36.

[42] *Freud to Abraham*, July 20, 1908, *Letters*, p. 46.

[43] *Freud to Abraham*, July 23, 1908, *Letters*, p. 46.

[44] *Freud:* The Resistances to Psycho-Analysis, 1925, *S.E.*, 19, 222.

[45] *The Future of an Illusion*, 1927, *S.E.*, 21, 3-56.

[46] *Freud:* Address to the Society of B'nai B'rith, 1926, *S.E.*, 20, 273-274.

[47] *Virgil: The Aeneid*, trans. Allen Mandelbaum, New York, Bantam, 1961, Book II, pp. 52-53, lines 954-959, 974-979, *passim*.

[48] *Freud: Moses and Monotheism*, 1939, S.E., 23, 115.

[49] *Jones: Freud*, III, 1957, p. 221.

References

BAKAN, D. (1958). *Sigmund Freud and the Jewish Mystical Tradition*. New York: Van Nostrand.

BERGMANN, M.S. (1976). Moses and the Evolution of Freud's Jewish Identity. *Israel Annals of Psychiatry and Related Disciplines*, *14*/1, 3-26; reprinted *In:* Ostow M. (1982), *Judaism and Psychoanalysis*. New York: Ktav, pp. 115-142.

BERKOWER, L. (1969). The Enduring Effect of the Jewish Tradition Upon Freud. *American Journal of Psychiatry*, *125*/8, 1067-1073.

BERNFELD, S. (1944). Freud's Earliest Theories and the School of Helmholtz. *Psychoanalytic Quarterly*, *13*, 341-361.

CASSIRER BERNFELD, S. (1951). Freud and Archeology. *American Imago*, 8/2, 107-128.

CUDDIHY, J.M. (1974). *The Ordeal of Civility: Freud, Marx, Levi-Strauss, and the Jewish Struggle with Modernity*. New York: Basic Books.

DEUTSCHER, I. (1968). *The Non-Jewish Jew and Other Essays*. London: Oxford University Press.

DILLER, J.J. (1991). *Freud's Jewish Identity: A Case Study in the Impact of Ethnicity*. Cranbury, N.J.: Associated University Presses.

FREUD, S. (1900a). The Interpretation of Dreams. *Standard Edition*, 5.

— (1905c). Jokes and their Relation to the Unconscious. *Standard Edition*, 8.

— (1925d). An Autobiographical Study. *Standard Edition, 20*, 1-70.

— (1925e). The Resistances to Psycho-Analysis. *Standard Edition, 19*, 211-222.

— (1926). Address to the Society of B'nai B'rith. *Standard Edition, 20*, 273-274.

— (1927c). The Future of an Illusion. *Standard Edition, 21*, 3-56.

— (1939a). Moses and Monotheism. *Standard Edition, 23*, 1-137.

— & ABRAHAM, K. (1965a). *A Psycho-Analytic Dialogue: The Letters of Sigmund Freud and Karl Abraham*. New York: Basic Books.

GAY P. (1978). *Freud, Jews and Other Germans*. New York: Oxford University Press.

— (1987). *A Godless Jew: Freud, Atheism, and the Making of Psychoanalysis*. New Haven: Yale University Press.

— (1988). *Freud: A Life for Our Time*. New York: W.W. Norton.

— (1990). *Reading Freud: Explorations and Entertainments*. New Haven: Yale University Press.

GILMAN S.L. (1993). *The Case of Sigmund Freud: Medicine and Identity at the Fin de Siècle*. Baltimore: Johns Hopkins University Press.

GRIGG K.A. (1973). All Roads Lead to Rome: The Role of the Nursemaid in Freud's Dreams. *Journal of the American Psychoanalytic Association, 21*, 108-126.

JONES E. (1953). *The Life and Work of Sigmund Freud, vol. 1: The Young Freud, 1856-1900*. New York: Basic Books.

— (1955). *The Life and Work of Sigmund Freud, vol. 2: Years of Maturity, 1901-1919*. New York: Basic Books.

— (1957). *The Life and Work of Sigmund Freud, vol. 3: The Last Phase, 1919-1939*. New York: Basic Books.

KLEIN D.B. (1981). *Jewish Origins of the Psychoanalytic Movement*. New York: Praeger.

LOEWENBERG P. (1970). A Hidden Zionist Theme in Freud's «My Son, the Myops...» Dream. *Journal of the History of Ideas, 31*/1 (January-March), 129-132.

— (1971). Sigmund Freud as a Jew: A Study in Ambivalence and Courage. *Journal of the History of the Behavioral Sciences, 7*/4, 363-369.

— (1992). The Pagan Freud, *In:* Wistrich R.S. (ed.), *Austrians and Jews in the Twentieth Century*. New York: St. Martin's Press, pp. 124-141.

Mc GRATH W.J. (1974). *Dionysian Art and Populist Politics in Austria*. New Haven: Yale University Press.

— (1986). *Freud's Discovery of Psychoanalysis: The Politics of Hysteria*. Ithaca: Cornell University Press.

RICE E. (1990). *Freud and Moses: The Long Journey Home*. Albany/New York: SUNY Press.

ROBERT M. (1976). *From Oedipus to Moses: Freud's Jewish Identity*. Garden City, New York: Anchor/Doubleday.

ROSENBLIT M.L. (1983). *The Jews of Vienna, 1867-1914: Assimilation and Identity*. Albany: State University of New York Press.

SCHORSKE C.E. (1980). Politics and Patricide in Freud's «Interpretation of Dreams», *In: Fin-de-Siècle Vienna: Politics and Culture*. New York: Alfred A. Knopf, pp. 189-193.

SHENGOLD L. (1979), Freud and Joseph, *In:* Kanzer M. & Glenn J. (eds), *Freud and His Self-Analysis*. New York: Jason Aronson.

SIMMEL G. (1908). The Stranger, *In:* Wolff K.H., trans. and ed., *The Sociology of Georg Simmel.* New York: Free Press, 1950.

SIMON E. (1957). Sigmund Freud, the Jew. *Leo Baeck Institute Yearbook*, II. London: East and West Library, pp. 270-305.

STONEQUIST E.V. (1937). *The Marginal Man: A Study in Personality and Culture Conflict.* New York: Charles Scribner's Sons.

VEBLEN T. (1919). The Intellectual Pre-Eminence of Jews in Modern Europe. *The Political Science Quarterly*, *34*; reprinted *In:* Ardzrooni L. (ed.), *Essays in Our Changing Order.* New York: Viking Press, 1934.

VIRGIL. *The Aeneid.* New York: Bantam, 1961.

VITZ P.C. (1988). *Sigmund Freud's Christian Unconscious.* New York: Guilford Press.

WALTER B. (1946). *Theme and Variations: An Autobiography.* New York: Alfred A. Knopf.

WISTRICH R.S. (1989). The Jewish Identity of Sigmund Freud, *In: The Jews of Vienna in the Age of Franz Joseph.* Oxford: Oxford University Press, pp. 537-582.

— (1990). The Jewishness of Sigmund Freud, *In: Between Redemption and Perdition: Modern Antisemitism and Jewish Identity.* London: Routledge, pp. 71-85.

YERUSHALMI Y.H. (1991). *Judaism Terminable and Interminable: An Exploration of Freud's «Moses and Monotheism».* New Haven: Yale University Press.

Cahiers Psychiatriques Genevois, Special Issue, 1994, pp. 151-167

FREUD'S RELATION TO PHILOSOPHY AND BIOLOGY AS REFLECTED IN HIS LETTERS

André Haynal

> «*Psycho-analysis ... as may be supposed, did not drop from the skies ready-made. It had its starting-point in older ideas, which it developed further; it sprang from earlier suggestions, which it elaborated.*»
>
> (Freud, 1924f, *S.E.* 19: 191)

I have already, in my introduction, stressed the immense influence which psycho-analysis has had on this century in the different fields of culture, human sciences and medicine, particularly psychiatry and what is called nowadays psychological medicine.

Freud has given us a new «vision» of human beings; in Foucault's words, he is one of those who have invented a *new discourse* on them. There is no longer any doubt that he was the creator of an important *synthesis*, with an extraordinary impact on the cultural history of this century. I was most interested in the question of what the «pieces» were from which this synthesis was constructed. It seems that we cannot reply to this question without examining the cultural context.

Synthesis: this is in fact the key-word to what follows: I am going to present a few pages of a much more extensive work which I am preparing on Freud's intellectual *sources*. I shall not be able to embark upon the fascinating subject of Freud's complex interactions with his cultural, and especially literary, world as a whole, and I shall limit myself to submitting a few ideas on his relationship with philosophy, and summarising a few others on his relationship with biology.[1] Thomas Mann, as late as 1936, said:

Translated from French by Dr. Christine Trollope, London.

«Sigmund Freud, founder of psycho-analysis as a general method of research and as a therapeutic technique, trod the steep path alone and independently, as physician and natural scientist, without knowing that reinforcement and encouragement lay to his hand in literature. He did not know Nietzsche, scattered throughout whose pages one finds premonitory flashes of truly Freudian insight; he did not know Novalis, whose romantic-biologic fantasies so often approach astonishingly close to analytic conceptions; he did not know Kierkegaard, whom he must have found profoundly sympathetic and encouraging for the Christian zeal which urged him on to psychological extremes; and finally, he did not know Schopenhauer, the melancholy symphonist of a philosophy of the instinct groping for change and redemption. Probably it must have been so. By his unaided effort, without knowledge of any previous intuitive achievement, he had methodically to follow out the line of his own researches; the driving force of his activity was probably increased by this very freedom from special advantage» (Th. Mann, 1936).

Philosophy

Freud, fascinated by the intuition of the Germanic romantic poets and writers on the *undercurrents, the hidden side of psychic life*, wished to make it the subject of a *science*, in *creating* this new science. His interest in biology, even in medicine, was preceded by an interest in philosophy which later evolved in parallel. Much criticism has been uttered of Freud's unwillingness to recognise this fact. In my opinion it is due to the cultural situation at *that precise moment in history*; it comes only shortly after the constitution of the natural sciences such as physics and chemistry, later psychology. These sciences separate from each other at this very moment through the elaboration of their own methodology, *breaking away* from philosophy and *a fortiori* from *Naturphilosophie*. This progressive detachment and delimitation was particularly long and *difficult* in the case of psychology. In Central European countries during practically all Freud's life, it was often philosophers who held chairs in this field – of course raising competition and rivalry with experimentalists whose ambition was to introduce scientific methods in this domain.

Freud had already touched on philosophy during his last year at *school*, at the Leopoldstädter *Gymnasium*; notably, besides logic, psychology was also taught as part of it. Through the third edition of Lindner's *Manual of Psychology* (1858 [1872]), Freud was able to catch a glimpse of the thoughts of Herbart, one of the founders of the new psychology: *Johann Friedrich Herbart* (1776-1841), in two works conceived between 1813 und

1825, had set out to base his science on experience and mathematics. This central role of quantity is part of the thinking of Freud. Herbart, taking up Locke's idea of mental *representations* and Hume's definition of the *Ego* («the sum of representations at present conscious»), considers feelings as the effect of representations among themselves, thus arriving at a psychology seen as a science of mental *dynamics*. In Lindner's book, even today fascinating to read, Freud was able to examine ideas such as «Dream is a prototype of the mental diseases» (*Seelenkrankheiten*, Lindner, 1872, pp. 221-222) that representations of dreams take the form of perceptions (*ibid.*, p. 221; in Freud, 1895d, they were «hallucinations», *S.E.* 2: 188), that depending on the importance of affects transitory disturbances can become lasting (*ibid.*, p. 225), and clearly, also, the idea of *psychodynamics* on the basis of associations between representations, and many others.

Apart from his readings, we know of two decisive encounters of Freud with philosophy: one with the ideas of Schopenhauer and Nietzsche in the *Leseverein der deutschen Studenten Wiens*, a Germanophile literary and philosophical circle to which he belonged between 1872 and 1878 (Brauns & Schöpf, 1989, p. 55), and the other, at the University, with his teacher Brentano.

Brentano

As a matter of fact, at the University of Vienna, besides his study of biology and medicine, Freud had enrolled, from the third to the sixth semester, in the course of Franz Brentano (1838-1917), then professor of philosophy (Merlan, 1959). Moreover, in his enthusiasm, he even attended other courses given by him[2] without enrolling in them, as we learn from his correspondence with Silberstein.[3] Brentano, like Schopenhauer, was one of those philosophers who, completely in «the atmosphere» of their time, found it essential to lean on the *natural sciences*. In his «habilitation» thesis[4] (Brentano, 1866) he expresses his *modern* theory in *traditional* Latin as if still between two worlds: «Vera methodus philosophiae non alia nisi scientiae naturalis» (The true method of philosophy is none other than that of natural sciences).[5]

Franz Brentano, «this splendid man, scholar and philosopher»[6] (Freud to Silberstein, 5.11.1874) came from a vastly cultured Catholic family; the famous romantic poet Clemens Brentano was his great-uncle. Franz first became a priest, then gave up his priesthood and left the Church in 1873 as a reaction against the Vatican I Council (1869). He then became a member of the Viennese intelligentsia. Thus he married *Ida von Lieben*, daughter of the banker and president of the Vienna Stock Exchange, whose sister,

Anna von Lieben, was later one of Freud's first important patients («Cecilia M.»). Freud developed in this same environment, which included his professor of psychiatry *Theodor Meynert*, his friend the physiologist *von Fleischl* (Stumpf, 1919), and his master and mentor *Josef Breuer*, who was at the same time carrying on an intense correspondence with Brentano (Bernfeld & Cassirer Bernfeld, 1981, p. 67; Sulloway, 1979, p. 54).[7]

At the very first sight, the Aristotelian Brentano is certainly one of those who could pass on to Freud the idea of Aristotelian *catharsis*,[8] a concept on which his fiancée's uncle, Jakob Bernays, had already published an important work (Bernays, 1880, p. 194). He was able to find the same concept in one of his great idols, Goethe,[9] and also in Nietzsche.

It is also well known that it was Brentano who suggested to him that he should translate the 12th volume of the works of the associationist John Stuart Mill, in a series published by Theodor Gomperz, work he accomplished during his military service.[10]

In the course which Freud followed, Franz Brentano, the author of *Psychology from an empirical point of view* (1874), was preoccupied with the question of the unconscious,[11] even though he arrived at rather negative conclusions, as compared with those which Freud was to reach later. For Brentano, in the classification of psychic phenomena, *intentionality* is at the forefront, prefiguring the relationship of psychism with its object in Freud. In movements of affectivity, the bipolarity of love and hate in Brentano's doctrine may or may not be one of the sources of inspiration of the notions of life-instinct and death-instinct in Freud.

According to a letter of 15.3.1875 to *Silberstein*, Brentano recommended that Freud and *Paneth* study Kant, and we know that Freud's library contained a copy of *The Critique of Pure Reason* with many notes in his handwriting. He discusses the problem of *Kant* in a letter to Silberstein dated 11.4.1878, saying that «synthetic *a priori* judgments» are called into question by the thoughts of the English empiricists, who refer, as he writes, to experience «instead of innate ways of understanding». Remarks of this sort are not those of someone ignorant of the philosophical heritage, even if later, for example in a letter to *Juliette Boutonnier* of 11.4.1930, he could claim: «Philosophical problems and formulations are so alien to me that I do not know what to do with them.»[12]

Schopenhauer and Nietzsche: the «Lebensphilosophen»

In 1896 we find this admission in a letter from Freud to Fliess: «I see how, via the detour of medical practice, you are reaching your first ideal of understanding human beings as a physiologist, just as I most secretly nourish the hope of arriving, via these same paths, at my initial goal of philosophy. For that is what I wanted originally ...» (Freud to Fliess, 1.1.1896, *in*: Masson, 1985, p. 159). And in the same year: «As a young man I knew no longing other than for philosophical knowledge, and now I am about to fulfill it as I move from medicine to psychology» (Freud to Fliess, 2.4.1896, *ibid*. p. 180).[13]

On his road, from the circle of German students already mentioned to the discussions of the Vienna Wednesday Society (*Mittwochsgesellschaft*), around 1908, Freud repeatedly encounters two philosophers who influenced his thinking over this period, *Schopenhauer* and *Nietzsche*, through people who were in very close contact especially with the latter: Paneth, in the *Leseverein*, Lou Andreas-Salomé, and Otto Rank whose intellectual horizons were fixed by Nietzsche's thought (what is more, in 1926 Rank gave Freud for his 70th birthday the complete works of Nietzsche bound in white leather, and when Freud emigrated to London, he choose to take this present with him).

Freud could even speak later of the «large extent to which psychoanalysis coincides with the philosophy of Schopenhauer» in specifying: «Not only did he assert the dominance of the emotions and the supreme importance of sexuality, but he was even aware of the mechanism of repression». He feels nonetheless compelled to add that these elements are «not to be traced to my acquaintance with his teaching» (Freud, 1925d, *S.E.* 20: 59). He goes on: «Nietzsche ... whoses guesses and intuitions often agree in the most astonishing way with the laborious findings of psychoanalysis, was for a long time avoided (*gemieden*) by me on that very account» (Freud, 1925d, *S.E.* 20: 60).[14] Even in 1935 he was still struggling with this question and found that «[his] interest, after making a lifelong *detour* through the natural sciences, medicine and psychotherapy, returned to the cultural problems which had fascinated [him] so long before, when [he] was a youth scarcely old enough for thinking... [It] might be described as a phase of regressive development» (Freud, 1935a, *S.E.* 20: 72). Self-criticism, provocation or ambivalence? In flagrant contradiction with a declaration made ten years earlier (Freud, 1926e, *S.E.* 20: 253) to the Vienna Psychoanalytical Society, saying that it is exactly the «*triumph*» of his life, which «lies in [his] having, after a long and roundabout journey, found [his] way back to [his] earliest path».

Arnold Zweig, Freud's close friend, easily grasped the relationship between the two when he wrote to Freud: «You have achieved everything that Nietzsche intuitively felt to be his task, without his being really able to achieve it with his poetic idealism and brilliant inspirations... And thanks to the fact that you are a scientist (*Naturforscher*), and furthermore a psychologist who advances step by step, you have attained what Nietzsche would so gladly have achieved himself: the scientific description and explanation of the human soul ...» (A. Zweig to Freud, 2.12.1930, *in*: Freud, 1968a, pp. 23-24). Freud makes no protest; far from it: «You should all the same write [the essay] which you wanted to do on the relationship between Nietzsche's influence and mine» (*ibid.*, 7.12.1930).[15] It is true that already much earlier, on 1.2.1900, he was writing to Fliess: «I have at present acquired Nietzsche, in which I hope to find the words for many things which are still dumb within me» (Masson, 1985, p. 398). This of course contradicts what he was to write with hindsight: «In later years I have denied myself the very great pleasure of reading the works of Nietzsche, with the deliberate object of not being hampered in working out the impressions received in psychoanalysis by any sort of anticipatory ideas. I had therefore to be prepared – and I am so, gladly – to forgo all claims to priority in the many instances in which laborious psychoanalytic investigation can merely confirm the truths which the philosopher recognised by intuition.» (Freud, 1914d, *S.E.* 14: 15-16). This paradox between acquaintance and non-acquaintance, knowledge and non-knowledge, may be drawn from life in the discussion of the Vienna Wednesday Society where, for example on 1st April 1908, Freud declares first that he has «finally given up studying philosophy» (Nunberg & Federn, 1962, p. 359) and «does not know» Nietzsche (*ibid.*), then adds that «Nietzsche recognised neither infantilism nor the mechanisms of displacement (*Verschiebung*)» (*ibid.*), which surely bears witness to his *knowledge* of this author. Otherwise how could he criticise what Nietzsche *has not recognised*? And if he has «given it up», he must have been interested in it earlier...!

How then are we to understand his allegation that he could never «get beyond the first half page whenever he has tried in his attempts to read Nietzsche» (session of 28.10.1908, Nunberg & Federn, 1967, p. 32)? Is it a question of protecting his own progress and defending himself against the unpleasant feeling of losing autonomy in his own research processes,[16] as was often to be the case in his life? Again at the Wednesday Society, in 1908, he gives explanations tending in the same direction: «... partly because of the resemblance of Nietzsche's intuitive insights to our laborious investigations, and partly because of the *wealth* of ideas ...» (Vienna Wednesday Society, session of 28th October 1910 – my italics). In the session of 1.4.1908 he was already confessing: «... occasional attempts at reading it were smothered by an *excess* of interest.» (*ibid.*, session of April 1st, 1908 – my italics). But his fears appear clearer still in his letter to Abraham of 20.1.1911 which he ends by saying: «Juliusburger has done a very good thing with his quotations from Schopenhauer, but my original-

ity is obviously *on the wane.*» (Freud to Abraham, 20.1.1911 – my italics). Originality, priority were obviously also some of his worries...

Here should follow a systematic analysis of *comparisons of contents* which goes beyond the context of this paper. Allow me merely to remind that on the subject of his dream theory, *central* to his work, Freud *himself* quotes words from Nietzsche: «In dreams, 'some primeval relic of humanity is at work we can now scarcely reach by a direct path'»[17] (Freud, 1900a, *S.E.* 5: 549) (the paragraph was formulated in 1919, it is true, in an edition prepared in collaboration with Otto Rank), and to expound a *cardinal point* [17] of his theory (on repression and defences) he takes his stand on this same philosopher's words in *Beyond Good and Evil*[19]: «But none of us has been able to portray the phenomenon and its psychological basis so exhaustively and at the same time so impressively as Nietzsche in one of his aphorisms: '«I did this», says my Memory. «I cannot have done this», says my Pride and remains inexorable. In the end – Memory yields.' [*Jenseits von Gut und Böse*, IV, 68].» (Freud, 1901b, *S.E.* 6: 147). If, with Strachey (*S.E.* 6: 147) we admit that Freud had this quotation from the Rat Man, this would show once more to what extent he could meet Nietzsche's theories «at every street corner» in Vienna at this time.

Of course Freud's theories on dreams had many other intellectual sources; his colleague in Vienna, Richard von Krafft-Ebing (1894) was already presuming that unconscious desires (libido) could be detected in dreams (Sand, 1992). Freud certainly remembered from his Paris period that Jean-Martin Charcot (1890, p. 442) supposed that the psychological trauma which precipitated the hysterical symptom is often present in the patient's dreams, and that Pierre Janet (1892, pp. 167-179) thought that the causes of hysteria are depicted in dreams, and that through dreams the patient's unconscious relationship with himself may be understood.

It is difficult to imagine that Freud could not have known that *Nietzsche*, in 1888, claimed that all philosophy is interpretation, consisting of removing or tearing up masks. Nietzsche's brilliant intuitions have, without a doubt, inspired the direction taken by Freud, even if Nietzsche is considered as remaining within the domain of art while Freud tried to build a science. For example, the concept of sublimation is Nietzsche's, and so is the instinctual power which acts on man, or the programme of self-realisation, which Nietzsche takes from Pindar with his «become what you are». He also perceived underlying motivations, like in the case of altruism for example the wish for power over another which may be hidden behind sympathy and empathy. Of course he used the term «unconscious», like Nicolai von Hartmann after him, even though it was not in the sense of an unconscious *system*, but close to Dostoevski and in the traditions of La Rochefoucauld or Montaigne, and the term «*Es*» («id» or «it») comes from Nietzsche... The term of eternal recommencement also belongs here.

Schopenhauer and Nietzsche were without a doubt postmetaphysical anthropological philosophers, *«Lebensphilosophen»*, as they were called at the time. Freud also avoided «flight» into metaphysics – to use Nietzsche's expression (*Sämtliche Werke*, vol. 7, p. 467) – and continued his critique of the morals of culture and the genealogy of consciousness. As far as his entourage of the *«Mittwochsgesellschaft»* is concerned, Federn could say, at the session of 1st April 1908 (Nunberg & Federn, 1962), that Nietzsche «intuitively knew a number of Freud's discoveries; he was the first to discover the significance of abreaction, of repression, of flight into illness, of the instincts»; he adds «the normal sexual ones as well as the sadistic instincts» (p. 359). Rank, «reading Nietzsche», has «the impression that the sadistic/masochistic instinct and its suppression play the chief role in Nietzsche's life» (*ibid.*, p. 361). In Stekel's opinion, «in Nietzsche ... the philosophic drive stems from sexual curiosity; the sexual enigma becomes the enigma of the world (displacement)» (*ibid.*, p. 361).

Though Freud's preoccupation with instinctual forces is certainly inspired by Darwin's thinking also, we cannot overestimate *Schopenhauer*'s influence on his hypothesis of the impact of irrational forces on man's psychic life. According to Guttman (1980, vol. 5, p. 374), Freud mentions his name twenty-six times, and twice explicitly quotes his principal work, *Die Welt als Wille und Vorstellung* (The world as will and representation), and he constantly repeats that he considers him a great thinker.[20] In this work we find practically no important idea which does not emerge in Freud as well. Schopenhauer declares that madness (*Wahnsinn*) results from defence and repression mechanisms – and also sees the price to be paid for this defence by the psychic organisation; cure, in his view, consists in reversing these processes. He believes that sexuality is essential in human life, that inner experience is important, and that thinking is a secondary function; isn't that the case in what was later to be called «Freudian»?

His *«blinder Drang»* (blind urge) and his *«hungriger Wille»* (hungry will) are Freud's «drives», and the life and death instincts are nearer to Schopenhauer's *«Lebensbejahung»* (affirmation of life) and *«Lebensverneinung»* (negation of life) than to biology. Schopenhauer's analysis of suffering is the precursor of Freud's pleasure-unpleasure principle, even if there the formulation comes to Freud from Fechner's biology. Moreover Schopenhauer, and Freud as well, are not systematisers, but essayists giving a modern face to the outlook to the world.

So much so that Freud was to write in 1932: «You may perhaps shrug your shoulders and say: 'That isn't natural science, it's Schopenhauer's philosophy!' But ... why should not a bold thinker have guessed something that is afterwards confirmed by sober and painstaking research?» (Freud, 1933a, *S.E.* 22: 107).[21] He thus comes back again and again to the fear that his theories can be taken «for philosophy» and not for painstaking scientific research.

All this takes us away from philosophy, to the biological roots of Freud's thought ...[22]

When Freud in his youth decided to do *science*, he tried to indicate his position by scientific references such as Broca, Darwin, the *sexologists* — and he seems to have left the philosophers aside.[23] Later, around 1920, he returned to them – and brushed aside his biological and zoological memories, for example in his declaration to Abraham: «It is making severe demands on the unity of the personality to try and make me identify myself with the author of the paper on the spinal ganglia of the petromyzon. Nevertheless I must be he, and I think I was happier about that discovery than about others since.» (Freud, 1965a, p. 369). Already, in what has been said up to this point, Freud appears much less as a «lonely hero» than as a man of amazing culture, endowed with an admirable capacity for original synthesis, and, of course, as the creator of the special listening-post which, as we can never forget, forms the basis of his work: «If only we could make the best people understand that all our affirmations are taken from experience (as for me, from an experience which one could also try to interpret otherwise), and have not been completely invented or dreamt up at a desk!» (Freud to Pfister, 12.7.1909).

The search for roots in the field of biology

In order to create the science of man's depths, Freud felt the need for firm foundations: all his life he looked for them in the field of *biology*. His relationship with biology and medicine is at least as complex as his relationship with philosophy. Obviously we cannot follow here all its vicissitudes. It would be interesting to follow his filiations in this field, especially through Brücke, to the group around von Helmholtz, that giant of science who, as we know, not only made basic contributions to optics, electrodynamics, the subject of the conduction of nervous influx, the physiology of visual and auditory perception, physics, mathematics and meteorology, but was also the founder of a school based on the application of strict *determinism* to biology, which made possible the magnificent progress of psychophysiology in German-speaking countries in the course of the 19th century. The notions of *force* and *nervous energy* which he introduced with his circle, particularly *Wilhelm Wundt* (1832-1920), Helmholtz's

159

pupil, and *Gustav Theodor Fechner* (1801-1887) whom Freud quotes on many occasions, have become current and play the part of which we are aware in Freud's later work.

Unfortunately I cannot further stress the importance of the impact of *Meynert* (1833-1892) for a neurobiological doctrine of psychiatry, nor Freud's work and research on cocaine, undertaken from 1884 onwards, which is of undeniable importance, as P. Swales (1983) has shown. Freud tested the effects of cocaine on himself: he was already using the introspection method here, calling it (Freud, 1888b) *«innere Selbstbeobachtung»* (inner self-observation).

In 1884 appeared the «Croonian Lectures» of Hughlings Jackson, in which the author explained the concepts of «evolution» and «dis-involution» (Kuhn, 1983, p. 23) which Freud had already taken up in his studies on aphasia, and which prefigured the notion of *regression*.

1889 is the date of Freud's publication of a clinical study on cerebral hemiplegia carried out at the Kassowitz Clinic.[24] In the same year he brought out his work on *aphasia* (1891b)[25] in which he already explicitly postulates the existence of *unconscious* processes. He declares that the earliest impressions are more durable, that what comes later «will be damaged earlier than what has been primarily associated».[26] We also find in his elaboration the distinction between «word-representation» and «object-representation» (Freud, 1891b, *S.E.* 14: 87).

Meynert's *«Sprachapparat»* (speech-apparatus) already prefigures Freud's later *«psychischer Apparat»* (mental apparatus). We find in it the notion of *«Besetzung»* (cathexis) and even that of *«Überdeterminierung»* (overdetermination). Freud deals with his self-observation and the reader is referred to his own. There also appears the idea of the influence of disturbing emotions. Freud sees these residues as a struggle between two tendencies: one that wants to express itself, and the other, the inhibiting tendency linked with disease. Thus we see emerging a model of *conflict* and its result: *compromise*. He speaks of a usage that is «automatic» and another *«unterbewusst»* («subconscious») as though he were already distinguishing between what was later to be the «preconscious» and the «unconscious».

The theory of the function of the neurones, underlying his study on aphasia, culminates in his *Outline of scientific psychology* which was never to be published in his lifetime. It is nevertheless interesting to note that in this project he works decisively with the model of neurones, which is not self-evident at this time and shows an exact intuition with regard to the evolution of neurobiology. In the historical context of the great debate of «continuity» versus «contiguity», we have to take into account the fact that Wilhelm Waldeyer did not express his doctrine of neurones until 1891, and that the *decisive* work of Ramon y Cajal comes at the turn of the century (although Freud anticipated it according to Ritvo, 1990, p. 110).

In 1895 he wrote to Fliess: « Everything seemed to fall into place, the cogs meshed. I had the impression that the thing now really was a machine that shortly would function on its own.» (Freud to Fliess, 20.10.1895). Then he had to realise that this was a setback and needed a change of direction. His scientific bases were from then on determined by his encounter with *Darwinism* – which already dated back to his studies at the Gymnasium and his contact with Fr. Karl Claus, and which he espoused particularly in its Lamarckian form – and, in parallel, with the *sexology* of his epoch to which he refers explicitly at the beginning of the *Three Essays* (1905d, *S.E.* 7: 135). We should not forget that part of his articles were published in journals or encyclopaedias of sexology (e.g. Freud, 1906a (1905); 1908a; 1908c; 1908d). The work of Albert Moll, *Untersuchungen über die Libido sexualis* (Berlin, 1898) had without a doubt a major influence on Freud's theory of libido. The word «libido» itself was coined by his colleague at the Faculty of Vienna, *Richard von Krafft-Ebing* (1889, pp. 1-6) and used by his other colleagues *Meynert* (1889, p. 195) and *Moritz Benedikt* (1868, pp. 448-454); it was *Moll* who gave it its meaning of sexual instinct, to which Freud refers explicitly, for example in his encyclopaedic article (Freud, 1923a (1922); *S.E.* 18: 255). Moll's book *The sexual life of children* («*Das Sexualleben des Kindes*», 1909) was the subject of a discussion at the Vienna Psychoanalytical Society on 11.11.1908 (Nunberg & Federn, 1967, pp. 43-53). The *Psychopathia Sexualis* (1886) of Richard von Krafft-Ebing, his colleague in the psychiatry of Vienna, was one of the acts of foundation of the new science of sexology. Magnus Hirschfeld, in 1908, chose as his co-editor of the *Zeitschrift für Sexualwissenschaft* also an Austrian ethnologist, Friedrich Salomon Krausz. All this happened in Freud's cultural environment. The term «homosexuality» was proposed by an Austro-Hungarian writer, K.M. Kertbeny (in 1869).[27] Krafft-Ebing coined the terms «sadism» and «masochism», the first after the Marquis de Sade, and the second after Sacher-Masoch, thus leaning on descriptions from literary works. These presupposed biological sub-foundations led Freud in 1905 to *Three Essays on the Theory of Sexuality* and in 1915 to *Instincts and their Vicissitudes*. The central position of *sexuality in his system* is explained by the fact that for him it constitutes *the bridge* to the natural sciences, notably biology *and* towards Darwinism and philogenesis.[26] Let us not forget that in the *Origin of Species* (1859) Darwin prophetized that «psychology will be put on new foundations» of biology.

Freud was to keep, all his life, *nostalgia* for a foundation of his system which he considered *provisional*, and which at the same time he wished to base on *natural sciences*. A few quotations out of many may convince us of it, without any ambition to be exhaustive. *Hope* is never abandoned, even if «for the moment» it is not possible to do anything *but* psychology. Thus in the *Introductory lectures on psycho-analysis* (Freud, 1916-17), we can easily find several passages to this effect, like the following:

> [Psycho-analysis] tries to give psychiatry its missing psychological foundation. It hopes to discover the common ground on the basis of which the convergence of physical and mental disorder will become intelligible. With this aim in view, psycho-analysis must keep itself free from any hypothesis that is alien to it, whether of an anatomical, chemical or physiological kind, and must operate entirely with purely psychological auxiliary ideas. (Freud, 1916-17a (1915-17), *S.E.* 15: 21).

> The theoretical structure of psycho-analysis that we have created is in truth a superstructure, *which will one day have to be set upon its organic foundation*. But we are still ignorant of this. (Freud, *ibid.*, S.E. 16: 389 – my italics).

> Well then, is our psycho-analytic method a causal therapy or not? (...) it is not. (...) Supposing, now, that it was possible, by some chemical means, perhaps, to interfere in this mechanism, (...) this would then be a causal therapy in the true sense of the word, for which our analysis would have carried out the indispensable preliminary work of reconnaissance.» (Freud, *ibid.*, p. 436).

Four years later he again writes:

> Biology is truly a land of unlimited possibilities. We may expect it to give us *the most surprising information* and we cannot guess what answers it will return in a few dozen years to the questions we have put to it. They may be of a kind which will *blow away the whole of our artificial structure of hypotheses* (Freud, 1920g, *S.E.* 18: 60 – my italics).

There has been no lack of affirmations that psychoanalysis «is, even in its present» state, a natural science»:

> In the natural sciences, of which psychology is one... (Freud, 1925d, *S.E.* 20: 57).

> ... enabled psychology to take its place as a natural science like any other. (...) their being modified, corrected and more precisely determined... (Freud, 1940a, *S.E.* 23: 158).

> ... this hypothesis has put us in a position to establish psychology on foundations similar to those of any other science, such, for instance, as physics. (Freud, *ibid.*, p. 196).

> Psycho-analysis is a part of the mental science of psychology... Psychology, too, is a natural science. What else can it be?» (Freud, 1940b, *S.E.* 23: 282).

All this is accompanied by consciousness of the need for methodological purity:

> ...that they (psychoanalysts) should resist the temptation to flirt with endocrinology and the autonomic nervous system, when what is needed is an apprehension of

psychological facts with the help of a framework of psychological concepts (*psychologische Hilfsvorstellungen*) (Freud, 1927a, *S.E.* 20: 257).

In an open letter addressed to Einstein, he admits that perhaps the psychoanalytical concepts belong to mythology – but a mythology similar to that of one in physics concepts: thus, once more, psychoanalysis is «lifted» to the level of natural sciences:

> It may perhaps seem to you as though our theories are a kind of mythology and, in the present case, not even an agreeable one. But does not every science come in the end to a kind of mythology like this? Cannot the same be said today of our own Physics?» (Freud, 1933b, *S.E.* 22: 211).

Contrary to what Sulloway (1979) asserted, Freud was not a «cryptobiologist», but a psychoanalyst who sought to the end the basis of his system in the *biological* substructure of man – with due deference to those who would have liked it to be otherwise, for example Jean Laplanche, who in the title of his recent work (1993), speaks of *Fourvoiement biologisant de la sexualité chez Freud* (i.e.: Freud's sexual theories going astray into pseudobiology).

Notes

[1] See also Haynal, 1991.

[2] For the reproduction of his student's notebook, see Hemecker, 1991, pp. 135-140.

[3] Freud writes to Silberstein on 22-23.10.1874 (quoted after McGrath, 1986, p. 101) that he is regularly following two of Brentano's courses, but has only registered for one of them (Brauns & Schöpf, 1989, p. 57).

[4] A scientific paper in order to become a university teacher.

[5] Brentano was also a man of several cultures, with remarkable capacity of cultural synthesis. A scholastic Aristotelian by training, he became a modern philosopher midway between Kant and the English empiricists, with Freud and Husserl among his descendants...

[6] «ein prächtiger Mensch, Gelehrter u. Philosoph».

[7] Extracts from this correspondence have been published by Hirschmüller (1978, pp. 293-322).

[8] *Von der Theorie der Tragödie*, bei Aristoteles, De Poetica, 330, pp. 9, 58-59 and pp. 24-28.

[9] «Lady Macbeth... suffers from a true defensive neurosis»; «The healing of Orestes as described by Goethe is a case of successful catharsis» (Alfred Freiherr von Berger on the *Studies on Hysteria, in* Kiell, 1988, pp. 71-72).

[10] This volume translated by Freud contains four essays: *On the emancipation of women* (1-29) about which he writes to Martha with a certain scepticism (letter to Martha, 15.11.1883); *Plato* (30-110) (we should mention that while he was still at school he had already read the «Dialogues»); *The question of the workers* (111-159); *Socialism* (160-225).

It is perhaps interesting to note that John Stuart Mill carried on a correspondence with Brentano!

[11] This was precisely through John Stuart Mill, and in particular through the hypothesis of unconscious activity by H. Maudsley. Thus his reflections must be an important source of the constructions of Freud (who mentions Maudsley in the bibliography of the *Traumdeutung*, 1900a, *S.E.* 5: 702).

[12] «Philosophische Probleme und Formulierungen sind mir so fremdartig dass ich mit ihnen nichts anzufangen weiss» (Freud, *Nachtragsband*, 1987, p. 671).

[13] «Ich habe als junger Mensch keine andere Sehnsucht gekannt als die nach philosophischer Erkenntnis, und ich bin jetzt im Begriffe, sie zu erfüllen, indem ich von der Medizin zur Psychologie hinüberlenke» (Freud, *in*: Masson, 1985, German p. 190).

[14] «Schopenhauer and Freud agree on many points in their perspective systems and one is justified in comparing them. Both lean to a dynamic, energetic and pessimistic conception of life. Both attribute our ills to the domination of our animal and egoistic instincts. (...) Both also exalt creative and sublimated love; *amor intellectualis, amor veritatis*» (Bischler, 1939).

[15] Finally, if it is not Zweig, it will be Haynal...

[16] «I was... concerned... with keeping my mind unembarrassed (*S.E.* 20: 60) («[es] lag mir... an der Erhaltung meiner Unbefangenheit»). And when he adds that his preoccupation was not with priority, might that perhaps be a sort of denial? When he speaks of «*gemieden*» (avoided) and of «*enthalten*» (restrain oneself) is he not speaking of an intentional inhibition parallel to the «excess» of attraction we have mentioned? He had a similar attitude towards «speculation». Might there be a connection between his fear of being over-influenced by philosophy and by too great a tendency towards speculations, rather in the sense of what he writes on «the synthesis emerging» in him and which he restrains («*Niederhaltung*») (letter to Fliess, 16.4.1900).

[17] «Im Traume, 'ein uraltes Stück Menschentum fortübt, zu dem man auf direktem Wege kaum mehr gelangen kann'».

[18] See, for instance, «The theory of repression is the corner-stone on which the whole structure of psycho-analysis rests» (1924d, *S.E.* 14: 16).

[19] A title which obviously recalls *Beyond the pleasure principle* (Freud, 1920g).

[20] (1917a, S.E. 17: 143) and a courageous thinker (1900a, G.W. 2-3: 39); 1905 d, G.W. 5: 32); 1917a (1916), G.W. 12: 12, 1925d, G.W. 14: 86; 1925e, G.W. 14: 105; and also 1900a, G.W. 2-3: 69, 94, 270, note 1; 1911b, G.W. 8: 230, note 2; 1914d, G.W. 10: 53, 1933a, G.W. 15: 114 f.; 1921 c, G.W. 13: 110.

[21] «Moreover, there is nothing that has not been said already, and similar things had been said by many people before Schopenhauer. Furthermore, what we are saying is not even genuine Schopenhauer.» (Freud, 1933a, *S.E.* 22: 107.)

[22] To summarise these considerations we must note that among the philosophers whom Freud revered, «Divine Plato» was an artist and a contemplative; among the moderns, Schopenhauer and Nietzsche were nearer to the literary and artistic world than systematic and systematising professional philosophers; on the other hand Brentano could influence Freud by his strictness and by the idea of «empirical psychology» as Herbart has already done.

[23] Really all these philosophers, from Schopenhauer to Brentano, recognised the importance of *natural sciences* for a new anthropology, for a new synthesis enabling us to get to know the «nature» of human beings

[24] Where he worked for several years with *children!*

[25] In 1891, he moved to Berggasse 19, near the University and the University Clinics (*Allgemeine Krankenhaus*), in the 9th arrondissement popular with the intellectuals of Jewish origin. In the same street lived Theodor Herzl, and before Freud, in the same flat on the first floor, Victor Adler, the co-founder of the Austrian Social Democratic Party.

[26] «An arrangement of associations which developed later and at a high level will be lost, while an arrangement acquired earlier, and simpler, is maintained.» (Freud, 1891b, p. 87).

[27] Ferenczi himself, at the beginning of his activity, speaks of uranism – the first psychoanalysts, including Freud, spoke of «inverts», and of «inverted sexual sensations», etc.

[28] Particularly ontogenesis, as a recapitulation of phylogenesis (see Freud, 1913j).

References

BENEDIKT, M. (1868). *Electrotherapie.* Wien: Tendler.

BERNAYS, J. (1880). *Zwei Abhandlungen über die Aristotelische Theorie des Drama.* Berlin.

BERNFELD, S. & CASSIRER BERNFELD, S. (1981). *Bausteine der Freud-Biographik.* Frankfurt/M.: Suhrkamp.

BISCHLER, W. (1939). Schopenhauer and Freud: A Comparison. *Psychoanal. Quart.*, *8*: 40-58.

BRAUNS, H.P. & SCHÖPF, A. (1989). Freud und Brentano. Der Medizinstudent und der Philosoph. *In*: Nitzschke, B. (Hrsg.): *Freud und die akademische Psychologie. Beiträge zu einer historischen Kontroverse.* München: Psychologie Verlags Union.

BRENTANO, F. (1866). *Ad disputationem qua theses ... pro impetranda venia docendi ... defendet et ad praelectionem inauguralem publicam ... invitat Franciscus Brentano.* Aschaffenburg: Schipner.

— (1874). *Psychologie vom empirischen Standpunkt.* Leipzig: Meiner, 1924.

CHARCOT, J.M. (1890). Leçons sur les maladies du système nerveux, faites à la Salpêtrière. *In*: *Oeuvres complètes*, Vol. 3. Paris: Bureau du Progrès Médical, Delahaye & Lecrosnier.

DARWIN, Ch. (1859). *On the Origin of Species.* London: Watts & Co, 1959.

FREUD, S. (1888b). "Gehirn", *in*: Villaret, A. (Hrsg.): *Handwörterbuch der gesamten Medizin*, Bd 1, Stuttgart (not in English).

— (1891b). [On Aphasia, a Critical Study], Appendix B: Psycho-Physical Parallelism. *Standard Edition*, *14*, 206-215.

— (1895d). Studies on Hysteria. *Standard Edition*, *2*.

— (1900a). The Interpretation of Dreams. *Standard Edition*, *4-5*.

— (1901b). The Psychopathology of Everyday Life. *Standard Edition*, *6*.

— (1905d). Three Essays on the Theory of Sexuality. *Standard Edition*, *7*, 123-243.

— (1906a [1905]). My Views on the Part Played by Sexuality in the Aetiology of the Neuroses. *Standard Edition*, *7*, 269-279.

— (1908a). Hysterical Phantasies and their Relation to Bisexuality. *Standard Edition*, *9*, 155-166.

— (1908c). On the Sexual Theories of Children. *Standard Edition*, *9*, 205-226.

— (1908d). «Civilized» Sexual Morality and Modern Nervous Illness. *Standard Edition, 9*, 177-204.

— (1914d). On the History of the Psycho-Analytic Movement. *Standard Edition, 14*, 1-66.

— (1915c). Instincts and their Vicissitudes. *Standard Edition, 14*, 109-140.

— (1916-17). Introductory Lectures on Psycho-Analysis. *Standard Edition, 15-16*.

— (1920g).Beyond the Pleasure Principle. *Standard Edition, 18*, 1-64.

— (1923a [1922]). "Psychoanalysis" and "The Libido Theory", *Standard Edition, 18*, 235-259.

— (1924f). A Short Account of Psycho-Analysis, *Standard Edition, 19*, 191-209.

— (1925d). An Autobiographical Study. *Standard Edition, 20*, 7-70.

— (1926e). The Question of Lay Analysis. *Standard Edition, 20*, 183-250.

— (1927a). [The Question of Lay Analysis]. Postscript. *Standard Edition, 20*, 251-258.

— (1933a). New Introductory Lectures on Psycho-Analysis. *Standard Edition, 22*, 1-182.

— (1933b). Why War? (Einstein and Freud). *Standard Edition, 22*, 195-215.

— (1935a). Postscript to "An Autobiographical Study (1925d). *Standard Edition, 20*, 71-74.

— (1940a). An Outline of Psycho-Analysis. *Standard Edition, 23*, 139-207.

— (1940b). Some Elementary Lessons in Psycho-Analysis. *Standard Edition, 23*, 279-286.

— (1950a [1895]). Extracts from the Fliess papers. *Standard Edition, 1*, 177-387.

— (1963a). *Psycho-Analysis and Faith. The Letters of Sigmund Freud and Oskar Pfister, 1909-1939*. London: The Hogarth Press/New York: Basic Books, 1963.

— (1965a) & ABRAHAM, K. *A Psycho-Analytic Dialogue: The Letters of Sigmund Freud and Karl Abraham, 1907-1926*. London: The Hogarth Press.

— (1968a). *The Letters of Sigmund Freud and Arnold Zweig, 1927-1939*. London: The Hogarth Press/New York: Harcourt, Brace & World, 1970.

— (1987). *Gesammelte Werke, Nachtragsband, Texte aus den Jahren 1885-1938*. Frankfurt/M.: Fischer.

— (1988). *Brautbriefe. Briefe an Martha Bernays aus den Jahren 1882-1886*. Frankfurt/M.: Fischer.

— (1989). *The Letters of Sigmund Freud to Eduard Silberstein 1871-1881*. Cambridge, Mass.: Harvard University Press, 1990.

— & FERENCZI, S. (1992). *Correspondence, vol. 1, 1908-1914*. Cambridge, Mass.: Harvard University Press.

GUTTMAN, S.A. & al. (eds) (1980). *The Concordance of the Standard Edition of the Complete Psychological Works of Sigmund Freud*. Boston, Mass.: Hall.

HAYNAL, A. (1991). *Psychoanalysis and the Sciences*. London: Karnac/Berkeley: The University of California Press, 1993.

HEMECKER, W.W. (1991). *Vor Freud. Philosophiegeschichtliche Voraussetzungen der Psychoanalyse*. München: Philosophia Verlag.

HIRSCHMÜLLER, A. (1978). *Physiology and Psychoanalysis. The Life and Work of Josef Breuer*. New York/London: New York University Press, 1989.

JACKSON, J.H. (1884). Croonean Lectures for 1884 on the Evolution and Dissolution of the Nervous System. *Archives suisses de Neurologie et de Psychiatrie, 8*: 294-302, et *9*: 131-152, 1921.

JANET, P. (1892). Etude sur quelques cas d'amnésie antérograde dans la maladie de la désagrégation psychologique. *In: International Congress of Experimental Psychology.* London: Williams & Norgate, pp. 26-30.

KIELL, N. (ed.) (1988). *Freud Without Hindsight. Reviews of His Work (1893-1939).* Madison, Conn.: International Universities Press.

KRAFFT-EBING, R. von (1889). Über Neurosen und Psychosen durch sexuelle Abstinenz. *Jahrbuch für Psychiatrie,* Vol 8.

— (1894). *Psychopathia Sexualis.* New York: Bell Publ. Comp., 1965.

KUHN, R. (1983). Préface, *in:* Freud, S.: *Contribution à la conception des aphasies.* Paris: Presses Universitaires de France, pp. 5-38.

LAPLANCHE, J. (1993). *Fourvoiement biologisant de la sexualité chez Freud.* Paris: Synthélabo.

LINDNER, G.A. (1858). *Lehrbuch der empirischen Psychologie nach genetischer Methode.* Graz: Wiesner.

MANN, Th. (1936). Freud and the Future. *International Journal of Psycho-Analysis, 37:* 106-115.

McGRATH, W.J. (1986). *Freud's Discovery of Psychoanalysis. The Politics of Hysteria.* Ithaca/London: Cornell Univ. Press.

MASSON, J.M.M. (1985). *The Complete Letters of Sigmund Freud to Wilhelm Fliess 1887-1904.* Cambridge/London: Belknap (German: Sigmund Freud, Briefe an Wilhelm Fliess, 1887-1904. Frankfurt/M.: Fischer, 1986).

MERLAN, P. (1959). Brentano and Freud - a Sequel. *Journal of the History of Ideas, 10,* p. 451.

MEYNERT, Th. (1884). *Psychiatrie: Klinik der Erkrankungen des Vorderhirns, begründet auf dessen Bau, Leistungen und Ernährung.* Wien: Braumüller.

— (1889). *Klinische Vorlesungen über Psychiatrie auf wissenschaftlichen Grundlagen.* Wien: Braunmüller.

MOLL, A. (1898). *Untersuchungen über die Libido sexualis.* Berlin: Kornfeld.

— (1909 [1908]). *Das Sexualleben des Kindes.* Leipzig: F.C.W. Vogel.

NIETZSCHE, F. (1980). *Sämtliche Werke, Kritische Studienausgabe.* 15 vol. München: Deutsche Tachenbuch Verlag.

NUNBERG, H. & FEDERN, E. (eds) (1962). *Minutes of the Vienna Psychoanalytic Society, vol. 1, 1906-1908.* New York: International Universities Press.

— (1967). *Minutes of the Vienna Psychoanalytic Society, vol. 2, 1908-1910.* New York: International Universities Press.

RITVO, L. B. (1990). *Darwin's Influence on Freud. A Tale of Two Sciences.* New Haven/London: Yale University Press.

SAND, R. (1992). Pre-Freudian Discovery of Dream Meaning: the Achievements of Charcot, Janet, and Krafft-Ebing, *in:* Gelfand, T. & Kerr, J. (eds): *Freud and the History of Psychoanalysis.* Hillsdale, NJ: The Analytic Press, 1992, pp. 215-229.

STUMPF, C. (1919). Erinnerungen an Franz Brentano, *in:* O. Kraus (Hrsg.): *Franz Brentano; zur Kenntnis seines Lebens und seines Lehre.* München: O. Beck.

SULLOWAY, F.J. (1979). *Freud, Biologist of the Mind. Beyond the Psychoanalytic Legend.* New York: Basic Books.

SWALES, P. (1983). *Freud, Cocaine, and Sexual Chemistry. The Role of Cocaine in Freud's Conception of the Libido.* Private edition of the author.

167

Cahiers Psychiatriques Genevois, Special Issue, 1994, pp. 169-194

THE THREADS
OF PSYCHOANALYTIC FILIATIONS
OR PSYCHOANALYSIS TAKING EFFECT

Ernst Falzeder

> «*The difficulties in the way of giving instruction in the practice of psychoanalysis ... are quite particularly great and are responsible for much in the present dissensions ...*»
> (Freud, 1914d, p. 26)

> «*Psychoanalysis never improves character.*»
> (Eva Rosenfeld, in Heller, 1992a, p. 10)

> «*Tous un peu analysés par personne.*»
> *(Everybody analysed a little by nobody in particular)*
> (Granoff, 1975, p. 96)

Perhaps nowhere else in science are personal relationships, or, if you prefer, transference and countertransference relations, so closely intertwined with the handing over of knowledge, professional competence, and tradition as in psychoanalysis. Through the personal analysis of the analyst-to-be each psychoanalyst becomes part of a genealogy, of a family tree, that ultimately goes back to Sigmund Freud and the early pioneers of psychoanalysis.

Would it not be interesting to draw such a family tree? A close study of this genealogy and its history will certainly contribute to the historiography of psychoanalysis, but, given the enormous impact of psychoanalysis, perhaps also to 20th century history of science and culture in general. In view of this fact, it is surprising that nobody, either inside or outside of the psychoanalytic community, has so far established a fairly satisfying map of what Balint called «apostolic succession» (Balint, 1948, p. 170), and of what Granoff later termed «filiations» (Granoff, 1975) in psychoanalysis. Consequently, no one has, until now, considered in detail how the form and structure of these filiations have influenced the path which theory and practice have taken.

My own interest is in the history of *ideas*, in tracing lines of thought back to their origins, in making visible hidden threads spun between seemingly disconnected areas; I am not interested in Freud- and psychoanalysis bashing nor in their idolatry. A history of ideas, however, cannot be separated from a study of the persons who conceived these ideas. Although we have to be well aware of the danger of equating the personal with the scientific domain, a detailed examination can often show clear and revealing connections between personal experiences and fields of interest, leanings towards certain theoretical and therapeutical concepts and formulations. But this investigation also compels us to reconsider the question of whether a complete history of psychoanalysis can be written at all.

«Spaghetti Junction»

As often happens in scientific research, I was rather naive when I began this project[1], deeming it of secondary importance as such, but thinking it might nevertheless be useful as an informal source of reference for my editorial work on the Freud/Ferenczi correspondence. In addition, it was fun to see a map of psychoanalytic filiations develop on the wall in my study – I put a big sheet of paper there, and whenever I came across information in the literature, in archives, or in interviews, on who analyzed whom, I added an arrow to my map (see at the end of this volume).

I began to grasp the significance of this leisure pursuit when I realised that

1. in the literature this sort of information is nearly always given in passing, as if adding just a little bit of gossip or some background information for the «insider». It is (again, nearly always) not treated as essential material for understanding the history of psychoanalysis. But in personal letters or in private talks, quite to the contrary, this aspect is seen to be of paramount importance.

2. As the family tree grew, erratically, as it were, clusters and patterns became visible, centres of influence, and unexpected connections. Nodes, crossroads, and bridges appeared in this «spaghetti junction».

3. It became increasingly clear that this network pervaded many aspects of the lives of those involved, professional or private. When I wrote to Peter Heller, himself thoroughly involved in this network, that «blurring of the borders of professional and intimate relationships» seemed to have been the rule rather than the exception, he fully agreed and even added the dictum of Eva Rosenfeld: «Indiscretion – point of honor!» (Heller, 1992b).

Back to the Roots

What was the very first training analysis? A seemingly simple, but in fact a very difficult question. Analyses of colleagues tended to be very short (sometimes they lasted only for a couple of hours or days), rather resembling talks with a certain degree of mutuality. Can these be called analyses? Training analyses? What form must an analysis have and how long must it last to deserve this name? Moreover, from the beginning, "training" and "treatment" were inseparably linked. Already about his first pupil, Felix Gattel (cf. Schröter & Hermanns, 1992), Freud wrote to Fliess: «Pupils *à la Gattel* are easy to come by; in the end they regularly ask to be treated themselves» (2.3.1899, Freud, 1985, p. 347). This was also the case with Wilhelm Stekel, another one of his early analysands (Stekel, 1950, pp. 107-8, 115). Or, as Jung wrote to Freud in 1909: «Dr. Seif of Munich has been here for 3 days, and I have put him through his ψA paces, which he needed very much. He is a good acquisition» (31 Dec. 1909; Freud & Jung, 1974, p. 308).

Be that as it may, it seems to be undisputed that it all started with Sigmund Freud, who passed on his skill to a few pioneers. The shorter and the more direct the line that can be drawn to Freud himself, the greater is one's prestige. A famous son of Geneva, Jean Piaget, even claimed that his own analyst, Sabina Spielrein, had herself been analyzed by Freud, in order to ennoble his analytic family romance: «My analysis was undertaken with a direct student of Freud's until her complete satisfaction. In the jargon of those days, I became a "grandson" of Freud's» (*Journal de Genève*, 5 Feb. 1977; in Schepeler, 1993, p. 261). It may be an irony of history that Piaget was in fact the «grandson» of the person who might be the one to have undertaken the very first explicit «training analysis» — but this person was not Freud, it was Carl Gustav Jung. In 1907 a young medical doctor and neurologist from Budapest had come to the psychiatric clinic «Burghölzli» in Zurich to study Jung's «association method», and the latter had seized upon the occasion to psychoanalyze him along Freudian principles, although, much to Jung's chagrin, his analysand later ended up with Freud himself — I am, of course, speaking of Sándor Ferenczi...[2] To be sure, this «analysis» could not have lasted longer than a few days or, at most, weeks. However that may be, it is interesting that the first «training» analysis along «Freudian principles» may not have been conducted by the father of psychoanalysis himself, but by one of his then most ardent disciples while, at the same time, this disciple evidently had in mind to create a following of his own, too...

It is of interest, by the way, that a great number of later renowned representatives of psychoanalysis or of «dynamic psychiatry» worked or were guests at the Burghölzli, headed by Eugen Bleuler and his chief assistant Carl Gustav Jung. Let us mention, for example, Karl Abraham, Roberto Greco Assagioli, Ludwig Binswanger, Abraham Arden Brill, Trigant Burrow, Imre Décsi, Max Eitingon, Sándor Ferenczi, Otto Gross, August Hoch, Johann Jakob Honegger, Smith Ely Jelliffe, Ernest Jones, Alphonse Maeder, Hans Maier, Hermann Nunberg, Johan H.W. von Ophuijsen, Nikolai J. Ossipow, Frederick Peterson, Franz Riklin, Hermann Rorschach, Tatiana Rosenthal, Leonhard Seif, Eugénie Sokolnicka, Sabina Spielrein, Fülöp Stein, Wolf Stockmayer, Johannes Irgens Stromme, Jaroslaw Stuchlík, and G. Alexander Young – and this list is certainly by no means complete. Neither Jung nor Bleuler conducted «training analyses» in the modern sense, although Jung did «analyze» a couple of colleagues, thinking that a rapid summary procedure could both help them and turn them into followers, e.g. Otto Gross or Leonhard Seif. There were seminars of a more general nature, and there existed, from 1907, a «Freud society»: a forum for discussions where one sought to detect «Freudian mechanisms» in hospital patients. Hilda Abraham recounted that «the wives of the medical doctors not only listened to the discussions and participated in them, but they also told their own dreams. But, to the extent in which the comprehension of unconscious motives and impulses grew, the doctors prevented their wives from speaking about their dreams» (Hilda Abraham, 1976, p. 62; my translation).

When we speak about a psychoanalytic training system today, we have to bear in mind that this was no system at all in the beginning. At first, Freud was reluctant to the idea as such, apparently also due to the fact that he grasped the difficulties of teaching psychoanalysis very early. It was indeed his *pupils* who broached the idea of a «training analysis» proper: Jung[3], Ferenczi, Nunberg and Hitschmann among others. Ferenczi in particular, dissatisfied with his short *«tranches»* of analysis with Freud, advocated the idea of a deep and thorough analysis of the analyst (cf. Ferenczi, 1928 [282], 1928 [283]), seeing in it the second «fundamental rule» of psychoanalysis (1928 [283], pp. 88 89).

172

«Apostolic Succession»

It was only about half a century after the beginning of what Freud called the psychoanalytic movement that one of its important members and, at the same time, iconoclasts, Michael Balint, drew our attention to the resemblance between the analytic training system and «primitive initiation ceremonies» (Balint, 1948, p. 167). «We know that the general aim of all initiation rites is to force the candidate to identify himself with his initiator, to introject the initiator and his ideals, and to build up from these identifications a strong super-ego which will influence him all his life» (*ibid.*); and he added that «hardly any candidate can evade» being «subjected to this super-ego intropression[4]» (*ibid.*).

Initiation is aimed at turning pupils or *«Lehrlinge»* [apprentices] into devout followers, but what it also achieves is to make some of them rebels or *«Zauberlehrlinge.»* Didn't Freud compare himself, in alluding to Goethe's poem *«Der Zauberlehrling»* [The sorcerer's apprentice], with «the venerable old master» (Freud & Jung, 1974, p. 476), and didn't he, by analogy, implicitly compare Jung with the apprentice having caused avok?

A turning point in the history of analytic succession was the founding of the «Secret Committee» around Freud, in the beginning consisting of Freud himself, Karl Abraham, Sándor Ferenczi, Ernest Jones, Otto Rank, and Hanns Sachs. In my opinion, it has not been sufficiently acknowledged that the original idea of Ferenczi was «the wish that a small group of men could be *thoroughly analyzed* by [Freud himself], so that they could represent the *pure theory unadulterated by personal complexes,* and thus build an unofficial inner circle in the Verein and serve as centres where others (beginners) could come and learn the work» (30 July 1912; Freud & Jones, 1993, p. 146; my italics). Each of the Committee's members should, in other words, undergo a purification process with the Master himself, an initiation procedure that would enable him to act himself as a representative of «pure» theory and «exact» technique and to initiate others. Here we have indeed the idea of an apostolic succession, created against the background of the impending dissension of Jung.

Although Freud was fascinated by the idea of a secret council around him, he was reluctant to analyze its members. Only Ferenczi was analyzed by Freud himself in a way that bore some resemblance to a proper analysis (in three parts each of a couple of weeks during World War I; cf. Dupont, 1993); Max Eitingon received a sort of peripatetical form of instruction during walks with Freud in Vienna (Freud & Ferenczi, 1994a, p. 85).[5] Ernest Jones was analyzed by Ferenczi for two months in 1913 (Freud & Jones, 1993, passim; Freud & Ferenczi, 1994a, passim), a fact that may have contributed to their later tensions. The other three members of the Committee were not analyzed at all: Hanns Sachs, Karl Abraham, and Otto Rank.

There is an interesting dispute about the implications of Rank's not having been analyzed. Jones had offered to analyze Rank in 1914 (Jones to Abraham, 1 Jan. 1923; LOC), but this did not work out. Later, in 1922, when there were serious tensions between Rank and Jones, Freud took sides with Rank and wrote to the Committee «that during 15 years of an ongoing and intimate working collaboration with Rank, it hardly ever occurred to me that he, of all people, would still need a piece of analysis» [... *daß ich in 15jähriger, stetiger und intimer Arbeitsgemeinschaft mit Rank kaum jemals auf die Idee gekommen bin, der könnte noch ein Stück Analyse brauchen]* (15 May 1922; Butler Library, New York [BL; my translation]). But two years later, on the occasion of the publication of Rank's book *The Trauma of Birth* (1924), Freud complained to him that «you would not have written this book had you yourself gone through an analysis» [*daß Sie dies Buch nicht geschrieben hätten, wenn Sie selbst durch eine Analyse gegangen wären]* (23 July 1924)[6]. Rank rejected this reproach categorically: «In this context, I have felt curiously touched by the fact that you, of all people, suggest that I would not have adopted this concept had I been analyzed. This might well be so, but the question remains whether or not this is regrettable. I, for one, can only consider myself lucky, after all the results I have seen with analyzed analysts» [*In diesem Zusammenhang hat mich ganz sonderbar berührt, daß gerade Sie mir vorhalten, ich hätte diese Auffassung nie vertreten, wenn ich analysiert worden wäre. Dies mag wohl sein. Die Frage ist nur, ob das nicht sehr bedauerlich gewesen wäre. Ich kann das jedenfalls nach allem, was ich von Resultaten an analysierten Analytikern gesehen habe, nur als ein Glück bezeichnen]*[7] (9 Aug. 1924). But when ever greater pressure was put on Rank by his colleagues and by Freud himself to withdraw his theory of the birth trauma, he did have some «analytical talks with the Professor» (Rank to members of former Committee, 20 Dec. 1924), the outcome of which he described in an astonishingly submissive tone (reminding one, in fact, of the "self criticisms" in Stalinistic trials): «Suddenly, I reemerged from a state that I can now recognize as neurotic... I could understand my reaction [to Freud's illness] as stemming from my personal child- and family-history, from the Oedipus and brother complex. ... the Professor found my explanations satisfactory and he forgave me personally, too» [*Ich bin plötzlich aus einem Zustand, den ich jetzt als neurotisch erkennen kann, wieder zu mir selbst gekommen und habe ... meine Reaktion darauf aus meiner persönlichen Kinder- und Familiengeschichte – dem Ödipus- und Bruderkomplex – verstehen können. ... der Professor [hat] meine Aufklärungen als befriedigend gefunden und mir auch persönlich vergeben*] (*ibid.*). Here we have a striking example not only of an apostle and the «prodigal son», but also of an absolution, of an «*Ego te absolvo*» by the Master. We know, however, that Rank's «conversion» did not last and he later told Anaïs Nin that «Freud tried to analyze [him], but this was a failure» (Nin, 1966, p. 279) ...[8]

None of the closest collaborators of Freud had what we would consider today a proper analytic training, in contrast to the analysts of the next generation, most of whom were either analyzed by Freud himself or underwent the training at one of the institutes in Berlin, Budapest, Vienna or London. But these institutes were headed by the members of the Secret Committee, who thus exercised not only «political» control over the course of the psychoanalytic movement, but also direct influence on the trainees. Naturally, they themselves analyzed the most promising of the candidates, or also those who threatened to become troublemakers. In Berlin, Sachs and Eitingon had absolute control over the training during the first years of the institute, founded in 1920: Sachs was the only training analyst (during the first two years, he analyzed 25 candidates, Franz Alexander being the first to complete his training along the new lines), and Eitingon was the only control analyst. When we look at some analysands of the members of the Committee (see figures 1 to 6), we see that their influence can hardly be over-estimated.[9] (Only Max Eitingon does not figure prominently here, but this may be due to the very scarce material concerning this enigmatic figure.) Very early, however, there were different opinions about the impact of this influence. While Jones, who had analyzed six out of the eleven original members of the British Psychoanalytical Society, found that he therefore was «in good contact» with them (Freud & Jones, 1993, p. 336), Abraham wrote to the Committee: «In our group a lot of difficulties arose from the fact that most of the member have been analyzed by me» (17 Nov. 1920; BL).

As far as Anna Freud is concerned (see figure 7), her huge unpublished correspondence, recently made accessible in 131 containers in the Library of Congress, shows her prominent position in the psychoanalytic movement, particularly after her father's death. She exercised decisive influence on the publication of biographical works on Freud, on the form in which his correspondences were published, or not published at all, and on the publication policy of journals like the «Psychoanalytic Study of the Child.» Her *analysand* Ernst Kris, editor of Freud's letters to Wilhelm Fliess, for example, was given orders by her of what to include in the publication of this correspondence, and what to omit.[10] Her most extensive and wide ranging correspondence, by the way, is the one with Kurt Eissler (analysand of her friend August Aichhorn and of Richard Sterba), founder of the Freud archives.[11]

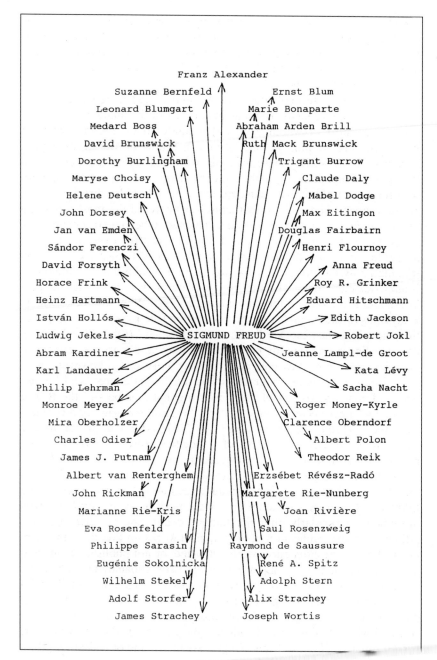

Franz Alexander

Suzanne Bernfeld   Ernst Blum

Leonard Blumgart   Marie Bonaparte

Medard Boss   Abraham Arden Brill

David Brunswick   Ruth Mack Brunswick

Dorothy Burlingham   Trigant Burrow

Maryse Choisy   Claude Daly

Helene Deutsch   Mabel Dodge

John Dorsey   Max Eitingon

Jan van Emden   Douglas Fairbairn

Sándor Ferenczi   Henri Flournoy

David Forsyth   Anna Freud

Horace Frink   Roy R. Grinker

Heinz Hartmann   Eduard Hitschmann

István Hollós   Edith Jackson

Ludwig Jekels   SIGMUND FREUD   Robert Jokl

Abram Kardiner   Jeanne Lampl-de Groot

Karl Landauer   Kata Lévy

Philip Lehrman   Sacha Nacht

Monroe Meyer   Roger Money-Kyrle

Mira Oberholzer   Clarence Oberndorf

Charles Odier   Albert Polon

James J. Putnam   Theodor Reik

Albert van Renterghem   Erzsébet Révész-Radó

John Rickman   Margarete Rie-Nunberg

Marianne Rie-Kris   Joan Rivière

Eva Rosenfeld   Saul Rosenzweig

Philippe Sarasin   Raymond de Saussure

Eugénie Sokolnicka   René A. Spitz

Wilhelm Stekel   Adolph Stern

Adolf Storfer   Alix Strachey

James Strachey   Joseph Wortis

Figure 1.

176

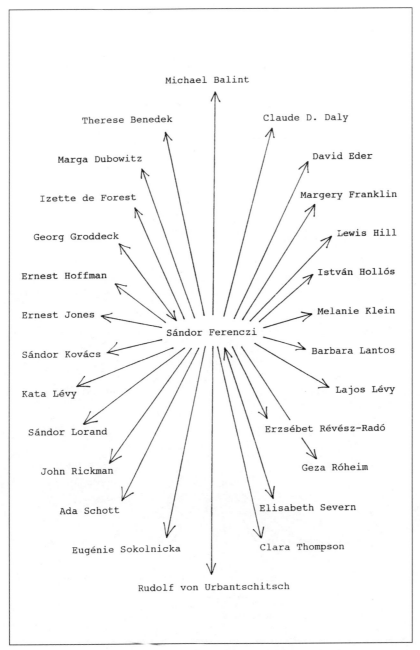

Figure 2.

177

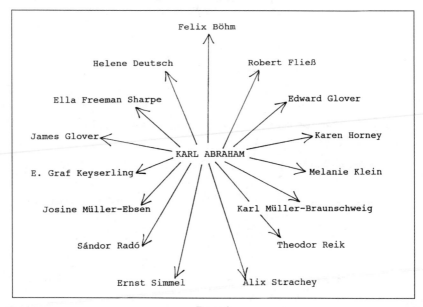

Figure 3.

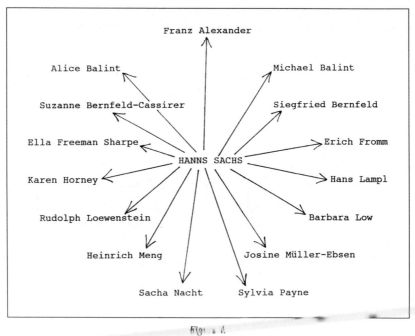

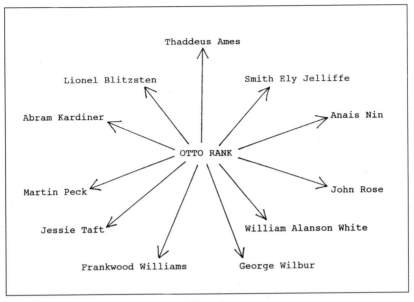

Figure 5.

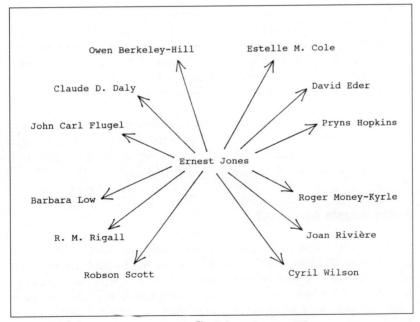

Figure 6.

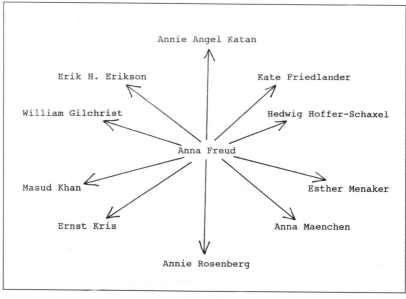

Figure 7.

There are very few other analysts of comparable importance: Paul Federn or Franz Alexander for instance, but above all *Melanie Klein*, herself analysand of Ferenczi and Abraham. A look at the number and the prestige of her supervisees and analysands (see figure 8; cf. also Grosskurth, 1986) does indeed make clear, what was also at stake in the so-called Freud/Klein controversies (King & Steiner, 1991) within the British Society.

Apart from the number and stature of analysands a training analyst had, several other facts can be deduced from the material I gathered, facts that complicate the picture we have of the history of psychoanalysis and that call for an explanation.

Postgraduate Analysis?

It was very common – indeed the rule – that analysts had more than one analysis. But why was this so? Why do we hardly find anyone, even among the most eminent analysts, who could make do with just one analysis? Many, if not most of them had two, some had three, some had even four, and some were analyzed by no less than five different analysts (e.g. Erich Fromm with Theodor Reik, Wilhelm Wittenberg, Karl Landauer,

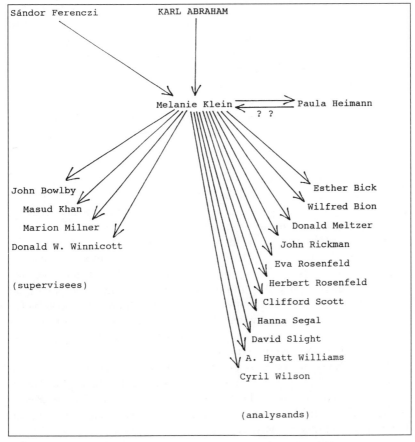

Sándor Ferenczi   KARL ABRAHAM

Melanie Klein ⇄ Paula Heimann
? ?

John Bowlby
Masud Khan
Marion Milner
Donald W. Winnicott

(supervisees)

Esther Bick
Wilfred Bion
Donald Meltzer
John Rickman
Eva Rosenfeld
Herbert Rosenfeld
Clifford Scott
Hanna Segal
David Slight
A. Hyatt Williams
Cyril Wilson

(analysands)

Figure 8.

Hanns Sachs, and by his later wife Frieda Fromm-Reichmann) (Harmat, 1986; Krutzenbichler & Essers, 1991; Leupold-Löwenthal, 1986; Rattner, 1990).

There were three main opinions about which sort of personal analysis the analyst should have. (1) Some found it sufficient to learn the profession more or less autodidactically, occasionally seeking advice from Freud when they ran into difficulties. Freud himself expressed this view a couple of times (e.g. about Rank [see above] or towards Bernfeld [Bernfeld, 1952, p. 442]). (2) There was the opposite argument, especially stressed by Ferenczi, that the training analysis should be a sort of «super analysis,» as long, deep and complete as possible. (3) Finally, we have Freud's conclusion, maybe also influenced by his experiences with Otto Rank, that analysts should periodically reenter analysis, each of these «tranches» not lasting for too long. To John Rickman he wrote on June 30, 1928, that he had «come to learn that the unconscious of the analyst stirred up by his growing analytical experience claims periodical renewals or rather continuations of his own analysis. He may deteriorate to a serious measure if he does not reply to this appeal; the more he gets mature the better the results of this continued investigation» (unpublished, LOC [English in original]; cf. also Freud & Weiss, 1970, p. 40). When Ernest Jones complained about the poor results of psychoanalysis among analysts themselves, and promoted «what may be called post-graduate analysis,» i.e. the idea that analysts «must continue their analysis from time to time later on» (18 Sept. 1933; Freud & Jones, 1993, p. 729), Freud was eager to assert that this was in fact his own idea: «For years I have been advocating your idea of a "Postgraduate Analysis," and am also trying to put it into effect. I find such supplementary analyses unexpectedly interesting and helpful. Therefore, in this instance I am stressing my priority!» (15 Oct. 1933; Freud & Jones, 1993, p. 731). His final conclusion is found in print in *Analysis terminable and interminable* (Freud, 1937c), where he first confirmed the necessity of a training analysis – although he thought that «for practical reasons this analysis can only be short and incomplete» (*ibid.*, p. 248) –, and secondly that «[e]very analyst should periodically – at intervals of five years or so – submit himself to analysis once more, without feeling ashamed of taking this step» (*ibid.*, p. 249).[12]

In fact, many, if not most analysts seem to have acted according to Freud's advice, but with one remarkable restriction: instead of considering this a standard part of their professional training, this whole area is treated either with shame or with curious pride. Are there other reasons for these postgraduate analyses?

Apart from the necessity to counteract the «*déformation professionnelle*», there is ample evidence that psychoanalysts seem not only to have had the same problems other human beings have, which would surprise nobody, but indeed had more than their share, and that many of them remained unhappy, not helped by their personal analyses. In fact, a great number of the early psychoanalysts committed suicide; of the 149 persons who were members of the Viennese Psychoanalytic Society between 1902 and 1938, at least nine killed themselves (Paul Federn, Max Kahane, Tatiana Rosenthal, Herbert Silberer, Eugénie Sokolnicka, Wilhelm Stekel, Victor Tausk, and Rosa Walk), that is, six percent or one out of seventeen (Mühlleitner, 1992). When Jakob Honegger, a former assistant of Jung's, with whom Jung had had some sort of mutual analysis, committed suicide, Freud remarked dryly: «Do you know, I think we wear out quite a few men» (Freud & Jung, 1974, p. 413). In addition, a good number of them had drug or alcohol problems (Ruth Mack Brunswick, Otto Gross, Walter Schmideberg ...).

Training Through Love?

We have evidence of many *training* analyses that were or became erotic relationships,[13] and that what we know may only be the tip of the iceberg. Let me name just a few examples: Georg Groddeck and (his later wife) Emmy von Voigt (Will, 1984); Michael Balint and (his later, second wife) Edna Oakeshott (Archives Balint, Geneva); Otto Rank and his wife Beata (Lieberman, 1985); August Aichhorn and Margaret Mahler (Stepansky, 1988); Wilhelm Reich and (his later wife) Annie Pink (Reich, 1988); Rudolph Löwenstein and Marie Bonaparte (Bertin, 1982); René Allendy *and* Otto Rank with Anaïs Nin (Cremerius, 1987; Krutzenbichler & Essers, 1991); Carl Gustav Jung and Sabina Spielrein (Carotenuto, 1980; Kerr, 1993), *and* Toni Wolff (e.g. Donn, 1988), *and* Maria Moltzer (Shamdasani, 1990, p. 54; cf. Freud to Ferenczi, 23 Dec. 1912; Freud & Ferenczi, 1994a, p. 446) and almost certainly others (Jung also analyzed his wife Emma because she «staged a number of jealous scenes, groundlessly» [Jung to Freud, 30 Jan. 1910; Freud & Jung, 1974, p. 289]); Victor Tausk and Lou Andreas-Salomé (*and* his patient Hilde Loewi) (Krutzenbichler & Essers, 1991); Erzsébet Révész-Radó and Sándor Radó, as well as Sándor Radó and his second wife Emmy (Ferenczi to Freud, 23 May 1919, 29 June 1919, LOC; Krutzenbichler & Essers, 1991; Reich, 1952), and so on.

The interference of affects, in particular sexual ones, with the allegedly "abstinent" atmosphere of an analysis *lege artis* preoccupied the early analysts from the beginning. At a meeting of the Viennese Psychoanalytic Society on November 3, 1909, Hitschmann stated that «the examination of the patient's sex organs by the attending analyst... [were] absolutely necessary and it is a sign of prejudice [*Befangenheit* – shyness] if Sadger failed to do this» (Nunberg & Federn, 1967, p. 299). Wilhelm Reich even claimed that «there were cases when the psychoanalysts, pretending to examine the genitals, a medical examination, introduced their fingers into the vaginae of their patients. *This happened quite often*. I knew that ... some psychoanalysts were not honest. ... They pretended that nothing specific happened, and then they masturbated the patient during sessions» (Reich, 1952, p. 96; my italics and translation). Freud himself advocated a more cautious procedure, well aware of the dangers: «Physical examination is certainly most desirable but unfeasible in analysis; it must be done by another physician» (Nunberg & Federn, 1967, p. 301). It is indeed understandable that Freud found a text on countertransference sorely needed, but at the same time stated that it had to be *secretly* circulated among analysts only (Freud & Jung, 1974, p. 476) ...

The fact that sexual relationships during analyses have been and still are notorious, has gained legitimate attention in recent years (cf. Anonyma, 1988; Fischer, 1977; Krutzenbichler & Essers, 1991). What has been less acknowledged is that sexual relationships have in fact been running as a red thread also through the analytic *training* network from its beginning. I am sure that each analyst could add examples from his own local society, which are usually treated with silence, and only rarely are made semi-public, as in the cases of Masud Khan or Karen Horney. It might be worth the effort to find out what percentage of analysts married training analysands. However, erotic relationships are not the only deviation from «classical» technique, as Ferenczi called it, that we come across.

«Familienbande»?

Karl Kraus once stated that *Familienbande* is one of the «deepest words» in the German language. Usually used to describe the ties and bonds between family members, it can also take on the second meaning of the word *Bande* in German, namely a gang, a «family» of gangsters. Kraus' pun could well be used in the context of psychoanalysis, too, because the mingling of analysis with kinship is only too clear. Not only did husbands or lovers analyze each other, or were analyzed by the same analyst, not only did parents have their children analyzed by their own analysts or even analysand, but it was common practice that parents analyzed their own children, aunts their nephews, men the children of their lovers. Still in 1925, Lou Andreas-Salomé even remarked to Alix Strachey «that the parents were the only proper people to analyze the child.» When Alix reported this to her husband James, she added: «a shudder ran down my spine» (Meisel & Kendrick, 1985, p. 200).

The most famous example is surely Anna Freud's analysis with her father (October 1918 – spring 1922, May 1924 – summer 1925), a fact first put in print by Paul Roazen (Roazen, 1969). In addition to Young-Bruehl's fine biography (1988), the unpublished parts of the Freud/Lou Andreas-Salomé correspondence and of his letters to Anna herself (both LOC) throw light upon this unprecedented procedure. Very early, she started sending dreams to her father («I have even dreamed of you tonight, but it was not nice at all»; 21 Sept. 1911). Of the 18 such instances between 1911 and 1930, some are very touching, e.g. «I dreamed that I had to defend a farm belonging to us against enemies. But the table was broken and I was ashamed before the enemies when I pulled it» (17 July

1915); «Recently I dreamed that you are a king and I am a princess, and that one wanted to bring us apart by intrigues. It wasn't nice and very exciting» (6 Aug. 1915); «I had a terrible dream. I dreamed that the bride of Dr. Tausk had rented the apartment in Berggasse 20 opposite us in order to shoot you, and each time you wanted to go near the window, she appeared there with a pistol. I was terribly frightened ...» (24 July 1919). Freud only rarely responded with short interpretations («You have to add jealousy to your dream interpretation»; 30 July 1919), he rather did not mention the dreams at all or gave a humorous reply – to her complaints that she suffered from repeated examination dreams, he simply answered: «Very agreeable that your repeated exams are "tax-free"[14]» (14 July 1915). In his letters to Lou Andreas-Salomé, Freud frequently wrote about Anna, and also about her analysis with him: «Being inhibited towards the male side because of me, she has had much misfortune in her friendships with women. She has developed slowly, is not only in her looks younger than her age. Sometimes I urgently wish her a good man, sometimes I frighten away from the loss» (3 July 1922). And, on May 13, 1924: «I have accepted a seventh analysis with special feelings: my Anna, who is so unreasonable to cling to an old father. The child causes me much sorrow; how she will bear the lonely life, and whether I will be able to get her libido out of the hiding-place, into which it has crept.» A year later, on May 10, 1925: «Anna's analysis will be continued. She is not easy and has difficulties in finding the way to apply upon herself, what she sees so clearly now in others. ... But, frankly speaking, the whole direction does not "suit" me. I fear that the suppressed genitality will play her a nasty trick some time. I cannot get her away from me, but then nobody helps me with it.»

Freud was not the only one to analyze a child of his. There were also the analyses of Karl Abraham with his daughter Hilda (Abraham, 1976 [1913]), of Carl Gustav Jung with his daughter Agathli (Jung, 1910), of Ernst Kris with his two children Anna and Tony (Heller, 1992c, pp. 67-68), of Hermine Hug-Hellmuth with her nephew (who later killed her) (MacLean & Rappen, 1991); Melanie Klein analyzed all her children and had her grandson analyzed by her trainee Marion Milner (Grosskurth, 1986). We know about the inextricable networks of Freud and the Brunswicks (cf. Roazen, 1992). Anna Freud's first patients were two of her nephews, «Heinerle» Halberstadt and Ernst Halberstadt (Gay, 1988, p. 436) (who was also analyzed by her friend Willi Hoffer). Franz Alexander, who had had some form of training with Freud himself (Rattner, 1990, p. 513), analyzed Freud's son Oliver (Freud to Anna Freud, 13 Apr. 1922; LOC).[15] There has been much discussion about whether Freud had had a *liaison* with Minna Bernays, but what I find even more startling is the idea, put forward by Appignanesi and Forrester (1992, p. 144) that he might have analyzed her. Sigmund Freud did not only analyze Marie Bonaparte and her lovers Heinz Hartmann and Rudolph Loewenstein (who himself analyzed Bonaparte), but also her daughter Eugénie; her son Pierre was analyzed by Heinz Hartmann (Bertin, 1982). Erich Fromm analyzed Karen Horney's daughter Marianne, while having a relationship with Horney. As a child, Marianne – as well as her sister Renate – had already been analyzed by Melanie Klein; Brigitte, the third daughter (who was to become a well-known actress), was also to have been treated by Klein, but, being 14 years old and strong-willed, she refused to go for analysis at all (Grosskurth, 1986; Quinn, 1987).

Peter Heller (see figure 9) was analyzed as a child by Anna Freud between 1929 and 1932; his father, Hans Heller, by Ludwig Jekels; his mother, Gretl Heller, by Hanns Sachs. Later, Peter Heller, besides consulting his father's analyst Jekels, was analyzed by Heinz Lichtenstein, and by Lichtenstein's own analyst, Ernst Kris, who himself had been analyzed by Anna Freud, Heller's first analyst. When the former patient later discovered that his analysis with Kris did, «however indirectly, ... come under her [Anna Freud's] supervision and – still more indirectly – under the purview even of her companion, my mother-in-law, who financed the long-drawn-out treatment» (Heller, 1992c, p. 69), and that not only had these people written about his analysis with utmost indiscretion in their correspondence, but that these letters were accessible to the public, he published parts of them adding some commentaries (Heller, 1992c).

Through Peter Heller's first wife, Katrina («Tinky») Burlingham, this network is tied to another one, the fascinating Burlingham/Freud network (Burlingham, 1989; Young-Bruehl, 1988). All the children of Dorothy Burlingham, the lifelong friend of Anna Freud, were analyzed by the latter at least twice. Of these children, Katrina, in addition, was also analyzed by Berta Bornstein, Robert (Bob) also by Kurt Eissler, Bob's wife, called «Mossik», by Edward Kronold (Kronengold) and by Marianne Kris (daughter of Freud's friend Oscar Rie, analysand of Freud and Franz Alexander), who also analyzed Mabbie Burlingham. Michael, the forth child, seems to have been content with his analyses with Anna Freud. Dorothy Burlingham herself was analyzed at first by Theodor Reik, and then, this analysis having run into difficulties, by Sigmund Freud himself. This analysis lasted, by the way, from 1927 until shortly before Freud's death in 1939, that is, for thirteen years and this, while Dorothy Burlingham lived for most of the time in the same house as the Freuds. Dorothy's husband Robert, from whom she had separated, was treated by the American analyst Amsden in Budapest, and, possibly, also by

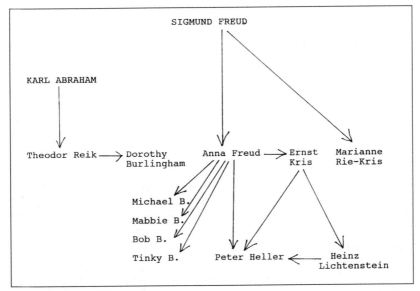

Figure 9.

Ferenczi in New York (Ferenczi to Freud, 10 Oct. 1926, 30 Nov. 1926; Freud to Ferenczi, 11 July 1928; LOC).

Conclusions

In summary, what we find in the factual history of psychoanalysis, are repeated patterns or series of affect-laden relationships, be they incestuous, hostile, erotic, or power relations, mixed with varying doses of analysis, leading to much confusion and suffering among those involved. I have not treated hostile relations that are indeed a chapter *per se*. As for the question of power and its use and misuse in analysis, this is probably the most unsettling topic of them all, but it is also the one least studied and the most difficult to grasp, because in most cases it is not as evident as in the case of Gregory Zilboorg and one of his patients, a successful public relations executive: «First there was the watch the patient was wearing (but with a different band, at Zilboorg's request), then there were tickets to the Joe Louis fight (first or second row, at Zilboorg's request), then a radio. Finally Zilboorg, who needed cash to pay taxes, offered to supplement his analysis of the patient with advice on business undertakings, since the patient – because of his drinking – needed all the help he could get. Zilboorg proposed that the patient pay him a fee of five thousand dollars, in advance and in cash, for his dual role as analyst and business consultant. At this point the patient, even in his dependent state, began to feel used. He paid Zilboorg the first thousand dollars in hundred-dollar bills but then left treatment» (Quinn, 1987, pp. 342-343).

Be that as it may, for the period I primarily studied (until about World War II), I have to state that I seldom came across a training analysis *lege artis*, as it was introduced by the Berlin group in 1920 at their institute, and agreed upon internationally in 1925 at the 9th International Psychoanalytic Congress (September 3-5) in Bad Homburg. When theory and practice do not correspond, in fact contradict each other, theory does not *reflect* reality, but stands for ideals not realized in reality, or can even be used to ward off reality and mystify it. According to my material, (1) self-analysis was either not practised after analysis at all, or it did not help much, (2) the dissolution of the so-called transference neurosis hardly ever took place after analysis, (3) hardly ever can one discern something like «abstinence,» (4) the blurring of the borders of professional and intimate relationships was the rule and not the exception, and (5) even allegedly normal, unneurotic people, famous analysts, needed two, three, four, or more long-term analyses without ever overcoming certain problems that would almost certainly, were they known, exclude them from analytic training today[16], and each new biography of a leading pioneer analyst shows with uncanny predictability the dark continent behind the official glamour. Like any other powerful method, psychoanalysis has its inherent dangers. Freud had already drawn the analogy between psychoanalysis and «the effect of X-rays on people who handle them without taking special precautions» (Freud, 1937c, p. 249). Incidentally, X-rays were discovered by Wilhelm Conrad Röntgen in 1895, the year in which Breuer's and Freud's *Studies on Hysteria* were published. Like the early radiologists, the pioneer psychoanalysts, and their patients, suffered the side effects of the newly discovered method. The more we know about its possible deleterious consequences, the better we are able to take the special precautions required. To do so, however, we have to study the *failed* cases, to learn still more about the dark side of the history of psychoanalysis, without succumbing to the temptation to idealise, to condemn or to deny our heritage. In this sense, it is my hope that a rewriting of the factual history of psychoanalysis will help us to better understand contemporary problems and to deal with them more efficiently.

Perhaps the time has come to investigate, *sine ira et studio*, the connection between the «private» lives and experiences of the pioneers and the theories springing from them, to investigate the connection between their «experiences» [*Erlebnisse*] and «insights» [*Einsichten*]. To do so, the his-

188

torian must necessarily be indiscreet: like in analysis itself, it is the secret, the repressed, the warded-off, and perhaps precisely the shameful detail that has the greatest explanatory power.

After all, is it not psychoanalytic tradition at its best to let the repressed or disgraceful knowledge «gain a hearing» (Freud, 1927c, p. 53)? And hasn't radical honesty been the trade-mark of psychoanalysis from its inception? «[A]nalysis... is in the first place an honest establishment of the facts» [*die Analyse... ist... zuerst eine ehrliche Feststellung*] (25 July 1922; Freud & Pfister, 1963, p. 87), and «becoming deceitful and [to] hide the essentials... is in direct conflict with the spirit of ψA» (31 Oct. 1909; Freud & Jones, 1993, p. 32). Let me conclude with another statement of Freud's saying that «these psycho-analytical matters are intelligible only if presented in pretty full and complete detail, just as an analysis really gets going only when the patient descends to minute details from the abstractions which are their surrogate. Thus discretion is incompatible with a satisfactory description of an analysis; to provide the latter one would have to be unscrupulous, give away, betray, behave like an artist who buys paints with his wife's house-keeping money or uses the furniture as firewood to warm the studio for his model. Without a trace of that kind of unscrupulousness the job cannot be done» (5 June 1910; Freud & Pfister, 1963, p. 38). Psychoanalysts and historians might be well advised to take Freud seriously even when studying him and the one hundred years of the movement he started.

Postscriptum

Attempting to draw a family-tree of psychoanalysis entails at least two major problems: (1) this is not an ordinary family tree. There are not only "illegitimate children," not only analyses with different "parents" or repeated analyses with the same "mother" or "father," not only reversals in the sense that analysands analyzed their former analysts, there are not only mutual analyses, but there is even the case of a son trying to analyze his own physical mother, Jean Piaget (Schepeler, 1993)! (2) Such a map cannot show *what sort of influence* was exerted in these analyses, how this was *experienced* by the analysands, and how they *reacted* to it. And more: «Such uncovered filiations will make it that much more complicated to trace the development of... analysts: for not only may the effect of their initiation process be postponed when they are in analysis with someone else; they may be also countertransferentially influenced by the analysts of their spouses and children, or by their patients concurrently or in a delayed manner, or by workshops, ongoing seminars, and so on.» In summary, the more we know about the past, the more we begin to realise that «it is impossible to write a totally sufficient history of analysis» (Mahony, 1993). Not only psychoanalysis itself, but also its historiography might be an impossible profession ...

Thanks

Research for this paper was funded by the Fondation Louis Jeantet, Geneva, Switzerland. My thanks go to André Haynal and Patrick Mahony for their comments and advice.

Notes

[1]   I had already been working on such a map of psychoanalytic descent for about two years when I came across a statement of Ernest Gellner who, in an avowedly critical vein, called for such a research (1985, p. 55).

[2]   I am indebted to Sonu Shamdasani for drawing my attention to this fact and to the pertaining document (a transcript of Aniela Jaffé's interviews with Jung; Library of Congress, Washington DC [LOC]) which, for legal reasons, can only be paraphrased here.

[3]   Jung seems to have been the first to advocate such a training analysis: «I count it as one of the many merits of the Zurich school of analysis that they have... demand[ed] that everyone who wishes to carry out analyses on other people shall first himself undergo an analysis by someone with expert knowledge» (Freud, 1912e, p. 116). «[I]t was *he* [Jung] who demanded the "analytic community" of students and treating students like patients» (Ferenczi to Freud, 26 Dec. 1912; Freud & Ferenczi, 1994a, p. 449).

[4]   A term coined by Ferenczi (1933 [308][58], p. 279).

[5]   Freud also analyzed van Emden during afternoon walks in Karlsbad (*ibid.*, p. 294).

[6]   The hitherto unpublished Freud/Rank correspondence was kindly made available to me by his daughter, Hélène Veltfort Rank (San Francisco) and by Judith Dupont (Paris) whom I also thank for permission to quote from Rank's letters. Quotations from unpublished letters of Sigmund and Anna Freud are reproduced with kind permission of A.W. Freud *et al.* in arrangement with Mark Paterson.

[7]   Anna Freud commented upon this letter to Max Eitingon: «The most incomprehensible thing about it is that even though there is so much said openly, he [Rank] is still full of hidden, cheap malice – this becomes clear if you know that the psychoanalysed patients [*sic*] he speaks of are all former patients of Papa's» (in Young-Bruehl, 1988, p. 149).

[8]   Nin, however, is not always reliable as a historical source. Also according to her (*ibid.*), Freud wanted Rank to marry his daughter, although we are left uncertain which of his daughters he had in mind. Freud also wanted Ferenczi to marry his daughter Mathilde, but he strongly disapproved of Jones' efforts to court Anna...

[9]   Let us remember that these "analyses" differed substantially in form and duration while Medard Boss, for example, possibly only had a few talks with Freud, the analyses of Marie Bonaparte or Ruth Mack Brunswick lasted for many years.

[10] Cf. for example her letter to Kris of February 11, 1947: «should be kept;» «cut only the second part of the first paragraph;» «to be omitted!»; «cut the stories of perversions!»; «Cut by all means!»; «Cut the phrase: "my own father not excluded", etc.

[11] I am indebted to Peter Heller for information regarding the Anna Freud correspondence.

[12] Because the dangers inherent in the «constant preoccupation with all the repressed material» stir up «in the analyst as well all the instinctual demands which he is otherwise able to keep under suppression» (*ibid.*).

[13] Or erotic relationships that turned into analyses – it is often difficult to decide.

[14] Students had to pay a fee – the so-called Taxe – for each examination.

[15] Paul Harmat (1986, p. 244) assumes that Alexander analyzed Freud's son Ernst, but this could be a mistake for Oliver.

[16] «I always play the game (and that's my favourite game) to [say] any time that a training committee [meets] – all the committees make very foolish decisions at times, must, because in borderline cases you can't advise. Impossible. Would say "Don't be so high up, impressed by your own importance. Let's suppose that the following people would put in an application, and you know everything that you know of them, everything. If it happened today, let's say: Jung, Adler, Stekel, Anna Freud, Melanie Klein, Otto Rank, Ferenczi, Karen Horney. Which of them would you accept? Which of them would you reject?"» (Balint, 1965, p. 47).

References

ABRAHAM, H. (1976). *Karl Abraham, Sein Leben für die Psychoanalyse.* München: Kindler.

ABRAHAM, K. (1976 [1913]). Klein Hilda: Tagträume und ein Symptom bei einem siebenjährigen Mädchen. *In:* Abraham, H. (1976). *Karl Abraham, Sein Leben für die Psychoanalyse.* München: Kindler, pp. 178-182.

ANONYMA (1988). *Verführung auf der Couch. Eine Niederschrift.* Freiburg: Kore Verlag.

APPIGNANESI, L. & FORRESTER, J. (1992). *Freud's Women.* London: Weidenfeld & Nicolson.

BALINT, M. (1948). On the Psycho-Analytic Training System. *International Journal of Psycho-Analysis, 29/3,* 153-173.

— (1965). *The Reminiscences of Michael Balint.* Psychoanalytic Project, Oral History Research Office, Columbia University, New York (quoted with kind permission of Enid Balint-Edmonds).

BERNFELD, S. (1952). Über die psychoanalytische Ausbildung. *Psyche,* 1984, *38,* 437-459.

BERTIN, C. (1982). *Die letzte Bonaparte, Freuds Prinzessin, Ein Leben.* Freiburg i.Br.: Kore, 1989.

BURLINGHAM, M. J. (1989). *The Last Tiffany. A Biography of Dorothy Tiffany Burlingham.* New York: Atheneum.

CAROTENUTO, A. (Ed.) (1980). *A Secret Symmetry. Sabina Spielrein Between Jung and Freud.* London: Routledge & Kegan Paul/New York: Pantheon, 1984.

CREMERIUS, J. (1987). Der Einfluß der Psychoanalyse auf die deutschsprachige Literatur. *Psyche, 41,* 39-54.

DONN, L. (1988). *Freud and Jung, Years of Friendship, Years of Loss*. New York: Collier Books, Macmillan Publishing Company, 1990.

DUPONT, J. (1993). L'analyse de Ferenczi par Freud vue à travers leur correspondance. *Le Coq-Héron*, N° 127, 51-56.

FALZEDER, E. (1994). My Grand-Patient, my Chief Tormentor. A Hitherto Unnoticed Case of Freud's and the Consequences. *Psychoanalytic Quarterly* [forthcoming].

FERENCZI, S. (1928 [282]). The Problem of Termination of the Analysis. *Final Contributions to the Problems and Methods of Psychoanalysis*. New York: Basic Books, 1955, 77-86.

— (1928 [283]). The Elasticity of Psycho-Analytic Technique. *Final Contributions to the Problems and Methods of Psychoanalysis*. New York: Basic Books, 1955, 87-101.

— (1933 [308[58]]). Amnesia. *Final Contributions to the Problems and Methods of Psychoanalysis*. New York: Basic Books, 1955, 278-279.

FISCHER, D. (1977). *Les analysés parlent*. Paris: Stock.

FREUD, S. (1912e). Recommendations to Physicians Practising Psycho-Analysis. *Standard Edition, 12*, 111-120.

— (1914d). On the History of the Psycho-Analytic Movement. *Standard Edition, 14*, 7-66.

— (1927c). The Future of an Illusion. *Standard Edition, 21*, 5-56.

— (1937c). Analysis Terminable and Interminable. *Standard Edition, 23*, 216-253.

— (1985). *The Complete Letters of Sigmund Freud to Wilhelm Fliess, 1887-1904*. Ed. Jeffrey M. Masson. Cambridge, Mass.: Harvard University Press.

— & FERENCZI, S. (1993). *Briefwechsel, Band I/1, 1908-1911*. Wien: Böhlau.

— & FERENCZI, S. (1994a). *Correspondence, Vol. 1 (1908-1914)*. Cambridge, Mass.: Harvard University Press.

— & FERENCZI,. S. (1994b). *Briefwechsel, Band I/2, 1912-1914*. Wien: Böhlau.

— & JONES, E. (1993). *The Complete Correspondence of Sigmund Freud and Ernest Jones 1908-1939*. Ed. R. Andrew Paskauskas. Cambridge, Mass.: Harvard University Press.

— & JUNG, C.G. (1974). *The Freud/Jung Letters. The Correspondence Between Sigmund Freud and C. G. Jung*. Ed. William McGuire. Cambridge, Mass.: Harvard University Press, 1988.

— & PFISTER, O. (1963). *Psychoanalysis and Faith. The Letters of Sigmund Freud and Oskar Pfister*. Ed. Heinrich Meng & Ernst L. Freud. New York: Basic Books.

— & WEISS, E. (1970). *Sigmund Freud as A Consultant: Recollections of a Pioneer in Psychoanalysis*. With an Introduction by Martin Grotjahn. New York: International Medical Book Corporation.

GAY, P. (1988). *Freud, A Life for Our Time*. New York: Anchor Books, Doubleday, 1989.

GELLNER, E. (1985). *The Psychoanalytic Movement or The Cunning of Unreason*. London: Paladin.

GRANOFF, W. (1975). *Filiations. L'avenir du complexe d'Oedipe*. Paris: Éditions de Minuit.

GROSSKURTH, Ph. (1986). *Melanie Klein, Her World and Her Work*. New York: Alfred A. Knopf.

HARMAT, P. (1986). *Freud, Ferenczi und die ungarische Psychoanalyse*. Tübingen: Edition Diskord.

HELLER, P. (Ed) (1992a). *Anna Freud's Letters to Eva Rosenfeld*. Madison: International Universities Press.

— (1992b). Letter to the author, September 16, 1992.

— (1992c). Reflections on a Child Analysis with Anna Freud and an Adult Analysis with Ernst Kris. *Journal of the American Academy of Psychoanalysis, 20,* 49-74.

JUNG, C.G. (1910). Psychic Conflicts in a Child. *Collected Works, Vol. 17 (The Development of Personality [1910; 1925-1943]).* Princeton: Princeton University Press/London: Routledge & Kegan Paul.

KERR, J. (1993). *A Most Dangerous Method. The Story of Jung, Freud, and Sabina Spielrein.* New York: Alfred A. Knopf.

KING, P. & STEINER, R. (Eds) (1991). *The Freud-Klein Controversies 1941-45.* London, New York: Tavistock, Routledge, 1992.

KRUTZENBICHLER, H. S. & ESSERS, H. (1991). *Muß denn Liebe Sünde sein? Über das Begehren des Analytikers.* Freiburg: Kore Verlag.

LEUPOLD-LÖWENTHAL, H. (1986). *Handbuch der Psychoanalyse.* Wien: Orac.

LIEBERMAN, E. J. (1985). *Acts of Will, The Life and Work of Otto Rank.* New York: The Free Press.

MACLEAN, G. & RAPPEN, U. (1991). *Hermine Hug-Hellmuth.* New York/London: Routledge.

MAHONY, P. (1993). Discussion of Ernst Falzeder, "My Grand-Patient, My Chief Tormentor." *Canadian Psychoanalytic Society,* Montréal, October 21, 1993.

MEISEL, P. & KENDRICK, W. (Eds) (1985). *Bloomsbury/Freud. The Letters of James and Alix Strachey, 1924-1925.* New York: Basic Books.

MÜHLLEITNER, E. (1992). *Biographisches Lexikon der Psychoanalyse. Die Mitglieder der Psychologischen Mittwoch-Gesellschaft und der Wiener Psychoanalytischen Vereinigung 1902-1938.* Unter Mitarbeit von Johannes Reichmayr. Tübingen: Edition Diskord.

NIN, A. (1966). *Diary, 1931-1934.* Ed. Gunther and Stuhlman. New York: Swallow Press and Harcourt, Brace & World.

NUNBERG, H. & FEDERN, E. (Eds) (1967). *Minutes of the Vienna Psychoanalytic Society, Volume II, 1908-1910.* New York: International Universities Press.

QUINN, S. (1987). *A Mind of Her Own. The Life of Karen Horney.* New York: Summit Books.

RANK, O. (1924). *The Trauma of Birth.* New York: Brunner, 1952.

RATTNER, J. (1990). *Klassiker der Tiefenpsychologie.* München: Psychologie Verlags-Union.

REICH, W. (1952). *Von der Psychoanalyse zur Orgonomie. Das Interview über Sigmund Freud im Auftrag des S. Freud-Archivs 1952.* Ohne Ortsangabe: Edition Freiheit und Glück, 2nd edition 1984.

— (1988 [1919, 1937]). *Passion of Youth, An Autobiography, 1897-1922.* New York: Farrar, Straus & Giroux.

ROAZEN, P. (1969). *Brother Animal.* New Brunswick, NJ: Transaction Books, 1990.

— (1992). Freud's Patients. First-Person Accounts. *In:* Gelfand, T. & Kerr, J. (Eds). *Freud and the History of Psychoanalysis.* Hillsdale, NJ/London: The Analytic Press, pp. 289-306.

SCHEPELER, E.M. (1993). Jean Piaget's Experiences on the Couch: Some Clues to a Mystery. *International Journal of Psycho-Analysis, 74,* 255-273.

SCHRÖTER, M. & HERMANNS, L.M. (1992). Felix Gattel (1879-1904): Freud's First Pupil. Part I. *International Review of Psycho-Analysis, 19,* 91-104.

SHAMDASANI, S. (1990). A Woman Called Frank. *Spring, A Journal of Archityte and Culture, 50,* 26-56.

STEKEL, W. (1950). *The Autobiography of Wilhelm Stekel. The Life of a Pioneer Psychoanalyst.* Ed. Emil A. Gutheil. New York: Liveright.

STEPANSKY, P.E. (Ed.) (1988). *The Memoirs of Margaret S. Mahler.* New York, London: The Free Press, Collier Macmillan Publishers.

WILL, H. (1984). *Georg Groddeck. Die Geburt der Psychosomatik.* München: Deutscher Taschenbuch Verlag, 1987.

YOUNG-BRUEHL, E. (1988). *Anna Freud. A Biography.* New York: Summit Books, 1990.

Part II

Freud and
his intimate Sándor Ferenczi

BIBLIOGRAPHICAL NOTE

Introductory texts to the problem Freud-Ferenczi, see:

ARON, L. & HARRIS, A. (Eds.) (1993): *The Legacy of Sándor Ferenczi.* Hillsdale, N.J.: The Analytic Press.

HAYNAL, A. (1987): *The Technique at Issue. Controversies in Psychoanalysis from Freud and Ferenczi to Michael Balint.* London: Karnac, 1988. US Edition: *Controversies in Psychoanalytic Method. From Freud and Ferenczi to Michael Balint.* New York: New York University Press, 1989.

HAYNAL, A. (1991): *Psychoanalysis and the Sciences. Epistemology - History.* London: Karnac, 1993. US Edition: Berkeley: University of California Press, 1993.

STANTON, M. (1991): *Sándor Ferenczi. Reconsidering Active Intervention.* Northvale, N.J.: Jason Aronson.

The Freud-Ferenczi correspondence is currently being published in its integrality by Böhlau Verlag (Vienna, Austria), the French translation by Calmann-Lévy (Paris), the English translation by Harvard University Press (Cambridge, Mass, USA), edited by Eva Brabant, Ernst Falzeder and Patrizia Giampieri-Deutsch under the academic supervision of André Haynal.

Cahiers Psychiatriques Genevois, Special Issue, 1994, pp. 199-204

FERENCZI'S SEARCH FOR MUTUALITY: IMPLICATIONS FOR THE FREE ASSOCIATION METHOD: AN INTRODUCTION

Axel Hoffer

It seems fitting to begin with what I consider Freud's greatest single contribution to the study of the human mind. The history of science tells us that each major step in the advancement of human knowledge is made with a new tool and method of investigation. The new tool may be a visual one like a light microscope, which was followed by a newer tool – at higher magnification – the electron microscope

The elegantly simple yet profoundly complex tool which Freud gave us to improve our vision is, of course, the method of free association, referred to as the «fundamental rule». Using this tool, the analyst encourages the analysand to attempt the impossible, namely to put into words anyting and everything which comes to mind – thoughts, feelings, images, sensations and anything else that «falls into» [*einfallen*] the mind. Analysis of the conflicts about that freedom to associate – and the corresponding difficulties of the analyst in listening evenly and freely – comprise the essence of the analyst's way of pursuing new insights into the human mind in conflict. The method of free association gave us the tool to probe the unconscious.

But that tool is not an impersonal, scientific DNA probe. It is used within the context of a unique relationship which we call an analytic relationship. The nature of the relationship which makes optimal free associations possible remains the subject of heated and vital controversy. On February 14, 1930, Ferenczi wrote to Freud:

> «My hope – which I believe is not unjustified – is that an analytically free exchange is also possible between reliable friends... Do you think that such a mutual openness would be impossible?» [My translation, quoted with permission of Judith Dupont.]

Ferenczi's question to Freud sets the stage for the presentations which follow. Is speaking freely and openly in a mutual, trusting relationship between friends the same as free association in analysis? If not, how is it different? What kind of relationship promotes the optimal use of the tool which Freud gave us?[1] Our field continues to explore the opportunities and limits of the analytic relationship.

From the beginning and virtually to the end of his relationship with Freud, the father of psychoanalysis, Ferenczi sought a mutual, free and open exchange. The history of Ferenczi's frustrated quest – including his rejected offer to analyze Freud (26 February, 1926)[2] – serves as the background for the presentations which follow. His quest culminated in his bold experiments with patients in «mutual analysis» (Ferenczi, 1932) which may be understood in part as a displacement of his wish to analyze his former analyst. The following articles focus on issues raised in the complex relationship between Freud and Ferenczi including theories of trauma; the ramifications of Ferenczi's analysis of Jones; mutual analysis and mutuality in analysis; and finally, new conceptualizations of transference and countertransference. I will limit my remarks to briefly highlighting my own view of the uniqueness of the analytic relationship. The consequence of the fateful blurring of the relationship between Freud and Ferenczi – from pupil, colleague, friend, confidant to analyst-analysand and back again – invite deeper understanding. Blurring of relationships was common in the early days, as the history of our field indicates.[4] Furthermore, the fact that the analytic candidate becomes in reality a colleague of his former training analyst has implications for our field that merit our continued attention. Finally, Ferenczi's contributions are only now being appreciated as the theoretical forerunners of contemporary interpersonal, object relations, self-psychological and relational theories. My own view stresses the importance of the analyst's evenly-hovering, non-judgmental attention to the analysand's free associations which include affects, images and conflicts. The analytic relationship is unique in two respects. Firstly, in no other relationship is one consistently called upon to share anything and everything that comes to mind «by putting... self criticism out of action» (Freud, 1940, p. 174). The analysand is there because he wants to know himself through allowing the analyst to know him; the analyst provides this intimate relationship to enhance the patient's capacity to free associate. Free association opens a window into a person's heart, mind and soul. Secondly, only in an analytic relationship is the purpose of the relationship – its very *raison d'être* – to explore as fully as possible both sides of each conflict in only one member of the dyad. The asymmetrical focus on the analysand is, in my opinion, a prerequisite for the analyst non-judgmentally to view the patient's conflicts from the patient's point of view. These aspects of the analytic relationship create a relationship of unique intimacy.

Thus, an analytic relationship is purposefully neither mutual nor ordinary (Hoffer, 1992). It is therefore particularly important to maintain our awareness of the continual pull on the analyst to convert the analytic relationship into an ordinary one and to deal with that pull analytically by analyzing the countertransference rather than acting on it. I propose that enhancing the analysand's freedom to associate, necessary for the deepest elucidation of conscious and unconscious conflict, requires a relatively anonymous, asymmetrical relationship and is constrained in a mutual one. I conclude that converting an analytic relationship into an ordinary, mutual one limits the freedom of both parties to attend to the free associations of the analysand.

Notes

[1] I want to acknowledge some remarks made by Dr. Ana-Maria Rizzuto (1992) which inspired my exploration of this subject.

[2] Ferenczi's offer to analyze Freud.

The letters containing Ferenczi's offer to analyze Freud and the latter's response are moving and instructive. For Ferenczi, analysis represented a loving gift to help his friend and mentor with his physical and emotional distress. For Freud, the refusal of the offer meant an acceptance of the limitations of analysis and the life span. Ferenczi understood the refusal as a resistance to analysis and an unwillingness to trust anyone enough to enter into the intimacy inherent in an analytic relationship. My view is that a relationship which enhances free associations and the deepest elucidation of conflict cannot be a mutual or reciprocal one. Psychoanalysis requires relative anonymity in an asymmetrical relationship in which the consistent focus of attention is on the analysand. Ferenczi's poignant offer of psychoanalysis from one analyst to another can be appreciated as a well-intended, loving gift. Had it been accepted it may well have been helpful and therapeutic; yet it is better understood as a gift than as psychoanalysis. The relevant parts of the correspondence have been excerpted below. In response to Freud's complaining of not feeling well because of some «cardiac complaints», Ferenczi wrote:

Letter #1048 Fer
26 February 1926

I am firmly convinced that – even if nicotine plays a role in this matter – the psychical can be decisive in the so-called myocarditides and cardiac stenoses. As much as I energetically pleaded for the operation for relief of your jaw-suffering, I am equally decided that the heart can and should be supported not only medically but also psychically. Perhaps this is the occasion on which I can say to you that I actually find it to be tragic that you, who gave psychoanalysis to the world, [find it] so difficult – indeed are not in a position – to entrust yourself to someone. If your heart complaints continue and if medications and diet don't help, I will come to you for several months and will place myself at your disposal as analyst – naturally: if you don't throw me out.
With best greetings to all.

Your Ferenczi

Freud's reply, on 27 February 1926, is as follows:

Letter #1050 F

Dear Friend,

Heartfelt thanks for your moving proposal. But you know, my main anxiety is that of a useless existence; how should I befriend myself with one so damaging for my loved ones! The psychical root may indeed be, but let us not forget that dying also has a psychical root and it remains quite doubtful that it can be controlled by analysis, finally, if one doesn't at age seventy have a good right to rest of every kind... If you want to move to Vienna, my analysis doesn't have to be the motive. I will turn over to you those patients that come to me.

Warmly your

Freud

Ferenczi's reply is dated 1 March 1926:

Letter #1051 Fer

Dear Professor

Very pleased about the news of the improvement in your condition... Naturally neither can nor should [one] be pressured into analysis, but please keep in your [mind's] eye that as soon as your disinclination (should I say resistance?) is half-way overcome, I can immediately come to Vienna... I thought of a stay of few months.

Your

Ferenczi

And finally on 3 March 1926, Freud repeats:

Letter #1052 F

I answer your repeated warm offer to take me into analysis because of some presumed psi [psychological] factors with the argument that one would not think of such a therapy with any other septuagenarian with toxic etiology and anatomical findings. It is not to be assumed that I would have more benefit from such an attempt.

(Quotations by permission of Mark Paterson and Judith Dupont: translation by the author)

The original letters in German follow:
Letter #1048 Fer
26 February 1926

Ich bin fest überzeugt, dass – selbst wenn Nikotin bei der Sache mitspielt – Psychisches bei den sogenannten Myokarditin und Stenokardien entscheidend sein kann. So sehr ich bei der Lösung Ihres Kieferleidens energisch für den Eingriff plädierte, so entschieden glaube ich, dass das Herz nicht nur medizinal, sondern auch psychisch gestützt werden kann und soll. Vielleicht ist das der Anlass, bei dem ich Ihnen sagen kann, dass ich es eigentlich als tragisch finde, dass Sie, der Sie die Welt mit der Psychoanalyse beschenkten, so schwer – ja gar nicht in der Lage sind, sich jemandem anzuvertrauen. – Wenn Ihre Herzbeschwerden andauern und wenn die Medikamente und die Diät nicht helfen, so komme ich auf einige Monate zu Ihnen und stelle mich Ihnen als Analytiker zur Verfügung – natürlich: wenn Sie mich nicht hinauswerfen.

Mit besten Grüssen an alle

Ihr Ferenczi

Letter #1050 F
27 February 1926

Lieber Freund

Herzl[ichen] Dank für Ihren rührenden Vorschlag. Aber Sie wissen, meine Hauptangst ist die vor einer nutzlosen Existenz; wie soll ich mich mit einer für meine Lieben schädlichen befreunden!... Die psychische Wurzel mag schon sein, aber vergessen wir nicht, auch das Sterben hat seine psychische Wurzel, und es bleibt recht zweifelhaft, ob gerade die durch Analyse beherrscht werden kann, endlich, ob man nicht mit siebzig Jahren ein gutes Recht auf Ruhe jeder Art hat... Wenn Sie nach Wien übersiedeln wollen, braucht meine Analyse nicht das Motiv zu sein. Ich gebe Ihnen an Patienten ab, was zu mir kommt.

Herzlich Ihr

Freud

Letter #1051 Fer
1 March 1926

Lieber Herr Professor,

Freute mich sehr über die Nachricht von der Besserung in Ihrem Befinden... Zur Analyse kann und darf natürlich nicht gedrängt werden, aber bitte im Auge behalten, dass ich sobald Ihre Abneigung (soll ich Widerstand sagen?) halbwegs überwunden ist, sofort nach Wien kommen kann... Ich dachte an einen Aufenthalt von wenigen Monaten.

Ihr

Ferenczi

Letter #1052 F
3 March 1926

Ihr wiederholtes herzliches Anerbieten, mich wegen eines zu vermutenden psi Faktors in Analyse zu nehmen, beantworte ich mit dem Argument, dass man an eine solche Therapie auch bei keinem anderen Septuag mit toxischer Ätiologie und anatomischem Befund denken würde. Es ist nicht zu vermuten, dass ich mehr Vorteil von solchem Versuch haben würde.

---

[3]   See E. Falzeder, «Psychoanalytic Filiations», in this volume.

References

FERENCZI, S. (1988 [1932]). *The Clinical Diary of Sándor Ferenczi*. Cambridge, Mass.: Harvard University Press.

FREUD, S. (1940a [1938]). An Outline of Psycho-Analysis. *Standard Edition*, *23*, 139-207.

— & FERENCZI, S. (1993). *Correspondence, vol. 1, 1908-1914*. Cambridge & London: Harvard University Press.

HOFFER, A. (1992). Asymétrie et mutualité dans la relation analytique: leçons actuelles à tirer de la relation Freud-Ferenczi. *Le Coq-Héron*, *125*, 3-9.

— (1993). Asymmetrie und Gegenseitigkeit in der analytischen Beziehung: Lecktionen für heute aus der Beziehung zwischen Freud und Ferenczi. *Psyche*, *47*, 1026-1040.

Cahiers Psychiatriques Genevois, Special Issue, 1994, pp. 205-215

THE NOTION OF TRAUMA ACCORDING TO FERENCZI: PROGRESS OR REGRESSION IN PSYCHOANALYTIC THEORY?

Judith Dupont

In psychoanalytical literature, as well as in discussions among colleagues, Ferenczi is often compared or opposed to Freud. Both Freud and Ferenczi have their determined supporters, each favouring their own author at the expense of the other.

Presumably, this passionate attitude is partly due to the impact of the heavy trauma experienced by the psychoanalytical community because of the disagreement between Freud and Ferenczi in the early 1930's. Michael Balint gives an account of it in Chapter 23 of his book *The Basic Fault* (1968): «The impact of this event was so painful that the first reaction of the analytic movement to it was denial and silence, broken only in recent years, since when all sorts of fictitious statements about Freud and Ferenczi have found their way into print: Freud was described as a ruthless autocrat... Ferenczi as a mean, cowardly schemer...» (p. 149).

Such unqualified judgements are equally applied to their respective positions about trauma: according to some, Freud was able to realize that most of the traumas reported by their patients were phantasies, while Ferenczi, blinded by his personal pathology, was ready to believe anything and everything his patients told him. According to others, Freud, a bourgeois himself, could not admit that so much vileness could occur in «good families», while Ferenczi was able to see things as they were.

All these highly emotional assessments show how strongly the two men are associated in peoples' minds – just as they were in reality. Their correspondence gives evidence of that. Freud: «We covered a long way

This paper was first published in French in *Le Bloc-Notes de la Psychanalyse*, Nr. 13, 1993, Geneva. Many thanks to Christopher Fortune who went through the English version of this paper.

together... always hand in hand» (Freud, 25 Oct. 1927) in an «intimate community of life, feelings and interests» (Freud, 11. Jan. 1933). This long journey, as in every rich and deep relationship, was riddled with encounters of an emotional, intellectual and professional nature, as well as with conflicts and misunderstandings. The conflicts that arose between these two men can be explained by the complexity of this long relationship, rather than by basic theoretical differences. So we can read in a letter of Freud, on 20 Jan. 1930: «In fact, we must humbly state that even the theoretical differences between us don't go farther than that which is inevitable between two independent workers when there is no permanent exchange of ideas and consequently a mutual influence between them.» As we see, he rather reproaches Ferenczi for a slackening of their correspondence; effectively, their letter exchanges became less frequent as Ferenczi tried to disengage himself from the heavy influence of Freud's thinking, in order to go on with his own research. It is their followers' passions that lead to simplifications which ignore a more complicated reality.

In fact, both authors advocated much more finely shaded positions. Freud never totally rejected the traumatic aetiology of neuroses; Ferenczi never denied the role of pathogenic phantasies. But Freud defended the point of view that the trauma was much more often of a phantasmatic nature than previously thought, Ferenczi considered that it was much more often real as Freud came to conclude as a result of his disappointment about the truthfulness of his hysteric patient's accounts. Freud's and Ferenczi's conceptions of trauma are not contradictory, but reflect a quantitative difference: they disagreed on the frequency of traumatic aetiology. Nevertheless, I would like to add that Ferenczi's study of the impact and mechanisms of «psychic shock» went so deep that one can indeed support the idea of a specifically Ferenczian notion of trauma.

So, here, as in many cases, rather than trying to oppose the two conceptions, it seems more fruitful to see two research orientations. Thus, I consider that Ferenczi did not return to an outdated theory, but pursued his research along an abandoned, but not exhausted, vein of analytic theory: an image he often comes back to.

In the beginning, Freud describes the traumatic event as essentially sexual, taking place in early childhood. But this infantile trauma is not the direct cause of the neurosis; it is a later event, during puberty or post-puberty, which revives the original trauma and produces the neurosis. So, two moments are necessary to constitute a neurosis: «Hysterics suffer mainly from reminiscences!» (Freud, 1893, p. 7.)

Then, progressively, the thesis of the pathogenic phantasy supplants the one of the actual trauma, though not eliminating it: «Here then, we foresee complications, a greater wealth of determinants for the onset of illness; but we may also suspect that there is no need to abandon the traumatic line of approach as being erroneous: it must be possible to fit it in and subsume it somewhere else.» (Freud, 1916-17, p. 276.)

Ferenczi in the course of his practice, met more and more often with possibilities to «fit in the traumatic line of approach». So he came to reconsider the problem or the traumatic aetiology of neuroses and to refine even the definition of trauma.

Little by little, taking his clinical observations as a starting point, Ferenczi refined his conception of trauma. He studied the problem from every angle, in various contexts. He completed his idea by a number of small additions. Consequently, the picture he gives is more like an impressionist painting than a precise drawing of an architect. But it is not less evocative. Consequently I will also have to follow this impressionist process as my way to describe the various aspects of the notion of trauma according to Ferenczi.

Like Freud, Ferenczi considered that two moments were necessary to make a trauma pathogenic, as every trauma does not have a pathogenic effect. A trauma correctly handled and discussed by the surrounding circle of persons can even forward a normal maturation process. But it can become pathogenic if it is denied by the people who are important to the child, primarily the mother. What makes the trauma pathogenic is hypocrisy, inducement of guilt feelings, rejection, moreover suprise effect, or repeated traumas.

Sometimes one can observe the two moments simultaneously: as described by Freud and as described by Ferenczi. For example: six years old Bernadette was raped by a neighbour. After threatening her not to say a word about what happened, he took her back to her parents, who were having tea in the garden with some friends. «What a nice girl your little Bernadette is!» said the neighbour. «Isn't she?» answered the mother, kissing her little daughter. The child remained silent about the whole event, but became awkward and aggressive. Some years later, the parents divorced. Bernadette and her sister stayed with their mother and had no more contact with their father. One evening, at the age of ten, Bernadette, after a lesson of sex education at school, asked her mother for more information. That was the moment Bernadette suffered a real «psychic shock» in Ferenczi's sense: so, she thought, did the neighbour try to make her have a child? Later, at puberty, Bernadette developed severe anorexia, which led her finally to psychoanalysis.

Gradually, Ferenczi completed his conception of the mechanism of trauma as acting: «The recollections which neocatharsis evoked or corroborated lent an added significance to the original traumatic factor in our aetiological equations.» Then, some lines where he goes back to his debate with Freud: «The precautions of the hysteric and the avoidance of the obsessional neurotic may, it is true, have their explanation in purely mental fantasy-formations; nevertheless the first impetus towards abnormal lines of development has always been thought to originate from real psychic traumas and conflicts with the environment – the invariable precursors of the formation of nosogenic mental forces, for instance, of conscience.» (Ferenczi, 1930, p. 120.)

Ferenczi showed how the frustration principle applied by analytical technique can, in some cases, reproduce the rigid authority of parents and thus represent a repetition of the original trauma. The trauma, he writes, is often a consequence of «really improper, unintelligent, capricious, tactless or actually cruel treatment» (ibid., p. 121). Or yet, a consequence of misunderstanding, denial, or abandonment by the people important for the child.

Ferenczi insisted on the frequency of sexual traumas, even in the most puritan families. (I propose here a cinematographic reference: Ingmar Bergman's «Fanny and Alexander», a widely autobiographical picture, which constitutes a striking illustration of the above.)

It happens, wrote Ferenczi, that the adults indulge in some erotic games with the child, often presented as expressions of tenderness. The child responds willingly, «more vehemently and far earlier» (ibid., p. 121) than supposed before. Nevertheless, his expectation is that of playing and tenderness. But the adult responds in a passionate mode, incomprehensible to the child. Driven by guilt feelings, the adult scolds and punishes the child; the suddenness of this turnaround is a major traumatic factor. (One can find here an answer to those who reproach Ferenczi for denying infantile sexuality. When Ferenczi speaks of the «innocence» of the child, he does not pretend that he is devoid of any sexual emotion, he only means that the child experiences these emotions without guilt feelings.)

Trauma may also result from insufficient stimulation, such as deprivation of love, as well as of overstimulation. Where Freud wrote about «congenital weakness of the capacity for life», Ferenczi rather saw the action of an ultra-precocious trauma (Ferenczi, 1929). The first reaction to a shock is a «temporary psychosis», a break from reality. From that follows a psychotic splitting, a destruction of the feeling of the Self, of the defenses, or even of the actual form of the personality. The individual might make himself completely flexible in order to better integrate the shock, or react by fragmentation or even atomization of the personality in the case of repeated traumas. Some of these fragments are made of dead or killed parts of the psyche, somehow encysted and sequestered by the surviving part.

Ferenczi insists, in his description of the shock mechanism, on the sudden, inexpected character of the traumatic event. The individual reacts with paralysis of the whole psychic activity, mobility, perceptions, thinking capacity; a state of passivity, of non-resistance sets in. The traumatized child, physically and psychically weakened, is defenceless and has no other choice than to identify with the aggressor, surrendering to all his desires, even anticipating them. (The notion of identification with the agressor was taken up later by Anna Freud in 1936; many authors credit her with this idea.) This kind of self-destruction can even be accompanied by feelings of pleasure: the pleasure in offering oneself as a sacrifice to superior powers. This pleasure in one's own defeat is expressed through admiration for the power and the greatness of the adversary. At the same time, the individual conforts himself with the feeling or his own wisdom and intellectual superiority. The aggressor is introjected, he becomes intra-psychic. In that way, the situation of tenderness can be hallucinatorily maintained.

But thus, the guilt feelings of the adult are equally introjected. What, before, was an innocent game, becomes reprehensible and deserves punishment. Hence the splitting: the child is simultaneously innocent and guilty; he no longer trusts his own senses. On the other side, the aggressor, driven by his own guilt feelings, denies the facts, and may even become brutal and increase the child's feelings of guilt by an extreme moral rigidity. When the child tries to communicate to the people around him, primarily his mother, something of what he has experienced, it often happens that he gets scolded because he talks «nonsense». For instance, this four years old boy, forced by his older cousin to play sexual games, who wanted to complain to his mother. But his mother was immersed in a fascinating book and did not want to be disturbed by «these silly stories». After that, the child became more or less mute, and his subsequent schoolwork was severely disturbed.

Another reaction to trauma is what Ferenczi calls «traumatic progression». The traumatized and split child suddenly develops remarkable capacities of intelligence and wisdom; he becomes the nurse, or even the psychiatrist of his parents. It is in this connection that Ferenczi created his notion of the «wise baby», who takes over all the responsibilities from his incompetent parents.

As a consequence of the splitting, the break, the object relationship turns into a narcissic relationship: part of the personality mothers the other part, in some way becoming his «guardian angel». If a second trauma then redoubles the first, the guardian angel might be unable to face up to it, and this could even lead to suicide. In his *Clinical Diary*, Ferenczi links his own physical death, which he knows to be imminent,

209

with the trauma he experienced on being «abandoned» by Freud (or what he felt to be an abandonment).

All these descriptions, these successive light touches, are summed up in five papers written between 1928 and 1932. The most impressive of them is his famous paper *Confusion of Tongues Between Adults and the Child* (1985 [1932]), where he gives the most complete formulation of his conception of trauma. We know the story of this paper: when Ferenczi read it to Freud, in Vienna, before presenting it to the Wiesbaden Congress in September 1932, Freud was deeply shocked by it. His reaction, as well as the massive rejection by the psycho-analytical community, in turn represented for Ferenczi a severe psychic commotion. (In this respect it is interesting to note that when Balint, in 1938 in London, asked Freud to read the paper again, the latter found it full of fascinating ideas.)

Between March 1931 and December 1932, Ferenczi devoted five short notes to the problem of trauma. They were collected and published posthumously in one paper by the *Internationale Zeitschrift für Psychoanalyse* (1934), and can be found separately in *Final Contributions* (pp. 236, 238, 249, 253, 276). In this series of notes, we can follow, *in statu nascendi* as it were, the development of his thought about this notion.

One of these notes is titled *On the Revision of the Interpretation of Dreams* (p. 238). It is about the traumatolytic function of the dream: the repetition of the trauma in the dream is equivalent to an attempt to find a better solution for the traumatic event. The weakening of the critical mind in the dreaming state can favour this better solution. When the attempt fails, the dream turns into nightmare. Ferenczi suggests that these traumatic residues, striving for repetition, could be unconscious impressions which in fact were never conscious. These residues take advantage of the wish-fulfilling function of the dream in order to find a solution.

Ferenczi evoked this «second function» of the dream in a supplement to a letter to Eitingon, of 31 May 1931. He also sent a copy of this letter to Freud. Ferenczi was aware, indeed, of the importance Freud attached to questions of priority. Freud himself mentioned this idea of repetition of the trauma in dream, in *Beyond the Pleasure Principle*. Consequently, Ferenczi does not omit to write to him on the 14th of July 1931: «Of course I know that the dream function I brought to the fore is the one you have described and explained in *Beyond the Pleasure Principle*, as characterizing the dreams of traumatized people. Though, my experience drives me to insist on this idea more forcefully than you did in your "Interpretation of dreams". In other words: I wish to give a more general meaning to the point of view of the mastering of trauma in sleep and dream.»

After having thus clarified his conception of trauma, its nature and its mechanisms, Ferenczi, above all a doctor – he was even reproached for his so-called *furor sanandi* – thought about therapeutic techniques which would allow him to reach back to the original trauma and treat its effects.

His techniques of relaxation and neocatharsis first led Ferenczi to reconsider the role of traumas in the formation of neuroses. «... no analysis can be regarded (at any rate in theory) as complete, he writes in *The Principle of Relaxation and Neocatharsis* (1930, p. 120) unless we have succeeded in penetrating to the traumatic material». This technique of relaxation offered him his first therapeutic tool. He realized that with the help of relaxation and permissiveness he could further regression in the patient, a regression which could reach a state of trance. During this trance, just as in dream state, patients were able to reexperience the original trauma, or even to experience it for the first time if the trauma took place in a state of unconsciousness. Indeed, in this case, there is no recollection possible, and the neurosis formed in that way would be inaccessible to a so-called classical analysis. But Ferenczi hoped that this first experience in a state of trance would make the neurosis more accessible to memory, thus allowing a better solution of the trauma in the protecting analytical situation.

But he also realized the dangers involved by the initiation of such a regressive process. So he warned the analysts that in this state of extreme fragility of the patient they must increase their control on their countertransference and on their own resistances, because too much sadism under the pretext of frustration, or too much tenderness under the pretext of relaxation and flexibility, could lead them to lose control of the situation.

Thus, Ferenczi reports on some reverses met with in the course of his therapeutic experiments with regression: the patients went from repetition to repetition, each time followed indeed by some relief, but only temporarily. They switched from emotion without understanding to understanding without emotion, but could never reach any conviction. Also, in spite of all the efforts of the analyst, the patient felt more and more frustrated, unhappy and hopeless. A great deal of tact was then necessary on the part of the analyst in order to restablish the dialogue and avoid a breaking off in a state of mutual bitterness and disappointment.

In *Confusion of Tongues Between Adults and the Child*, Ferenczi insists on the necessity to take the infantile regression literally, and take into account the real depth of the splitting, in order to understand the fact that a regressed patient is no longer able to reason, and reacts only to attitudes, not to words.

This observation retained Michael Balint's attention; taking up Ferenczi's last clinical experiments, he was able to approach more closely to the solution. As Ferenczi writes in an unpublished note of 26th of September 1932, written in Luchon during his last holidays, when he knew already how ill he was: «Balint takes up things there where I got stuck.»

Balint describes three areas in the mind: 1) the Oedipal area, involving three persons, where the language used is an adult conventional language; 2) the area of the Basic Fault, involving two persons only, where the adult conventional language is of no more use; 3) the area of Creation, where the individual is alone and tries to produce something out of himself.

Ferenczi's description in his paper quoted above corresponds precisely to the area of the Basic Fault. So, the possibility must be given to the patient to regress to this area, in order to reach the original trauma. At this level of regression, the patient is totally helpless, deprived of adult language, but endowed with increased sensibility and extraordinary clear-sightedness. It is of no use to pretend understanding and sympathy, one cannot deceive him. The most extreme sincerity and empathy is then required on the part of the analyst, in order to spare the patient from experiencing the same hypocrisy, denial and rejection as he had originally.

But this regression, necessary to the healing process, can take different directions, one favourable, the other impossible to keep under control. Balint called them benign or malignant forms of regression. Ferenczi's reverses originated in his inability to identify the factors which were determining the evolution in one or the other direction. He well understood that something had to be given to patients regressed until this pregenital level, and that this «something» must be very carefully measured. But he could not determine what could, and should be granted, or what might initiate an uncontrollable evolution. Or, maybe he did not live long enough to discover it.

It was Michael Balint who established the distinction between benign and malignant regression. In the first case, the patient is able to reexperience the trauma and then start life again with new energies, though still carrying the indelible scar left by the past, that is, his basic fault according to Balint's terminology. This is the process he called a «new beginning». In the second case, the malignant regression brings no solution, but initiates an endless spiral of repetitions of the trauma, and constantly renewed demands impossible to satisfy. The analyst must be extremely careful and clearsighted about the nature of the satisfactions granted to the patient in order to control the outcome of the regression. These satisfactions must always remain at the level of foreplay, simply showing that the desires and needs of the patient are perceived and recognized.

Ferenczi, throughout his life, was concerned by the problem of trauma. He certainly had his personal reasons for that. He mentioned several traumatic events in his papers, his *Clinical Diary*, and his correspondence with Freud: some incidents with a nanny, with older boys, as well as his feats as a great masturbator. Then, he was the 8th child of a big family: we know, for instance, that little Sándor hated his sister who came just before him – called Gizella! – and that the sister following him died when he was four. In a letter to Groddeck, on Christmas day 1921, he mentions the cold rigidity and puritanism of his mother. His relationship with her always remained difficult.

So, it seems that Ferenczi, as all researchers in psychoanalysis for that matter, drew his research material principally from himself, from his own experience, which certainly motivated him to become a psychoanalyst, but also oriented his analytic practice, which he conducted with rare sensitivity.

The whole of the *Clinical Diary*, as well as Ferenczi's way of giving account of the sessions and evolution of his patients (all of whom had suffered severe traumas) bears witness to the traumatic past of Ferenczi himself. His special sensitivity for such patients seems to have been generally recognized. It is certainly not just by chance that these difficult patients were sent to him from everywhere in the world.

Finally, many passages of his *Clinical Diary* can be seen as a reaction to the trauma inflicted on Ferenczi by Freud himself. Principally, it concerns the unfinished analysis of Ferenczi by Freud, and the lack of understanding or even rejection by Freud of Ferenczi's researches conducted during the thirties. These researches were precisely about ways of expression, mechanisms and treatment of trauma.

At the time, Ferenczi practically forced Freud to accept him for analysis. But could he have asked anybody else to do it? It was certainly not the best of conditions to undertake an analysis, to be simultaneously pupil, friend, and collaborator of one's analyst, his fellow traveller and his permanent accomplice in the internal political manoeuvres of the analytical society. Freud had a very clear perception of that, and tried to warn Ferenczi. That is all he could do. The predicted complications did not fail to happen. This analytic experience, even shortened as it was, certainly had a great part in the upheavals that cast a gloom on the last years of their relationship. On the other hand, Ferenczi too was right when he reproached Freud for not having analyzed the whole of his negative transference. Possibly Freud was overtaken by the passionate demands of Ferenczi, noticeable in their correspondence of this period, and preferred to consider that the analysis was «closed», even if «not finished» (Freud, 24 Oct. 1916), rather than take the risk of losing control of it in a way Balint would have called a malignant regression.

The second big shock probably took place when Ferenczi set out to conquer his independence. Independence cannot be given, only taken. For Ferenczi it was vital, and at the same time impossible. He describes it in a very pathetic way in his *Clinical Diary*. Instead of being supported by this «superior power», represented for him by Freud, he felt «trampled» by it. He experienced Freud's lack of understanding for his ultimate researches as an actual personal abandonment. The tone of Freud's letters at that time was sometimes very hard indeed: once he reproached Ferenczi for living «a belated puberty», then he blamed him for refusing to take his criticisms into account. We can note here something remarkable on the part of a supporter of pathogenic phantasy: Freud believed, without expressing any doubts, the report of Dm., one of Ferenczi's female patients, who tells him about the way Ferenczi sometimes came to kiss her. In a now famous letter (13 Dec. 1931) he reproaches Ferenczi for his «kissing technique» and its prejudicial consequences. Of course, his credulity is based on Ferenczi's slips in his professional conduct in his early years of practice (the Elma affair). Ferenczi's answer is less well known, because it was omitted in Jones's biography of Freud. He explains the reasons that could lead Dm. – reasons she recognized – to somewhat exaggerate her account of the events (Ferenczi, 1985 [1932], pp. 3-4).

In his *Clinical Diary*, Ferenczi gave free rein to his grievances against Freud. These are very subjective remarks, of course – how could it be otherwise? – but Ferenczi describes what he feels. In some poignant phrases he formulates his distress: he feels he cannot overcome the shock of Freud's «abandoning» him, and that he was dying of it.

So, Ferenczi, who taught us so much about trauma, is himself an exemplary case of a patient who, having suffered repeated traumas, was not in position to receive any proper treatment because there was no available analyst to undertake it, and no appropriate therapeutic tools. Ferenczi himself was the one who began to elaborate them, but illness did not leave him the necessary time to obtain complete success. Balint took things up where Ferenczi got stuck...

References

Many valuable writings have been published on the question of trauma according to Ferenczi. It is impossible to enumerate all of them, in spite of their interest. So, besides Freud and Ferenczi, I will quote only one, Michael Balint, who not only thoroughly studied the notion of trauma according to Ferenczi – his analyst, master and friend – but who took it as starting point for his own researches.

BALINT, M. (1932). Character Analysis and New Beginning. In: *Primary Love and Psycho-Analytic Technique*. London: Tavistock, pp. 151-164.

BALINT, M. (1959). *Thrills and Regressions*. London, Hogarth.

— (1968). *The Basic Fault*. London: Tavistock Publications.

FERENCZI, S. (1928). The Elasticity of Psycho-Analytic Technique. *In: Final Contributions to the Problems and Methods of Psycho-Analysis*. New York: Brunner & Mazel, 1980, pp. 87-101.

— (1929). The Unwelcome Child and His Death Instinct. *In: Final Contributions to the Problems and Methods of Psycho-Analysis*. New York: Brunner & Mazel, 1980, pp. 102-107.

— (1930). The Principle of Relaxation and Neocatharsis. *In: Final Contributions to the Problems and Methods of Psycho-Analysis*. New York: Brunner & Mazel, 1980, pp. 108-125.

— (1920, 1930-32). Notes and Fragments. *In: Final Contributions to the Problems and Methods of Psycho-Analysis*. New York: Brunner & Mazel, 1980, pp. 236, 238, 249, 253, 276.

— (1933). Confusion of Tongues Between Adults and the Child. *In: Final Contributions to the Problems and Methods of Psycho-Analysis*. New York: Brunner & Mazel, 1980, pp. 156-167.

— (1985 [1932]). *The Clinical Diary*. Cambridge, Mass.: Harvard Universities Press, 1988.

FREUD, A. (1936). *The Ego and the Mechanisms of Defence*. London: Hogarth, 1979 (see also *The Writings of Anna Freud*, vol. II).

FREUD, S. (1916-17). Introductory Lectures on Psycho-Analysis. *Standard Edition, 15-16*.

— (1920g). Beyond the Pleasure Principle. *Standard Edition, 18*, 1-64.

— & BREUER, J. (1895d). Studies on Hysteria. *Standard Edition, 2*.

— & FERENCZI, S. (1992). *Correspondence, vol. I, 1908-1914*. Cambridge, Mass.: Harvard University Press, 1994; *vol. III* (to be published).

Cahiers Psychiatriques Genevois, Special Issue, 1994, pp. 217-223

A DIFFICULT ENDING: FERENCZI, «R.N.», AND THE EXPERIMENT IN MUTUAL ANALYSIS

Christopher Fortune

In this paper I will present a piece of my research on the relationship between Sándor Ferenczi and his critically important patient, Elizabeth Severn. I will tell the story of the last difficult months in late 1932 of their historic experiment in mutual analysis, and the ending of their eight-year analytic relationship itself, not long before Ferenczi's death. It is an extension of my chapter (Fortune, 1993) in the recently published *The Legacy of Sándor Ferenczi*. My research over the last seven years has included extensive interviews with Elizabeth Severn's aged daughter.

I will give only a very brief background to the mutual analysis, and to Elizabeth Severn – code-named «R.N.» by Ferenczi in his *Clinical Diary* (1988). The diary's pages are filled with references to «R.N.», and establish her profound influence on Ferenczi's last radical work. For example, she was the catalyst for the experiment in mutual analysis. How did Elizabeth Severn come to be in this remarkable situation with Ferenczi?

Elizabeth Severn was born in 1879 in a small town in the American mid-west. Little is known of her parents. She was in all likelihood subjected to severe early child abuse. A sickly child, she was plagued with fears and anxieties. Throughout her childhood, teenage, and early adult years, she experienced chronic fatigue, violent headaches and eating disorders. She later reports having amnesia about her life before twelve-year-old. Frequently bedridden, she suffered a number of nervous breakdowns from which she recovered in mental sanitoriums. Medical treatment provided only temporary relief. In her early twenties, at about the turn of the century, she married, had a daughter, but within a few years she ended the

The preparation of this paper was supported by the Social Sciences and Humanities Research Council of Canada.

marriage and left her husband – a radical act for a woman in those times. Through her ongoing treatment she was exposed to psychological and «healing» techniques based on the «power of positive thinking» and Theosophy. Severn became convinced she had healing powers herself and began to see patients, calling herself a metaphysical therapist.

In 1913, she published her first book, *Psycho-therapy: Its Doctrine and Practice*, based on her ideas on willpower, dreams, visualization and telepathic healing. Although she lacked any formal academic or professional credentials, she identified herself as having a «Ph.D.» She continued to use the title «Dr.» throughout her life.

Severn's chronic symptoms, including exhaustion, headaches, severe depression and suicidal impulses continued. Her symptoms fit the profile of many of today's patients who have suffered severe abuse as children. She sought help from a number of psychiatrist-analysts, including Otto Rank, but none were able to alleviate her suffering. In 1924, the forty-four-year-old Severn was referred to Sándor Ferenczi. Desperate, and believing that he was perhaps her last hope, she travelled to Budapest to begin an analytical treatment with Ferenczi that would radically expand the bounds of classical psychoanalysis.

By the time Elizabeth Severn met Ferenczi, she was an extremely strong willed and determined woman, who's life had been a quest to untangle the mystery of her chronic psychic pain.

Ferenczi was impressed by Severn, although a little anxious, as they set about the analysis. He writes that he responded to her «majestic superiority of a queen», with «intrepid masculinity» (Ferenczi, 1988, p. 97). By 1926, after a few years of intensive analysis, Severn's treatment stalled. Using his indulgence and elasticity techniques, and openly overcompensating, Ferenczi writes that he «redoubled [his] efforts» and gradually «gave into more and more of the patient's wishes» (p. 97). His «superperformances» included sessions twice a day – often at her home – sometimes for four to five hours, weekend sessions, and if necessary, at night. Ferenczi even continued Severn's analysis during vacations abroad. Efforts such as these led Freud to talk of Ferenczi's «*furor sanandi*» – his rage to cure.

In 1928, a breakthrough came. Utilizing relaxation and regression techniques, including trance states, Severn and Ferenczi lifted a veil of early amnesia. They reconstructed the events of a severe case of sexual, physical, and emotional abuse by her father, beginning at age one-and-a-half. The recovered unconscious material was horrendous and bizarre, including «memories» not only of incest, but of a murder, and of being drugged and prostituted to other men. Ferenczi writes that the «traumatic shocks» of her childhood left Severn in a state of almost total psychic disintegration with severe amnesia about the events before she was twelve years old – a «confusion of chaotically jumbled memory impressions from her past» (Ferenczi, 1988, p. 10).

Although unsure of the objective reality of Severn's recovered images, through the analysis they began to uncover and piece together the missing details of Elizabeth's childhood and fragmented self. Severn's condition became acute. In 1929, Ferenczi writes to Groddeck that she has entered a «critical phase» (Ferenczi and Groddeck, 1982, p. 117). In 1930, Ferenczi writes optimistically that Severn's case is «exhausting but worthwhile» and that he hopes «to announce what it means to complete an analysis» (p. 122).

It's not clear when, but Ferenczi writes in his diary that the «catharsis bogged down» (Ferenczi, 1988, p. 24). For two years, Ferenczi determinedly continued his devotions to Severn. His attentive behaviour convinced Severn that she had found her «perfect lover». Alarmed, Ferenczi backed off, reducing his attentions. Severn reacted to Ferenczi's withdrawal by challenging him that she suspected he harboured hidden negative feelings – hate and anger – towards her, which blocked her analysis. She demanded to analyze those feelings in *him*, or, she said, her analysis would remain at an impasse. Ferenczi resisted for a year, then reluctantly agreed to submit to Severn's analysis of him (p. 99).

On the couch Ferenczi admitted: «I did hate the patient in spite of all the friendliness I displayed.... Curiously», he writes, «this had a tranquilizing effect on the patient, who felt vindicated» (p. 99). Ferenczi described other positive effects. Severn's analysis deepened, she became less demanding and she strengthened her belief in her «memories» of early trauma. As well, mutual analysis uncovered Ferenczi's own early traumas and the roots of his «superkindness» and «superperformances». However, despite the analytical rewards, Ferenczi soon saw the practical difficulties and problems of mutual analysis.

In early March 1932, Ferenczi's ambivalence was growing and he seemed to consider ending the experiment (p. 46). This precipitated a crisis for Severn. Through mutual analysis, she had gained a more equal position with Ferenczi, her own analysis had progressed and she felt more confident. She balked at a return to one-way analysis. Besides, she felt Ferenczi's unanalyzed complexes could still torture her. Severn warned Ferenczi that his clinical work was dependent on her and couldn't be continued without her. Ferenczi felt threatened. He writes in his diary:

> In fact the patient had already made various plans for lifelong co-operation... [and mentioned] the uniqueness of her case and of our joint technique, which penetrates into deep metaphysical regions (Ferenczi, 1988, p. 47).

Feeling betrayed, Severn considered leaving Budapest. Ferenczi himself thought of ending Severn's analysis altogether (p. 47). It was a stalemate. Ferenczi attempted to correct what he judged as his «excessive self-sacrifice» (p. 46) by drawing a stricter boundary for the relationship. He writes that he was trying a more «active» approach to pressure Severn to «renounce unrealizable fantasies» (p. 156). Ferenczi proposed a compromise to Severn: «[that] I would pursue *my* analysis only for brief periods each day and only as far as it was relevant to her analysis.» He writes that, «after a prolonged, deathly silence and total despair», Severn agreed (p. 47).

Severn was also worried about money. The few financially well-off patients that had followed her to Budapest to continue therapy had dropped away. Quite possibly she lost them during her earlier breakdown when Ferenczi had her admitted to a sanitorium for four months in 1930. Throughout their eight-year relationship, Ferenczi occasionally appears to have waived his analytical fees in an effort to help her stay in analysis.

There were logistical problems inherent in mutual analysis. For example, who should go first? After trial and error, by late March, Ferenczi writes that «every double session begins with the analysis of the analyst» (p. 71). However, following his own analytic session, Ferenczi had trouble concentrating when it was Severn's turn on the couch – even falling asleep. In response, Ferenczi «shamefacedly» agreed to Severn's earlier suggestion that her own analysis cease until she completed her analysis of him. Their roles became completely reversed. But, to Ferenczi's relief, this situation lasted only two days, as Severn couldn't do without her analysis. At the core of this back and forth was a dilemma based in lack of confidence in each other as analysts. Ferenczi writes, that since neither of them were free of «complexes», both of them were afraid they would be abused, or at least misunderstood, by what was unanalyzed in the other (p. 72).

For the next nine months, until December 1932, Ferenczi and Severn struggled with the vicissitudes of mutual analysis. Severn oscillated between extremes of anger and affection towards Ferenczi. She writes that Ferenczi's «complexes» had inhibited her analysis and delayed her cure, and that he had been a «failure» in her case. She still suffered a number of chronic symptoms. She constantly wrestled with the idea of leaving Budapest.

The fall of 1932 was stressful on another front for Ferenczi. His growing estrangement from Freud had reached a crisis. In a painful last meeting in late August in Vienna, before Ferenczi was to present his *Confusion of Tongues* (1933) paper at the Wiesbaden Congress, Freud rejected him and his paper which affirmed the significance of early sexual trauma. Shortly thereafter, Ferenczi developed Pernicious Anemia, the disease from which he would ultimately die eight months later.

In the late fall of 1932, it appears again that Severn's own analysis stopped and she was solely analyzing Ferenczi. There is a strong suggestion that Ferenczi offered to pay Severn for her analysis of him. One can speculate that in his weakened condition he may have wished to extricate himself from mutual analysis, yet still support Severn in her need to be acknowledged for her analytical abilities. Severn's daughter wrote to her mother to be careful that Ferenczi was paying her for a real analysis, not simply humoring her (M. Severn to E. Severn, 14 December 1932). Although Ferenczi earlier mentions his fears of being vulnerable to Severn (Ferenczi, 1988, p. 72), it is quite possible, in his weakened state, that he became dependent on Severn as his analyst.

As these last months inevitably drew to their tragic conclusion, Ferenczi reduced his analytic workload. Distressed, Severn wrote to her daughter of a number of developments which upset her, saying Ferenczi avoided discussing the termination of her analysis and her imminent departure from Budapest. She wrote that Ferenczi was concerned that she keep his analysis by her a secret. She also implied that in order to protect Ferenczi, she felt she needed to proclaim herself «cured» (M. Severn to E. Severn, 23 December 1932).

It is not surprising that they struggled at the end. Ferenczi was physically and emotionally exhausted. Severn was on a roller-coaster of emotion at the prospect of the ending of their eight-year relationship. Many of her symptoms still persisted, and she felt that her analysis was not finished. Their mutuality had enmeshed them deeply. As Janet Malcom writes: «All analyses end badly. Each «termination» leaves the participants with the taste of ashes in their mouths» (Malcom, 1982, p. 102).

It appears from Severn's last letters that, in the end, she and Ferenczi parted with some degree of equanimity and goodwill. In late February 1933, Severn said good-bye to Ferenczi and took the train to Paris to stay with her daughter. However, she arrived in such a state of mental and physical collapse that her daughter wrote Ferenczi a «terrible letter» of protest (M. Severn, personal communication, 8 May 1986). But Ferenczi was too weak to reply. He died 22 May 1933 at his home in Budapest.

Epilogue

By mid-June 1933, Severn had recovered enough to make her way to London where she restarted her therapy practice. That fall, she published *The Discovery of the Self* (1933), the book she had started in Budapest in 1932. Her book does not mention mutual analysis, and there are few references to Ferenczi (she didn't dedicate the book to him). One can only speculate on Severn's silence. Quite possibly, she simply respected his request and treated their analysis as private. She may also have felt some guilt for Ferenczi's final exhaustion (Ferenczi, however, only ever mentions his «disappointment with Freud» as a contributing factor of his illness [Ferenczi and Groddeck, 1982, p. 127]). Also, Severn may have still felt critical of Ferenczi and not wanted to reveal this. Knowing that the orthodox psychoanalytic community disapproved of Ferenczi's last clinical work, Severn may have been concerned about bringing further negative attention to Ferenczi, and to herself.

In another work (Fortune, 1993), I have written in detail about Severn's book. In summary, the book attempts to pull together her early «psychotherapy» methods with her later analytic influences, and sets them within her overarching metaphysical-spiritual philosophy. She writes that analysis is limited – too regressive, and while she values it, she champions a more «positive» healing approach beyond analysis. She writes in solidarity with Ferenczi's views on trauma, repetition, re-mothering, and the processes of fragmentation, dissociation, and splitting. However, she does not defer to Ferenczi's priority, or authority, but writes from her own perspective as a therapist and equal collaborator. For example, she claims to have led Ferenczi to the development of the «relaxation technique» (Severn, 1933, p. 95).

Many questions remain unanswered about this historic relationship. I asked Severn's daughter an obvious one: «Do you think your mother's analysis with Ferenczi was beneficial?» She replied:

> Her analysis was so complicated, the dreams so extraordinary, so deep and so incessant, that he could never really get to the bottom of it all, much less anybody else. He helped her more than anybody else. He tried very hard. He did everything he possibly could. But by the end he was beginning to break down because of his own mind and the problems he was facing.

Severn's daughter had no doubt, however, that Ferenczi «ultimately saved my mother's life» (M. Severn, personal communication, 29 January 1989).

After Ferenczi, Elizabeth Severn went on to live and practice therapy for another quarter of a century. She died of leukemia in New York in 1959 at 79 years of age.

Conclusion

In conclusion, I believe that Ferenczi's and Severn's analytical relationship produced a mixed result. Clearly, psychoanalysis has benefitted

222

from the rich legacy of insights gained from this experiment. Ferenczi may have needed a person with Severn's strength to challenge him and see through to his own unresolved countertransference issues. However, the demands of this relationship may have also contributed to his exhaustion. Severn's life may have been «saved», but her chronic symptoms, while more deeply understood, were certainly not resolved.

In this paper, I have focused on the rich complexity of the last phases of Ferenczi's experiment in mutual analysis and of his historic analytical relationship with Elizabeth Severn. I hope to have shed some light, but have undoubtedly raised many questions to be explored in the future.

References

FERENCZI, S. (1933). Confusion of Tongues Between Adults and the Child. *Final Contributions to the Problems and Methods of Psycho-Analysis*. London: Karnac, 1980, pp. 156-167.

— (1932). *The Clinical Diary of Sándor Ferenczi*. Cambridge, Mass.: Harvard University Press, 1988.

— & GRODDECK G. (1982). *Correspondance (1921-1933)*. Paris: Payot.

FORTUNE, C. (1933). The Case of «RN»: Sándor Ferenczi's Radical Experiment in Psychoanalysis. *In:* Aron L. and Harris, A. (Eds), *The Legacy of Sándor Ferenczi*. Hillsdale, N.J.: The Analytic Press, pp. 101-120.

MALCOLM, J. (1982). *Psychoanalysis: The Impossible Profession*. New York: Vintage.

SEVERN, E. (1913). *Psycho-Therapy: Its Doctrine and Practice*. London: Rider & Co.

— (1933). *The Discovery of the Self: A Study in Psychological Cure*. London: Rider & Co.

Cahiers Psychiatriques Genevois, Special Issue, 1994, pp. 225-233

FERENCZI'S ANALYSIS OF JONES IN RELATION TO JONES' SELF-ANALYSIS

R. Andrew Paskauskas

In trying to come to grips with Jones' ambiguous relationship to Ferenczi I have, on previous occasions, given Jones the benefit of the doubt and tried to argue Jones' case like a lawyer defending his client (Paskauskas, 1993, p. 723, n. 3). On this occasion, however, I want to delve more deeply into this historical problem and explore evidence which might lead us to surmise that Jones may possibly have harbored an unconscious hatred towards Ferenczi. To do this we must examine the psychological structure of Jones' relationship to both Ferenczi and Freud during the crucial period of Jones' analysis with Ferenczi in the summer of 1913.

I will begin by examining what we know about Ferenczi's analysis of Jones, which we can do with reference to the Freud-Jones letters (Paskauskas, 1993) and the letters between Freud and Ferenczi (1992); after that I will highlight the portions of Jones' self-analysis that we can reconstruct from his letters to Freud and two of his published case histories (Jones, 1912, 1913).

We must first note that Jones' initial decision to go into analysis with Ferenczi was sparked primarily by Jones' remorse regarding his break with Loe Kann, his common-law wife, who was in analysis with Freud between 1912 and 1914. Indeed, it was in the midst of the trying conditions and the imminent break with Loe that Jones went to Budapest and began his analysis with Ferenczi around early June 1913. The following passage

I would like to express my deep gratitude to Janet C. Powell who read an early version of this paper and made valuable suggestions. For permission to quote passages from the Freud-Ferenczi correspondence, I thank Judith Dupont. Regarding passages from the Freud-Jones correspondence, I thank Harvard University Press.

from a letter to Freud reveals the extent of his disaffection and depression:

> The idea of losing my wife has not yet penetrated fully into my mind. I have difficulty in «taking it in». She has meant so much to me for years, and I held so fast unconsciously on to the *Bedingungslosigkeit* (unconditionality) of her love, that it will cost me pretty severe depression before getting over the blow of seeing her love given to another, especially her *full* love, which I had always dreamed of winning. It is of course worse for me that I know how much I have contributed to the present situation. I only hope that happiness for her will be at least a gain amidst the surrounding loss. For me the next year or two will be especially critical, in many ways, so that the help of this analysis comes just at the right time (Paskauskas, 1993, 3.6.1913, p. 200).

This was probably one of the lowest periods of Jones's life. «I will try of course to pick up the threads again», Jones wrote to Freud, «but my *Lebenslust* (pleasure for life) is not over great.» (*ibid.*, p. 201).

Jones' analysis with Ferenczi can be viewed historically as an attempt by Jones to reconcile his feelings towards Loe. The analysis allowed Jones to deal more adequately with his own emotional state. He realized that his relationship with Loe could only continue as a friendship, and he tried to adapt accordingly (*ibid.*, 17.6.1913, p. 204). Compare the account presented much later by Jones in his autobiography, in which we find no hint of these personal problems, where he writes that:

> When I returned to Vienna in May, I was planning to set up again in practice in London, but as a result of a talk with Freud I decided to make use of the opportunity of not being tied by time and to undertake a didactic analysis with Ferenczi in Budapest. I was the first psychoanalyst to do this. At the time it was a revolutionary idea, but it has since become part of the normal procedure for studying the subject. My analysis, like the rest of my life, was intensive. I spent an hour twice a day on it during that summer and autumn, and derived great benefit from it. It led to a much greater inner harmony with myself, and gave me an irreplaceable insight of the most direct kind into the ways of the unconscious mind which it was highly instructive to compare with the more intellectual knowledge of them I had previously had (Jones, 1959, p. 199).

Now, if we turn to a discussion of the actual analysis we find that it was conducted in German, not over a span of four months, as claimed (*ibid.*, pp. 199, 224), but over a period of two months, stretching from about the beginning of June 1913 towards the latter part of July; in fact, an extremely short time frame compared to today's lengthy didactic analyses.

Jones was pleased with Ferenczi as an analyst. Except for German lessons and a brief interruption in July when Loe undertook a short visit to Budapest, Jones devoted all his energies to Ferenczi, both inside and outside the analysis (Paskauskas, 1993, 3.6.1913, pp. 200-201; 8.7.1913, pp. 209-210; 22.7.1913, pp. 212-214). Indeed, he found him to be very «tactful and kind» (*ibid*, p. 200). Jones also spoke of Ferenczi as being «exceedingly intelligent, as well as kind, and I greatly admire his technique of dealing with me» (*ibid*, p. 203).

Generally speaking, the two colleagues worked well together from the outset of the analysis. Of particular historical significance here is the fact that Jones may have brought up material during his initial sessions with Ferenczi that stemmed from his self-analysis. I infer this from a passage contained in a letter of 7 June 1913 from Ferenczi to Freud:

> I think the analysis with Jones is going to work. For the time being, he interprets too much, *and only provides old material that is already known to him.* He has already produced the (positive) transference in the treatment. He is very intent upon being sincere (that I know from the comparison of his accounts with those which I know from you.) Otherwise he feels rather content (Freud & Ferenczi, 1992, p. 519, my italics).

As the analysis proceeded, Ferenczi was able to uncover several important areas of psychological repression. For example, an unconscious personal resistance to Freud soon surfaced. Jones blamed Freud for the loss of Loe and his friend and mentor Wilfred Trotter. On 11 June 1913 Jones communicated the following explanation to Freud:

> You were of course right about an unconscious personal resistance in regard to yourself... my unconscious, with the logic peculiar to itself, had been blaming you for the loss first of my greatest friend (Trotter), then of my wife, i.e. the man and woman who were dearest to me. With such a great loss it is little wonder that I mechanically sought for someone to blame, especially when I had so much self-blame that needed projecting (Paskauskas, 1993, p. 203).

Jones, however, insisted on pointing out the transitory nature of these negative feelings. He thus continued in the following manner:

> However there isn't any doubt but that this will be only a passing phenomenon, even in the unconscious, for consciously my attitude is quite the opposite, and has been all through. There is no question about appreciating your attitude, for the delicate correctness of this is sky-clear, and I am only sorry that you should have been placed in such a painful situation.

Similarly, both positive and negative feelings towards Ferenczi also surfaced in the course of the analysis. For instance, although Jones was «very agreeable as a friend and colleague», Ferenczi reported to Freud, on 17 June 1913, that:

> ... his dreams are full of scorn and disdain for me, which he must admit, without really being able to believe in these hidden pecularities of character. He also seems to be afraid that I feed everything that I discover in the analysis to you. That is why I beg you never to mention our correspondence in front of Mrs. Jones. I find Jones in many respects scientifically much more valuable for us at present, than before the analysis. By that I do not mean that the analysis has already changed him, but that

previously I underestimated him a little. He is however restrained in output by his super-goodness: he forbids himself any independence, which then avenges itself through a preference for intrigue, secret triumphs and underhandedness. I hope that the weeks here will be useful to him. I find him already a little less unassuming, that is, more sincere (with others and with himself). He learns German assiduously and makes good progress in it (Freud & Ferenczi., 1992, p. 522).

Ferenczi also discovered very strong, but concealed aggressive tendencies in Jones that proved to be the basis of certain impulsive behaviours. Ferenczi's analysis helped Jones to reconcile these tendencies and to achieve greater control over the impulses (Paskauskas, 1993, 17.6.1913, p. 204). He was patient with Jones' eccentricities and changes of mood. The two spent much time together in scientific talks, and seemed to understand each other very well. Thus, on 23 June 1913 Ferenczi wrote to Freud: «Jones is my best and most likeable patient, he is able, intelligent, obedient, at the same time a truly trustworthy friend; I hope we will be able to build upon him» (Freud & Ferenczi, 1992, p. 524). For his part, Jones spoke of Ferenczi as possessing «a beautiful imagination, perhaps not always thoroughly disciplined, but always suggestive. He has been exceedingly kind to me here, and I shall always remember it» (Paskauskas, 1993, 8.7.1913, p. 210). At the conclusion of the analysis Jones wrote:

> Well, my analysis is drawing towards a close, and I have found it so valuable that I am wondering if I can manage to get in another month next year. It has without doubt been successful in making me face more clearly various character traits and dangerous tendencies, and I trust that it will prove its value also when it comes to be tested in actual life. I cannot praise Ferenczi too highly for his skill and tact throughout, and he has also succeeded in making it congruous with the analysis to be very kind «out of school», so that on the whole I have had a very enjoyable time in Budapest (*ibid.* 22.7.1913, p. 213).

Ferenczi, for his part, did have some reservations, which on 26 July 1913 he expressed to Freud in the following way:

> Jones works diligently; I hope that the analysis will be useful to him in every respect; he still cannot entirely emancipate himself from his latent tendencies (although he is very optimistic about that) (Freud & Ferenczi, 1992, p. 531).

But in the end, on 5 August 1913, Ferenczi admitted his warm feelings toward Jones in these words:

> Jones took his leave of me four days ago. I regret it deeply. We became intimate friends. I taught him love and respect; it was a pleasure to have such an intelligent, keen and distinguished pupil. The result of the analysis on him was very favourable. His convictions became more securely consolidated, his independence enhanced... mastery of his neurotic tendencies will hopefully soon follow – however, in the mean time, I do not venture to place a more positive prognosis (*ibid.*, p. 500).

After the analysis Jones decided to put out an English version of Ferenczi's papers. In August of 1913 he wrote to Freud that «my first two months will be given to translating Ferenczi» (Paskauskas, 1993, 18.8.1913, p. 221). The volume came out in 1916 with a preface by Jones as a kind of «*hommage à Ferenczi*» (Jones, 1916).

Although on the surface level, we may view relations between Jones and Ferenczi as having being excellent in the period during and immediately after the analytic sessions of the summer of 1913, nevertheless, we must accept the fact that negative feelings towards Ferenczi had surfaced at an early point in Jones' analysis (Freud & Ferenczi, 1992, p. 522), and that these feelings may have formed the basis of a negative transference.

Unfortunately, we cannot go much further in our attempts to uncover the details of Ferenczi's analysis of Jones. However, we can delve more deeply into the structure of Jones' transference towards Ferenczi by examining the critical elements of Jones' self-analysis.

Although it is difficult to date precisely the beginning of the self-analysis, it is clear that by the middle of 1910 Jones was engaged deeply in the process. In that year Jones admitted to Freud that from childhood on up to young adulthood he had sustained a condition of mild neurosis which consisted of obsessive tendencies and anxiety. He revealed to Freud that:

> ... I consider myself fairly «normal», perhaps not quite so much as the average. I had a number of *Zwang* and *Angst* symptoms, especially in juvenile life, never very serious, though quite pathological – since then analysed (Paskauskas, 1993, 28.6.1910, pp. 62-63).

More specifically, Jones was affected by a phobia of heights, emotional distress regarding any authority figure, persistent nightmares, as well as a number of obsessive acts which for many years he was neither able to control nor to account for. Jones typically described his phobia of heights as a manifestation of «morbid anxiety (dread, nervousness, giddiness, palpitation, tachycardia, and sweating, etc.)» (Jones, 1913, p. 508). The symptoms were most severe whenever he stood on an edge that overlooked deep water. His specific experience of the associated anxiety took different forms: he might simply experience a fear of falling, he might experience a fear of jumping over; or, if another man was close by when Jones was near a dangerous edge, he would fear that he might be thrown over (*ibid.*, p. 508).

To Freud, and in a disguised fashion in print, Jones provided several examples of traumatic experiences, which had given rise to feelings of intense anxiety: at the age of three, when the family doctor hung Jones in a high water butt; at the age of seven, when a teacher suspended Jones upside down by his ankles over a wall looking down a hill and threatened to let him drop; at the age of nine, when his father forced the young, unwilling Jones to walk around the top of a high tower; and, finally, at the age of ten, when he was manoeuvered unexpectedly to sit on a high window ledge (Paskauskas, *ibid.*, p. 63; Jones, 1913, pp. 509-510).

Jones' phobia of heights was closely tied to his anxiety concerning «any authority or master, from school up,» accompanied by «a certain dread and especially a fear of being blamed, of being found out in wrong-doing» that «arose from a strong guilt-complex,» and until adulthood had given him «more suffering than anything else in life» (Paskauskas, 1993, 30.1.1912, p. 130).

In addition to the phobia and the problem of anxiety, at least two obsessive acts frustrated Jones' existence from the age of twelve up to early adulthood. First, in writing letters, or in jotting down addresses, Jones would persistently make use of a special symbol to undersign his documents, and he had always assumed that it stood for «science» (*ibid.*, 12.2.1910, p. 44). A second obsession, which manifested itself, was the placing of a wooden stethoscope, which he never used, on his consulting room desk between himself and the patient's chair. He did this compulsively, repeating a practice that he enacted on the hospital wards in London when he was a medical intern, and imitating another doctor. whom Jones greatly admired (*ibid.*, 28.6.1910, p. 63).

Psychoanalysis provided Jones with explanations for both these compulsive acts by revealing the crucial role played by Jones' family in shaping his psychological development. For example, his self-analysis revealed an unconscious erotic attraction towards the mother, coupled with an intense unconscious hatred for the father; affects which in a similar fashion were also carried over into his relationships with his two younger sisters, Elizabeth and Sybil, his common-law wife, Loe Kann, and the men in his life that he admired. Let us consider the dynamics of these relationships in more depth.

In *A Simple Phobia*, Jones revealed that he was «a fretful child, much given to crying» (Jones, 1913, p. 509); that he was «very sickly and ailing» and «his mother was of an unusually affectionate disposition», and that «he was the only child» and « unduly pampered by his mother, who doted on her first-born, and nursed him night and day» (*ibid.*, p. 512).

The extent to which the Œdipus complex was repressed in Jones, came out vividly in his dreams. One specific dream, revealed in a letter to Freud, «concerned an indescribably beautiful mass of architecture, palaces with marvellous corridors». Jones traced it back to an anal fixation in relation to the mother. As he admitted to Freud, the dream «turned out to be an infantile one about the genitalia of my parents, particularly my mother (anal)» (Paskauskas, 1993, 10.11.1910, p. 76).

Although other dreams and experiences revealed the classical Œdipus complex at work in Jones' psyche (*ibid.*, 30.7.1912, pp. 146-147), his relationship to his father was complicated by the presence of an additional male figure: the family doctor, «a man who was closely identified in his mind with his father» (Jones, 1913, p. 513). The doctor lived with the Jones family, and Jones admired him a great deal. As Jones explained to Freud, the doctor was «a handsome dare-devil fellow. We were in a small country-place, and he lived with us till I was three years old». That «the doctor was loved by all the women of the neighbourhood», made a lasting impression on Jones. «When the doctor died», Jones wrote to Freud, «my mother cried, and I heard her tell my father how kind he had always been to her, and how he had kissed her consolingly the last time he attended her. I recall feeling jealous, or, to be more accurate, wondering if my father was jealous» (Paskauskas, 1993, 28.6.1910, p. 63).

The extent to which Jones identified with the doctor can be discerned by his behaviour at a crucial point in his adolescence. When Jones was twelve years old the doctor died and, as Jones told Freud, «the enormous crowd of weeping women», that he saw at the doctor's funeral, made a deep impression on him (*ibid.*, p. 63). Several years after this incident he decided at the age of fifteen to enter medicine. Although the decision was «sudden», analysis revealed that it was based on his admiration for the doctor and his desire to be like him (*ibid.*, p. 63).

Jones' relationship to the doctor was psychologically complex. For Jones, on the one hand, the doctor represented a «Knight in shining armour», a kind of ladies man whom Jones identified with in choosing to become a doctor himself. Jones also had explained that in several dreams the doctor attacked him with a sword, which, for Jones, symbolized the stethoscope, and the doctor's penis. To Freud, he wrote: «stethescope (*sic*) = sword = penis. ("The pen is mightier than the sword", and pen and stethescope each represent the chief weapon of two great professions.)» (*ibid.*, p. 64). The «sword» itself symbolized Jones's masculinity. Thus, as a womanizer, a «Knight in shining armour», like the family doctor, Jones was conscious of sexual attractions to patients and had to protect himself, and them, from his own prowess. He wrote to Freud:

> I was always much struck by the story of one of the British Knights of the Round Table, I forget if it was Sir Lancelot or Sir Galahad. who slept with a maiden with a drawn sword between them to keep him from temptation, and to reassure her of her safety. The meaning, therefore, of the wooden stethoscope on my desk is quite clear. I still keep it there! (*ibid.*)

On the other hand, however, the family doctor was a powerful male figure who brought out the feminine side of Jones' character. As Jones wrote to Freud:

> ... I have no doubt that I was in love with him, and that at the age of 3 8/12, when my younger sister was born, I had the double phantasy that she was the child (a) of the doctor and myself, (b) of myself and my mother.

Jones goes on to say that:

> Now, I well remember, when about ?7 (*sic*) years old, being examined by the doctor who used a single, wooden stethescope, and it is easy to recall the erotic sensation I got, during the rhythmic chest movements, from the pressure of the instrument. I must at that time have unconsciously symbolized it as his penis (*ibid.*, p. 63).

At this point, let me emphasize that, from the psychoanalytic standpoint, the two key figures of Jones' youth (his father and the family doctor) seem to parallel the two great figures of his formal analysis (Ferenczi and Freud).

In the first place, just as the family doctor's influence shaped Jones' early years as a would-be doctor, so Freud's personal influence was significant in shaping Jones' formative years as a psychoanalyst. When he had initially met Freud at Salzburg in April of 1908, Jones had for the first time in his life met a man who, in spite of his authority and rank, could understand him and not blame him for any wrong-doing. In 1912 Jones confessed to Freud that:

> ... you were the only man of position I had ever met who knew what it was to feel young in heart, meaning that you had the power of comprehending the trials and difficulties of youth. I felt at the same time that I would listen to criticism and guidance from you in a way that I had never before been willing to from anyone. The more I have got to know you the plainer has become that first impression (*ibid.*, 30.1.1912, p. 130).

Second, it is also clear from the historical documents that Jones took on a «feminine role» in his relationship to Freud, just as he had done with the family doctor during his infancy. In 1910 Jones explained his position to Freud in this way:

> ... I feel it is a more sensible ideal to aim at developing one's own capacity in whatever direction that may lie than in merely trying to be «original». The originality-complex is not strong with me; my ambition is rather to know, to be «behind the scenes,» and «in the know», rather than *to find out*. I realise that I have very little talent for originality; any talent I may have lies rather in the direction of being able to see perhaps quickly what others point out: no doubt that also has its use in the world. Therefore my work will be to try to work out in detail, and to find new demonstrations for the truth of ideas that others have suggested. To me work is like a woman bearing a child; to men like you, I suppose it is more like the male fertilisation (*ibid.*, 19.6.1910, p. 61).

What is not so obvious, however, is the fact that Jones may well have experienced an unconscious identification with his dead mother (Freud, 1917e) at about the same time that he made a firm commitment to Freud to dedicate his life to psychoanalysis. From the psychoanalytic standpoint it is tempting to posit this as an important mechanism in the formation of Jones' close psychological attachment to Freud, especially with respect to his self-defined feminine role.

Consider, for example, that Jones' mother died in the spring of 1909 and that her death in fact coincided almost exactly with the period in which Jones made a firm decision to commit his life to Freud's work. Indeed, shortly after the Worcester celebrations of September 1909, the young Jones was moved to write that «about six or eight months ago I determined not only to further the cause by all means in my power, which I had always decided on, but also to further it by whatever means you personally decided on, and to follow your recommendations as exactly as possible» (*ibid.*, 17.10.1909, p. 29).

If we now take a look at the psychological dynamics at work here, does this mean that Freud, from Jones' perspective, takes on a role that was formerly played by the family doctor during Jones' infancy? If so, then does this also imply that Ferenczi takes on the role of the dreaded father, whom, as mentioned, Jones unconsciously hated? If we can answer the latter question in the affirmative, then it might help us understand more fully Jones' castigation of Ferenczi in later years (*ibid.*, 3.6.1933, p. 723, n. 3).

To close, I would like to challenge the professional analysts to speculate further on the possible unconscious mechanisms at work here and to delve more deeply into the psychological implications of this web of historical material, especially the factors that may allow us to gain a deeper insight into Jones' life-long commitment to Freud, as well as his ambiguous relationship with Ferenczi.

References

FREUD, S. (1917e). Mourning and Melancholia. *Standard Edition, 14*, 239-260.

— & FERENCZI, S. (1992). *Correspondence, vol. 1, 1908-1914.* Cambridge, Mass.: Harvard University Press, 1994.

JONES, E. (1912). A Forgotten Dream (Note on the Oedipus Saving Phantasy). *Journal of Abnormal Psychology, 7*, 5-16.

— (1913). A Simple Phobia. *In: Papers on Psycho-Analysis,* 2nd ed., revised and enlarged. Toronto: MacMillan Company of Canada, 1918.

— (1916). Translation of S. Ferenczi. *In: Contributions to Pschoanalysis.* Boston: R.G. Badger.

— (1959). *Free Associations. Memories of a Psycho-Analyst.* New York: Basic Books.

PASKAUSKAS, R.A. (Ed.) (1993). *The Complete Correspondence of Sigmund Freud and Ernest Jones, 1908-1939.* Cambridge, Mass.: Belknap.

Cahiers Psychiatriques Genevois, Special Issue, 1994, pp. 235-255

THE CONFUSION OF TONGUES THEORY: FERENCZI'S LEGACY TO PSYCHOANALYSIS

Arnold Wm. Rachman

The significance of «The Confusion of Tongues» theory

As Ferenczi's clinical work rejoins the mainstream of psychoanalytic thought, a revolution presently begun, his capacity to conceptualize the analytic process and the nature of human relations will also become appreciated. Although, better known as a clinician than a theory builder, or a systematizer, Ferenczi did leave psychoanalysis with a very significant theoretical framework which has been largely ignored by traditionalists and not given sufficient attention by even the liberal wing of psychoanalysis. I am, of course, referring to the *Confusion of Tongues Between Adults and Children: The Language of Tenderness and Passion* (Ferenczi, 1932/1949), delivered by Ferenczi at the 12th International Psychoanalytic Conference, at Wiesbaden on September 4, 1932. The attempts to suppress and censor this paper and its influence have been chronicled elsewhere (Cremerius, 1983; Fromm, 1959; Masson, 1984; Rachman, 1989; 1993 a, b, c, d; 1994 a, b; 1995).

These attempts at suppression and censorhip were actually very successful since the paper and the implications for technique and theory were lost to psychoanalysis for several generations (Cremerius, 1983; Masson, 1984; Rachmann, 1994, 1995).

With the rediscovery of Ferenczi's life and work in the last decade or so, it is time to delve more deeply into Ferenczi's legacy, and begin to realize that his last presentation and paper contain the outline of a significant contribution to psychoanalytic theory. In fact, one can hypothesize that Freud realized how significant an alternate view his «favorite son» had developed, since the idea was the first dissident view that altered the œdipal theory of neurosis, presented by the outstanding clinician of his time (or, in this author's opinion, Ferenczi was a clinical genius and psychanalysis's greatest practitioner). Ferenczi's theory had significant implications for the understanding of trauma, the conduct of psychoanalysis, and issues of disturbed human relations (Rachman, 1994; 1995).

The suppression and censorship of The Confusion of Tongues paper

Freud's reaction to the paper

Sándor Ferenczi was not a child psychoanalyst, but he had a profound intellectual, emotional, and professional interest in children. In personal interactions with children, he was warm, friendly, loving, and animated (Lehrner, 1932). As André Haynal has recently noted, Ferenczi was very close to *the child within the adult* (Haynal, 1993). Melanie Klein wrote that she had a debt of gratitude towards Ferenczi and that he had «a streak of genius» (Grosskurth, 1986, p. 73). Indeed, it was Ferenczi (Klein's first analyst) who encouraged her to go into the psychoanalysis of children.

This special gift of empathy and understanding of children and the traumas they endured *within their own families* fueled Ferenczi's clinical work. He also made many significant attempts to understand how the child can cope with the trauma of seduction.

The Confusion of Tongues Paper delivered at the 12th International Psychoanalytic Congress on Sunday, September 4, 1932 at The Hotel Rose in Wiesbaden, Germany, was Ferenczi's courageous and significant attempt to present an alternate version to the œdipal theory of neurosis. It was the first object relations theory, emphasizing the actual relational dimensions of parent/child interaction which give rise to psychopathology and personality difficulties. Freud's decision to suppress Ferenczi's theory was a complicated and overdetermined reaction. Among the plausible explanations for censorhip are: (1) Freud's desire to protect his œdipal explanation of neurosis as the cornerstone for psychoanalytic theory; (2) Freud's mistaken conclusion that Ferenczi's relaxation therapy and Confusion of Tongues Theory were «regressive» measures fueled by psychopathology rather than creativity; (3) Freud's anxiety that Ferenczi's dissidence signaled his desire to reject him and leave mainstream psychoanalysis as Jung and Rank had done; (4) Freud's denial that sexual seduction was a relevant clinical variable in the psychanalysis of the 1930's or in his own life (Krüll, 1986; Rachman, 1993, 1994), (5) Freud's disdain for non-neurotic patients who need empathy rather than interpretation, and need to deal with relational rather than drive-conflict issues (Kohut, 1984; Mitchell, 1988; Rachman, 1989).

Ferenczi's removal from mainstream psychoanalysis

The void in psychoanalytic literature regarding Ferenczi's Confusion of Tongues theory is clearly due to a successful attempt at suppression and censorship of his dissident views, first by Freud, and then the orthodox psychoanalytic community. I have reviewed this darkest moment in psychoanalytic history in several publications (Rachman, 1989; 1993a, b; 1994; 1995). Clearly, the removal of Ferenczi's ideas and methods, from mainstream psychoanalysis, particularly his «relaxation therapy» (Ferenczi, 1930) and the theory of childhood trauma caused by sexual seduction (Ferenczi, 1933/1949), created a void so that he was ignored as a significant figure in the history of psychoanalysis. What is more, his ideas were not viewed as having sufficient merit for serious psychoanalytic thinkers. The process of censorhip was so complete that up until the 1970's, Ferenczi's work was not formally studied at any IPA approved psychoanalytic training institute in North America. He was only briefly mentioned, if at all, at dissident institutes, such as William Alanson White (Ortmeyer, 1992), or in my own analytic training, at The Postgraduate Center For Mental Health in New York. Lewis Wolberg, the late Founder and Medical Director of the Postgraduate Center, was analyzed by Ferenczi's analysand Clara Thompson. Wolberg, interestingly enough was a modern pioneer in the active method of psychoanalysis and was considered to be flexible, innovative and daring. In all my training, which took place from 1964-1968, whether it be course work, supervision, special lectures or seminars by invited scholars and personal analysis, Ferenczi's name was never spoken, nor did it ever appear on a reading list. I was able to rectify this oversight when I taught the first course on Ferenczi's work in 1989 at the Postgraduate Center.

Recently I was astounded to hear that the suppression of Ferenczi's paper and its implications had not only occurred in English-speaking countries, but also in Ferenczi's native land. It is all the more remarkable, since Ferenczi was the founder of Hungarian psychoanalysis. Hidas, one of the current leaders of Hungarian psychoanalysis and president of the Ferenczi Society, has brought this suppression to light (Hidas, 1993). Ferenczi's paper cannot be found in any Hungarian journal, even though Ferenczi has one hundred papers published in the Hungarian medical journal *Gyógyászat*. The paper was first published in Hungary in 1971

237

(thirty-nine years after it was presented at Wiesbaden), in a book by Béla Buda entitled *Psychoanalysis and its Modern Tendencies*, published at a commemorative meeting on Ferenczi's work. After 1971, the paper disappeared again from Hungarian psychoanalysis. According to Hidas (1993), this paper and any discussion of it are not to be found in contemporary Hungarian psychoanalysis.

The Confusion of Tongues theory

I would like to present my understanding of Ferenczi's theory in an elaboration which attempts to anchor it in an object relations perspective[1] in three basic areas of human functioning:

1. The parent/child experience, especially where seduction and trauma have intruded into the relationship.

2. The analyst/analysand encounter which has the potentiality for retraumatization.

3. The experience in any dyadic relationship where issues of seduction, power, status, and control predominate.

In this way we can appreciate the significant contribution Ferenczi has made to the understanding and treatment of human relationships in any form where manipulation, abuse of power and inequality predominate.

The Confusion of Tongues theory is basically a description of a relational psychology of child/parent interaction. Ferenczi's theory was a reinterpretation of the œdipal tragedy. It is an elaboration of the interpersonal, relational dimension of the family drama, based on the real experiences between parents and children, not solely on the child's intrapsychic developmentally-driven fantasy life. This version of the œdipal drama encourages the clinician to examine the nature of the object relations between family members, acknowledge actual trauma, help individuals to differentiate their pathologies from the caretakers, and develop strategies to recover from the persons and interpersonal damage of abusive relationships.

The parent/child experience where seduction and trauma predominate

1. The parent, usually the father, misinterprets the natural need for affection and relatedness by his child, usually the daughter, as «lust», which

is his *own* projection onto the child. This does not mean the child doesn't have sexual feelings. There is a phase appropriate element of sexuality and sensuality embedded within the overall, total parent/child interaction. But the overtly sexual interaction *must* be kept at the level of fantasy. When the parent, under the pressure of his/her own unhealthy narcissistic and inappropriate needs, distorts the total motivation of the child, reducing it to a predominately sexual, erotic one, the stage is set for pathological, incestuous, acting out with the child.

2. The parent *confuses* the natural phase appropriate *longings for tenderness*, sensuality, affection, and attachment oriented play by the child *for erotic sexuality*, thereby reducing the complexity of normal attachment strivings for merely one of its components. In object relations terms, the parent initiates a «part-object» relationship, and uses the child as a «discharge object» rather than as a whole object, in which the capacity for sublimation and concern predominates.

3. The child's sense of reality can be seriously altered in such an interaction with an adult, where the adult exercises status, power, and control over the child. Ferenczi first emphasized sexual seduction of the child but also mentioned parental unresponsiveness to the child's needs (Ferenczi, 1932/1988; 1933). What is more, the parent is emotionally unavailable to help the child understand what has happened to him/her. This is especially true when the adult denies the reality of the seductive experience or the unresponsiveness, attempting to convince the child that a different experience has taken place. In the case of sexual seduction, the parent attempts to convince the child that a «loving experience » has occurred. In the case of emotional unresponsiveness, neglect or abuse, the child also feels abandoned and at the mercy to his/her own feelings, without parental acknowledgement that a disturbing experience has occurred. This insidiously invalidates the child's perception of reality.

4. The child becomes confused about the reality of his/her experience. What is more, a child can actually deny his/her subjective experience while adapting to the parent's distorted reality. The child is then left in a confused state which, once dissociated, remains essentially the same. Because the sexual experience is traumatic the child splits off the traumatic experience, including the image of him/herself at the time as a victimized, helpless, overwhelmed, frightened, angry, and confused individual (Bollas, 1991; Modell, 1991; Searles, 1986; Stierlin, 1959).

5. Once repressed, this dissociated state fails to change (it remains unconsciously timeless), becomes semi-autonomous, and continues to influence the adult personality, unconsciously. It thereby exerts an ego-weakening, disruptive effect on healthy adult functioning, especially in the area of mature object relations.

6. The parental seducer can seriously influence the child's sense of reality, *because* the child's reality testing is still in the process of developing. A child's sense of reality can easily be destabilized when trauma and associated «reactive fantasies» intrude. The distinction is being made here between reactive fantasies and innate sexual fantasies. Fantasies that occur as a reaction to real trauma are distinguished from the traditional (Freudian) notion that there are innate sexual fantasies caused by innate drives. One can summarize the subjective experience of the child as follows: «I was seduced because I am bad, or I did something to make it happen: I feel guilty and I need to be punished: there is something wrong with me.»

7. The child is developmentally inclined to believe the parent's presentation of reality because acceptance of parental authority is associated with love, protection, and object attachment. Seduction fosters a profound sense of betrayal, not in just the parent, but in the capacity to perceive reality accurately. This then engenders a serious difficulty in trusting one's perceptions. Manifestations of this difficulty appear in masochistic patients who repeatedly enter into abusive relationships from which they are unable to protect themselves, or extricate themselves (Miller, 1980; 1986; Rachman, 1992).

8. Besides the alteration of reality, parental authority also prevents the child from talking about their sense of confusion. The child is confused, realizing at some level that his/her experience is derived from the parent's, but they cannot give voice to this difference, since it is associated with the danger of loss of parental love, retaliation, and abandonment. In essence, the child becomes «tongue tied», both literally and figuratively. This is further compounded by the fact that at this immature level of cognitive development, the child actually needs the parent's help to understand and verbalize what has happened to her or him. This requires truthful explanations given in the context of emotional support, something which the abusive parent is quite unable to do (Ferenczi, 1928, 1933; Rachman, 1993 a, b, c). Emotional support cannot come from a parent who is narcissistically intruding his/her needs onto a child and is hence insensitive to the child's needs.

9. Because the child is not helped to understand and verbalize the effects of the seduction, a pathological split-off nucleus (of traumatic affect, self-image, relational interaction) develops and becomes the basis for later psychopathology by arresting and distorting moral development. This effects all subsequent developmental stages and tasks, including the ego functions of drive regulation, reality testing, self and affect regulation, and object relations during each stage.

10. The major defenses that Ferenczi described that enable the child to cope with the actual sexual seduction are: splitting, dissociation, denial, detachment, blunted affect, confusion and identification with aggressor.

   a) Splitting means that the child is unable to integrate the extremes of the parent's actual behavior, from non-seductive to suddenly seductive, invasive, intrusive, and massively overstimulating. It is not merely a defense against contaminating the good image of the parent with the child's innate aggression towards the bad image, but stems from the parent's extreme erratic behavior. (This is a non-Kleinian view of splitting.) This explanation is more of an actual object relational view than Klein's because the splitting is related to the quality of the parent's extreme behavior in the present and not based predominately on the child's fantasies and distortions of reality. The parent's *real* behavior is so extreme and unexpected that the child's ego is unable to integrate such a «split» in the parent's action.

      1. Consequently the intensity of the trauma and the painful effects that ensue are so great that it disrupts and impedes the synthetic and integrative functions of the child's ego (Rachman, 1991). This results in the persistence of a developmental lack of integration, which is typically referred to as «splitting». It is manifested in the person shifting from one extreme state to another, in which the images of the self or the other are extreme opposites, which are not integrated into a whole, balanced realistic component. Therefore, the parent, or the self (for every object there is a self, since for every object image there is a self image that goes with it), remains either all good or all bad, when the person is in either extreme emotional, or «self state». But to view this phenomenon merely as a defense against object directed aggression misses the earlier developmental interferences with normal integration caused by the parent's actual seductive or abusive behavior.

2. The earlier the sexual trauma, the greater the capacity to integrate is arrested. If the seduction occurs befor the age of three, it is likely the child will remain arrested in a state of severe fragmentation, in which the self and object world, and other important aspects of reality functioning will be experienced with massive discontinuities, irregularities, and bewildering confusion.

b) Confusion means the individual is left, both during and after the seduction, in a confusional state. From the object relations viewpoint, the child has internalized an introject that disrupts reality-oriented thinking and prohibits thinking about what actually occurred. Consequently, the child, and subsequently the adult, doubts his/her own perception of reality, and is often unable to perceive the actual abuse in later abusive relationships to which he/she masochistically clings.

c) Detachment is a defense against getting emotionally reattached to an abusive object and re-experiencing the trauma. Psychologically, it consists of removing oneself intrapsychically from an interpersonal field and from one's painful feelings.

d) Dissociation is a phenomenon in which the split-off parts become quasi-autonomous and take on lives of their own, dominating the person's consciousness and behavior. This results in internal objects and split-off parts of the self which exist as static, unmodified, pathological motivational systems, in which the original trauma is repeatedly re-enacted and replayed. This constitutes an object relations view of the repetition compulsion (Fairbairn, 1952), to relive, and repeat earlier internalized object relations. Freud's ego psychology did emphasize the attempt to achieve mastery over the earlier trauma by repeating it, but missed the person's need to remain attached to earlier abusive objects, despite stated conscious aversion to those very objects.

e) Blunted affect is the habituation of emotional detachment and also a manifestation of feeling «dead inside» (Bollas, 1991). The child feels he/she has been psychically murdered («soul murder», Shengold, 1989). Incest survivors talk about being «murdered» by the abusive parent for they feel that the trusting, affectionate, loving child-self in them has been destroyed by the abuse. They no longer have access to a wide range of normal feelings, the consequence of chronic affect defenses against vulnerability, pain, abuse, fear and betrayal. It is as if a piece of them has died, ever since the experience of sexual seduction.

f) Identification with the aggressor was discovered by Ferenczi in his attempt to understand the psychodynamics of victimization. This defense mechanism has been attributed to Anna Freud, which she supposedly introduced in her 1936 book, *The Ego and the Mechanisms of Defense.* But the chronology of discovery favors Ferenczi. In the German original of the Confusion of Tongues paper, published in 1933, the term appears for the first time. On the bottom of page 11, Ferenczi writes of «*ängstlicher Identifizierung and Introjektion...*», fearful identification with and introjection of the threatening or attacking person[2] (Ferenczi, 1933). In the original English translation by Michael Balint, Ferenczi described this mechanism as follows: «The same anxiety, however, if it reaches a certain maximum, compels them [children who have been seduced] to subordinate themselves like automata to the will of the aggressor, to divine each one of his desires and to gratify these; completely oblivious of themselves, they identify themselves with the aggressor» (Ferenczi, 1933/1949, p. 162). According to Ferenczi, «the parental seducer» is able to continue the molestation because the child's ego is not fully developed and can be submerged by «...the overpowering force and authority of the adult» (p. 162).

Identification with the aggressor is a complicated mechanism that can help explain the masochistic bond that develops in an abusive situation. The child, instead of «rebelling» or rejecting the hated and abusive object, psychologically attaches itself to the parental seducer. It is a desperate but effective way to gain, or continue, an «affectionate» tie with the parent, maintaining the fiction (delusion, if you wish), that the seduction is an act of tenderness. By introjecting the bad object, the child attempts to master the trauma by becoming like the oppressor. In instances of massive trauma, where the individual is overpowered, demoralized, or numbed in his/her senses, in a pathologic environment which offers «no exit» (Kafka, 1948), identification with the aggressor becomes the only alternative for maintaining the psychological life force of the individual. As has been pointed out, the trauma of sexual seduction usually occurs in an unconsolidated developing child, lacking the emotional capacities to reject the aggression or the means to «flee the scene» of the family for a protected safe alternative. It is just these vulnerable conditions of childhood that make seduction a heinous act, characterized by many incest survivors as: «The work of the devil»; «an act of profound evil» (Rachman, 1993c). Identification with the aggressor is a child's way to cope with the overpowering trauma of incest, which constitutes an exercise in power, control, and aggression of an authority over a subordinate.

It can also explain the phenomenon of a child acting out sexual abuse with someone else: a child abused by a parent then molests a sibling or friend. This dynamic is not seen in the experience of a child solely as a wish to be powerful, inflict harm on others, or master anxiety. One can distinguish an inherent communicative function, or an effort to convey the child's internal state to another person. It is an attempt to force the other to feel what he feels, which is contained in the idea of projective identification («putting» one's own internal state into the other person, by acting with them, in such a way as to induce in the other person what one is feeling: compelling one to know their experience on a visceral level). Essentially, the child is signalling its distress about the trauma by causing the other person to feel it (Ogden, 1979).

Identification with the aggressor, therefore, is not just an interpersonal manifestation of an essentially intrapsychic process, but contains a relational function. The individual wants his/her distress to be understood and ameliorated by a significant other. This is what is meant by the notion of «containment» of projective identifications in normal development or in psychoanalytic treatment.

Ferenczi's Confusion of Tongues

If we can accept the relational perspective as part of the issue of the concept of identification with the aggressor, then we can attempt to apply it to Ferenczi's functioning as well. There is some suggestive evidence that Ferenczi himself may have suffered a childhood seduction and emotional trauma. The emotional trauma centers around his relationship with his mother. Ferenczi was one of a very large family, where maternal nurturance was diluted by the need to attend to such a large brood in a busy household, where the family business functioned as a gathering place for a host of people. What is more, Ferenczi refers to his mother as a «harsh» individual (Grubrich-Simitis, 1986).

These pieces of information suggest Ferenczi may have experienced an ongoing failure in empathy as a child, which left him with a special sensitivity to the emotional trauma of others. He transformed his own trauma into viewing the child's experience of trauma, especially «the child in the adult» experience.

Additional evidence for childhood trauma now comes from the publication of Ferenczi's *Clinical Diary*. There are several passages which suggest he was the victim of a childhood sexual seduction (Ferenczi, 1932/1988):

1. «The analyst's association in fact move in the direction of an episode in his infancy. "Szaraz dajka" (nurse) affair, at the age of one year» (p. 13).

2. «... The identity between the analyst and the analysand: both had been forced to do more and endure more sexually than they had in fact wanted to» (p. 15).

3. «While telling the "analyst" about this, I submerged myself deeply in the reproduction of infantile experiences; the most evocative image was the vague appearance of female figures; probably servant girls from earliest childhood; then the image of a corpse, whose abdomen I was opening up presumably in the dissecting room; linked to this the mad fantasy that I was being pressed into this wound in the corpse. Interpretation: the after-effect of passionate scenes, which presumably did take place, in the course of which a housemaid probably allowed me to play with her breasts, but then pressed my head between her legs, so that I became frightened and felt I was suffocating. This is the source of my hatred of females: I want to dissect them for it, that is, to kill them. This is why my mother's accusation «you are my murderer» cut to the heart and led to (1) a compulsive desire to help anyone who is suffering, especially women; and (2) a flight from situations in which I would have to be aggressive. Thus inwardly the feeling that in fact I am a good chap, also exaggerated reactions of rage, even at trivial affronts, and finally exaggerated reactions of guilt at the slightest lapse» (pp. 60-61).

Sexual trauma in childhood has been a factor in the lives of other psychoanalytic pioneers: Freud (Krüll, 1979); Jung (McGuire, 1974); Rank (Goldwert, 1986).

Professional hypocrisy: healing through relationship

The second area of the Confusion of Tongues Ferenczi identified was between the analyst and the analysand. No doubt this angered Freud and the analytic community, since the implication was that the analyst could be involved in a emotional and interpersonal seduction of his analysand, which would lead to retraumatization. To suggest that Freud and his followers, through their behavior in the psychoanalytic session may actually be causing the individual to repeat the trauma of his childhood, however unknowingly that was being done, was an outrage.

Now Ferenczi was not only calling analysts potential private seducers of their children, but also seducers of their patients. With this contention Ferenczi apparently alienated the entire analytic community.

Ferenczi identified a «confusion of tongues in patients» caused by the «professional hypocrisy» of the analyst. He introduced the concept of «professional hypocrisy» to describe this version of a Confusion of Tongues (Ferenczi, 1933, p. 158):

> We greet the patient with politeness when he enters our room, ask him to start with his associations and promise him faithfully that we will listen attentively to him, give our undivided interest to his well-being and to the work needed for it. In reality, however, it may happen that we can only with difficulty tolerate external or internal features of the patient, or perhaps we feel unpleasantly disturbed in some professional or personal affair by the analytic session (Ferenczi, 1933, p. 159).

Ferenczi was identifying a confusion of tongues in the psychoanalytic situation, characterized by the analysand experiencing the analyst as unempathic. The analysand cannot speak of the experience. «Something had been left unsaid in the relation between physician and patient, *something insincere...*» (p. 159, italics added). Ferenczi was identifying the relational dimension in the psychoanalytic situation, where the analyst is not willing to create a democratic, mutual, emotionally sincere relationship with the analysand. The analyst, he suggested, hides behind the tradition of interpretation of transference and resistance when faced with negative feelings being expressed by the analysand. Such a tradition does not incorporate, as Ferenczi recommended, an ongoing analysis of the countertransference, nor a stance which encourages the analyst to examine his contribution to the analytic process. In the Confusion of Tongues paper, Ferenczi urged psychoanalysis to commit itself to a two-person psychology, the analysis of the analyst in relationship to the analysand. Interpolating the message of Ferenczi's clinical thinking into an axiom, we would say: «If patients are to get better, the analysts must also get better and become, for each patient, a better analyst» (Scharff, 1990).

Ferenczi made a remarkable contribution on behalf of the analysand in the psychoanalytic situation. By encouraging analysands to give full expression to their feelings about the analyst and then not forming a resistance or even transference interpretation, he validated the analysand's perception of what he or she was experiencing. The analytic situation is reality. The analysand is upset because of something the analyst said or did. This is not to deny that the patient's reaction to the analyst has transferential implications, but the transferential meaning is explored after the reality of the psychoanalytic situation is identified and verified. The transferential reaction amplifies and intensifies the meaning of the reality, anchors it in a historical context, but does not obfuscate the realness, reality, or relational dimensions of the therapeutic encounter. Prior to Ferenczi's innovations, the analyst defined what was real and what was reality. The relationship was not the focus. Now reality was defined from the analysand's perspective. What was real were the feelings and thoughts being expressed by the analysand. The reality of the psychoanalytic situation was a significant part of the therapeutic process. Prior to Ferenczi's contribution, what was thought to be real were the unconscious fantasies layered underneath the overt reality. Finally, he conceived of the analytic relationship as curative. What transpired between the analyst and the analysand in the analytic situation, how they experienced one another and how they worked through their relational issues, would determine the outcome of the treatment.

Ferenczi argued for a «renunciation of the "professional hypocrisy"» by the analyst in order to distinguish the analysis from the «unbearable traumatogenic past» (p. 160). He argued that all analysts «commit blunders» (p. 159). As Kohut pointed out forty years later, unempathic intervention and omissions are an inevitable part of an analysis. But Ferenczi made another daring suggestion as part of his discovery of the Confusion of Tongues experience. A curative element is introduced, he suggested, if the analyst is sincere with the analysand:

> ... the admission of the analyst's error produced confidence in his patient... the restrained coolness, the professional hypocrisy... a dislike of the patient... such a situation was not essentially different from that which in his childhood has led to the illness... we created a situation that was indeed unbearable (p. 159). Small wonder that our effort produced no better results than the original trauma. The setting free of his critical feelings, the willingness on our part to admit our mistakes and the honest endeavor to avoid them in future, all these go to create a confidence in the analyst. *It is this confidence that establishes the contrast between the present and the unbearable traumatogenic past* (p. 160).

It is truly ironic that Freud did not allow Ferenczi to explicate his ideas on seduction, both in the object relations of the child/parent relationship, and what is even more to the point, in the interaction between the analyst and the analysand. Freud would have heard that seduction of any kind in the psychoanalytic situation is to be avoided.

Reality and relationship in the analytic situation

The Confusion of Tongues theory which re-established sexual trauma as causative of psychological disorder, was extended to include emotional trauma. Driven by the intense and disturbing transference reactions with difficult cases, Ferenczi furthered his understanding of the empathic failings that fuel rage, denunciation, harshness and narcissistic absorption. He realized that these difficult patients had been traumatized, wounded by their relationships to parents. Parental needs had taken precedence over the child's needs. In understanding the issue of trauma as empathic failure in a flawed relationship, Ferenczi was continuing the theoretical line of thinking he began in his monograph *Development Aims of Psychoanalysis* (Ferenczi and Rank, 1925).

The next line of reasoning was to conceptualize the psychoanalytic situation from the vantage point of trauma theory. What Ferenczi originally discovered in 1925 and continued to verify until his last work in 1932 was that there was a «healing through relationship». The relationship between the analyst and the analysand healed the trauma of childhood, whether the trauma was sexual, physical, or emotional. The analyst was encouraged to come out from behind his clinical facade and create an encounter in the here-and-now of the psychoanalytic situation that emphasized the basic constituents of a healing relationship. The healing ingredients were safety, trust, empathy, honesty, responsiveness, and love.

But Ferenczi realized that such demands on the analyst for active and continued empathic participation did not arise only from sheer goodwill or a desire to heal. The analytic process needs to incorporate new measures to ensure healing. He proposed four such measures: analysis of the analyst, therapist self-disclosure, countertransference analysis, and mutual analysis. The analysis of the analyst, «down to rock bottom», was of particular importance. Analysts, he observed, should be analyzed so that they could experience an emotional reliving of their own core traumas, so that they would be able to empathize fully with the analysand's traumas and carry them fully through the necessary benign regression to reach their core traumas. He wished analysts to be able to thoroughly work through the wounds of trauma in the transference and real relationship – something, unfortunately, he felt he was not able to do in his analysis with Freud (Ferenczi, 1932/1988). He was therefore the first psychoanalyst to lobby for a training analysis as a personal analysis, not a didactic analysis. Ferenczi wanted the healers to be as well analyzed as the people they wanted to heal. He also encouraged analysts to be honest and self-disclose their feelings or thoughts when confronted with them by their analysands. The cure for confusion of tongues was clarity, reality, and especially honesty. If an analyst could find a therapeutic way to admit to the negative feelings the analysand sensed he was having towards him/her, he/she would have a new corrective emotional experience with a parental figure who was willing to be responsible for his contribution to the disturbance in the relationship (Ferenczi, 1928; Rachman, 1993a). In this way, the «traumatized child-in-the adult» would gradually come to feel that he/she was in a relationship with a nontraumatizing parental figure.

Ferenczi was the first analyst to take Freud's discovery of countertransference reactions seriously. In fact, he took it so seriously that one could say his two-person psychology is built upon the bedrock of countertransference analysis. The countertransference and its self-analysis, as well as the procedures he championed to aid the self-analysis, such as experiential (not didactic) analysis of the analyst, analyst self-disclosure, and mutual analysis, create and maintain the richest areas of exploration.

«Lines of Advance in the Further Development» of the Confusion of Tongues theory

When Ferenczi moved beyond the conceptualization of the Confusion of Tongues as a parent/child phenomenon and introduced the concept of «professional [clinical] hypocrisy» to broaden the experience to analyst/analysand interaction, he laid the foundation for a theory of human relations. The ideas contained in his theory address fundamental issues in human relations both within and beyond the consultation room. I would like to outline some applications of this theory to a variety of situations:

1. The use of the paper as a bibliotherapy adjunct in the analysis of the incest trauma. Recently I have been experimenting with giving Ferenczi's paper to analysands who are in the process of analyzing their sexual trauma, when they need a cognitive aide to supplement their struggles to confront the meaning and effect of childhood seduction. In the small sample I have gathered, there has been a very dramatic positive response to reading the paper. One such example concerns an incest survivor who is a mental health professional. She was so moved by Ferenczi's description of the Confusion of Tongues experience that she was able to better understand her own psychodynamics in relation to her childhood experience with her father (the parental abuser) as well as its implication for her contemporary relationships with men. In addition, she is planning to write a paper on her experience with these ideas as well as incorporate them into a video she is creating to train mental health professionals to develop greater empathy in the understanding and treatment of incest survivors.

2. The Confusion of Tongues which develops in adolescence between youth and their parents, when discrepancies in relating and construction of reality are fueled by the adolescent identity crisis (Erikson, 1959; Rachman, 1975, 1993d). At such moments in the life cycle, parents and adults authority figures often react with affective hypocrisy.

3. A reassessment of Freud's Case of Dora (Freud, 1905e), which focuses on the Confusion of Tongues between Freud and Dora. Freud, by his admission, could not imagine giving Dora the «affection she longed

for», that is, to show «a warm personal interest in her». He diagnosed her need for affection as a sexual desire. Is this not a Confusion of Tongues, in that Freud interprets the demand for affection as a demand for sex? (Rachman & Mattick, 1993).

4) A broadening of the concept of the Confusion of Tongues to include an inherent issue in all relations, parent to child, analyst to analysand, teacher to student, one adult to another; that is to say, any relationships which have the potential to be relationships of power and control. In this Ferenczi anticipated Foucault's (1980) focus on power relations, and the idea of the introjection of the controlling relationship of another to oneself and Laplanche's idea (1989) of primal seduction where unconscious sexual signifiers are inherent in the relationship. Forrester (1990) is presently studying these extensions in the work of Foucault and Lacan, as well as his own theoretical formulations.

5) An attempt to understand the relationship between Hedda Nussbaum and Joel Steinberg, which made the news headlines (Hackett, McKillop and Wang, 1988), because it highlighted how abuse and victimization can become the central dynamic in a dyadic relationship (Rachman, 1992).

The Wiesbaden trauma and recovery

It is now over sixty years since Ferenczi delivered this paper at the Wiesbaden Conference and over forty years since it was first published in English in the *International Journal of Psychoanalysis*. Balint clearly stated that Ferenczi suffered a trauma as a result of the analytic community's negative and suppressive reaction to the idea contained in the paper (Balint, 1968). What better analyst to help us understand this experience as trauma than Ferenczi's outstanding pupil, analysand, friend and inheritor of the mantle to the Hungarian school.

Balint also felt that the analytic community suffered a trauma, splitting it into Freud and Ferenczi camps. Balint attempted to heal the wounds of the trauma by several means. He worked creatively to expand and integrate Ferenczi's ideas into mainstream psychoanalysis of the post-pioneering period through his contributions to the object-relations framework of the British Psychoanalytic Institute's «middle group» (Bacal, 1985, 1988; Balint, 1968; Casement, 1985, 1990; Forrester, 1990, Kahn, 1969, Stewart, 1989). Balint clarified Ferenczi's work as not being the product of confusion, acting out, dementia, or rebellion. The Confusion of Tongues ideas were rather the result of a daring experimental clinician as Dupont has said (Dupont, 1988), who was both willing and able to work with seriously disturbed individuals who demanded and needed alterations in the standard psychoanalytic method and theory. I have recently begun a study of Ferenczi's clinical cases. His reports illustrate that his difficult cases were what many of us in contemporary psychoanalysis would term incest survivors. It is no accident that, as Ferenczi is rediscovered, his work seems so compatible with modern pioneers who changed our thinking and functioning, such as Winnicott and Kohut, who also worked with similar populations. Ferenczi's ideas and some of his methods have seriously influenced and have been incorporated into three major schools of psychoanalysis: object relations; interpersonal / humanistic; self psychology.

Balint also felt, I think unfortunately, that the trauma could be ameliorated if time would only heal the wounds of conflict. In this regard, he took a conciliatory role with Ferenczi's detractors. This created a «silent vacuum» which did not counteract in a vigorous way Jones's character assassination of Ferenczi (Rachman, 1994). Generations of analysts either did not study Ferenczi's work, especially the Confusion of Tongues ideas, or were told this material was not worthy of study, since it was «not psychoanalysis». When Jones's Freud biography was published, accusing Ferenczi of «madness» (Jones, 1957; Rachman, 1993a), Balint had a very gentle exchange of letters in the *International Journal of Psychoanalysis* (Balint, 1958; Jones, 1958). At no time was there the vigor that Fromm showed in his discussion of Ferenczi's trauma (Fromm, 1959), nor did Balint release the Freud/Ferenczi correspondence or the *Clinical Diary* (Ferenczi, 1932/1988), and demonstrate Ferenczi's side of his emotional struggles with Freud that would have indicated the plot to suppress and censor Ferenczi. It wasn't until the Le Coq-Héron group reported the translations of letters pertaining to the censorship and Dupont edited the *Clinical Diary* that we had a more meaningful and vigorous defense of Ferenczi's struggles with the Confusion of Tongues paper (Sylwan, 1984).

I would like to categorically state, that as we celebrate the 100th anniversary of the founding of psychoanalysis, Ferenczi's Confusion of Tongues paper was one of the greatest intellectual and emotional achievements in the history of psychoanalysis. The emotional courage Ferenczi displayed in writing and delivering this paper is only matched by Freud's presentation before the Society for Psychiatry and Neurology in Vienna on April 21, 1896, when he outlined a revolutionary theory of mental illness entitled *The Aetiology of Hysteria* (Freud, 1896c). Ferenczi's ideas were not only prophetic for their time, but are completely relevant to contemporary psychoanalysis. In fact, I believe these ideas can help us better understand human relations both within and beyond the consultation room (in the family, classroom, political arena, and so forth).

In summary, I would like to quote the final words of Ferenczi's paper. He said to that group of psychoanalysts gathered at the Hotel Rose in Wiesbaden, on Sunday morning, September 4, 1932:

> I shall be pleased if you would take the trouble to examine in thought and in your practice what I said to-day and especially if you would follow my advice to pay attention more than hitherto to the much veiled, yet very critical way of thinking and speaking to your children, patients, and pupils and to loosen, as it were, their tongues. I am sure you will gain a good deal of instructive material (Ferenczi, 1933/1949, p. 166).

Notes

[1] Some of these formulations were developed in discussions with Marc Wayne, C.S.W., B.C.D.

[2] I am grateful to Paul Mattick, Ph. D., for the translation of this phrase.

References

BACAL, H. (1985). Optimal Responsiveness and the Therapeutic Process. *In*: Goldberg, A. (ed.), *Progress in Self-Psychology*, vol. 1, pp. 202-226. New York: Guilford Press.

— (1988). Reflections on «Optimum Frustration». *In*: Goldberg, A. (ed.), *Progress in Self-Psychology*, vol. 4, pp. 127-131. Hillsdale, N.J.: Analytic Press.

BALINT, M. (1958). Sándor Ferenczi's Last Years (letter to the Editor). *International Journal of Psycho-Analysis, 39*, 68.

— (1968). *The Basic Fault: Therapeutic Aspects of Regression*. London: Tavistock.

BOLLAS, C. (1991). The Trauma of Incest. *In*: *Forces of Destiny: Psychoanalysis and Human Idiom*. London: Free Association Books.

BUDA, B. (Ed.) (1971). *A pszichoanalízis és modern irányzatai*. [*Psychoanalysis and its Modern Tendencies*]. Budapest: Gondolat.

CASEMENT, P.J. (1985). *Learning from the Patient*. New York: Guilford Press, 1990.

— (1990). *Further Learning from the Patient*. London: Routledge.

CREMERIUS, J. (1983). Die Sprache der Zärtlichkeit und der Leidenschaft. Reflexionen zu Sándor Ferenczis Wiesbaneder Vortrag von 1932. *Psyche, 37*: 988-1015.

DUPONT, J. (1988). Ferenczi's "Madness". *Contemporary Psychoanalysis, 24*, 250-261.

ERIKSON, E.H. (1959). *Identity and the Life Cycle*. New York: International Universities Press.

FAIRBAIRN, W.R.D. (1952). *Psychoanalytic Studies of the Personality*. London: Routledge.

FERENCZI, S. (1928). The Elasticity of Psychoanalytic Technique. *In*: *Final Contributions to the Problems and Methods of Psycho-Analysis.* New York: Basic Books, 1955, pp. 87-101.

— (1929). The Principle of Relaxation and Neocatharsis. *In*: *Final Contributions to the Problems and Methods of Psycho-Analysis.* New York: Basic Books, 1955, pp. 108-125.

— (1933). *Confusion of Tongues Between Adults and the Child: The Language of Tenderness and Passion.* The first English translation appeared in the "Sándor Ferenczi Number", M. Balint (Ed.), *International Journal of Psycho-Analysis, 30,* N° 4, 1949; reprinted *in*: *Final Contributions to the Problems and Methods of Psycho-Analysis.* New York: Basic Books, pp. 156-167, 1955; a new translation made by J.M. Masson and M. Loring, *in*: Masson, J.M., *The Assault on Truth: Freud's Suppression of the Seduction Theory.* New York: Farrar, Straus & Giroux, Appendix C, pp. 283-295, 1984. In German: Sprachverwirrung zwischen der Erwachsenen und dem Kind. *Bausteine zur Psychoanalyse,* Bd III, S. 511-525.

— (1985 [1932]). *The Clinical Diary of Sándor Ferenczi.* Cambridge, Mass.: Harvard University Press, 1988.

— & RANK, O. (1924). *The Development of Psychoanalysis.* New York: Nervous and Mental Disease, 1927; reprinted London: Karnac, 1986.

FORRESTER, J. (1990). Michel Foucault and the History of Psychoanalysis. *In*: *The Seduction of Psychoanalysis.* Cambridge, G.B.: Cambridge University Press.

FOUCAULT, M. (1980). *Power/Knowledge.* New York: Pantheon Books.

FROMM, E. (1959). *Sigmund Freud's Mission.* New York: Harper & Row.

FREUD, A. (1936). *The Ego and the Mechanisms of Defence.* New York: International Universities Press, 1966.

FREUD, S. (1896c). The Aetiology of Hysteria. *Standard Edition, 3,* 187-221.

— (1905e): Fragment of an Analysis of a Case of Hysteria. *Standard Edition, 7,* 1-122.

GOLDWERT, M. (1986). Childhood Seduction and the Spiritualization of Psychology: The Case of Jung and Rank. *Child Abuse and Neglect., 10,* 555-557.

GROSSKURTH, P. (1986). Melanie Klein, Her World and Her Work. New York: A.A. Knopf.

GRUBRICH-SIMITIS, I. (1986). Six Letters of Sigmund Freud and Sándor Ferenczi on the Interrelationship of Psychoanalytic Theory and Technique. *International Review of Psycho-Analysis, 13,* 259-277.

HACKETT, G., McKILLOP, P. & WANG, W. (1988). A Tale of Abuse: The Horrifying Steinberg Trial. *Newsweek,* December 12th.

HAYNAL, A. (1993). Ferenczi and the Origins of Psychoanalytic Technique. *In*: Aron, L. & Harris, A. (eds). *The Legacy of Sándor Ferenczi.* Hillsdale, N.J.: Analytic Press, pp. 53-74.

HIDAS, G. (1993). Flowing Over – Transference, Countertransference, Telepathy: Subjective Dimensions in the Psychoanalytic Relationship in Ferenczi's Thinking. *In*: Aron, L. & Harris, A. (eds). *The Legacy of Sándor Ferenczi.* Hillsdale, N.J.: Analytic Press, pp. 207-215.

JONES, E. (1957). *The Life and Work of Sigmund Freud, vol. 3, The Last Years.* New York: Basic Books.

— (1958). Response to M. Balint's "Sándor Ferenczi's Last Years" (letter to the Editor). *International Journal of Psycho-Analysis, 39,* 68.

KAFKA, F. (1948). *The Metamorphosis, The Penal Colony, and Other Stories.* New York: Shocken.

KHAN, M.M.R. (1969). On the Clinical Provision of Frustrations, Recognitions, and Failures in the Analytic Situation. *International Journal of Psycho-Analysis, 50,* 237-248.

KOHUT, H. (1984). *How Does Analysis Cure?* Chicago: University of Chicago Press.

KRÜLL, R. (1979). *Freud and His Father*. New York: Norton, 1986.

LAPLANCHE, J. (1989). *New Foundations for Psychoanalysis*. Oxford, G.B.: Blackwell.

LEHRNER, (1932). *Film*: "Freud and Other Analytic Pioneers". A.A. Brill Library. New York Psychoanalytic Institute.

MASSON, J.M. (1984). *The Assault on Truth: Freud's Suppression of the Seduction Theory*. New York: Farrar, Straus & Giroux.

McGUIRE, W. (1974). *The Freud/Jung Letters*. Princeton, N.J.: Princeton University Press.

MILLER, A. (1980). *The Drama of the Gifted Child*. New York: Basic Books.

— (1986). *Thou Shalt Not Be Aware*. New York: Farrar, Straus & Giroux.

MITCHELL, I. *et al.* (1988). Phenomenology of Depression in Children and Adolescents. *Journal of the American Academy of Child and Adolescent Psychiatry*, *27*, 12-20.

MODELL, A. (1991). A Confusion of Tongues or Whose Reality Is It? *Psychoanalytic Quarterly*, *60*, 227-244.

OGDEN, T.H. (1979). On Projective Identification. *International Journal of Psycho-Analysis*, *60*, 357-373.

ORTMEYER, D. (1992). Sándor Ferenczi Symposium Division of Psycho-Analysis. *American Psychological Association Conference*, Philadelphia, Pa., April.

RACHMANN, A. Wm (1975). *Identity Group Psychotherapy With Adolescents*. Springfiels, Ill.: Charles C. Thomas.

— (1989). Confusion of Tongues: The Ferenczian Metaphor for Childhood Seduction and Emotional Trauma. *Journal of the American Academy of Psychoanalysis*, *17*, 181-205.

— (1991). Psychoanalysis, Sexual Seduction and the Contemporary Analysis of Incest. *American Academy of Psychoanalysis*, New York City, December 8.

— (1992). The Confusion of Tongues Between Hedda Nussbaum and Joel Steinberg. *International Conference of the Psycho-Historical Society*. John Jay College of Criminal Justice, New York City, June.

— (1993a). Ferenczi and Sexuality. *In*: Aron, L. & Harris, A. (eds). *The Legacy of Sándor Ferenczi*. Hillsdale, N.J.: Analytic Press, pp. 81-100.

— (1993b). Theoretical Issues in the Treatment of Childhood Sexual Trauma in Spinal Cord Injured Patients: The Confusion of Tongues Theory of Childhood Seduction. *American Association of Spinal Cord Injury Psychologists and Social Workers*. Las Vegas, Nevada, September 8th.

— (1993c). The Evil of Childhood Seduction. *American Academy of Psychoanalysis*, New York City, December.

— (1994). *Sándor Ferenczi: The Psychoanalyst of Tenderness and Passion*. Northvale, N.J.: Jason Aronson (in press).

— (1995). The Suppression and Meaning of The Confusion of Tongues Presentation. *In*: Rachmann, A. Wm. (ed), Sándor Ferenczi: Psychoanalysis' Favorite Son. *Psychoanalytic Inquiry* (in press).

— & MATTICK, P. (1993). The Confusion of Tongues Between Frend and Dora (*Unpublished Manuscript*).

ROAZEN, P. (1975). *Freud and His Followers*. New York: Alfred A. Knopf.

SCHARFF, D.E. (1990). Review of «Relational Concepts in Psychoanalysis,» by S.A. Mitchell. *Psychoanalytic Psychology*, *7*, 429-438.

SEARLES, H.F. (1979). The Patient as Therapist to His Analyst. *In: Countertransference and Related Subjects*. New York: International Universities Press.

— (1986). *My Work With Borderline Patients*. Northvale, N.J.: Jason Aronson.

SHENGOLD, L. (1989). *Soul Murder*. New Haven: Yale University Press.

STEWART, H. (1989). Technique at the Basic Fault/Regression. *International Journal of Psycho-Analysis*, *70*, 221-230.

STIERLIN, H. (1959). The Adaptation to the Stronger Person's Reality. *Psychiatry*, *22*, 143-152.

SYLVAN, B. (1984). An Untoward Event: Ou La Guerre du Trauma de Breuer à Freud, de Jones à Ferenczi. *Cahiers Confrontation*, *2*, Automne, 1-115.

Cahiers Psychiatriques Genevois, Special Issue, 1994, pp. 257-263

SANDOR FERENCZI: AMALGAMATING WITH THE EXISTING BODY OF KNOWLEDGE

Judith E. Vida

> *«The historian communicates a pattern which was invisible to his subjects when they lived it and unknown to his contemporaries before he detected it.»*
> (George Kubler, *The Shape of Time, 1962*).

Sándor Ferenczi died in May, 1933. In 1948, Michael Balint wrote for him a new obituary to introduce the first English translation of *Confusion of Tongues*. This is the paper that had precipitated Ferenczi's near-break with Freud and was badly received at the Wiesbaden Congress of 1932 when Ferenczi read it against Freud's wishes. In part, the new obituary took the form of a lamentation. Balint surveyed Ferenczi's fate in the annals of psychoanalysis even as he reaffirmed his conviction that a new generation of psychoanalysts would eventually return to Ferenczi as someone from whom there was a great deal still to be learned.

Ferenczi, he wrote,

> was always admired for his freshness, originality, and fertility, but was hardly ever understood, and often completely misunderstood. He was seldom studied thoroughly, seldom quoted correctly, was often criticized, and more often than not erroneously. More than once his ideas were rediscovered later and then attributed to the second "discoverer" ... (p. 244).

Balint thought Ferenczi's idiosyncratic clinical language compounded the problem:

> For Ferenczi, words and technical terms were only – more or less – useful means of expressing mental experience; the experience was the important thing that had to be described as strikingly as possible...(p. 245) Even the most common, the most everyday, the most routine experience was never rounded off and finished for him; he never filed anything away as finally dealt with or definitely solved (p. 246).

In my view, this crystallizing of open-ended experience has been a chief agent of Ferenczi's being misunderstood. When a clinical experience is presented as Balint described, there is room for a participatory engagement. The reader comes away with an impression or understanding of the material which feels quite thoroughly his own. By virtue of not having made a definitive pronouncement, Ferenczi will have stimulated new thought and new connections *in the mind of the other*. It is this fundamental property of engagement with Ferenczi that makes it so difficult to trace with clarity the enormity of his influence. Ernest Jones (1933), noting 25 years of correspondence and intense friendship between Ferenczi and Freud, acknowledged that it was impossible to say for certain which idea originated with whom. In this context, it is interesting to recall Freud's own observation about Ferenczi that all analysts became his pupils (1933).

Certainly the leading edge of Ferenczi's originality was in his use of idiosyncratic language, in the freshness of his style, and in his precocious capacity to look at structure and process virtually independently of content. Paul Federn, in his own keenly observed obituary for Ferenczi (1933), wrote:

> In every one of his works, we see his great power of grasping the element of similarity in processes which other people had till then regarded as widely dissimilar and of thereby discovering new explanations – new to himself as well as to the rest of us. He was encouraged in the exercise of this capacity by the example of Freud. It requires intellectual *courage* to devote one's psychic resources to the establishing of connections hitherto undreamed-of, and intellectual *energy* to muster the necessary psychic force for the severing of established relations... (p. 475).

John Gedo made a retrospective survey of Ferenczi's work, which he wrote in German in 1966, and published in English in 1976. Gedo expected himself «to be impressed once more by [Ferenczi's] brilliance» but, far beyond that, found himself witness to the taking shape of Ferenczi's creativity within what he described as an «immense quarry of psychoanalytic ideas, most of which are not specifically credited to their originator when they are used today» (p. 361).

Gedo, wondering about the apparent diminution of creativity in psychoanalysis since the early days, asked if the active presence of Freud's unique «creative genius» had facilitated such creativity in others. Or perhaps the limitations of self-analysis and personal analysis in those days may have added an intensely personal motivation for new discovery, as he believed it had with both Freud and Ferenczi. But he also invoked the spectre of Ferenczi's idealizing transference to Freud to explain Ferenczi's «failure» to put himself forward:

> One finally gains the impression that, had Freud himself failed to evolve at the structural model of the mental apparatus in the early 1920's, this crucial advance in

theory might very well have been accomplished by Ferenczi. To put it another way, Ferenczi was so close to such a formulation that his inability to synthesize the scattered elements of his theoretical thinking into one cohesive statement was all that prevented him from matching Freud's achievement in *The Ego and the Id* (p. 367).

What Gedo interpreted as «inability», I am inclined to see as the consequence of a state of internalized deference from which, by 1927, Ferenczi was beginning to shake loose, ushering in his profound rethinking of clinical practice. It must be remembered that even as late as 1976 Gedo did not have access to *The Clinical Diary*, which was first published in French in 1985, and finally translated into English in 1988. This document, without precedent in the annals of psychoanalysis, demonstrated substantially the degree to which Ferenczi's originality had become freed up in the last years of his life. Gedo concluded his survey with the judgment that Ferenczi's «contribution to the field prior to 1930 is second only to Freud's» (p. 377). Noting the irony that it was Ferenczi who had observed that humankind receives the great with ambivalence, Gedo mused: «Perhaps we solve the conflict of our ambivalence about Freud through splitting: Freud is idealized, and his closest collaborator, Ferenczi, becomes the recipient of our hostility...» (p. 377).

Historically, it certainly seems that Ferenczi's creativity has been judged according to the positive or negative valence of one's idealization of Freud. In a companion article to Gedo's, Heinz Kohut (1976) examined the problems posed by this idealization. Not only did he think that the intellectual history of psychoanalysis was made more difficult to assess, but the individual practicing psychoanalyst «... in his training ... is driven either into an idealization of the creator of psychoanalysis or into a defensive reaction formation against this attitude» (p. 379).

The vehicle for this is the structure of psychoanalytic training, which traditionally begins with intense study of *The Interpretation of Dreams*, whereby intimate exposure to the details of Freud's inner life exerts a powerful pull to identification and idealization: «Such empathic closeness with total sectors of another person's mind, extending from conscious to unconscious levels, is not available to us in our day to day relationships» (p. 384). I think this holds particularly true for the period of time *before* candidates begin to practice as psychoanalysts; after that, the identifications and idealizations take hold and are reinforced by the myriad rituals and observances of psychoanalytic professional activities. Kohut rejected the notion that the idealization of Freud lent a «semireligious» quality to the psychoanalytic «movement». Moreover, he concluded that idealization was essential to maintain group cohesiveness among psychoanalysts as well as supporting self-esteem and professional identity.

Frank Sulloway in 1979 presented a comprehensive and clearly reasoned intellectual biography of Freud which examined many of the hallowed myths of the psychoanalytic tradition and found them to be unsupported by readily accessible historical documentation. Freud's own investment in his role as mythic hero or «conquistador», consciously or unconsciously, was demonstrated to have been carefully tended. Sulloway did not shy away from outlining the cultlike aspects of psychoanalysis. Like Kohut, he zeroed in on the initiation-«rite-of-passage» aspects of the training analysis, but he went farther in pointing out the dangers of the psychoanalytic system in which a hypothesis is verified by either a yes or no response, for an example of which we need look no farther than Kohut's statement that the candidate is «driven either into an idealization of... [Freud] or into a defensive reaction formation against... [him]» (Kohut, 1976, p. 379).

On October 30, 1932, Ferenczi (1955) jotted this down in his personal notes: «In fact *there is* in the end something that cannot, need not, and must not, be interpreted – or else analysis becomes an endless substitution of emotions and ideas mostly by their opposites» (p. 263). To create a new possibility for getting outside this reverberating closed loop, I want to introduce, however briefly, into our discourse the work of George Kubler, a distinguished art historian, who expanded the notion of art to include the «whole range of man-made things», even ideas, in his monograph *The Shape of Time: Remarks on the History of Things* (1962). Kubler, drawing upon his lifetime's work in art history in time periods ranging from prehistory to the modern, decided to employ the perspective of «the individual in terms of his situation» (p. 36) to make a case for the concept of historical sequence grounded in a demonstrable process of continuous change. This is a reversal of the common practice of «biographical narration... [which] tends to display the entire historical situation in terms of an individual's development» (*ibid.*) which is also the usual perspective of psychoanalysis.

Kubler's view that each important development is both an historical event and a solution to a problem is borne out by Henri Ellenberger's well-known, masterful piece of scholarship, *The Discovery of the Unconscious* (1970). That work documents the efforts of many individuals over a period of centuries to explain and to harness the powers of this mysterious mental capacity. Freud was neither alone nor unique in his historical period to be thus fascinated. Of this sort of phenomenon Kubler observed, «... An occasional person, born by chance into a favoring time, may contribute beyond the usual measure of a single life span» (p. 33).

Such an innovator is

> ... the first to perceive a connection among elements to which the key piece had only just come into view. Another could have done it as well as he, *and* another very often does, as in the celebrated coincidence of Charles Darwin and Alfred Wallace... because of similar training, equal sense of problem, and parallel powers of perseverance (pp. 63-64).

This useful piece of perspective is generally obscured by the institutionalized idealization of Freud. As Peter Rudnytsky (1991) has put it,

> The life and works of Freud can never be equalled as a source of psychoanalytic inspiration and insight. Yet in the years since Freud's death, many of his ideas have been called into question, and psychoanalytic theory has undergone extensive modification... Freud is at once insuperable and out-of-date (p. 14).

The publication of Ferenczi's *Clinical Diary*, as Balint had thought it might, has clearly established that Ferenczi's progression of experiments in psychoanalytic technique did succeed in defining the problems of psychoanalysis as therapy (Vida, 1993). Ferenczi was thus able to go far beyond both Freud's discovery of transference, and Freud's notion of countertransference as something the analyst had to suppress. The *Diary* penetratingly illustrated the insufficiency of Freud's aphoristic recommendations regarding technique. Ferenczi's discovery that countertransference was an inevitable participant in every psychoanalytic treatment, and that it could be put to constructive use, prefigured both the development of attachment theory and the ascendancy of relational perspectives in psychoanalysis. None of this could be perceived during Ferenczi's lifetime. Because of Freud's ultimate pessimism about the therapeutic usefulness of psychoanalysis (1937), we are freer to regard Ferenczi as a principal innovator of psychoanalytic *technique*, perhaps even as the precursor of our contemporary psychoanalytic *therapy* (Haynal, 1994). Kubler defined precursors as those with «the power to produce the solutions to a general need long before the majority experience the need itself. Indeed the way the need is framed often owes its final form to these premature talents» (p. 109).

Despite our general cultural practice of mythologizing the contributions of certain heroic individuals, Kubler insisted that invention is a fundamentally collaborative activity, both directly and indirectly. «Despite the inventor's solitary appearance he needs company; he requires the stimulus of other minds engaged upon the same questions...» (p. 115). Furthermore, Kubler observed, «Some sequences require contributions from many different kinds of sensibility» (p. 52). The history of the development of psychoanalysis amply bears out both these notions. It is fitting, thus, to note Gedo's reference to Ferenczi as Freud's «collaborator».

As an inventor whose intuitive insights transcended the practice of his contemporaries, and whose significance has grown in the decades since his death, Ferenczi deserves a place alongside Freud. Kubler described a biphasic pattern for invention: following any new discovery was its «amalgamation with the existing body of knowledge» (p. 64). Furthermore, «... in the absence of supporting conditions and reinforcing techniques, the invention [can languish] in obscurity... until those conditions are produced that allow [it] to reenter the inventive conscience of another [time]» (p. 96). Within the psychoanalytic tradition, a number of individuals can be discerned who, in the generations following Freud and Ferenczi, emerged from their own identifications with versions of classical psychoanalytic theory and practice to arrive at original perspectives regarding psychoanalytic therapy through a process of internal development strikingly similar to Ferenczi's. I am, of course, referring to such individuals as Winnicott, Searles, Kohut, Herbert Rosenfeld, and Bernard Brandchaft. This is how, I believe, Ferenczi's amalgamation into the existing body of psychoanalytic knowledge is being accomplished.

Kubler observed that «... any solution points to the existence of some problem to which there have been other solutions and that other solutions to this same problem will most likely be invented to follow the one now in view. As the solutions accumulate, the problem alters» (p. 33). During the second hundred years of psychoanalysis, the pathways of problems and solutions may lead, very likely, to developments as unimaginable to us as our contemporary practice would be to Freud. It is interesting to realize that we may not be able to predict who will be identified as the innovators of today.

References

BALINT, M. (1948). Sándor Ferenczi. In: *Problems of Human Pleasure and Behavior*. New York: Liveright, 1957, pp. 243-250.

ELLENBERGER, H.F. (1970). *The Discovery of the Unconscious. The History and Evolution of Dynamic Psychiatry*. New York: Basic Books.

FEDERN, P. (1933). Sándor Ferenczi Obituary. *International Journal of Psycho-Analysis, 14*, 467-484.

FERENCZI, S. (1949). Confusion of Tongues Between the Adult and the Child (The Language of Tenderness and Passion). *International Journal of Psycho-Analysis, 30*, 225-230.

— (1955). Notes and Fragments. In: *Final Contributions to the Problems and Method of Psycho-Analysis*. London: Maresfield, 216-279.

— (1988). *The Clinical Diary of Sándor Ferenczi*. Cambridge, Mass.: Harvard University Press.

FREUD, S. (1933). Sándor Ferenczi Obituary. *International Journal of Psycho-Analysis, 14,* 297.

— (1937). Analysis Terminable and Interminable. *Standard Edition, 23,* 209-253.

GEDO, J.E. (1976). The Wise Baby "Reconsidered". *In*: Gedo, J.E. & Pollock, G.H. (eds), *Freud: The Fusion of Science and Humanism.* New York: International Universities Press, pp. 357-378.

HAYNAL, A. (1994). Introduction. *In*: *The Correspondence of Sigmund Freud and Sándor Ferenczi, vol. 1, 1908-1914.* Cambridge, Mass.: Harvard University Press, pp. XVII-XXXV.

JONES, E. (1933). Obituary. Sándor Ferenczi, 1873-1933. International Jovinal of Psycho-Analysis, 14, 463-466.

— (1955). *The Life and Work of Sigmund Freud, vol. 2.* New York: Basic Books.

KOHUT, H. (1976). Creativeness, Charisma, Group Psychology: Reflections on the Self-Analysis of Freud. *In*: Gedo, J.E. & Pollock, G.H. (eds), *Freud: The Fusion of Science and Humanism.* New York: International Universities Press, pp. 379-425.

KUBLER, G. (1962). *The Shape of Time: Remarks on the History of Things.* New Haven: Yale University Press.

RUDNYTSKY, P. (1991). *The Psychoanalytic Vocation: Rank, Winnicott, and the Legacy of Freud.* New Haven: Yale University Press.

SULLOWAY, F. (1979). *Freud, Biologist of the Mind: Beyond the Psychoanalytic Legend.* New York: Basic Books. With a new Preface, Cambridge, Mass.: Harvard University Press, 1992.

VIDA, J. (1993). Ferenczi's Clinical Diary. Roadmap to the Realm of Primary Relatedness. *Journal of the American Academy of Psychoanalysis, 21,* 623-635.

Closure

Commentary

Cahiers Psychiatriques Genevois, Special Issue, 1994, pp. 267-270

METAPSYCHOANALYSIS

Olivier Flournoy

100 Years of Psychoanalysis. The Early Freud: Thus was entitled the Congress which was convened in Geneva. As is the case for most conventions about psychoanalysis the question which comes immediately to mind is the following: 100 years of psychoanalytic science or of psychoanalytic history? Is this meeting assembling psychoanalysts or historians of psychoanalysis?

Or are we supposed to be both at the same time? In which case we might be only half of one and half of the other. If we are psychoanalyst-historians that means that we run the risk of acting as wild analysts. Instead of considering our relationship with our analysands, we interpret the history of psychoanalysis and furthermore we interpret Freud himself, and others, without their being in a position to answer back. This is wild psychoanalysis. If we are historian-psychoanalysts then we are not authentic historians and worse, we are too easily open to voyeurism. «Wild historians» one might say. Aren't we wild psychoanalysts or wild historians when for example we talk about Freud's sexual life when we know strictly nothing about it and when psychoanalysis has repeatedly proven that the reality of facts, of written testimonies, of confidences or even of gossip, is not the «manifest» reality we are interested in?

Still, one cannot ignore the insatiable curiosity of the public and of the participants of such conventions for all that concerns the life of the first analysts and that of the first amongst them. It is as if Freud's message, psychoanalysis, rounded on him and left us dissatisfied and deeply curious about him.

Without denying the importance of Freud's masterly work, one cannot but assume that this situation is due to the difficulty of his endeavour. At this point, I wish to underline one aspect of the difficulties Freud encountered when faced with the task – no doubt partly due to a hostile environment – of making *his* psychoanalysis independent from academic psychology. While conducting his self-analysis (P. Mahony reminded us of its curative power), Freud submitted himself to an important work of introspection, undoubtedly a bold and original undertaking, but one of a psychological nature.

With *The Interpretation of Dreams* based on his auto-analysis, Freud wrote a psychological work of great significance centered around himself but not around the analyst-analysand relationship which was to become the main characteristic of psychoanalysis. In its seventh chapter devoted to the theory of the psychical apparatus and its functioning, Freud once again underlined the psychological origin of the theory by calling it meta-psychology. This metapsychology, supposed to represent the core of psychoanalytic theory, is afflicted with two major drawbacks, according to a contemporary psychoanalytical viewpoint.

Firstly, it does not take into account the specific interpersonal experience of analysis, concerned as it is with the functioning of a single apparatus. This creates a methodological problem: a scientific theory should be based on a congruent experimental method and as stated above this it not the case. Two undesirable after-effects emerge as a consequence:

1. the possibility of viewing the psychical apparatus as identical in all people and this leaves the door open to wild analysis and even to arrogance;

2. anybody could declare himself a psychoanalyst after studying this metapsychology since it does not require experience, which leaves the door open to all sorts of misuses.

The second drawback of metapsychology centers around the fact that while considering itself universal, it is compelled to suggest death as the ultimate goal of the psychical apparatus if scientifically oriented or «felicity in the other world» if it leans towards mysticism.

These flaws appear clearly in the very details of the theory. Two main principles govern the psychical apparatus. The pleasure-principle which requires the increase of psychical excitation leading to displeasure and its decrease towards pleasure. This means that pleasure and satisfaction are linked to this decrease. But this also entails the disappearance of pleasure with the end of the excitation. Without it there is neither pleasure nor displeasure. And without excitation there is no psychical activity, no life. Consequently the pleasure principle aims towards death.

The reality principle which is meant to replace it entails being reasonable, taking the so-called reality into account, not giving in to the deceiving immediate satisfactions and at the same time postponing any pleasure. And this, day after day, indefinitely – that is the interminable analysis – until death (or until after death?). We are again faced here with death as an ultimate goal.

The psychical mode of functioning requires energy. The instincts as described in the metapsychology characterise it. The first theory of instincts concerns the libido, this sexual energy specific to psychoanalysis. According to the psychoanalytic point of view the libido aims at something quite precise: the enactment of the Oedipus complex, homicide and incest, both lethal happenings. Only the castration-threat – castration equals death of sex – will enable this enactment to be avoided. A sad prospect indeed which, if it corresponds to a certain tragic vision of mankind, does not answer the wishes of analysands.

The second theory of instincts, the momentous fight between life and death instincts, speaks for itself. It is the death instinct which will gain the upper hand with its destructive aftermath, death as an aim, death of oneself, death of the other, even murder or suicide. In the end it also means the death of the instincts and by the same token the death of psychoanalysis.

What then does the metapsychology aim at? Renouncement to pleasure, instincts, passion, submission to the dull and harsh reality of reason, which should convince us to accept our mortal condition, but this time without too much fuss. Why then, one may ask, is such a realistic metapsychology so open to criticism? It is – and here Freud would not disagree – because the practice of psychoanalysis aims at something totally different. It aims at becoming aware of the violent and domineering power of «sexed mankind», of these sexed beings as it shows through the political, economical, social life, or else the family. It aims at being aware of the power of the individual as sexed, whether he acquires it with his reason while denying the sex, or through sex, the homosexual ignoring half of mankind and the heterosexual seducing whoever happens to be around for personal advantages. It is this power which is metaphorically represented by the Oedipus complex with its horrible triad: murder, incest, castration.

Through the acknowledgement of the above, psychoanalysis also aims at something more which justifies its undertaking: it aims at the pleasure derived from speaking, at the shared pleasure of pointing at and recognizing the pitfalls of power instead of surrendering and acting them out. And it is a stake, a challenge, its challenge, which is undoubtely very much in the limelight nowadays.

If Freud was remarkably successful in his self-analysis, he could also not help but spread a certain confusion between psychology and psychoanalysis to the detriment of the latter. This ambiguity contributes to making psychoanalysis the only science in the world – but can this apply to a science? – which 100 years later incites its followers to study with delight the personality of its creator instead of focusing on the experience itself, our everyday experience which accounts for its scientific and ethical value.

This is why I believe that it is about time psychoanalysts interested in research in the field of experience reconsider metapsychology on the basis of intersubjective experience enriched by self-analysis and not funded exclusively on the latter. Their first goal should be to modify the pleasure principle, the pleasure requiring excitation as shown by experience: the analysand is urged to start dreaming, waking up, remembering, saying. And above all, phrasing the discovery of the Oedipus complex as shown by his dreams and associations, and enjoying doing so instead of giving in to the so-called pleasure of dreamless nights which means repression of the complex consigned to the gloomy oblivion of the unconscious. It is this metapsychology I wish to name *metapsychoanalysis* (Flournoy, 1994).

References

FLOURNOY O. (1994): *Défense de toucher ou La jouissance du dit. Essai de métapsychanalyse*. Paris, Calmann-Lévy.

FREUD S. (1900a): The Interpretation of Dreams. *Standard Edition*, 4-5.

INDEX

by Maud Struchen

Gellner, E.: 190, 192
Gersuny: 87
Giampieri-Deutsch, P.: 197
Gicklhorn, J.: 81, 97
Gicklhorn, R.: 81, 97
Gilman, S.L.: 146, 149
Glenn, J.: 125, 132, 133, 147, 149
Gluck, Pr.: 83
Goethe, J.W.: 38, 64, 89, 93, 97, 154, 163, 173
Goldberg, A.: 252
Goldwert, M.: 245, 253
Gomperz, Th.: 154
Graf, Hanna: 123-128, 131, 132
Graf, Herbert (*see* Little Hans): 121
Graf, Max: 121-123, 125-127, 130-132
Granoff, W.: 169, 170, 192
Grèce, Princesse Eugénie de: 186
Grèce, Prince Pierre de: 186
Grigg, K.A.: 147, 149
Grimm (Brothers): 112
Grinstein, A.: 74, 92, 97, 116, 119
Groddeck, G.: 183, 194, 213, 219, 223
Gros, Dr: 60
Gross, O.: 172, 183
Grosskurth, Ph.: 180, 185, 186, 192, 236, 253
Grotjahn, M.: 192
Grubrich-Simitis, I.: 25, 30, 91, 93, 97, 244, 253
Guttman, S.A.: 158, 166
Guttstadt, A.: 97

Hackett, G.: 250, 253
Halberstad, Ernst: 185
Halberstad, «Heinerle»: 185
Hamilcar Barca: 76
Hammond, W.: 90, 97

Hanna (Hans' sister): *see* Graf, Hanna
Hannibal: 76, 77, 137
Hans: *see* Little Hans
Hans' father: *see* Graf, Max
Hans' mother: 121-129, 131, 132
Hans' sister: *see* Graf, Hanna
Harmat, P.: 181, 191, 192
Harris, A.: 197, 223, 253, 254
Harris, R.: 44, 54
Hartmann, H.: 186
Hartmann, N. von: 157
Hasdrubal: 77
Haynal, A.: 163, 164, 166, 197, 236, 253, 261, 263
Hegar, A.: 60, 85, 86, 88, 97
Heine, H.: 142
Heller, Gretl: 186
Heller, Hans: 186
Heller, Peter: 169, 171, 185, 186, 191, 192
Heilbrunn: 85
Helmholtz, H. von: 146, 148, 159
Hemecker, W.W.: 163, 166
Henoch, E.H.: 57, 86, 97
Herbart, J.F.: 152, 153
Heredity and the Aetiology of Neuroses (Freud): 30, 96
Hermanns, L.M.: 171, 193
Herz, M.: 61, 66, 67, 86, 98
Herzl, Th.: 165
Heubner: 82
Heydenreich: 59
Hidas, G.: 237, 238, 253
Hirschfeld, M.: 161
Hirschmüller, A.: 26, 30, 37, 39, 64, 81, 86-90, 98, 163, 166
Hitschmann, E.: 172, 183
Hoffer, Axel: 201, 204
Hoffer, Willi: 185
Homans, P.: 116, 119
Honegger, J.J.: 172, 182

Sacher-Masoch, L. von: 161
Sachs, H.: 173-175, 181, 186
Sade, D.A.F. de: 161
Sadger, I.: 183
Sand, R.: 157, 167
Sándor Ferenczi (Freud): 263
Saussure, Ferdinand de: 39
Saussure, Raymond de: 14
Schaefer, D.: 147
Schäfer, S.: 60, 61, 66, 86, 99
Scharff, D.E.: 246, 255
Schepeler, E.M.: 171, 189, 193
Schiff, E.: 81
Schiller, F. von: 103, 104
Schliemann, H.: 68, 91
Schmidt, Dr.: 86, 99
Schmideberg, W.: 183
Schopenhauer, A.: 152, 153, 155, 156, 158, 164, 165
Schöpf, A.: 153, 163, 165
Schorske, C.: 137, 138, 146, 149
Schröder, J.L.C. van der Kolk: 59, 85
Schröter, M.: 89, 93, 171, 193
Schur, M.: 63, 74, 81, 93, 99
science, scientific, scientist: 13, 33, 35, 57, 103, 109, 116, 139, 141, 151-153, 155-159, 161-164, 166, 169, 170, 199, 228, 267, 268, 270
Searles, H.: 239, 255, 262
Seif, L.: 171, 172
Severn, Elizabeth (R.N.): 217-223
Severn, Margaret: 221, 222
The Sexual Enlightenment of Children (Freud): 83
The Sexual Theories of Children (Freud): 131
Sexuality in the Aetiology of Neuroses (Freud): 107, 118
Shakespeare, W.: 113, 132
Shamdasani, S.: 183, 190, 194

Shengold, L.: 78, 92, 99, 147, 149, 242, 255
A Short Account of Psycho-Analysis (Freud): 166
Signorelli, L.: 76, 78
Silberer, H.: 182
Silberstein, E.: 153, 154, 163, 166
Silverman, M.A.: 130, 131, 133
Simmel, G.: 140, 141, 147, 150
Simon, E.: 146, 150
Simon, J.: 135
Smith-Rosenberg, C.: 46, 54
Sokolnicka, E.: 171, 182
Some Elementary Lessons in Psycho-Analysis (Freud): 166
Some Points for a Comparative Study of Organic and Hysterical Motor Paralyses (Freud): 39
Spielrein, S.: 171, 172, 183, 191, 193
Spinoza, B.: 13, 142
Spitz, R.: 80, 84, 86, 99
Sprengnether, M.: 128, 133
Stalin, J.V., Stalinistic: 142, 174
Stanton, M.: 197
Starobinski, J.: 39
Stein, F.: 172
Steinberg, J.: 250, 254
Steiner, R.: 180, 192
Stekel, W.: 158, 171, 182, 191, 194
Stengers, J.: 84, 86, 99
Stepansky, P.E.: 119, 183, 194
Sterba, R.: 175
Stewart, H.: 250, 255
Stierlin, H.: 239, 255
Stockmayer, W.: 172
Stonequist, E.V.: 140, 147, 150
Strachey, Alix: 111, 116, 146, 184, 193
Strachey, James: 49, 51, 54, 91, 130, 146, 157, 184, 193
Strean, H.S.: 130, 133
Stromme, J.I.: 172

281

Cahiers Psychiatriques Genevois

BULLETIN D'ABONNEMENT

Pour 2 numéros: Suisse: 50 Frs
                  Etranger: 60 Frs

Nom: _____

Prénom: _____

Adresse: _____

Code postal: _____   Ville: _____

Les Cahiers suivants sont encore disponibles au prix de
30 francs l'exemplaire:

N°6   Toxicomanies
N°7   Alcoologie
N°8   Dépression
N°9   Médecine psychosomatique
N°10 Psychose et changements
N°11 Psychiatrie infantile
N°12 Psychiatrie et neurosciences
N°13 Psychiatrie et modèle biomédical
N°14 Perspectives épidémiologiques
N°15 Nouvelles orientations

0 Je désire m'abonner aux Cahiers Psychiatriques Genevois
0 Je désire recevoir le(s) numéro(s) suivant(s):

A retourner aux:
Editions Médecine et Hygiène
case postale 456
CH-1211 Genève 4
Tél. 022 / 346 93 55 - Fax 022 / 347 56 10